CRIME & JUSTICE *in*
AMERICA

AN INTRODUCTION TO CRIMINAL JUSTICE

Joycelyn M. Pollock

Texas State University-San Marcos

anderson publishing
A member of the LexisNexis Group

Crime and Justice in America: An Introduction to Criminal Justice

Copyright © 2008
        Matthew Bender & Company, Inc., a member of the LexisNexis Group
        Newark, NJ

  ISBN-10: 1-59345-333-7
  ISBN-13: 978-1-59345-333-6

Phone: 877-374-2919
Web site: www.lexisnexis.com/anderson/criminaljustice

Library of Congress Cataloging-in-Publication Data

Pollock, Joycelyn M., 1956-
  Crime and justice in America : an introduction to criminal justice / Joycelyn M. Pollock.
    p. cm.
  Includes index.
  ISBN 978-1-59345-333-6 (softbound)
  1. Criminal justice, Administration of--United States. I. Title.
HV9950.P65 2008
364.973--dc22

2007049798

Cover design by Tin Box Studio, Inc./Cincinnati, Ohio   EDITOR Elisabeth Roszmann Ebben
ACQUISITIONS EDITOR Michael C. Braswell

Preface and Acknowledgments

Is there a need for yet another Introduction to Criminal Justice book? I think there is and I hope this book meets that need. This textbook has been developed in response to a perceived need for a shorter, less expensive, introductory text for instructors who desire an alternative to the comprehensive textbooks that are currently available. I have attempted to provide the "bare bones" of theory, law, and organizational descriptions without going into too much detail in any area.

The most unique characteristic of this text, I believe, is the "In the State of . . ." exercises that help the instructor adapt the text to a particular state. Too often, it seems, students become confused when textbook descriptions do not match their own state's criminal justice system. I strongly urge instructors to have students keep a notebook of these completed exercises so they can have a reference to understand the system in their own state.

Another characteristic of the book that sets it apart from some other textbooks is the inclusion of women and minorities in each chapter, rather than relegating relevant information to a single chapter. I believe this provides a more cohesive treatment of the subject of minorities and women in the criminal justice system and offers it in a way that is better utilized and understood than the single-chapter method.

I have also attempted to provide a unifying theme of due process throughout the book, and as it relates to each subsystem of the criminal justice system. Since law is the bedrock of the system, it has been given a more prominent emphasis here than perhaps in other textbooks. The concept of due process is especially relevant to current discussions concerning the war on terrorism and I have attempted to provide extremely current information as well as theoretical background for students to understand the legal principles behind the current controversies. Furthermore, I have tried to show the specific connections between the federal government's activities in the war on terrorism and the goals and responsibilities of local law enforcement.

I must thank Mickey Braswell for the idea and opportunity to create this book. He provided the impetus and guidance for the development of the text and allowed me the opportunity to create it. He read and offered guidance on early drafts of the chapters and the book has benefited from his advice. I most sincerely thank him for his vision, insights, and guidance along the way. It has been a real honor to work and become friends with Mickey and Susan Braswell and everyone at Anderson/LexisNexis over the years, and I am extremely grateful for the friendship and support that has come my way.

I want to also thank Gini Deibert, a colleague here at Texas State University–San Marcos, for her assistance in writing the chapter on the juvenile justice system. Since her expertise lies with juvenile justice issues, her assistance was invaluable. She graciously provided excerpts of interviews with juvenile offenders that provided a firsthand observation of probation. Tom Martinelli, an expert in law enforcement ethics training and a former Detroit police officer, read the chapters on law enforcement and helped me refine some of the issues and topics in those chapters. Sarah Stone, my graduate assistant this term, has been a great help in developing study tools for students that are relevant and targeted to student needs and abilities. Quint Thurman, the chair of the Criminal Justice Department here at Texas State University–San Marcos, was instrumental in the early stages of this text. He has been an extremely powerful force in the growth and development of our program here at Texas State and provides a great deal of support, enthusiasm, and encouragement for all professional activities. I want to thank him for all that he does for the department and every one of the faculty members who teach here.

Because of intervening projects, this book has been a long time in coming and I want to thank the folks at LexisNexis for their patience, as well as their assistance in the final stages. Elisabeth Ebben has been a pleasure to work with, as always, and has improved the book considerably with her ideas and skills. Melissa Gliebe of Tin Box Studio, Inc., and Linda Sullivan of DBest, Inc., provided a great design and worked diligently to improve the visual aids in the text.

Finally, I want to thank my husband, Eric Lund, and son, Gregory Byrne, for their continuing love and support. They continue to cheerfully keep the house running, get the dinner on the table, and the dogs and cats cared for, while I spend way too many hours away from them.

To Greg and Eric, as always . . .

Contents

Chapter 5 *Police Operations*　　**105**

Chapter 6 *Policing and the Legal Process*   **131**

SECTION III THE LAW AS SOCIAL CONTROL

Chapter 7 *Law and Society*   **157**

SECTION IV CORRECTIONS AS SOCIAL CONTROL

Chapter 1

CHAPTER OUTLINE

Criminal Justice as Social Control

What You Need to Know

★ Television presents a highly artificial perspective of crime, criminals, and the criminal justice system.

★ Common law is the compilation of early decisions by magistrates in England. Common law is the basis of the legal system in the United States.

★ Felonies are usually serious crimes punishable by more than a year in prison and misdemeanors are less serious crimes punishable by up to a year in jail (in most states).

★ Police power is the power to make laws. The federal government's ability to create law is limited to the enumerated powers as stated in Article I of the Constitution. All other police power resides in the states.

★ The "flow chart" of the criminal justice system starts with arrest and ends with release. Certain basic steps are common to all states.

★ Expenditures for the criminal justice system have been increasing even though there was a dramatic decline of crime in the 1990s through the early 2000s.

★ An ideology is a body of doctrines or beliefs that guide an individual or group. Two ideologies relevant to criminal justice issues are the *crime control* and *due process* ideologies.

Blood, bloated corpses, high-speed chases, true-blue detectives, and evil criminals who revel in their wickedness are the images of crime on television. They are not reality. Criminal justice became one of the fastest growing majors on college campuses in the 1980s and 1990s. Since the CSI shows first

---

BOX 1.1

What Are Forensics?

"Forensic" is an adjective used to describe something as related to the legal system. A forensic pathologist is someone who conducts autopsies to determine cause of death; a forensic scientist uses a range of science to answer questions about crime; a forensic handwriting analyst is called upon to testify in forgery or fraud cases, and so on. You might remember that your high school debate class also might have used the word forensics, which has a second meaning of "the art or study of debate." This is because the root of the word comes from the Latin word forensis, meaning "forum." Legal cases were tried in front of a forum of citizens who decided guilt or innocence based on the skill of the orator who defended the guilty, thus the connection between the two uses of the word.

---

appeared on television several years ago, a profession that had been arcane and "geeky" became the hottest new occupational interest. Forensic investigation majors have now been created in many universities to tap the huge market of interested students, many of whom may not realize that crime scene analysts typically have science degrees and if you didn't enjoy your high school biology or chemistry class, it may not be the profession for you. The definition of **forensic science** is "science that serves the court"; in other words, *forensic* is an adjective that is used to describe something as related to the legal system. Some of the applications of the term are shown in Box 1.1.

Before the *CSI* shows, the television series *Law and Order* introduced countless viewers to the criminal justice system via the perspective of the police and prosecutors. Many viewers today know most of what they know about the criminal justice system through these television series and others. This is not necessarily a new trend. In earlier decades, *Adam 12*, a series about two LAPD officers, depicted them reciting the *Miranda* warning to arrestees almost every week. Before long, we all knew that:

Neal Preston/CORBIS

(L-R) Actors David Berman (as assistant coroner David Phillips), Robert David Hall (as coroner Al Robbins), and William Petersen (as Gil Grissom) examine a corpse in a scene from *CSI: Crime Scene Investigation. CSI: Crime Scene Investigation* and *Law & Order* have become so influential with viewers as imitations of life in the criminal justice system that some legal experts worry that they are distorting the expectations of actual jurors.

"You have the right to remain silent. If you give up that right, anything you say can and will be used against you in a court of law. You have the right to an attorney, and if you cannot afford one, one will be appointed to you." Viewers may not have known where the *Miranda* warnings came from, or when police needed to recite them, but they remembered the warning in the same way they did advertising jingles for chewing gum or coffee. Some officers ruefully admit that, in some ways, the most realistic police show was *Barney Miller*, a comedy/drama about New York City police detectives who dealt with a steady stream of strange and humorous victims and offenders, interspersed with mundane stories about the detectives' personal lives.

BOX 1.2

The CSI Effect

Lawyers and journalists have coined the term "CSI Effect" to describe the incredible effect this television show has had on criminal court trials and jury deliberation. What seems to be happening is that viewers confuse reality with television and expect that every criminal case should have the type of scientific evidence portrayed in the show. When prosecutors are unable to present DNA evidence, fingerprints from any type of material, findings from scent identifiers, and so on, jurors may acquit defendants, believing that if the evidence doesn't exist, the case must be weak. Defense attorneys also complain about the show's effect, arguing that jurors believe that scientific evidence is infallible and don't consider human error or technological glitches when such evidence is utilized by the prosecutor. Evidently, the show has even influenced criminals and some police say that criminals are more likely today to pour bleach around crime scenes in an attempt to destroy DNA and trace evidence.

Source: Willing, R. (2004). "CSI Effect Has Juries Wanting More Evidence." *USA Today*, August 5: B1.

Television today would have us believe that crime scene investigators solve most crimes (*CSI* series), or that medical examiners solve the crimes (*Crossing Jordan*), prosecutors (*Shark*), or even that forensic anthropologists most often solve crimes (*Bones*). Of course, most television dramas portray police detectives solving most crimes (i.e., *Law and Order*). In reality, the majority of crimes are cleared because of witnesses or citizens that point police to the offender.

What spurs our fascination with crime? Every decade of television has had its share of crime drama shows. Some of these are displayed in Box 1.3. In fact, crime dramas with either law enforcement or courtroom scenes seem to be the most common type of series other than medical dramas. Perhaps these professions are chosen because they are more likely to provide gripping tales of life and death. It is difficult to squeeze nail-biting drama out of a television show about accountants or teachers, for instance.

AP Photo/Peter Cosgrove

Crime scene investigators prepare to enter a home in Deltona, Fla., Friday, Aug. 6, 2004, where six people were found slain earlier in the day. A friend checking the house for a Burger King employee who missed Friday's early-morning shift discovered six adults slain in a scene investigators called exceptionally violent.

It is important to remember, however, that these television shows may color our perception of reality. For instance, when you ask someone what they think of when you say crime, they are probably going to say murder or rape or some violent crime; not a relatively low-dollar theft, which is much more common in reality. If you ask who they think of when you say criminal, they may think of the murderer or "gangbanger" portrayed on a popular television show, rather than the legions of petty offenders who pass through our courts every day. These perceptions have the power to influence our decision making and opinions about real issues. For instance, when habitual felon or "three strikes" laws are debated, most people believe that they apply only to seriously violent offenders, the

BOX 1.3

Television Crime Dramas

1960s: Perry Mason, N.Y.P.D., Dragnet, Mannix, Felony Squad, Scales of Justice, Burke's Law, For the People

1970s: Adam 12, CHIPs, Barney Miller, Baretta, Columbo, Hawaii Five-0, Mod Squad, Quincy, M.E., Starsky & Hutch, Streets of San Francisco, Police Woman, Serpico, The D.A., The Guardians, Sword of Justice, The Blue Knight, McMillan and Wife, Owen Marshall, Counselor at Law, The Rookies, Police Story, McCloud, S.W.A.T.

1980s: Cagney & Lacey, Hill Street Blues, Miami Vice, Night Court, In the Heat of the Night, L.A. Law, Matlock, McClain's Law, Police Squad, Crime Story, Houston Knights, Mancuso, FBI, True Blue

1990s: Law and Order, N.Y.P.D. Blue, Homicide: Life in the Streets, The Commish, Profiler, High Incident, Murder One, NY Undercover, The Practice, Against the Law, Broken Badges, Equal Justice, Scene of the Crime, Street Justice, Undercover, Bodies of Evidence, Third Watch, Cold Case Squad, The Detectives, Walker, Texas Ranger, JAG, The Wright Verdicts, The Thin Blue Line, The Sentinel, Public Morals type that they see on television generally. In reality, such laws often apply to property offenders, drug offenders, and others who voters are not necessarily thinking of when voting for such laws.

1. THE FUNCTION OF SOCIAL CONTROL

What is the function of the criminal justice system? You probably said "to punish wrongdoers" and that is partially correct. The underlying function of the system, however, is social control. There are other institutions of society that socialize us and control our behavior. Schools, churches, and neighborhood associations are examples of other institutions of social control. However, sometimes those institutions are unsuccessful in controlling a person's behavior and, when that happens, the criminal justice system steps in.

Every society needs to control the actions of citizens when they threaten the social order. One of the most well-known concepts in philosophy and the sociology of law is the **social contract**. This concept comes out of the work of Thomas Hobbes (1588-1679), John Locke (1632-1704) and Jean-Jacques Rousseau (1712-1778).[1] According to Hobbes, before civilization, man lived in a "war of all against all" and life was not very pleasant. A more peaceful existence for everyone could only come about if every person agreed to give up the liberty to aggress against others in return for society's protection against aggressors. Rousseau's "social contract" is the idea that citizens agree to abide by the law in return for the law's protection. Of course, it is not really the case that we all consciously agree to such a contract. Our agreement is implicit when we choose to accept the benefits of living within a society. Part of the

---

BOX 1.4

The Code of Hammurabi

Hammurabi was a ruler of Babylon. Hammurabi's reign [1795-1750 B.C.] is noted for many things, but one of the greatest is his celebrated code of law. It is not the earliest code of laws, but one of the most complete. It is also noteworthy in that this ruler made public the entire body of laws, arranged in orderly groups, so that the citizenry would know what was required of them. The code was carved upon a black stone monument, eight feet high, and clearly intended to be in public view. This noted stone was found in the year 1901, not in Babylon, but in a city in the Persian mountains. It consists of 282 laws. A few examples are offered below:

BOX 1.4 — *continued*

3. If any one bring an accusation of any crime before the elders, and does not prove what he has charged, he shall, if it be a capital offense charged, be put to death.

6. If any one steal the property of a temple or of the court, he shall be put to death, and also the one who receives the stolen thing from him shall be put to death.

8. If any one steal cattle or sheep, or an ass, or a pig or a goat, if it belong to a god or to the court, the thief shall pay thirty-fold therefore; if they belonged to a freed man of the king he shall pay tenfold; if the thief has nothing with which to pay he shall be put to death.

25. If fire break out in a house, and some one who comes to put it out cast his eye upon the property of the owner of the house, and take the property of the master of the house, he shall be thrown into that self-same fire.

132. If the "finger is pointed" at a man's wife about another man, but she is not caught sleeping with the other man, she shall jump into the river for her husband.

146. If a man take a wife and she give this man a maid-servant as wife and she bear him children, and then this maid assume equality with the wife: because she has borne him children her master shall not sell her for money, but he may keep her as a slave, reckoning her among the maid-servants.

195. If a son strike his father, his hands shall be hewn off.

196. If a man put out the eye of another man, his eye shall be put out.

197. If he break another man's bone, his bone shall be broken.

198. If he put out the eye of a freed man, or break the bone of a freed man, he shall pay one gold mina.

199. If he put out the eye of a man's slave, or break the bone of a man's slave, he shall pay one-half of its value.

idea of the social contract is that if we break the law, we have agreed to the consequences; specifically, prosecution and punishment.

The earliest tribal societies had leaders who mediated conflicts and handed down punishment. As society became more complex, layers of authority developed between the king/ruler and the populace, so that even as early as Hammurabi, "laws" were written down to be administered when offenses occurred. Gradually rudimentary court systems were created, and then, eventually, law enforcement emerged as a public agency (as opposed to private protection paid for by those who could afford it). The emergence of law and law enforcement is a very interesting historical process and one can see that it is part of the process of a community becoming "civilized."

2. THE AMERICAN LEGAL SYSTEM

Our legal system comes from English **common law.** Starting around the 1500s, magistrates appointed by the kings and queens of England handed down decisions regarding both civil disputes and criminal offenses. Over time, these decisions were written down to be used as guidance when similar cases were brought before that magistrate or others. The common law was the compilation of all those decisions. In the 1700s, William Blackstone, a famous English jurist, undertook the mammoth effort of organizing and identifying the principles of law that derived from these decisions. Blackstone's Law Commentaries collected the common laws together in one source for the first time.

After the American Revolution, the common law was still the pervading law of the land, but as states were created, many began to write their own **penal codes**, which are basically an organized list of laws of the state. You may have seen an Internet item that lists obscure and ridiculous old laws that supposedly still exist, such as no kissing in public or no shooting buffalos from a moving train. This is largely urban legend, because penal codes are periodically reviewed and rewritten by legislators, aided by the bar association of each state. On the other hand, it is an interesting exercise to become more familiar with the penal code of your own state and see some of the quirky, old, and/or ignored laws that do still exist.

★ Exercise: In the State of . . .

1. Go to **www.dumblaws.com/index.php.**

2. Look up the "dumb laws" listed for your state.

3. Check the link provided to read the original law or, when the link is not provided, obtain a copy of your state penal code. This is often available over the Internet. Use the Google or Yahoo search engines to find a link to your state's penal code. Try to find the law mentioned.

The exercise provided on page 7 is the first of many in this book designed to help you become more familiar with the criminal justice system of your own state. One of the challenges in writing a criminal justice text is that the criminal justice system and the laws of each state are slightly different. Thus, in each chapter, there is an exercise designed to help you become more familiar with your own state's criminal justice system. Today the Internet is an invaluable tool to quickly and conveniently discover most of this information. An important thing to remember, however, is that Web sites can be created by anyone. When researching criminal justice issues, it is best to look for official sites, such as state attorneys-general sites, federal sites such as the Bureau of Justice Statistics, and university sponsored sites. Of course, other sites can be used as well (such as the one identified in this exercise). However, be careful to double-check facts when using Web sites that are not affiliated with official sources.

Laws define the "do's and don'ts" of society. They can be broken down into felonies, misdemeanors, ordinances, and violations. **Felonies** are the most serious misbehaviors and are usually punishable by a year or more in prison. Most of the crimes you think of (murder, rape, assault) are felonies, although sometimes a crime might be either, such as larceny/theft, which may be a felony or a misdemeanor depending on the dollar amount of the theft. **Misdemeanors** are less serious (such as simple assault) and can be punished by up to a year in jail. It is possible that in your state misdemeanors must be committed in the presence of a police officer for them to be able to arrest the offender without an arrest warrant. In some states, when misdemeanors happen outside the presence of police, a victim must go to the prosecutor's office and file a complaint. The prosecutor will ask a magistrate to sign an arrest warrant if he or she decides there is probable cause. States usually further subdivide felonies and misdemeanors to classes or levels indicating their seriousness.

State legislatures have the power to create criminal laws. City ordinances (i.e., skating on the sidewalk), are created by city councils or the local political entity, and are usually punishable by fines. City code violations (i.e., keeping livestock within city limits) are also created by local political bodies and punished by fines.

Law enforcement exists at the state and local level to enforce these laws, although as you are probably aware, police officers and prosecutors have a great deal of discretion. Just because a law is broken does not necessarily mean there will be an arrest or prosecution. Typically, a state will have a state law enforcement agency (highway patrol) that enforces the state's highway laws, but can also be called in to help investigate local crime. There is usually a county-level law enforcement agency (county sheriff and deputies). Most of us are familiar with the city police officer, but there are also other types of law enforcement officers, depending on the state, such as constables, park or airport police departments, port authority police, transportation police, university police departments, and so on. These specialized police forces must be created by the state legislature.

There are also different layers of courts that prosecute the laws. City ordinances and code violations are typically heard in municipal courts, while misdemeanors and felonies are heard in county and state courts. Every state has a court structure that allows for appeals, and the highest appellate court in the state is often called the state supreme court, not to be confused with the United States Supreme Court, the highest court in the country.

The federal criminal justice system parallels the state systems. Federal laws are passed by Congress and can be found in the United States Code. You can purchase a "compact" version that is only 700 pages! One thing to remember is that Article I of the United States Constitution specifically enumerates the powers held by the federal government. All other powers are held by states. The Tenth Amendment to the United States Constitution made this division of power clear by stating: *"The powers not delegated to the United States by the Constitution, nor prohibited by it to the States, are reserved to the States respectively, or to the people."* **Police power**, the authority to set and enforce most laws, lies with the states. The federal government's role in crime control has historically been strictly limited and must be derived from one of its other powers, i.e., the power to protect the borders or regulate interstate commerce.

> To look at the U.S. federal code, go to http://uscode.house.gov/

Despite the limitations created by the Constitution, we have a large number of federal laws that must be enforced by federal law enforcement agencies. We are most familiar with the FBI, but other federal agencies, such as the border patrol, customs, post office inspectors, and treasury agents also investigate and enforce federal criminal laws.

As you know, the Department of Homeland Security was created after the terrorist attacks of September 11, 2001. The purpose of creating this department was to streamline and create better communication among the many federal law enforcement agencies that are involved with protecting the country from terrorist acts. Box 1.5 shows how the various agencies are linked into one large organization whose mission is to protect the country from terrorist threats.

> For information on DHS, see: http://www.dhs.gov/index.shtm

It is important to note that federal laws and procedures have made a distinction between domestic crimes and international terrorism when allocating powers of investigation and prosecution to federal agencies. Typically, federal agencies, such as the FBI and CIA, have greater powers when investigating international offenders who are suspected of terrorism than when they are investigating "regular" crimes. Of course, there are often blurry lines between domestic crimes, such as bank robbery or smuggling drugs, and international terrorism. One of the most hotly contested elements of the USA PATRIOT Act was increased law enforcement powers in domestic investigations when there is reason to believe a connection to international terrorism exists. We will revisit the PATRIOT Act and law enforcement's role in protecting this nation from terrorism in Chapter 15.

BOX 1.5

Department of Homeland Security

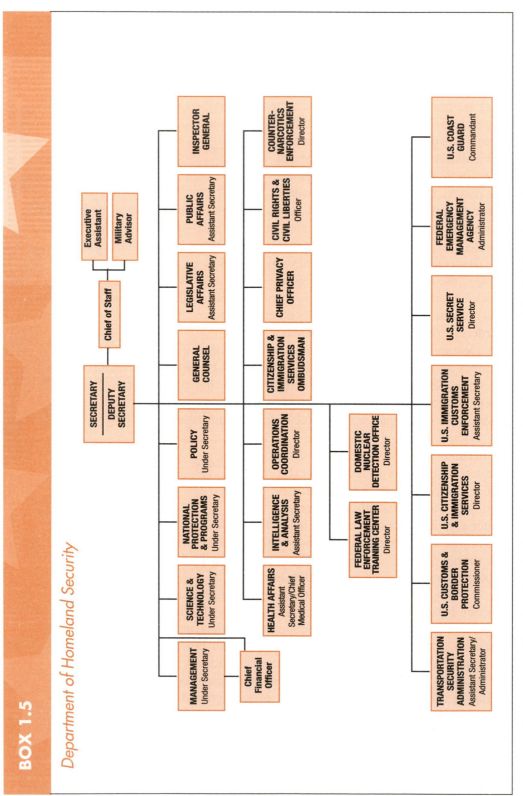

Source: Department of Homeland Security. http://www.dhs.gov/xabout/structure/editorial_0644.shtm. Accessed April 1, 2007.

3. FLOWCHART OF THE SYSTEM

In Box 1.6, a rough flowchart of a felony offender's experience going through the criminal justice system is presented. An individual may exit the system through:

★ non-prosecution at any stage up to conviction;

★ acquittal;

★ successful completion of a pretrial diversion program;

★ successful completion of probation;

★ successful completion of parole;

★ completion of jail or prison sentence.

BOX 1.6

The Criminal Justice System

The criminal justice system is typically divided into three subsystems: police, courts, and corrections. The use of these three subsystems has become a standard way to describe the system. Police take center stage up to arrest; their role is to investigate crimes, arrest the suspect, and gather evidence. Courts are obviously involved in the process of adjudication, which determines guilt or innocence and sets the amount of punishment for the guilty. Corrections takes over after sentencing. Of course, real life doesn't have such simple categories. Police investigate offenders who are on probation or parole. Pretrial adjudica-

BOX 1.7

The Criminal Justice Process

Booking: is basically an administrative entry into jail. The suspect's fingerprints are taken, officers take his or her property, issue jail clothing, and sometimes, the suspect undergoes some form of health screening before being placed in the jail population.

First Appearance: is usually within the first 24 hours of arrest (and it must take place within a "reasonable" period after arrest). In this short hearing before a magistrate, the charges are read and the magistrate determines if there is sufficient probable cause for the arrest. The magistrate may also begin the process of determining if the suspect is indigent, in which case an attorney will be appointed.

Preliminary Hearing: is basically to determine whether there is sufficient evidence to go forward with a trial. Often the preliminary hearing is waived. In some states, the grand jury system completely takes the place of the preliminary hearing.

Grand Jury Hearing: is with a jury appointed by the administrative judge of a jurisdiction. This group hears the evidence presented by a prosecutor to determine if there is probable cause to go forward to trial. If they agree that there is, they issue an *indictment*. Not all states use the grand jury system.

Arraignment: is where the offender may plead guilt or innocence and, if indigent, have an attorney appointed if one has not been appointed yet.

Pretrial Diversion: may occur at any time before trial and after charges have been filed. Typically, the suspect must admit guilt and agree to conditions that range from work and restitution programs to community service.

Plea Bargaining: is an agreement between the defendant, represented by his or her attorney, and the prosecutor to plead guilty in exchange for a recommended sentence.

Pretrial Hearings: are when judges decide procedural issues relevant to the trial, such as the admission of evidence or change of venue.

Trials: may be "bench trials," which means that they are held only in front of a judge with no jury. If the defendant requests a jury trial, voir dire takes place before the jury is seated, which basically involves ensuring that jury members will be unbiased in their judgment.

Sentencing Hearing: is a separate proceeding, although appointed attorneys are required to continue to represent the offender through the sentencing hearing (and first appeal). There may be some time between the trial and the sentencing hearing in order for a presentence report to be written. While some states allow juries to sentence, others release the jury and have the judge do the sentencing.

Prison/Probation: is the basic sentencing decision in felony cases. Some states have strictly limited which crimes are eligible for a probation sentence; in other states, potentially any felon can be sentenced to probation.

Parole: comes *after* a prison sentence, while probation is *instead of* a prison sentence (in most cases). They are very similar in that both involve supervised release into the community.

tion programs often use probation officers to supervise clients who haven't been found guilty. Probationers who violate the conditions of their probation may go back to court for a Motion to Revoke Probation hearing. Thus, it is important to understand what happens to the offender during the whole process from arrest through discharge from the system.

Once an offender is arrested, with or without an arrest warrant, the individual has started his or her entry into the "system." In Box 1.7, the steps of the system are described briefly. It is important to note that there are differences between the states in these steps. We will more carefully explore the various steps taken in the criminal justice flowchart in a later chapter.

4. COSTS OF THE SYSTEM

The criminal justice system is an incredibly expensive operation. As Box 1.8 shows, the costs of the system have been increasing exponentially for the last 20 years and now reach 80 billion dollars just for state expenditures! States spend more for criminal justice than they do for education or health and human services. In fiscal year 2001, federal, state, and local governments spent more

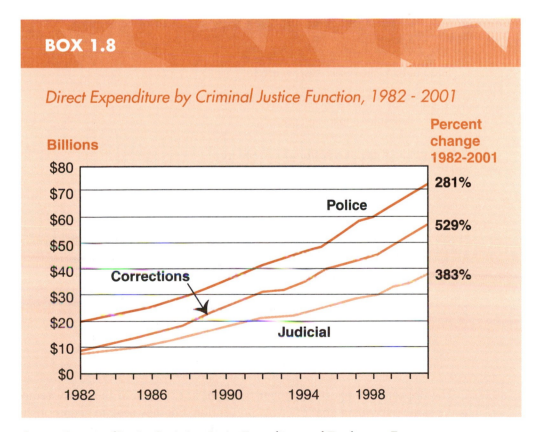

BOX 1.8

Direct Expenditure by Criminal Justice Function, 1982 - 2001

Source: Bureau of Justice Statistics, *Justice Expenditure and Employment Extracts.*
Retrieved 2/15/07 from: http://www.ojp.usdoj.gov/bjs/glance/tables/exptyptab.htm.

than $167 billion for police protection, corrections, and judicial and legal activities. It is estimated that criminal justice functions cost every person in the United States $600.00 per year.[2]

What is interesting about the huge increase in expenditures for criminal justice functions is that in the decade of the 1990s through the early 2000s, we experienced a dramatic decline in all types of crime. As we shall see shortly, some crime rates have declined to 30-year lows. The declining crime pattern was experienced across the country, in cities as well as small towns. We will discuss the crime decline in more detail in the next chapter.

5. MISSION AND GOALS OF THE SYSTEM

The basic mission of the criminal justice system is to prevent victimization by preventing criminal behavior. Each of the subsystems has its own specific, but complementary, goals to achieve this general mission. The goals of *law enforcement* are:

- ★   to prevent crime by patrol;

- ★   to educate the public on crime prevention; and

- ★   to investigate crime and arrest those suspected of committing a crime.

The goals of the *court system* are to:

- ★   determine guilt or innocence through due process; and

- ★   determine a just sentence.

The goals of the *correctional system* are:

- ★   punishment: we believe that criminals must be punished because they deserve it;

- ★   deterrence: we believe that what we do to offenders will make others decide not to commit crime and also will encourage that offender not to commit additional crime;

- ★   rehabilitation: we believe that programs and what is done to the offender in the system may create some internal change that will make him or her become more law-abiding;

- ★   incapacitation: if nothing else, we believe that we should hold the offender in a manner that will prevent him or her from committing any crimes, at least for that period of time.

The important thing to remember is that basically each of the subsystems has the same overriding goal of crime prevention, but they seek to accomplish that goal in different ways. Most analyses and discussions of the criminal justice system utilize a **systems approach**, meaning that the various elements of police, courts, and corrections are viewed as working together as an integrated whole toward a single goal. In general, this is true, although the various subsystems sometimes have contradictory objectives. In fact, some police officers might say that the court system works "against" the police by letting offenders out as fast as police lock them up. Despite the sometimes contradictory objectives of the subsystems, a systems approach is helpful because it allows us to consider two major concepts that are relevant to our understanding of the criminal justice agencies.

The first is the concept of open versus closed systems. An **open system** is one that is permeable and responsive to outside influences. The criminal justice system, for instance, can be described as a fairly open system because it must and does respond to outside influences such as public opinion, legislative changes in the law, executive prioritizing, and so on. A **closed system** is one that does not respond to outside influences and, though the criminal justice system itself is open, there may be examples of certain agencies in the system that are closed. Historically, prisons were fairly closed systems that were outside of public scrutiny and fairly autonomous. This is no longer the case, however, and even prisons must respond to outside pressures from the public, prisoners' rights advocates, and the legislature.

The second concept is that of **homeostasis**—the idea that any system will adjust to changes by adapting in such a way to maintain "business as usual." This is important and can arguably explain why we are spending just as much money (actually more!) after a decade-long drop in crime as we did during the years with the highest crime rates. Systems theory argues that there is a tendency for systems to maintain a status quo. In criminal justice, we might point to the fact that rarely do we ever close prisons despite reduced crime rates, and rarely do changes in the law dramatically affect the courtroom work group's decision-making procedures. In general, the system responds to outside pressures by minor adjustments or reinterpretations that tend to allow a continuation of "business as usual." We will discuss these concepts in more detail in later chapters.

6. IDEOLOGIES IN CRIME AND JUSTICE

An **ideology** is a body of doctrines or beliefs that guide an individual or group. It is a way of organizing knowledge, in that we interpret things we see and hear in reference to our existing belief systems. In fact, we may even ignore information that doesn't fit our existing ideology and remember information that does. In 1968, Herbert Packer[3] described two models of law enforcement that are extremely helpful in understanding the issues and decisionmaking that occur in reference to the entire criminal justice system, not just law enforcement. In fact, what he termed *models* could also be called ideologies. Packer called his two models "*crime control*" and "*due process.*"

In the **crime control ideology**, the basic belief is that controlling crime and punishing the criminal is more important than anything else, best expressed by a Supreme Court justice who argued that the criminal should not be set free because "the constable blundered." Some of the beliefs that are consistent with Herbert Packer's crime control ideology are:

★ Reducing crime is the most important function of law enforcement.

★ The failure of law enforcement means the breakdown of order.

★ The criminal process guarantees social freedom.

★ Efficiency is a top priority.

★ The emphasis is on speed and finality.

★ There is a presumption of guilt, once the suspect is in the system.

Packer's **due process ideology** supports controlling crime, but in this ideology, crime control is not the most important goal. The most important mission of the criminal justice system is the enforcement of law in a fair and just manner, as characterized by the comment: "It is better to let 10 guilty men go free than punish one innocent." Beliefs that are consistent with this ideology include:

★ There is a possibility of error in the system.

★ Prevention of mistakes is more important than efficiency.

★ Protection of the process is as important as protection of innocents.

★ The coercive power of the state is always subject to abuse.

★ Every due process protection is there for a reason and should be strictly adhered to.

These basic ideologies are very pervasive in our thinking and opinions regarding criminal justice issues. You can see evidence of them in the television shows we discussed earlier, in politicians' statements, in television and radio talk show host's rantings, and in "letters to the editor" in the local newspaper. If one's ideology is purely "crime control," then some consistent beliefs would include:

★ Criminals are the "enemy" and fundamentally different from "good" people.

★ Police are the "army" that fights the enemy, using any means necessary to control, capture, and punish them.

★ "Good" people accept and understand that police are in a "war" and must be allowed deference in their decisionmaking because they, not us, are the experts and only they "know the enemy."

★ Due process protections, such as the *Miranda* warnings, exclusionary rule, and search warrants "hamstring" the police from doing their job.

On the other hand, if one has a basic ideology of due process, then other beliefs are more consistent, and might include:

★ Criminals are not a distinct group; they also shop, pay taxes, have kids and parents, may be victims themselves, and often are one's next-door neighbor.

★ Police have limited ability to affect crime rates one way or the other because crime is a complex social phenomenon and, in fact, the history of law enforcement originates in order maintenance, not crime control.

★ Police, as "public servants," serve all people, and it is important to remember that suspects are not criminals until a court of law finds them so.

★ The law is more important than catching criminals, so if police officers break the law to catch a criminal, then they become criminal themselves.

★ Due process protections, such as the *Miranda* warnings, exclusionary rule and search warrants are an inherent element of the job of police; therefore, when they ignore, subvert, or skirt these protections, they are not doing their job.[4]

One's belief system influences how new information is received. For instance, the USA PATRIOT Act was lauded by those with a crime control ideology as a step in the right direction in that it allocated greater powers of search to law enforcement officers investigating terrorism. On the other hand, for some with a due process ideology, it was perceived as a direct attack on civil liberties and previous privacy protections enacted by Congress.

Of course, most of us do not have pure ideologies and so you might feel that you lie between these two, or, indeed, have a different overriding ideology entirely. The point of examining ideologies is simply that they sometimes obscure our understanding or acceptance of new information. There is a distinct possibility that your receptiveness to certain facts in this book, and every other book you read, is colored by your ideology. If, for instance, you don't believe something in this book is true, then you should go explore the facts, either by the footnote provided, or by your own research. The piece of information may be wrong, it may be out of date, or it may be that it simply doesn't fit your idea of the way things are, which is shaped by your ideology. Of course the writers of textbooks (including this one) have their own ideologies; therefore, their presentation of facts may be influenced by their own ideology. The goal of every textbook writer is to present a balanced view of the facts; however, facts are sometimes more complicated than we think and, although we may strive for objectivity, it is not always easy to do. One of the most difficult things, for instance, in writing research papers is to seek out all the facts and write a balanced review of the research, rather than use only those facts that fit the conclusion that you want to reach. At the end of this chapter is a short guide to writing a research paper. While there are more detailed instructions available in other sources, this short discussion may help you to identify and narrow a topic and organize the material in a logical and cogent manner.

7. CAREERS IN CRIMINAL JUSTICE

It is possible that you are reading this book because you are interested in a career in the field of criminal justice. One of the interesting features of the field is the wide variation in professions. Criminal justice encompasses drug counselors and border patrol agents, prison guards and public defenders. You've probably heard that "you'll never get rich" in this field, and that is true. Box 1.9 shows some low and high average salaries for certain selected professions associated with criminal justice.

Although there are no riches to be earned in this field, there are not that many professions that have such potential to change lives. Almost all the occupations and professions in this table (except for private security and private attorneys) are public servants. Public servants are individuals whose salary comes from the public purse; therefore, they have special duties to put the public's interest before their own. They have discretion and power over the lives of others, and therefore must be held to high standards of integrity and ethics. If public servants do not respect the law, then everyone is at risk and corruption inevita-

BOX 1.9

Annual Salaries

Position	Lowest $	Average $	Highest $
Police officer	26,910	45,210	68,880
Police chief		72,924 - 92,983	
Police sergeant		49,895 – 59, 454	
FBI (GS 10-13)		53,185 - 64,478	
Private detective	19,260	32,110	58,470
Security guards	14,390	20,320	33,270
Correctional officer	22,630	33,600	54,820
Probation officer	26,310	39,600	66,660
Attorney		94,930 (wide variation)	
Judges	29,920	93,070	141,750
Counselor	15,480	24,270	39,620

Source: Bureau of Labor Statistics. Retrieved 6/1/07 from: http://www.bls.gov/oco/.

bly follows. In the chapters that follow, we will examine in greater detail not only the offenders who pass through the criminal justice system, but also the women and men who are the agents of social control and the law.

8. CONCLUSION

In this chapter we learned some basic facts about the criminal justice system. Obviously the television shows that portray the system do not present completely accurate views of what happens in real life. We should be concerned that sometimes false perceptions influence decisions, such as what is described in the "CSI effect."

Criminal justice is basically an institution of social control. The powers invested in system actors come from the American Constitution, which places most "police powers" in the state. States pass laws, cities pass ordinances, and they all are enforced by law enforcement at the state and local level. The flowchart of the criminal justice system displays how an offender enters the system and how he or she can exit. We use systems theory to understand what we call the criminal justice system, but we must also recognize that the various subsystems may sometimes have contradictory objectives. Positions that are consistent with the ideologies of crime control or due process can be seen in the media. Ideologies are inevitable but they may prevent one from accepting facts that do not fit one's "view of the world." It is important to constantly challenge one's ideologies with facts as they develop. In the next chapter, we will further explore crime and how we measure it.

REVIEW QUESTIONS

1. What is common law?

2. What are the differences among felonies, misdemeanors, and violations?

3. What is police power? Who has the power to pass laws?

4. What powers were given specifically to the federal government?

5. Name and describe each of the steps of the flowchart of criminal justice.

6. How much do we spend on criminal justice agencies?

7. What has been the pattern of crime in the last decade?

8. What is systems theory and what are open and closed systems?

9. Explain the concept of homeostasis.

10. What is an ideology? Explain the crime control and due process ideologies.

VOCABULARY

closed system – does not respond to outside influences

common law – English magistrates' decisions regarding both civil disputes and criminal offenses; eventually they became a body of legal decisions that formed the basis of the American legal system

crime control ideology – the basic belief that controlling crime and punishing the criminal is the most important goal of the criminal justice system

due process ideology – the belief that the most important mission of the criminal justice system is the enforcement of law and protecting the rights of the individual

felonies – the most serious misbehaviors, usually punishable by a year or more in prison

forensic science – science that serves the court; in other words, *forensic* is an adjective that is used to describe something as related to the legal system

homeostasis – the idea that any system will adjust to changes by adapting in such a way as to maintain "business as usual"

ideology – a body of doctrines or beliefs that guide an individual or group; it is a way of organizing knowledge in that we interpret things we see and hear in reference to our existing ideologies

misdemeanors – less serious offenses (such as simple assault) that can be punished by up to a year in jail.

open system – one that is permeable and responsive to outside influences

penal codes – an organized list of laws of the state

police power – the authority to set and enforce most laws

social contract – a concept proposed by philosophers Hobbes, Locke, and Rousseau that explains that individuals give up the liberty to aggress against others in return for protection from being victimized themselves

systems approach – a type of analysis utilizing the definitions and characteristics of a system

FOR FURTHER READING

Bailey, Frankie and Donna Hale (1997). *Popular Culture, Crime and Justice*. Belmont, CA: Wadsworth/ITP.

Muraskin, Rosalyn and Shelly Domash (2006). *Crime and the Media: Headlines vs. Reality*. Upper Saddle River, NJ: Prentice Hall.

Packer, Herbert (1968). *The Limits of the Criminal Sanction*. Stanford, CA: Stanford University Press

Potter, Gary and Victor E. Kappeler (1998). *Constructing Crime: Perspectives in Making News and Social Problems*. Prospect Heights, IL: Waveland Press.

Rafter, Nicole (2000). *Shots in the Mirror: Crime Films and Society*. New York, NY: Oxford University Press.

Surette, Ray (1997). *Media, Crime, and Criminal Justice*, Second Edition. Belmont, CA: Wadsworth, ITP.

APPENDIX: WRITING A RESEARCH PAPER

You may be required to write a research paper; therefore this last section provides some guidance. Papers may range in length from 3 to 25 pages, so the comments below must be adjusted to fit the length of the paper assigned.

Choosing a topic. One of the most important steps in writing a good paper is choosing a topic. Luckily, in the field of criminal justice, there is a veritable wealth of topics to choose from that are interesting, current, and even controversial. You should try to discover a topic that is less typical; for instance, instead of the death penalty, you might do a cross-cultural comparison of the death penalty. If the paper is a small one, it is important to limit the topic. In fact, the easiest way to do that is to ask a research question: Do all states have the death penalty? Then three to five pages will be sufficient to describe states' laws and differences between the states. You will not need to do a whole history, presentation of legal issues, and methods of execution for such a topic title.

For possible topics, you can look in your textbook table of contents, scan the book itself or even read the local newspaper for current, topical issues. Some possible topics (assuming an average length paper) are:

> The extent of the use of juvenile waivers to adult court
>
> Changes in school discipline and use of school safety officers
>
> Television and its link to violence
>
> Drug use among teens – is it going up or down?
>
> Gun control research – does it reduce crime?
>
> The CSI effect on criminal prosecution
>
> The effectiveness of community policing
>
> Methods to improve ethical behavior in policing
>
> Issues in the use of tasers: legal issues, misuse, effect on lethal force
>
> The effectiveness of residential drug treatment versus out-patient treatment

The effectiveness of sex offender treatment

The need for gender-specific programming

Habeas Corpus and recent Supreme Court decisions

USA PATRIOT Act's effect on law enforcement

Illegal aliens' involvement in crime

Issues of female police officers: performance, sexual harassment

The effect of domestic violence mandatory arrest policies

The causes of the crime decline of the 1990s

Community policing evaluations

These would all be too broad for paper lengths under 10 pages and so you would need to revise them. For instance, instead of looking at the effectiveness of drug or sex offender treatment in general, you might want to research one particular program or modality. Similarly, instead of a paper on habeas corpus in general, you may want to concentrate on two cases that deal with habeas corpus. The point is that you want to be able to present the issue or question and then comprehensively discuss it in the pages assigned.

Outline. The second step is to outline the paper, but if you don't know anything at all about your subject, you will need to do some research first. Today, the Internet makes research incredibly easy. You can use your library's online data search engine or, if you do not have access to one, you can use Google Scholar. Simply enter your topic and you will be able to access a number of academic journal articles on your subject. Remember that academic journals, not popular magazines, are usually required for research papers. Also, you may not be able to use "practitioner journals" such as *Corrections Today* or *Law Enforcement Digest*. Academic journals such as *Crime and Delinquency, Criminology, Justice Quarterly, Journal of Crime and Justice,* and *Prison Journal* are the most common sources for a research paper. Instructors seldom allow Wikipedia or other non-official Internet sources as acceptable bibliographic citations. Of course you should also actually go to your library (remember that building?) and look for current books on your subject.

After finding several articles or books on your topic, read them and note the issues that are present in your topic. Certain themes, issues, or points, should become repetitive and these will form the basis of your outline. Start your outline with an introduction section that explains to the reader what the paper is about and a short description of the topic. This section should be no more than one page (or paragraph for short papers) but it must be on the first page, not come later. Then present the sub-topics in some logical order. For some topics, it may be a chronology; for others, it may be that you present positive points, then negative points. It is best to go from the general to the specific. Set your outline up in a document in bold font and perhaps in a larger font size. The advantage of word processing is that you can cut out sections and move them around if you need to as the paper develops. At this point, it is wise to check with your instructor to make sure that the outline fits the requirements of the assignment.

Enter Notes. The next step is to enter your research notes. You should never copy from your sources! Generally, research papers are too short to include quotes anyway so just resolve to write every word yourself. When you read the article, you should enter notes into the word document under the appropriate bold face heading with a reference. See the example below. Refrain from copying since when you begin to write, you will forget whether it is a quote or whether it is your sentence. Continue to enter in facts from the articles as you read them. Once all your references have been read and relevant facts entered, you can see where the gaps are in your outline. Then you need to either go find that information from new sources or rearrange your outline to eliminate those topics or issues. The general rule of thumb is that you should have the ratio of a reference per page assigned; which means that for a 10 page paper you need 10 references and so forth.

In the box provided, you see an outline for a paper on probation where some beginning notes are filled in. You must have complete reference citation for every fact entered as a note. Once your outline is filled in with notes, you can begin writing.

The Use of Probation Today

History
John Augustus, Boston shoemaker, 1841 (reference, year)

Mission and Scope of Use

Probation in State X
State organization chart

Criticisms of Probation
Slap on the wrist? (reference, year)
Percent of people who are in favor of it (reference, year, page number)

Future of Probation

Write the paper. If the paper is long, it is important to provide subheadings. These can be the outline headings. You should always have an introductory paragraph or page that explains what the paper is about, and a conclusion paragraph or page that basically identifies the few key points you want the reader to remember. Do not introduce new information in the conclusion.

Referencing your sources is very important so as you take notes, make sure you have a system for identifying where they came from. It is important to reference with an author, year *and* a page number every time you use a number (i.e., the number in prison or the percent of people who recidivate). You must also reference with a page number when you use a direct quote. For all general information you may cite only to the author and year of the publication without a page number (but check with your instructor).

The most common reference citation style in criminal justice is the *modified* APA style. APA style manuals may be purchased and style sheets can be found on the Internet. Your instructor may provide a style sheet for you. Generally, the modified style puts the author's name, year and page number (if necessary) in parentheses in the text. For instance, if I entered a fact from my note above and I obtained the information from this textbook, it might read something like this:

> The "father" of probation was John Augustus, a Boston shoemaker. He asked the court to release an offender arrested for public drunkenness into his custody in 1841 (Pollock 2007).

If I had used a direct quote or used a number from the source, I would need the page number as well.

> John Augustus eventually helped supervise 267 offenders (Pollock 2007, 31) [or (Pollock, 2007: 31).]

There are many ways to cite, however, so find out whether there is a particular citation style that you are required to use. Regardless of which style you use, you must be consistent throughout the paper.

Write the conclusion. The last step in writing is providing a good conclusion paragraph. Typically, you do not insert any "editorializing" in the body of the paper, but it is sometimes acceptable to insert your own opinions and conclusions in the final section of the paper. After writing your paper, it is very important to check it for grammatical errors and omissions in citation. Make sure your references are complete and do not include any source as a reference that is not used in the text of the paper. In the checklist provided, you can see some of the most common writing problems. Make sure that you do not include them in your paper!

WRITING CHECKLIST
(These are the most common writing errors)

__1. Is there a beginning paragraph that explains what the paper is going to do and a concluding paragraph that summarizes the content?

__2. Is there proper citation *in the text*? Is there a cite after the source author's name? Follow the assigned style or be consistent in your use of any standard style of citation.

__3. Is there a citation for every fact that is not general knowledge? Are there citations *with page numbers* for direct quotes and any numbers or percents?

__4. Are there any sentences copied from another source without quotes and/or without having a reference cite? Remember even changing a word in a sentence is still considered plagiarism.

__5. Are there any paragraphs that are longer than about a fourth of a typed page? If so, break up into smaller paragraphs. Are paragraphs too short (less than three sentences)?

__6. Are there any sentences that run on for more than three lines? If so, break up into two sentences.

__7. Are there any Web pages used as references? If so, is the cite in the text the author's name (not the web address) and does the reference in back indicate the date you retrieved the Web site?

__8. Are numbers spelled out in words if single digits and displayed as numerals in double digits and above? Also, if a sentence starts out with a number, it must be spelled out.

__9. Are affect (think "influence") and effect (think "consequence") used correctly?

__10. Are verb "strings" correct? ("they are running, walking, and singing;" or, "they ran, walked, and sang;" NOT: "they are running, walked and sing")

__11. Are verbs consistently in past tense or present tense. He ran to the store and talked to the owner; NOT He is running to the store and talked to the owner.

__12. Are female/male (adjectives) and men/women (nouns) used correctly?

__13. Is there no more than one quote per page?

__14. Are any quotes that are over three lines long indented and single spaced?

__15. Are all noun/verbs in agreement, depending on whether they are plural or singular?

__16. Are there any "I" statements? (Typically this is not appropriate in a research paper).

__17. Are there any conclusory or opinion statements in the text? (Typically this is not appropriate in a research paper).

__18. Is research referred to appropriately in the text? Typically, one writes: "Smith (1987) in his research on prisoners . . ."; use of the title of the article or book is generally not appropriate.

__19. Are law cases italicized or underlined with the citation provided?

__20. If a secondary source is cited, is it appropriately referenced? (i.e., Smith, as cited in Jones, 1990: pgs).

__21. Are *were* and *where* used correctly?

---

[1] See, Hobbes, T. (1651/1982). *Leviathan*. New York: Penguin Classics. See also Rousseau, J. (1762/1968). *The Social Contract*. New York: Penguin Classics.

[2] Bureau of Justice Statistics. Retrieved 12/23/05 from ojp.usdoj.gov/bjs/glance/exptyp.htm.

[3] Packer, H. (1968). *The Limits of the Criminal Sanction*. Stanford, CA: Stanford University Press.

[4] Pollock, J. (2007). *Ethical Dilemmas and Decisions in Criminal Justice*, Fifth Edition. Belmont, CA: ITP/Wadsworth, pp. 190-191.

Chapter 2

Crime in Society

What You Need to Know

★ The majority of crime is mundane, low-dollar property crime.

★ Crime is defined by our laws and the definition of what is a crime can change.

★ The two most important sources of crime data are the Uniform Crime Reports (UCR) and the National Crime Victim Survey (NCVS).

★ Crime has declined dramatically in the last 15 years, but this decline has leveled off in the past couple of years.

★ The three strongest correlates of crime are sex, age, and, for certain crimes, race.

What is crime? This seems like an easy question, and it is, in a way. However, the answer is not necessarily murder, robbery, or rape. Those may be examples of crime, but the definition of **crime** is simply "those actions that are prohibited by law." The definition exemplifies one of the fundamental problems of criminology. If criminology is the study of why people commit crime, then one can see why such a study may be difficult if the definition of crime changes. For instance, in past years abortion was a crime, and now it is not (at least in the first three months of a pregnancy), but it might be in the future. Gambling is usually illegal, unless it is buying a state lottery ticket or unless the state has legalized that specific form of gambling. So how does one construct an explanation for why people commit such "crimes" when sometimes they are and sometimes they are not crimes at all?

What is deviance? Crime and deviance may be considered synonyms, but they are definitely not. **Deviance** can be defined as behaviors that are contrary to the norm. Deviance has a negative connotation, but it simply means that the behavior is unusually infrequent. Most crime is deviant. There are very few serial killers (thank goodness!) and even relatively few burglars compared to the total population. On the other hand, some "crime" is not deviant at all. Can you think of some? (Hint: How many people break speeding laws?) Even simple assault is not really deviant. In fact, perhaps you have been a victim or perpetrator of simple assault and never realized it. The definition of simple assault in one state is:

> (1) intentionally, knowingly, or recklessly causes bodily injury to another, including the person's spouse;

> (2) intentionally or knowingly threatens another with imminent bodily injury, including the person's spouse; or

> (3) intentionally or knowingly causes physical contact with another when the person knows or should reasonably believe that the other will regard the contact as offensive or provocative.[1]

So, if you pushed or even hugged someone who you knew would consider it to be provocative or offensive, you have committed simple assault. This is a Class A misdemeanor unless some other conditions are met, therefore, it is not a very "serious" crime. Most simple assaults are not brought to the attention of the criminal justice system. However, many other, more serious crimes are also never reported. This creates what is known as the **dark figure** of crime, which is crime that does not find its way into official numbers. Crimes such as domestic violence, acquaintance rape, and even theft, are more likely than other crimes to be part of this dark figure of crime.

Because the dark figure of crime is so high, it makes any theorizing about criminals highly questionable. We do not know if the offenders who never come to the attention of authorities are similar to those who do. We do not know if these unknown offenders have similar motivations and patterns of criminal offending. Studies that are based only on known offenders may be faulty in that they are not able to base findings on all offenders—only those we know about.

1. DEFINING CRIMES

Crime is called a "constructed reality" because it is created based on the definitions and perceptions of the observers, formal system actors (such as police), victims, and the actions of the perpetrator. Box 2.1 illustrates the sequence of decision making. Person A shoves Person B. Is it simple assault? It would be only if Person A did it intentionally, believing it to be offensive to Person B. Is it a crime? It is only if it meets the legal definition as provided above. Is it prosecutable? It might be only if Person B reports it (unless a police officer happened to be standing nearby). Will it be prosecuted? A variety of factors affect the decision to prosecute, including the wishes of the victim, the resources of the prosecutor's office, the nature of the evidence, and, some say, perhaps the race and ethnicity of the offender and/or victim.

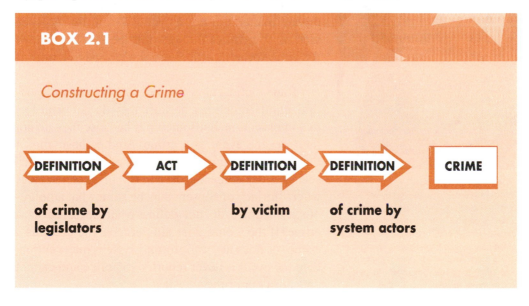

BOX 2.1

Constructing a Crime

DEFINITION ➤ ACT ➤ DEFINITION ➤ DEFINITION ➤ CRIME

of crime by legislators   **by victim**   **of crime by system actors**

1.1 Definition of Crime by Legislators

Before we can punish any act as a crime, a law has to be created by legislation. As we learned in the last chapter, most of our laws come from common law; however, state and federal legislators are constantly fine-tuning our criminal codes and adding new laws or changing existing laws.

In most states, carrying a weapon onto state property, such as a university, is a crime, unless one is a licensed peace officer on duty. Since the tragedy at Virginia Tech University in 2007, when Seung-Hui Cho killed 32 students and professors and wounded dozens more, at least one state (South Carolina) has considered legislation that would make it legal to carry concealed weapons onto college campuses.[2] This illustrates the dynamic nature of law. Legal changes often occur in response to a specific event and some changes may take place before due consideration is given to their ramifications. Legislators typically pass legislation creating new laws in response to a news event and public attention toward a particular type of behavior. The public also has a great deal of influence when they want to increase the punishment for certain crimes. The perceptions and response to domestic violence, drunk driving, and drug use have undergone dramatic change in the last 30 years. Drug laws, especially, have changed in response to public sentiment and legislative initiatives.

1.2 Definition of Crime by Victim

AP Photo/Jeff Christensen

Model Naomi Campbell is led out of the Midtown North Police Precinct by police officers in New York City, Thursday, March 30, 2006. Campbell was charged with second-degree assault after hitting her housekeeper in the head with a phone during an argument in her Park Avenue apartment, police said. According to police, Campbell's 41-year-old housekeeper received four stitches.

Before a crime can be counted by officials, it must be reported by the victim. Why might someone *not* report a crime to authorities? The most common reason is that they believe police can't do anything about it, but they might also interpret the event as a private matter and not a crime. Domestic violence victims sometimes do not want the involvement of the police even though they are obviously victims of assault.

Rape victims also may not report their own victimization, sometimes because they do not want formal intervention, but sometimes because they do not interpret the event as a crime. Studies have shown that female victims who are raped in "date-rape" scenarios by someone they know in circumstances where the lack of consent may be somewhat ambiguous sometimes do not define what occurred as a crime. If the victim does not perceive the event as a crime, or does not want formal system intervention, then the event is never reported to police and cannot appear in our crime statistics.[3]

1.3 Definition of Crime by System Actors

Police do not arrest in a large percentage of cases where an arrest is legally justified; perhaps in as many as half of all cases. Although arrests are usually made in serious felony cases, or in situations in which victims demand an arrest, even assaults may be dealt with informally rather than by initiating a formal report or arrest.[4] Understanding when and why police choose to make arrests is a necessary part of understanding crime statistics. We forget that crime reports are simply the crimes that victims choose to report, and arrest statistics represent only the cases in which police officers made an arrest. Both are only a portion of the total number of criminal incidents.

One of the most important questions in the study of criminal justice is whether police enforce the law unfairly and are more likely to target minorities for formal system responses. There are many studies that explore the issue, but it is not an easy topic to analyze because it must involve the researcher being able to access information on each police-citizen interaction that might have resulted in an arrest to determine if certain factors, such as race, age, sex, or demeanor, affected the decision.

One of the reasons we use homicide, robbery, and burglary as indicators of crime is that they are less subject to the discretion of system actors. When these acts occur, it is more likely that everyone agrees that they are crimes, and system actors are more likely to begin formal processing. As we discussed above, even assault may be subject to individual definitions and interpretations of the offender, victim, and system actors, therefore fluctuations in assault rates may be real differences in such behavior, or differences in perception and/or enforcement of the behavior that can be defined as assault.

2. VICTIM-HARMING CRIMES

It might be helpful to consider crime as victim-harming or victimless. **Victim-harming crimes** are those where there is a specific victim who has been injured or suffered a loss. **Victimless crimes** are those where there is no direct victim. Thus, most drug laws are victimless crimes, as are gambling, underage drinking, and so on. These acts are prohibited because society has deemed them injurious to at least the perpetrator and, sometimes, others, but not in a direct way. Some might argue, in fact, that no crimes are truly victimless because such actions may harm, even if indirectly, family members or friends of the perpetrator.

Crimes such as assault, rape, robbery, burglary, larceny/theft and others are victim-harming crimes. Even theft from large corporations or income tax evasion would be considered victim-harming because there is a loss that is suffered directly from the action. What about computer hacking? Simply breaking into a computer security system on a dare and not doing any damage could still be considered an injury because it requires the company to bolster its defenses; therefore, one might place computer hacking into the victim-harming category.

What about prostitution? (Victimless?) Teen prostitution? (Victim-harming?) Pornography? (Victimless?) Child pornography? (Victim-harming?). If you disagree, what are the elements of your argument as to why it should be the other category? What are some other crimes that are victimless crimes? What are some that are victim-harming? There are several different drug-related crimes, including simple possession, possession with intent to sell, and smuggling. Are some victim-harming and some victimless crimes? The reason we may want to distinguish victim-harming and victimless crimes is that if we want to understand what motivates people to commit a crime, then there might be dramatically different answers depending on the crime. One can see, for instance, that different explanations might be applied to why someone uses drugs or gambles, from why someone rapes or robs another. On the other hand, there are some criminologists who would argue that the same underlying reason could explain both victim-harming and victimless crimes.[5]

Crime is not usually glamorous. Crime is not often committed by offenders who painstakingly plan their act and play cat-and-mouse games with determined detectives as we see in the movies or on television. Mostly, crimes are mundane, committed by individuals who are not necessarily committed to a criminal lifestyle, and result in relatively modest losses to the victim. Even homicide is rarely as it is depicted on television. On television, homicide is often committed by strangers; in reality, many homicides occur between people who know each other and happen as a result of a dispute or altercation.

Before we can ask the question "Why do people commit crime?" we need to be aware of the characteristics of crime. In other words, we need to know the "who, what, and where" of crime. To understand crime patterns, we use a number of sources of crime data. These are not perfect and each has inherent weaknesses, but they are the source of everything we think we know about crime in this country.

3. SOURCES OF CRIME DATA

The two most common sources of crime data are the Uniform Crime Reports and the National Crime Victimization Survey. It is important to note that everything that we think we know about crime is derived primarily from these sources; thus, if there is some bias (inaccuracy) present in the way they present the pattern of crime, then what we know is not necessarily accurate.

3.1 The Uniform Crime Reports

The most well-known and used source of crime statistics in this country is the **Uniform Crime Reports**. This collection of local crime reports and arrest data began in 1929 and is now produced by the Federal Bureau of Investigation. The numbers come either directly from local law enforcement agencies or from a state agency that collects the data from local agencies and delivers it in a centralized format. In 2004, according to *Crime in the United States, 2004,* the reports represented 94.2 percent of the total population of the country (the remaining locales did not participate).[6]

The Uniform Crime Reports presents crime in terms of **rates**. A rate is the number of crimes divided by the population and then multiplied to display by a standard number. Using the mathematical formula, one computes the number of crimes committed per every 100,000 people in the population.

The advantage of a rate is that it allows us to compare patterns of crime in very different populations. For instance, with rates, we can compare the same city in two different periods, even if the city has grown. We can also compare

$$\text{Rate} \;=\; \frac{\text{\# crimes known to police}}{\text{\# total population}} \;\times\; 100{,}000$$

two different cities, even if one is very large and the other very small. Knowing, for instance, the raw number of burglaries in New York City, Portland, Oregon, and Detroit, Michigan, tells us something, but it doesn't tell us the relative risk of victimization in these cities because they do not have the same populations. The only way to compare the crime of two different populations is to compute the rate of each city, then compare the rates. In 2005, the *numbers* of reported burglaries and the *rates* for these cities[7] looked like this:

City	Population	Number of Burglaries	Rate
New York City	8,115,690	23,210	285
Portland	540,389	6,121	1,132
Detroit	900,932	15,304	1,698

Who would have thought that there were more burglaries per 100,000 people in Portland and Detroit than in New York? One might conclude that it was somehow connected with having a large population that made New York City's rate so low, but compare other big cities:

City	Population	Number of Burglaries	Rate
Houston	2,045,732	27,541	1,346
Los Angeles	3,871,077	22,592	583
Boston	567,589	4,531	798

These cities also had higher rates than New York City. So, despite the stereotype of high crime in the Big Apple, these numbers indicate that maybe the city is not as unsafe as we might think.

It should also be noted, however, that the FBI cautions against anyone using these numbers to compare the crime risk between cities because there are so many variables that go into them, including reporting practices, urban density, the department's reporting practices, and so on. If a city extends its limits out into the suburbs, the crime rate will be lower because crime occurs less often in suburban than in urban areas. Thus, New York's city limits may be drawn in such a way that it brings down the rate of burglary, compared to other cities. Also, burglaries may not be recorded in the same manner, or people may be less inclined to report them in New York City.

It is very important to have an accurate population base for rates to mean anything. If the population base is inaccurate, then so, too, will be the rate. If, for instance, the population base is out of date and the actual population has grown considerably, then the crimes (which inevitably would increase with a larger population) will be divided by an artificially small population indicating that the rate of crime in that locale (the amount of crime per person) is higher than what it actually is. In contrast, if the population used is inaccurate in the other direction and shows a much larger population than what actually exists (perhaps because people have been moving away from that area), and crimes are divided by this inaccurately high population, then the crime rate will appear to be lower than it actually is. Usually, the FBI uses the most recent Census numbers for the area, but these numbers may be vulnerable to rapid fluctuations in population/migration.

You can look at the crime rates for your state or even your city by going to the FBI Web site or by looking in a library for their yearly report, titled *Crime in the United States*. Crimes are reported by state, region, and by city-rural categories.

These numbers are gathered from law enforcement agencies via a standard reporting form so that, for instance, larceny means the same thing in all states despite different state laws defining the dollar amount that would change larceny from a misdemeanor to a felony. Because these are standard definitions, they may or may not conform to the state's definition for that particular crime. Also, because of the index crime definitions, it is difficult to use this source to find out about certain crimes such as domestic violence or identity theft, because the reporting is not set up to identify them.

The UCR provides the total number of reported crimes for the seven index crimes: murder and non-negligent manslaughter, forcible rape, robbery, aggravated assault, burglary, larceny-theft, motor vehicle theft, and arson. Box 2.2 shows how violent crime reports have decreased over the years, although the decreasing numbers seem to be leveling off. Box 2.3 shows property crimes.

The numbers of arrests are by no means a measure of crime, because they capture only the crimes in which a suspect was identified and a decision to arrest was made. It is interesting, however, that arrests also decreased during the period when we saw the large drop in reported crime. Arrest data is presented for 21 crime categories in Box 2.4. The table shows that arrests for most crimes have been decreasing over the last 15 years.

★ Exercise: In the State of . . .

1. Go to **http://www.fbi.gov/ucr/ucr.htm#cius.**

2. Go to the tables that provide information on the crimes reported by state.

3. Find the rate per 100,000 for your state for the crimes of murder, rape, robbery, and burglary.

4. Find the rates for at least three states you would like to compare your state to and construct a table.

5. How do they compare?

Many crimes go unsolved or are not cleared. Crimes are considered cleared when an arrest is made for an offense. The UCR reports the number of crimes cleared by arrest with a statistic called the **clearance rates.** The clearance rates vary greatly for different crimes. In 2004, The UCR showed national clearance rates. Homicide has the highest clearance rate (62.6%) while burglary has the lowest clearance rate (12.9%).[8]

One of the most often cited criticisms of the UCR is that it represents only reported crimes. If someone does not report a criminal victimization to the police, it does not get counted as a crime. Consequently, we note that there is a "dark" figure of crime that never appears in the UCR. The amount of unreported crime varies by the type of crime, but in general, it is estimated that about half of all crime does not appear in the UCR. This presents a distinct

BOX 2.2

Uniform Crime Reports–Violent Crime
(Estimated Crimes/Rate Per 100,000)

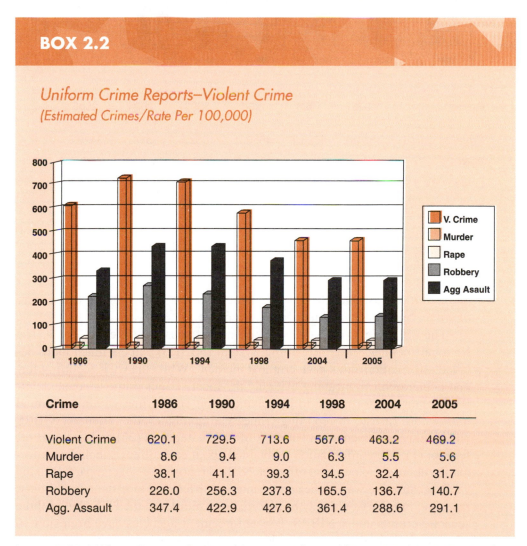

Crime	1986	1990	1994	1998	2004	2005
Violent Crime	620.1	729.5	713.6	567.6	463.2	469.2
Murder	8.6	9.4	9.0	6.3	5.5	5.6
Rape	38.1	41.1	39.3	34.5	32.4	31.7
Robbery	226.0	256.3	237.8	165.5	136.7	140.7
Agg. Assault	347.4	422.9	427.6	361.4	288.6	291.1

Source: UCR, Table 1. *Crime in the United States.* By Volume and Rate, 1986-2005. Retrieved from: www.fbi.gov/ucr/05cius/data/table/_.01/html.

BOX 2.3

Uniform Crime Reports–Property Crime

Crime	1986	1990	1994	1998	2004	2005
Property Crime	4881.8	5073.1	4660.2	4052.5	3514.1	3429.8
Burglary	1349.8	1232.2	1042.1	863.2	730.3	726.7
Larceny/theft	3022.1	3185.1	3026.9	2729.5	2362.3	2286.3
MVT	509.8	655.8	591.3	459.9	421.5	416.7

Source: UCR, Table 1. *Crime in the United States.* By Volume and Rate, 1986-2005. Retrieved from: www.fbi.gov/ucr/05cius/data/table/_.01/html

problem if one uses the UCR as a measure of crime. In fact, it is not a measure of crime, but only a measure of *reported* crime.

The FBI has also been collecting crime statistics in a different format. The National Incident Based Reporting System (NIBRS) gathers much more detailed information about each criminal incident. While the UCR reporting format is hierarchical, meaning that only the most serious crime is counted, NIBRS requires information to be submitted on each crime within a criminal transaction. Instead of reporting crimes via the eight index offenses, NIBRS will display information on Group A offense categories (22) and Group B offenses (11). More information is obtained about each offense, including information about the victim and offender. NIBRS reports are not comparable to the UCR because the way crimes are counted is different. For instance, a robbery, rape, and murder would only be reported as a murder in the UCR, but as three separate crimes under NIBRS. Law enforcement agencies have been slow to adopt the NIBRS reporting procedures, most probably because it is much more detailed, requiring more effort to enter the data.

BOX 2.4

Uniform Crime Report Arrests (by Rate/per 100,000)

Crime	1995	2000	2005
Murder/non-negligent Manslaughter	8.5	4.8	4.7
Forcible rape	13.5	9.8	8.6
Robbery	70.2	39.7	39.2
Aggravated Assault	223.0	173.9	152.2
Burglary	148.8	104.0	101.2
Larceny/theft	592.7	429.5	392.6
MVT	75.9	54.2	49.7
Arson	7.6	5.9	5.5
Other assaults	496.5	471.4	440.2
Forgery and counterfeiting	46.8	39.1	40.0
Fraud	162.9	117.4	106.4
Embezzlement	5.9	6.9	6.5
Stolen Property	65.1	43.2	45.6
Vandalism	118.5	101.3	94.8
Weapons	95.3	57.9	65.6
Prostitution	41.3	33.7	28.8
Sex offenses	36.8	33.6	27.2
Drug abuse violations	582.5	572.4	496.8
Gambling	8.0	4.0	2.2
Offenses against family and children	53.4	50.1	55.3
DUI	526.0	508.6	328.2
Liquor laws	221.6	239.3	128.4
Drunkenness	268.4	232.5	80.1
Disorderly conduct	285.9	231.5	293.3
Vagrancy	10.4	12.1	10.4
All other (except traffic)	1,486.3	1,324.2	933.2
Curfew and loitering	58.5	58.0	86.1
Runaways	96.6	51.4	19.7

Source: UCR, Table 30. *Crime in the United States,* 1995, 2000, 2005: Number and Rate of Arrests. Retrieved from: http://www.fbi.gov/ucr/cius and http://www.fbi.gov/ucr/05cius/data/table_30.html.

3.2 Victimization Studies

Another source of crime statistics comes from victimization surveys. The Bureau of Justice Statistics presents findings from the **National Crime Victimization Survey**. Begun in 1973, the U.S. Bureau of the Census has been interviewing household members in a nationally representative sample. The items in the survey capture more information than what is available through the UCR. For instance, one question asks the respondent whether the crime was reported to the police. This is the source for our information about how much of crime goes unreported.

Questions cover information on the victim (i.e., age, sex, race, ethnicity, income, and educational level), and, if known, the offender (i.e., age, sex, race). It also reports findings on the victimization itself, including time and place and level of injury or loss. Findings from the National Crime Victimization Survey can be accessed most easily through the Bureau of Justice Statistics, an agency that also presents other forms of crime statistics.

These two sources of crime data may be compared, but it is important to note their differences. The NCVS excludes homicide, arson, commercial crimes, and crimes against children under age 12 (the UCR includes these crimes). The UCR only collects arrest data on simple assault and sexual assaults other than rape, not reported crimes in these areas. Further, the NCVS calculates rates on the basis of 1,000 *households* while the UCR calculates rates based on 100,000 *persons*. Thus, it would be a mistake to treat findings from the two sources as comparable statistically. In general, the UCR gives us a broad picture of crime patterns (as reported to police) in the United States while the NCVS gives us more information about the characteristics of victimizations and reporting trends by victims.

To access the Bureau of Justice Statistics, go to: http://www.ojp.usdoj.gov/bjs/

Because the NCVS is based on a random sampling of the population and does not collect reports of all victimizations, it is subject to all the potential problems of sampling and survey weaknesses. If any principles of random sampling are violated, then the applicability to the general population is in doubt. However, it is important to note that the NCVS also showed a decline of reported crime victimization in the last decade, thus the two sources of crime data were consistent in measuring a crime decline.

3.3 Self-Report Studies

Another source of crime data is simply to ask the offender. Self-report studies ask individuals to report the crimes they have committed. Obviously there are problems inherent in such an approach, such as whether the individual is answering honestly or not. Self-reports are generally only obtained from targeted groups, specifically juveniles (who are still in school), and offenders (who are incarcerated). We do not administer self-report surveys door-to-door to samples of citizens. Self-report studies provide interesting information, but the findings must be considered in light of the characteristics of the sample. For instance, self-report studies of juveniles often use measures of behavior that stretch the definition of "crime" to the breaking point by including minor deviances, such as truancy and other forms of juvenile misbehavior. The definitions of wrongdoing are expanded in such studies because most students have not committed any criminal acts. Therefore, in order to get sufficient numbers for statistical analysis, the definition of "offender" is expanded. It should be kept in mind when reading these studies that these "offenders" are not necessarily who we think of as criminals.

Part of the reason that student self-report studies have difficulty obtaining sufficient numbers of offenders for statistical analysis is that by the time they are administered in junior or senior years, many high-risk juveniles have already dropped out or are not in school the day the study is administered. Therefore, the group of young people most likely to have committed crimes are likely to be absent from the study and the reports of criminal activity are likely to underrepresent the true nature of juvenile crime.

Like school samples, prisoner samples are also relatively easy to obtain, but are also non-representative. Prisoners do not represent all offenders (only those who are caught and sentenced to prison). They also may not admit or may exaggerate their criminal activities. In addition, these surveys are subject to the potential inaccuracies of all surveys in that respondents may forget or mis-remember when events occurred.

Self-report studies give us more information about the offenders' patterns of criminal activity—if we can trust the data. One of the uses of self-report studies is to see if official statistics accurately represent who commits crime. We have found from self-reports of juveniles, for instance, that many more juveniles have committed crimes than official arrests indicate. This raises the question, "When do system actors (police) utilize formal methods of social control versus informal?"

3.4 Cohort Studies

One other source of crime data are **cohort studies**, which follow a group of subjects over a long period. For instance, one cohort study followed all males born in Philadelphia in 1948.[9] Another longitudinal study conducted by the Harvard Program on Human Development and Criminal Behavior collected data on a cohort sample.[10] Typically the follow-up period extends throughout childhood and into adulthood. Proponents of longitudinal research argue that this method of data collection can illuminate how factors work at various times in one's life. Longitudinal research identifies those correlates of delinquency that emerge during the lifetime of the cohort members. For instance, Farrington, Ohlin, and Wilson[11] identified the following as correlates of delinquency and crime:

We know that the typical high-rate offender is a young male who began his aggressive or larcenous activities at an early age, well before the typical boy gets into serious trouble. We know that he comes from a troubled, discordant, low-income family in which one or both parents are likely to have criminal records themselves. We know that the boy has had trouble in school—he created problems for his teachers and does not do well in his studies. On leaving school, often by dropping out, he works at regular jobs only intermittently. Most employers regard him as a poor risk. He experiments with a variety of drugs—alcohol, marijuana, speed, heroin—and becomes a frequent user of whatever drug is most readily available, often switching back and forth among different ones.[12]

Thus, individual differences, family influences, school influences, and peer influences were all identified as potential predictors of the onset of, continuation in, and desistance from crime.

4. PATTERNS OF CRIME

According to the Uniform Crime Reports and the National Crime Victimization Survey, crime has shown a steady overall decline since the early 1990s. In Box 2.5, we see that: (a) there is much more property crime than violent crime, and (b) that property crime has shown a more dramatic decline than violent crime. The long timeline in Box 2.5 does not show enough detail to see that violent crime actually declined quite substantially from a high of 758 crimes per 100,000 in 1991 to a low of 475 in 2003. The violent crime decline is shown in the second table.

The National Crime Victimization Survey also indicates that Americans have experienced a dramatically declining crime rate over the last decade. In Box 2.6, victimization survey data shows that, for violent crime and property crime, the decline is comparable to that recorded in the Uniform Crime Reports.

5. THE GREAT AMERICAN CRIME DECLINE

The biggest "story" in criminal justice in the last 20 years was the dramatic drop experienced through the latter half of the 1990s. Although the decrease has leveled off in some locales in recent years, we experienced truly amazing drops in all crime, including homicide and other violent crimes. Why? It could be any of the following factors:

★   aging birth cohort of baby boomers

★   stabilization of drug markets

★   higher incarceration rates

★   community policing

★   "zero tolerance" policing

★   home health care and pre- and post-natal health services

BOX 2.5

Uniform Crime Rate Over Time

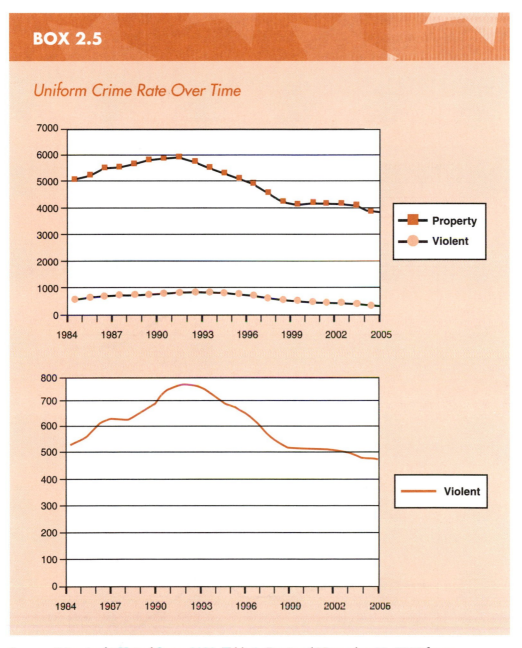

Source: *Crime in the United States*, 2003, Table 1. Retrieved November 11, 2007 from: www.fbi.gov/ucs/cius_03/xl/03tbl.01.xls.

★ violence prevention programs in schools

★ increased numbers of abortions in the late 1970s and 1980s[13]

There is no consensus as to whether any of these factors, either alone or in combination, account for the dramatic decline of crime. One thing that hasn't happened as a result, however, is any decline in the size of criminal justice system.

BOX 2.6

Bureau of Justice Statistics: Property and Violent Crime Victimization

Property crime rates

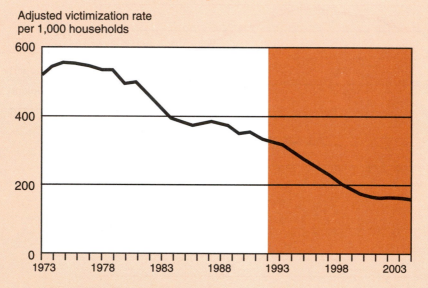

Adjusted victimization rate per 1,000 households

Violent crime rates

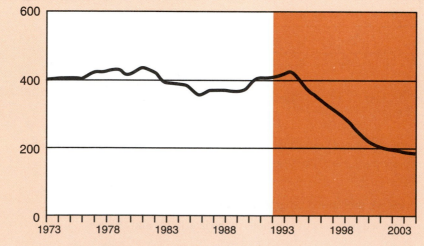

Adjusted victimization rate per 1,000 persons age 12 and over

Source: Bureau of Justice Statistics. Retrieved April 1, 2007 from: http://www.ojp.usdoj.gov/bjs/glance/cv2.htm.

It also appears that the great crime decline may be over. In Box 2.7, the introduction and summary of the 2006 Uniform Crime Reports is provided.

BOX 2.7

News Release (September 2007): FBI Releases its 2006 Crime Statistics

Washington, D.C. — For the second consecutive year, the estimated number of violent crimes in the nation increased, and for the fourth year in a row, the estimated number of property crimes decreased.

According to statistics released today by the FBI, the estimated volume of violent crime increased 1.9 percent, and the estimated volume of property crime decreased 1.9 percent in 2006 when compared with 2005 figures. The estimated rate of violent crime was 473.5 occurrences per 100,000 inhabitants (a 1.0-percent increase when the 2006 and 2005 rates were compared), and the estimated rate of property crime was 3,334.5 per 100,000 inhabitants (a 2.8-percent decline).

The FBI presented these data today in the 2006 edition of Crime in the United States, a statistical compilation of offense and arrest data as reported by law enforcement agencies throughout the nation. The FBI collected these data via the Uniform Crime Reporting (UCR) Program.

The UCR Program gathers offense data for violent and property crimes. Violent crimes are the offenses of murder and nonnegligent manslaughter, forcible rape, robbery, and aggravated assault; property crimes are the offenses of burglary, larceny-theft, motor vehicle theft, and arson. (Though the FBI classifies arson as a property crime, it does not estimate arson data because of variations in the level of participation at the agency level. Consequently, arson is not included in the estimated property crime total.) The Program also collects arrest data for violent and property crimes as well as 21 additional offenses that include all other offenses except traffic violations.

In 2006, more than 17,500 city, county, college and university, state, tribal, and federal agencies voluntarily participated in the UCR Program. These agencies represented 94.2 percent of the nation's population. A summary of the crime statistics presented in Crime in the United States, 2006, follows:

★ Nationwide, there were an estimated 1,417,745 violent crimes reported in 2006.

★ Of the violent crimes, the estimated number of murders and nonnegligent manslaughters increased 1.8 percent, and the estimated number of robberies increased 7.2 percent in 2006 when compared with 2005 data. The estimated number of aggravated assaults decreased 0.2 percent, and the estimated number of forcible rapes declined 2.0 percent.

★ There were an estimated 9,983,568 property crimes, excluding arson, reported nationwide in 2006.

★ Of the property crimes, burglary was the only offense to show an increase (1.3 percent) in volume when 2006 data were compared with the 2005 data. The estimated number of larceny-thefts decreased 2.6 percent, and the estimated number of motor vehicle thefts declined 3.5 percent.

★ In 2006, excluding arson, victims of property crimes collectively lost an estimated $17.6 billion: thefts of motor vehicles resulted in losses of more than $7.9 billion, larceny-thefts resulted in losses of $5.6 billion, and burglaries, $4.0 billion.

★ Slightly more than 44 percent (44.3) of violent crimes and 15.8 percent of property crimes were cleared by arrest or exceptional means by the nation's law enforcement agencies in 2006.

★ A total of 13,943 law enforcement agencies reported 69,055 arson offenses to the UCR Program in 2006.

★ The number of arsons reported in 2006 increased 2.1 percent when compared with the number of arsons reported in 2005.

★ The average dollar loss for arson offenses was $13,325 per incident.

★ The FBI estimated that law enforcement agencies nationwide made 14,380,370 arrests in 2006, excluding those for traffic offenses.

BOX 2.7

★ Law enforcement agencies made 4,832.5 arrests for each 100,000 in population nationwide for the 29 offenses for which the UCR Program collects arrest data.

★ The arrest rate for violent crime was 207.0 arrests per 100,000 inhabitants; for property crime, the rate was 524.5.

★ The rate of arrests for murder and nonnegligent manslaughter in 2006 was 4.5 per 100,000 in population. The rate of arrests for forcible rape was 8.2; for robbery, 43.2; and for aggravated assault, 151.1.

★ Of the property crimes, law enforcement made 102.5 arrests for burglary for each 100,000 in population, 370.0 for larceny-theft, 46.5 for motor vehicle theft, and 5.5 for arson.

Source: http://www.fbi.gov/pressrel/pressrel07/cius092407.htm.

6. CORRELATES OF CRIME

Of course, these summary statistics of crime do not tell us much about who commits crime, when and where it is committed, or against whom. A **correlate** of crime is a factor that is associated statistically with the incidence of crime. In other words, it can be a predictor of crime. The three strongest predictors of crime seem to be sex, age, and race. We say "seem to be" because the information we have available is based on arrest statistics. We know who is arrested for crimes, and we assume that those arrested represent those who commit crimes, but we cannot be completely sure. For instance, the **chivalry theory** proposes the idea that women are less likely to be arrested than men in similar circumstances, and if arrested, are less likely to be tried and convicted. There has been a great deal of research testing whether or not this occurs, and the weight of evidence indicates that it occurred to some extent, for some women, for some crimes, in the past, but seems to be less likely to occur today.[14]

Generally, we are fairly certain that women are much less likely to commit violent crime than men, and somewhat less likely to commit property crimes.

Karla Faye Tucker, shown in this undated photo, in Gatesville, Texas, lost an appeal Monday, Dec. 8, 1997, before the U.S. Supreme Court, clearing the way for the first execution of a woman in Texas since 1863. Tucker was convicted of the 1983 killing of a Houston man with a pickax.

In Box 2.8 we see that for all crime categories the number of arrests of men exceeded that for women. For some crimes, the differential was quite extreme (homicide and rape); for others, it was marginal (fraud and embezzlement). It also seems to be the case that in the five-year period reported, women experienced an increase in arrests while men were less likely to be arrested in some crime categories (rape, aggravated assault, motor vehicle theft, other assaults, forgery/counterfeiting, and sex offenses/other than prostitution and rape). This could be the beginning of a long-range trend, or it could be a temporary pattern and not appear in the next reporting period.

Another clear correlate of crime is age. Crime is typically committed by those between the ages of 18 and 25. Box 2.9 illustrates this trend and shows how crime declines after age 30.

Race, a third correlate of crime, is not as predictable. The race of the offender varies quite a bit depending on the type of crime. Unfortunately, the FBI statistics used to construct tables of those arrested does not include information on ethnicity; therefore, "whites" includes both whites and non-black Hispanic offenders. Box 2.10 shows that, considering their population percentage of about 13 percent, blacks are arrested at disproportionate rates, although for most crimes, not dramatically so. On the other hand, for some

BOX 2.8

Ten-Year Arrest Trends, by Sex 1996-2005

Offense	Male		Female	
	1996	2005	1996	2005
Total	6,773,900	6,261,672	1,845,799	1,982,649
Murder/mans	8,572	7,114	992	875
Rape	18,512	14,924	233	205
Robbery	73,192	60,096	7,788	7,745
Ag. Aslt	260,469	224,080	54,936	57,923
Burglary	195,124	153,888	25,674	27,085
Lar/Theft	595,297	421,828	310,666	270,765
MVT	86,405	67,522	13,913	14,638
Arson	9,972	8,114	1,628	1,602
Other Aslts	597,763	554,044	158,366	183,431
Forg/Ctf	45,250	43,068	26,853	27,670
Fraud	137,874	104,201	117,288	89,338
Embezz	5,545	5,979	4,607	6,108
Sex off	52,296	48,112	4,188	4,298
Drug Viol	688,006	832,707	142,678	202,137

Source: *Crime in the United States*, Table 33. Retrieved May 21, 2007 from: http://www.fbi.gov/ucr/05cius/data/table_33.html.

BOX 2.9

Age of Arrests — 2005

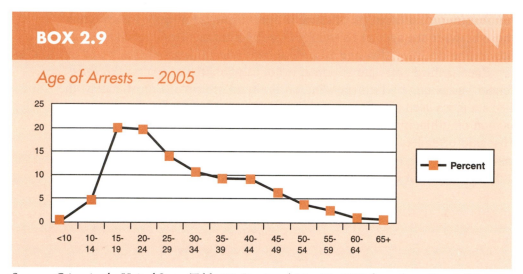

Source: *Crime in the United States*, Table 38. Retrieved May 21, 2007 from: http://www.fbi. gov/ucr/05cius/data/table_38.html.

BOX 2.10

Arrests, by Race —2005

Offense	Percent Distribution		
	White	**Black**	**Am. Indian/Asian**
Total	69.8	27.8	2.3
Murder/mans	49.1	48.6	2.3
Rape	65.1	32.7	2.2
Robbery	42.2	56.3	1.5
Ag. Aslt	63.3	34.3	2.4
Burglary	69.6	28.5	1.9
Lar/Theft	69.3	28.0	2.7
MVT	62.8	34.8	2.3
Assaults	65.1	32.3	2.5
Forg/Ctf	70.7	27.6	1.7
Fraud	68.7	30.1	1.2
Embezz	67.0	31.0	1.9
Sex off	73.6	24.3	2.1
Drug Viol	64.7	33.9	1.3

Source: *Crime in the United States*, Table 43. Retrieved May 21, 2007 from: http://www.fbi.gov/ ucr/05cius/data/table_43.html.

crimes, their arrest rates are highly disproportionate. Murder and robbery have very high rates of arrests for blacks and these two crimes are usually associated with black offenders in the public's mind. Although not displayed on the table, some of the more minor crimes have very high percentages of arrests for blacks as well. Almost 40 percent of the arrests for vagrancy were of blacks (38.4 percent), and an amazing 71.1 percent of arrests for gambling in 2005 were of blacks.[15] Because it is highly doubtful that 71 percent of those who engage in illegal gambling are black, we must look at whether other factors affect the arrest decision.

7. PUBLIC ATTITUDES TOWARD CRIME AND CRIMINALS

In Box 2.11, the public's views of crime and punishment are displayed. We see that public concern about crime was in a downward path until 2001. The terrorist attacks of September 11, 2001, no doubt contributed to the spike one sees in the number of people who believe crime has increased in the last several years, even though official statistics indicate that crime continues to decline.

The Gallup Poll indicates that the public has always favored social programs over more police and prisons. However, the Gallup poll also indicates that the public thinks courts don't deal harshly enough with offenders. In 2003, only six percent of respondents thought the criminal justice system was "too tough," but 65 percent thought it wasn't "tough enough." This is quite a bit less than the 83 percent who thought the courts were not tough enough in 1992.[16] Other sources indicate that the public may be favorably inclined to community sanctions when they feel they are strictly managed. In one study, when asked about 25 crimes, only 27 percent of respondents chose prison as the appropriate sentence when offered a range of community alternatives.[17]

The Sentencing Project, a private non-profit policy body, offers statistical reports on sentencing practices and promotes alternatives to incarceration. This organization offers evidence that there are many myths that exist, such as the following:

1. **Crime is increasing.** The public is not generally aware of the official statistics that show crime has been declining for a decade. There is a widespread belief that crime continues to increase year after year and this misperception fuels the desire for harsh punishments.

2. **Criminals are not being sentenced to prison or not sentenced harshly enough.** Although the public believes that prison is used rarely, it is now the most frequent sentence handed down. The public is not aware that "truth in sentencing" statutes have drastically increased the percentage of the sentence that an average criminal serves. For instance, Florida residents, when polled, believed that offenders only served about 40 percent of their sentence, but, in reality, offenders in Florida are required to serve 85 percent of their sentence.

BOX 2.11

Public Opinion Toward Crime and Punishment

Public's Views on Crime

Question: Is there more crime in your area than there was a year ago, or less? (Deleted "same" answers)

Public's Opinion on How to Address Crime Problems

Question: To lower the crime rate in the United States, some people think additional money and effort should go to attacking the social and economic problems that lead to crime through better education and job training. Others feel more money and effort should go to deterring crime by improving law enforcement with more prisons, police, and judges. Which comes closer to your view?

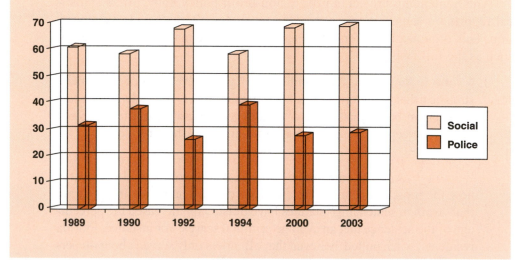

Source: Gallup Poll. Retrieved June 3, 2005 from: http://www.gallup.com/poll/1603/crime.aspx.

3. **The public is in favor of three-strikes laws and harsh sentences.**
When asked, respondents indicate their approval of three-strikes laws;
however, when presented with case scenarios that realistically portray
criminal defendants, they fa-
vor alternative sanctions. This
is so even though such offender profiles would be the
types of offenders who would

> To access the Sentencing Project,
> go to: www.sentencingproject.org

be subject to three-strikes sentences. Thus, it appears that the public
favors the concept of three strikes, but not necessarily how it is likely
to be implemented.

4. **The public supports "tough on criminal" platforms of politicians.**
Again, the concept is different from reality. Politicians may be surprised
to know that one study reported that policymakers estimated that only
12 percent of the public would be in support of alternative sanctions, but
actually 66 percent of respondents indicated their support. As seen in
Box 2.11 above, the majority of respondents favor social programs over
police and prison responses to crime prevention.[18]

8. CONCLUSION

In this chapter, we have discussed the reality of crime; however, we first
note that it is a "constructed reality" created by the perceptions of the victim
and system actors. Only a portion of all crimes find their way into official
statistics. Even the Uniform Crime Reports, our most commonly utilized
source for crime statistics, only can report those crimes that are reported to
the police. The "dark figure" of crime is that which is unreported. We do not
know whether or not these offenders are similar or different from those who
appear in official statistics.

In addition to the Uniform Crime Reports, we also have the National Crime
Victimization Survey which provides additional information. We know more
about victims' injuries and who is likely to report criminal victimization to the
police because of victimization surveys. However, they also have some weaknesses and are not strictly comparable to the UCR in how crime is reported.

The biggest news is that crime declined dramatically during the last part of
the 1990s and early 2000s. It now appears that the most dramatic decline has
slowed and, in some crime categories, and in some locales, the trend has reversed itself. We must be alert to new crime reports to determine if crime will
continue to rise, decline again, or remain stable. The strongest correlates of
crime are sex, age and, to a much lesser degree, race. We know that most crime
is committed by young men. Why this is so and what motivates individuals to
commit crime is the subject of the next chapter.

REVIEW QUESTIONS

1. Why is the definition of crime problematic for the study of criminal justice and criminology?

2. Why is the dark figure of crime problematic for the study of criminal justice and criminology?

3. What do we mean when we say crime is a "constructed reality"?

4. Describe and provide examples for victim-harming and victimless crimes.

5. Describe the Uniform Crime Reports and crime "rates."

6. What are the most commonly committed crimes? What are the most infrequently committed crimes?

7. What are clearance rates?

8. What has been the pattern of crime in the last 30 years?

9. Describe the three correlates of crime.

10. Describe public opinion concerning what should be done about crime.

VOCABULARY

chivalry theory – proposes the idea that women are less likely to be arrested than men in similar circumstances, and, if arrested, less likely to be tried and convicted

clearance rates – the percent of crime solved by arrests

cohort studies – a group of subjects followed over a long period with data collected multiple times during the course of their lives

correlate (of crime) – a factor that is associated statistically with the incidence of crime

crime – actions that are prohibited by law

crime rate – the number of crimes divided by the population and then multiplied to display by a standard number (usually 100,000)

dark figure of crime – crime that does not find its way into official numbers

deviance – behaviors that are contrary to the norm

National Crime Victimization Survey – survey of a nationally representative sample about their criminal victimization

victim-harming crimes – crimes that harm specific victims (either physically or financially)

victimless crimes – crimes where there is no direct victim

Uniform Crime Reports – collection of local crime reports and arrest data begun in 1929 and now produced by the Federal Bureau of Investigation

FOR FURTHER READING

Alvarez, Alex and Ronet Bachman (2003). *Murder American Style*. Belmont, CA: Wadsworth/ITP.

Blumstein, Alfred and Joel Wallman (eds.) (2000). *The Crime Drop in America*. Cambridge, England: Cambridge University Press.

Pollock, Joycelyn (2005). *Women, Prison and Society*. Belmont, CA: Wadsworth, ITP.

Tonry, Michael, Lloyd Ohlin, and David Farrington (1991). *Human Development and Criminal Behavior: New Ways of Advancing Knowledge*. New York, NY: Springer-Verlag.

Zimring, Franklin (2006). *The Great American Crime Decline*. New York, NY: Oxford University Press.

---

[1] Texas Penal Code. Retrieved 4/10/07 from: http://tlo2.tlc.state.tx.us/statutes/docs/PE/content/htm/pe.005.00.000022.00.htm#22.01.00.

[2] Retrieved 4/10/07 from "South Carolina Considers Gun Law" from: www.foxnews.com/story/10,2933,272974,00.html.

[3] See Cleveland, H., M. Koss, and J. Lyons. 1999. "Rape Tactics From the Survivor's Perspective." *Journal of Interpersonal Violence* 14, 5: 532-548.

[4] See Mendias, C. & E. Kobe (2006). "Engagement of Policing Ideals and the Relationship to the Exercise of Discretionary Powers." *Criminal Justice and Behavior* 33, 1: 70-77.

[5] See Gottfredson, M. & T. Hirschi (1990). *The General Theory of Crime*. Stanford, CA: Stanford University Press.

[6] Federal Bureau of Investigation (2004). *Crime in the United States, 2004*. Washington, DC: FBI. Unfortunately the FBI did not publish this statistic for 2005 or 2006.

[7] Federal Bureau of Investigation (2004). *Crime in the United States, 2005*. Table 8. Crime in the United States by State, by City, 2005. Washington, DC: FBI. Retrieved 9/5/2007 from www.fbi.gov/ucr/05cius/data/table_8.html.

[8] Federal Bureau of Investigation. Retrieved 8/1/06 from: www.fbi.gov/ucr/cius_04/offenses_cleared/index.html.

[9] Wolfgang, M., R. Figlio & T. Sellin (1978). *Delinquency in a Birth Cohort*. Chicago, IL: University of Chicago Press.

[10] Tonry, M., L. Ohlin, & D. Farrington (1991). *Human Development and Criminal Behavior: New Ways of Advancing Knowledge*. New York, NY: Springer-Verlag.

[11] Farrington, D., L. Ohlin & J. Wilson (1986). *Understanding and Controlling Crime: Toward a New Research Strategy*. New York: Springer-Verlag.

[12] Farrington, D., L. Ohlin & J. Wilson (1986). *Understanding and Controlling Crime: Toward a New Research Strategy*. New York City: Springer Verlag., p. 2.

[13] Steven Levitt's economic analysis indicated that the rising use of abortion by poor women after abortion became legal led to a reduced number of unwanted children who were at the highest risk for becoming delinquents and criminals.

---

[14] See Pollock, J. (2005). *Women, Prison and Society*. Belmont, CA: Wadsworth/ITP.

[15] From *Crime in the United States*, Table 43. Retrieved 5/21/07 from: http://www.fbi.gov/ucr/05cius/data/table_43.html.

[16] Retrieved 6/2/05 from http://www.gallup.com/poll/1603/crime.aspx.

[17] Bennett, L. 1991. The Public Wants Accountability. *Corrections Today* 53, 4: 92, 94-95.

[18] The Sentencing Project (n.d.). "Crime, Punishment and Public Opinion: A Summary of Recent Studies and their Implications for Sentencing Policy." Available at: www.sentencingproject.org.

Chapter 3

Why Do People Commit Crime?

What You Need to Know

★ Criminology is the study of crime and criminal motivation.

★ Classical thinkers believed that humans were rational and chose crime because it was in their best interest to do so.

★ Positivists look for the causes of crime and positivist theories fall into biological, psychological, or sociological categories.

★ Biological theories identify certain genetic influences that may predispose some individuals to crime.

★ Psychological theories can be subdivided into psychoanalytic, developmental, and learning theories.

★ Sociological crime theories can be further divided into social structure theories and social process theories.

★ Social structure theories identify societal elements as criminogenic and include subcultural theories, the strain/opportunity theory, radical/critical theories, social support, and social disorganization theories.

★ Social process theories identify interactive processes between the individual and the environment as criminogenic and include differential association, labeling theory, control theory, the general theory of crime, and general strain theory.

Almost everyone thinks they know why people commit crimes. Their answers may include family factors (bad parents), individual/personality factors (bad kids), peer factors (bad friends), and societal factors (bad economy/neighborhood). For hundreds of years, researchers have attempted to understand why some people choose to commit crimes. **Criminology** is the study of crime and criminal motivation. It is usually a separate course in most college curriculums, and so, in this short chapter, we do not attempt to discuss all the various theories that have been proposed to answer this question. Instead, we will look at the types of theories that have been proposed and tested. Recall from the last chapter that the strongest predictors of crime are sex, age, and, to a lesser extent, race. Thus, any theory of crime should be able to explain why young men (and, for some crimes, young black men) are more likely than any other group to commit crimes (or perhaps only be arrested for them).

Another way to approach the study of criminology is to think of crime on a continuum of deviance, as displayed in Box 3.1. At one end are acts that are extremely rare. They are committed by very few people and happen infrequently, such as serial murder, sadistic killings, and serial rapes. At the other end of the continuum are acts that are committed by a large number of people quite frequently, such as speeding or perhaps minor income tax evasion (such as overstating the amount contributed to charity). All other crimes fall on the continuum in relation to how frequently they are committed and/or how many people commit the act. It seems reasonable that an explanation of why people commit crimes on the far left side of the continuum would more likely be individual theories, that is, explanations that are unique to the individual because they are so different from others. Therefore, psychoanalytic theories make more sense for these types of offenders. Crimes toward the right of the continuum may be explained by a wider range of criminological theories.

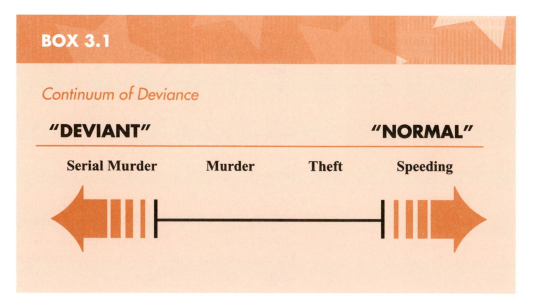

BOX 3.1

Continuum of Deviance

"DEVIANT"   "NORMAL"

Serial Murder   Murder   Theft   Speeding

1. THE CLASSICAL SCHOOL VERSUS POSITIVISM

The **Classical School** is usually described by the contributions of Cesare Beccaria (1738-1794) and Jeremy Bentham (1748-1832).[1] Both theorists, writing in the 1700s, operated under a fundamental assumption that men were rational and operated with free will. Therefore, the elimination of crime could be achieved by promising punishment for offenses, which would act as a deterrent to crime. Philosophers during this period did not view women in the same manner as men and viewed their mental abilities to be more akin to children, therefore their discussions applied specifically to men.

Jeremy Bentham proposed that the justice system must employ punishment in such a way that it was slightly more punitive than the perceived profit of the crime contemplated (in order to deter individuals from attempting the crime). Bentham's "**hedonistic calculus**" called for punishment adjusted in this way for each offense. According to Bentham, punishment should be no more than necessary to deter. It should be adjusted upward in severity in relation to a decrease in certainty. Punishment that was swift, certain, and proportional to the potential profit or pleasure of the crime was most effective. The focus of these thinkers was on the legal system; the assumption was that everyone would respond to the legal system in a similar, rational manner. The Classical School is usually a historical preface to the theories of crime that developed after the rise of Positivism.

1.1 Positivism

Positivism can be described simply as "scientific method" or the search for causes using scientific method. It is typically associated with Cesare Lombroso,[2] who is often referred to as the "Grandfather of Criminology." With Lombroso, the focus shifted from the legal system to the offender. The cause of crime, in fact, was assumed to lie in the individual. Lombroso believed that a few "born criminals" were born with genetic defects that made them commit criminal acts. It should also be noted that over the course of his career, he developed a more sophisticated typology of criminals. He recognized other types in addition to the purely biological criminal, and these types represented some of the same explanations we use today, such as opportunity, influence, and passion. Later positivists in the early 1900s also looked at individual causes, and both biological and psychological factors were examined. According to positivists, criminals were different from non-criminals and criminologists merely needed to understand those differences.

Lombroso also wrote a book about criminal women.[3] Women were presumed to be biologically and psychologically different from men, which accounted for their lower crime rates. However, some women were evolutionary throwbacks, according to Lombroso, and these "primitive" women were criminal because, in his theory, all primitive women were more masculine and criminal than "modern" law-abiding women.

We can say that the field of criminology really began with the positivists because they initiated the search for differences between criminal men and women and law-abiding men and women. Their findings do not hold up over the passage of time, but their approach is still the basic approach of most criminologists today—that is, to seek out differences that motivate some people to choose crime.

2. BIOLOGICAL THEORIES OF CRIME

Recall that the three strongest predictors of crime—sex, age, and race—are biological constructs. Of the three, only race shows strongly different patterns cross-culturally. Furthermore, race is mediated by interracial mixing so that most people do not represent pure racial phenotypes. Contrary to the complications race presents, the other two strongest correlates are age and sex. Thus, it would seem that biology should be at least explored as a factor in crime causation. However, research on biological factors has been given little attention in most criminology textbooks. Part of the reason biological approaches in criminology have been so completely rejected is that there are serious policy implications for such theories. It is argued that such theories lead to **eugenics**, which is the idea of improving the human race through controlled procreation, and other forms of control repugnant to our democratic ideals.

Biological factors may be: (a) inherited genetic traits, or (b) biological, but not genetic. For instance, a brain tumor that puts pressure on the violence center of the brain and results in irrational violence is obviously a biological cause of crime, but tumors are not thought to be inherited. Chemicals or other environmental toxins can also affect the brain and are non-genetic biological factors that may influence criminal choice. More controversial, however, is the idea that criminality is inherited.

Is there a criminal gene? Of course not, but the argument of biological criminologists is that there are some inherited characteristics that predispose individuals to criminal choices. The methodological problem has always been trying to isolate genetic influences from socialization influences. If you are like your mother or father, is it because you have inherited traits from them or because they raised you? Trying to separate these influences is very difficult to do.

Twin studies identify and track twins (both monozygotic twins who share a single egg and dizygotic who have separate eggs but a single sperm) and look to see concordance or discordance in such things as intelligence, delinquency, alcoholism, and other behavioral indices. **Concordance** occurs if both twins possess the affliction (i.e., alcoholism). Discordance means that the twins do not share the trait. Higher rates of concordance among monozygotic twins than dizygotic twins lend support to biological explanations because monozygotic twins share the exact same genetic makeup. Several studies have found higher concordance rates, but the problem remains that such similarity could be because monozygotic twins are treated more alike than dizygotic twin pairs.[4]

Studies have also looked at the concordance between the criminality of children and their adoptive parents and biological parents. The best study would be of monozygotic twins separated from biological parents, and from each other, at birth, but obviously, such samples are extremely small.

Generally, it is difficult to get any large sample sizes to study the effects of genetic inheritance on criminality, mental illness, or other factors. However, we know that there are medical conditions that may be inherited. We also now know that certain forms of mental illness have a genetic component. It is also believed that a predisposition to alcoholism or addiction is inherited and scientists believe they have discovered the "addiction gene" on the DNA strand. Further, it may be that certain personality traits, such as impulsivity and poor conditionability (or ability to learn), are also inherited. Personality traits have long been associated with delinquency/criminality. Such traits as impulsiveness, aggressiveness, extroversion, and other traits have played a role in very early studies as well as more recent ones. These traits do not inevitably lead to criminal choices, but they predispose the individual to such choices, especially when the individual grows up in criminogenic environmental conditions.

2.1 Hormones and Brain Chemistry

When a personality trait is believed to be inherited, scientists look for the actual physical components of the trait. These origins lie in the neural structures of the brain, brain chemistry, and hormones. For instance, if aggressive tendencies are inherited, it is possible that what is actually inherited is a higher-than-average level of testosterone, which has long been associated with aggression. There has developed a fairly impressive body of knowledge regarding the correlation between testosterone and aggression, although such research has also been subject to heavy criticism. Although both men and women have testosterone in the body, men have about 10 to 15 times more testosterone than women. Therefore, many argue that when we observe male aggression, we are observing the effects of testosterone. Basic problems with such research include accurate measurements of testosterone; a valid definition and operationalization of the construct of aggression; and understanding the interactive effect of testosterone production, aggressive behavior, and environmental cues. Testosterone production seems to be moderated by environmental factors, and obviously the translation of aggressiveness to behavior is subject to social control, self-control, meanings ascribed to behavior, and learning, which may account for the ambiguous findings in this area.[5]

Brain chemicals may also affect personality traits. A chemical found in the brain has intriguing qualities that may be linked to a predisposition to delinquency. Researchers have found that a low level of monoamine oxidase (MAO) is linked to psychopathy, alcoholism, sensation-seeking, impulsivity, extraversion, schizophrenia, and criminal behavior.[6] Men, on average, have about 20 percent less MAO than women, and this difference exists at all ages. Studies have reported findings that MAO levels are linked to delinquency. Boys with low MAO levels were found to be more impulsive and sensation-seeking than other boys and were more likely to have drug and alcohol problems.[7] Associations are consistently found between low MAO activity and various correlates of criminal behavior, such as impulsiveness, childhood hyperactivity, learning disabilities, sensation-seeking, substance abuse, and extroversion. MAO activity seems to be correlated with age, sex, and race. Testosterone evidently depresses MAO levels. In fact, testosterone levels are at their highest and MAO levels are at their lowest during the second decade of life (10-20, roughly corresponding with the crime-prone age years).[8]

Other research shows interesting connections between serotonin levels and negative emotionality and impulsivity.[9] Serotonin also seems to be linked with norepinephrine levels and, together, they may play a role in conditionability or the ability to learn.[10] There is evidence to indicate that individuals differ at a cellular level in their response to outside stimuli. Those with low levels of arousal tend toward behaviors that are risk-taking and sensation-seeking because these behaviors increase the cortical level of arousal. Risky behaviors are not necessarily antisocial. They could be sport-related activities or daredevil stunts. However, some individuals might be predisposed toward antisocial behaviors because these behaviors are exciting and produce the level of cortical arousal that extroverts seek. Thus, aggressive interactions, fast driving, shoplifting, robbery, and so on are risky and result in a thrilling rush of adrenalin that is much more pleasant for thrill-seekers than thrill-avoiders. Because thrill-seekers need a greater level of stimuli to respond, they do not learn as well, and do not absorb societal lessons that lead to law-abiding behavior.[11]

One model that incorporated physiological processes and learning theory postulates that traits that have been linked to delinquency; specifically, impulsivity, hyperactivity, sensation-seeking, risk-taking, and low self-control, are linked to neurophysiological mechanisms. Risky activities may release more endorphins in certain individuals than others because of brain chemistry. The differential experience of endorphins means that such behaviors become more internally rewarded for some than others, with the corollary prediction that they will continue to engage in such behavior.[12] Sex differences exist in cortical arousal levels, and men, in general, are more likely to have low cortical arousal.[13]

2.2 ADD, Hyperactivity, and Intelligence

There is consistent evidence that hyperactivity and Attention Deficit Disorder (ADD) are correlated with delinquency. It has been reported that those diagnosed with hyperactivity as children were 25 times more likely to exhibit later delinquency.[14] Deborah Denno[15] also reports that delinquency is linked to overactivity, perceptual-motor impairments, impulsivity, emotional lability, attention deficits, minor disturbances of speech, intellectual defects (learning disabilities), clumsiness, neuro-developmental lag, psychogenic factors, and minor physical anomalies. These features may be the result of genetic transmission, poor living environment, prenatal or birth trauma, or a combination of the above. It has been found that delinquents have significantly lower verbal skills, auditory verbal memory, interspatial analysis, and visual-motor integration in elementary school.

Such early evidence of cognitive deficits indicates that it is not simply a delinquent "lifestyle" and/or drug use that causes subsequent lower cognitive abilities; but, rather, there may be problems at birth that affect the child's performance in school. Evidence indicates that many children outgrow predisposing factors, but those who do not are more likely to become delinquent.

It is interesting to note that ADD and hyperactivity tend to be more common for boys than girls. Boys and men experience a higher incidence of prenatal and perinatal mortality and complications, reading and learning disorders, and mental retardation, as well as left hemisphere deficits.[16] In general, male children are more prone to learning dysfunctions due to brain differences.[17] Is it possible that the greater tendency of young men to engage in risky and/or violent behavior is not only culturally induced, but also may have a biological component?

There are numerous, hotly debated issues involved in the research concerning intelligence. The first is whether intelligence can even be defined and/or measured. The next point of controversy, assuming that we can agree upon some definition of intelligence, is whether intelligence is inherited. Again, while some researchers maintain that the evidence is clear and convincing, others argue that the correlation in IQ scores between parents and children, between twins, or between siblings is simply the product of family environment or other social factors (such as poverty), rather than a product of inheritance. Finally, there is the issue of the relationship between intelligence and delinquency or criminality.

Most researchers accept that there is a correlation between intelligence scores and delinquency/criminality. Some researchers argue that the relationship is purely spurious, because both are affected by some other factors, i.e., poverty, family dysfunction, or something else. Other researchers, however, believe that the relationship exists even after controlling for all other factors.[18] The relationship between intelligence and delinquency may be that intelligence affects school performance, which, in turn, affects delinquency because of opportunity (kids who drop out have more time to get into trouble). It could also be a direct relationship in that poor conditionability would lead to poor school performance and poor conditionability would lead to poor socialization to law-abiding norms. Intelligence may be related to family and environmental variables as well as genetic inheritance.

2.3 Summary

Theorists who support the idea of a biological predisposition to choose criminal behavior argue that personality differences do not inevitably lead to delinquency, no more than social factors inevitably lead to delinquency. The traits of impulsivity and thrill-seeking are due to biological differences, such as MAO and serotonin levels, as well as low cortical arousal. However, these biological differences merely predispose individuals to certain behavior patterns. The choice of crime versus other types of behaviors is influenced by social, familial, and environmental factors.

Biological theories can help explain the sex and age differential in criminality. There are sex differences in the relative levels of brain chemicals and hormones associated with delinquency. Furthermore, these chemicals and hormones fluctuate over the life course, therefore explaining why younger people are more impulsive and thrill-seeking than older individuals. These predispositions don't necessarily translate into delinquency, but there is a higher probability of such behavior when such biological predispositions exist.

3. PSYCHOLOGICAL THEORIES OF CRIME

Criminology has largely ignored psychological theories of deviance and crime.[19] This is largely because criminology has emerged as a discipline from the field of sociology, not psychology. Psychological theories can be categorized into psychoanalytic theories, developmental theories, and learning theories. Of these, both developmental theories and learning theories have their correlates in sociological criminology, so to say that psychology is ignored in criminology textbooks is perhaps a misstatement of facts. Perhaps we could say that psychological theories are merely sociologized.

3.1 Psychoanalytic Theories

Neither Sigmund Freud nor many of his followers had a great deal to say about crime. The psychoanalytic tradition would assume, however, that crime was the result of a weak superego or ego.[20] According to psychoanalytic theory, one does not develop in a normal manner when childhood trauma occurs or there is deficient parenting. Crime may occur because of unresolved feelings of guilt and a subconscious wish to be punished, or, more likely, because of weak superego controls over id impulses; that is, the individual cannot control impulses and pursues immediate gratification.

Generally, when a criminal commits very unusual or extreme acts, psychological explanations are utilized. The FBI has been instrumental in the growing use of "profilers" who construct psychological profiles of offenders based on the small sample of offenders who have been caught and interviewed. The book and movie *Silence of the Lambs* and many similar movies and television shows dramatize the work of psychological profilers. "Forensic psychologists" are used by many police departments for a variety of tasks, including offender profiling. As information is collected from these offenders, profiles are constructed and refined based on similarities and differences between them and how they commit their crimes. It should be noted, however, that the work of profilers is typically used for unusual criminals (such as serial or mass murderers, serial arsonists or serial rapists). Furthermore, profiles are not infallible. Recall that the predicted profile of the Washington sniper case was a white male 20 to 30 years of age, with a military background. John Malvo and John Mohammed did not fit the profile, but profiles are constructed from prior examples of such criminals, and the smaller the sample size, the greater the possibility of error.[21]

The most obvious contribution of psychological theory to an understanding of criminality is the concept of **sociopathy** or **psychopathy**. The psychopath has been differentiated from the sociopath in the following way: "[the psychopath is] an individual in whom the normal processes of socialization have failed to produce the mechanisms of conscience and habits of law-abidingness that normally constrain antisocial impulses" and the sociopath as "persons whose unsocialized character is due primarily to parental failures rather than to inherent peculiarities of temperament."[22] The Diagnostic and Statistical Manual (DSM-IV), used as the dictionary by mental health workers to diagnose and categorize all mental health problems, has replaced the terms "psychopathy" and "sociopathy" with the term "antisocial personality disorder." Regardless, these definitions describe an individual who is without a conscience and unable to

Sniper suspect Lee Boyd Malvo listens to court proceedings as he is surrounded by sheriff's officers during the trial of fellow sniper suspect John Allen Muhammad in courtroom 10 at the Virginia Beach Circuit Court in Virginia Beach, Va., Monday Oct. 20, 2003.

form sincere, affectionate bonds with others. This describes many, but not all, of those who engage in criminal behavior.

Psychological explanations for crime do address sex differences and incorporate biological traits, but not all in a manner that most would agree with today. For instance, in an early theory of female delinquency, Cowie, Cowie, and Slater[23] wrote that social and psychological factors, such as poverty or broken and/or poor home environments, seemed to be stronger factors in predicting female delinquents than male delinquency. Comparing delinquent girls with delinquent boys, the girls were found to come from lower income homes, with a higher level of mental health problems in the family, "worse" moral standards and worse discipline. Additionally, the girls more often came from a broken home, experienced more frequent changes of home, more conflict at home, and more disturbed intra-familial relations. These researchers were psychological/biological theorists in that they argued that biology ordinarily played a part in restraining women from criminal choices, so that it was only in situations of extreme stress that women were not controlled by these biological predispositions. Research on the different paths and childhoods of female and male delinquents continues today, but rarely ascribes criminal differences to biology, nor do many theorists believe that delinquent girls are more psychologically distressed than delinquent boys. Interestingly, there is some evidence to indicate that girls do follow a different path to delinquency.

3.2 Developmental Theories

Theories of development address both cognitive development and social development. The general hypothesis is that all individuals progress through similar stages of understanding and maturity regarding the world around them. Those who engage in criminal behavior have, for some reason, become "stuck" at lower stages of development. They are immature, either in their response to the world, their interactions with others around them, and/or in their putting self above others.

Piaget[24] and Kohlberg[25] are most commonly identified with the cognitive development field. Those who subscribe to the stage theory of cognitive development assume that the infant goes through qualitatively different stages of understanding. Only gradually does the child come to understand that others have needs and desires similar to him- or herself. Higher levels of maturity are necessary to understand such abstract concepts as altruism and compassion. Kohlberg carried Piaget's work into moral development, arguing that cognitive development was necessary in order to develop a moral conscience, and understandings of right and wrong varied depending on what cognitive level one had reached. For instance, very young children understand that stealing is wrong only because parents have told them so. It is much later that they come to understand more abstract reasons for why stealing is wrong.

Later, Carole Gilligan,[26] a student of Kohlberg's, concluded that women tended to cluster at lower stages in Kohlberg's stage sequence than did men. Although controversial, her theory was that women followed a "different" morality and were more likely to continue to utilize themes of relationships and caring, while men moved on to principles and law-based models of morality.

This work has seldom been applied directly in criminology to the question of why people choose criminality. One of the problems seems to be that one's ability to understand the moral implications of one's acts does not necessarily translate into behavior. That is, many people know something is wrong, but do it anyway. The research on moral stages, however, has been utilized in corrections and it has been found that offenders can improve their moral reasoning given appropriate learning environments.[27]

3.3 Learning Theory and Behaviorism

Basically, learning theory proposes that individuals act and believe the way they do because they have learned to do so. Learning takes place through modeling or reinforcement. **Modeling** stems from the desire to be like others, especially those whom one admires; therefore, children will act as they see their parents or peers act. The other form of learning is through **reinforcement**. That is, one will continue behaviors and beliefs for which one has been rewarded, and eliminate behaviors and beliefs that have been punished or not rewarded. Bandura,[28] for instance, argues that individuals are not necessarily inherently aggressive, but rather learn aggression. He and others also point out that learning is mediated by intelligence and temperament. Personality traits such as impulsivity, activity, and emotionality affect one's ability to absorb learning.

One of the most enduring explanations of why women commit less crime, by both laypeople and criminologists, is the idea that they learn to be law-abiding and that the social sanctions against deviance for women and girls are much stronger than what boys or men would experience. If true, learning theory is perfectly consistent with the lower crime rates observed for women. Further, it also explains why women tend to cluster in consumer crimes, because women may be more likely to learn how to commit credit card fraud or check forgery than armed robbery. It might also explain why younger people commit more crime—we might suppose they haven't yet absorbed societal messages that condemn such behaviors.

3.4 Summary

Psychological theories concentrate on individual factors of criminal choice. More sophisticated theories also refer to environmental factors. So, for instance, Andrews and Bonta[29] developed a psychological theory of crime that includes the characteristics of the immediate environment and individual characteristics to explain crime choices. They point to the attitudes, values, beliefs, and rationalizations held by the person with regard to antisocial behavior, social support for antisocial behavior (perceived support from others), a history of having engaged in antisocial behavior, self-management and problem-solving skills, and other stable personality characteristics conducive to antisocial conduct. Then they relate these to a behavioral explanation of criminality where rewards and costs of crime are mediated by these individual differences.

Such theories can only explain why women commit less crime if we presuppose that women learn different messages from society (learning theory) or develop different moral definitions (developmental theory). The theories are somewhat consistent with the age differential because it can be assumed that one continues to develop and learn through young adulthood and that maturity changes one's inclination to commit criminal acts. Also, it might be assumed that reward structures change during the life course and criminal choices may result in greater rewards for young people than for those with family and career responsibilities.

4. SOCIOLOGICAL THEORIES OF CRIME

If the focus of the Classical School was the legal system, and the focus of the Positivists was the individual, then the focus of early sociology was society itself. Societal factors were determined to be the causes of crime. However, while the Classical School assumed all men would respond rationally to the deterrence of punishment, sociological theories offer more complicated assumptions.

Adolphe Quetelet (1796-1874) and Emile Durkheim (1858-1917) are credited as early sociologists who established the foundations of sociological criminology. Quetelet discovered that crime occurred in reasonably predictable patterns in society, thus supporting the notion that there was something about society that caused crime rather than crime occurring at random or because of individual causes. Emile Durkheim offered the principle that crime was normal and present in all societies. The absence of deviance or crime, in fact, was evidence of cultural stagnation.

Sociological theories can be further divided into social structure theories and social process theories. Societal factors that influence criminality may come from the social structure (i.e., elements of society that induce criminality), or the social process (i.e., the interactions between the individual and society that influence criminal choices). Both approaches reject the idea of the "criminal as different." In these theories, it is assumed that anyone who happens to be exposed to these factors would become criminal; thus, the approach is similar to the Classical School (which assumed sameness among individuals).

4.1 Social Structure Theories

Social structure theories identify some aspects of society as leading to criminal choices. The so-called Chicago School in the 1930s and 1940s truly began the study of societal influences on criminality when sociologists at the University of Chicago observed that crime occurred more often in **mixed zones** of the city. In these zones, residential, commercial, and industrial activity could be observed. The zones were also characterized by low home ownership, property damage, graffiti, and high rates of alcoholism, domestic violence, and mental health problems. Early sociologists discovered that these mixed zones always had higher crime rates, even though different demographic groups moved in and out of them over the decades. For instance, in the nineteenth century, Irish immigrants were the population that lived in the zones, but they eventually moved out, to be replaced by Eastern and Southern Europeans, and then blacks moving up from the South. Thus, it seemed that there was something about the zone, rather than the people who lived within it, that generated crime. Observers noted that subcultures existed in the mixed zone and these subcultures promoted values and beliefs that were different from the dominant culture and encouraged criminal behavior (such as prostitution, gambling, and other forms of deviance).

Subculture theories and cultural deviance theories, first developed in the 1950s, observed that there are some groups in society that teach antisocial behaviors (instead of socialize its members to follow the norms of the dominant culture). If one lives in these areas of the city, then one will most likely become delinquent because the subculture defines such behavior as acceptable.[30] **Cultural deviance theory** identifies cultures that clash when individuals migrate to a new culture; i.e., immigrants from India who sell their daughters into marriage in the United States are committing a crime, but in their culture, this behavior is not wrong. **Subcultural theories** look at subcultures that exist within the dominant culture but have different values and belief systems. Gangs are an example of a subculture, although this stretches the classic definition of a subculture, because members of any gang also participate and are socialized, to some extent, by the dominant culture as well. Women were largely ignored in early subcultural theories even though they obviously lived in the mixed zones alongside the boys and men who were being socialized to criminality. More recently, gang research has identified female gang members and female gangs, but there are mixed findings as to whether girls are increasing their participation in gangs.[31]

Another factor observed in the mixed zones was lack of opportunity. The individuals who lived in these neighborhoods had very little hope of economic success. **Strain or opportunity theory**, popularized in the 1960s, argued that lack of opportunity is the cause of crime. Individuals who are blocked from legitimate means of economic success, such as employment, family, or education, will choose crime.[32] A later application of the theory enlarged it to groups, so that those who were blocked from opportunities would form groups (gangs) distinct from those who had legitimate opportunities.[33] Because everyone is socialized to believe that they can and should achieve material success, those who do not have the means feel particular stress. In other cultures that are more static, i.e., where the poor have no expectations or hope that they will achieve wealth, there is less pressure or inclination to use illegitimate means to get ahead.

If the strain/opportunity thesis was perfectly able to explain crime, then one would think that women should be more criminal than men because, arguably, they have had fewer opportunities to achieve financial success and, therefore, should experience more strain. On the other hand, if women's goals are different, for instance, to get married and to have children, rather than achieve economic success, then the theory would adequately explain the sex differential in crime. Whether this has ever been true, or whether it is true today, is a subject that many researchers have addressed. The results indicate that there are differences between men and women and strain may predict to some extent the criminal choices of both groups, but economic strain does not completely explain why some people commit crime, or why men are more likely to make criminal choices.

Radical, Critical, or Marxist Criminology was somewhat popular in the 1970s. This type of theory can also be considered a social structure theory because it identifies an element of society as criminogenic. Radical or critical criminology challenges the "science" of criminology and the nature of the exercise, concentrating as it does on the individual "deviant." Critical or radical criminology addressed the process of defining crimes and the nature of law as a method of social control by those in power. Under a Marxist theory of crime, crime exists in the capitalist society as "work." It is an essential element of capitalism. Typical criminal activity represents false consciousness; the "lumpenproletariat" does not know who their true oppressors are, thus they steal from and hurt each other. This approach would expand the definition of crime to activities engaged in by government and business; for instance, the death of workers because of unsafe working conditions should be defined as homicide.

Elements of **critical criminology** include an identification of class-based definitions of crime, a challenge to the ideology of equality, and the lack of objectivity in law.[34] Critics of these theories contend that their view of society is oversimplified and that power coalitions are more complicated and diverse than can be represented by such theories. Another criticism that can be made is that these types of theories are unable to explain the sex differential.

More recently, the ideas of the Chicago School have been revived with **social support theory** and **social disorganization theory**. Basically, both point to the community as a prime factor in crime causation. These theories tend to look solely at macro-level factors that are correlated with crime causation. They are similar in that social support theory identifies elements of the society that provide emotional and practical support to the individual and proposes that the more support there is in a community, the less crime occurs.[35] Social disorganization theory states a similar assumption, arguing that communities that exhibit signs of disorganization and lack of cohesion are more likely to experience delinquency and criminality.[36] Thus, in both theories, crime is predicted in the neighborhoods and for the people who have few resources such as church, friendly neighbors, clubs, and other social organizations.

4.2 Social Process Theories

Social process theories focus on the individual's interaction with the world around him or her. Thus, relationships become a central feature of these theories. Social process theories have more in common in this respect with psychological theories and, in fact, many could be described as social-psychological.

Differential association theory, introduced originally by Edwin Sutherland in 1939, is very similar to learning theory.[37] Differential association assumes that delinquency and criminality develop because of an excess of definitions favorable to crime offered by one's close associates. That is, if family and friends are criminal, profess criminal values, and teach criminal methods, one will become criminal. This theory assumes that learning takes place most importantly within intimate personal groups and that learning includes techniques of crime, as well as motives, drives, rationalizations, and attitudes. Later, others applied social learning principles to the theory to make it even more similar to learning theory.[38]

In order for this theory to be consistent with the sex differential in crime, one must assume that girls and boys receive different societal messages, with girls less likely to be reinforced for delinquent behavior. Burgess and Akers argued that: "From infancy, girls are taught that they must be nice, while boys are taught that they must be rough and tough . . . Girls are schooled in 'anti-criminal behavior patterns'."[39] Evidently all girls are taught from birth to conform to one model of female normality that is homogeneous across social, economic, and subcultural categories, while boys are exposed to a variety of different definitions of normality depending on class, race, and neighborhood. These factors predict delinquency for boys, but not for girls under this theory. Further, the theory doesn't explain why crime is more common among young people and drops off after young adulthood because, if one learned criminal definitions, there is no reason to assume they would change after maturity.

Labeling theory relies on symbolic interactionism. The theory is unique from those discussed above in that, like radical criminology, it focuses attention on the official labeler as well as the deviant. This theory assumes even though almost all of us have engaged in "primary deviance," only certain individuals are labeled as deviant. This results in their accepting and absorbing the deviant role and committing further delinquency because of the label.[40] Criticisms of labeling theory include the observation that no explanation for primary deviance is offered. Also, whether secondary deviance would not exist except for the labeling is probably untestable.[41] Labeling does not explain persistent criminality when offenders are not subject to labeling (such as hidden corporate criminality) and ignores the fact that official intervention (such as prosecution and punishment) might deter individuals from future criminality.

Recall that the Classical School assumptions disappeared with the rise of positivism in the 1800s. However, the premises of the Classical School have been revived with **rational choice theory**. This modern-day theory presumes that criminals rationally choose criminal action because the immediate rewards outweigh uncertain punishments.[42] Burglars, for instance, are influenced by such facts as the affluence of the neighborhood, the presence of bushes, nosy neighbors, alarms, dogs, placement on the street, access to major traffic arteries, and other factors. They identify and target the houses where they have the best chance of success. Although the theory makes sense with burglars, and other purely economic crimes, it is more difficult to apply to other criminals.

Routine activities theory is slightly different from rational choice, and might even be placed in the social structure category because it ignores criminal motivation, assuming a motivated offender exists all the time.[43] According to these theorists, for a crime to happen, there must be a motivated offender, suitable targets of criminal victimization, and the absence of guardians of persons or property. Any changes in routine activities lead to changing opportunities for crime. For instance, the increase in the number of working women after WWII meant that more homes were left unattended during the day, and this created the opportunity for burglaries to occur. Most sociological theories look at the motivation of the offender, and these authors argue that it is also fruitful to look at changes in opportunities or guardianship. Tests of this theory focus on demographic, macro-level changes in society. However, it is difficult to identify any societal changes that occurred in the last decade that might have accounted for the dramatic drop in crime. Critics argue that, by not looking at the criminal motivations of the offender, this theory is incomplete.

Control theory, as presented by Travis Hirschi in 1969,[44] stated that the delinquent or criminal is one who is not controlled by bonds to society—specifically attachment, commitment, involvement, and belief. Attachment involves relationships; commitment involves the dedication to legitimate work and leisure activities; involvement measures actual time engaged in such activities; and belief refers to the agreement and acceptance of goals and rules of society. In the research that supported the development of control theory, Hirschi used

Will & Deni McIntyre/CORBIS

Control theory states that school activities, such as band, provide one type of bond (involvement) that prevents delinquency. Other bonds are attachment, commitment, and belief.

self-report surveys of large numbers of young people and analyzed self-reported delinquency (validated by comparison to official records) and whether delinquency was correlated with the bonds to society described above. Control theory postulates that conformity occurs because of ties to society; deviance occurs when those ties are weak or nonexistent. Conformity is associated with good school performance, strong family ties, liking school, conventional aspirations, and respect for law.

Control theory provides a relatively adequate explanation for the sex differential in crime rates if we can assume that girls have more attachments and other bonds than boys. It is generally found that girls profess stronger ties to friends, family, and school, and they tend to possess more pro-social belief systems than boys.

Hirschi's control theory generated a wealth of theoretical and analytical response in criminology in the 1970s. A couple of decades later, in 1990, he and Michael Gottfredson[45] published a book describing the **General Theory of Crime**, which resulted in another flood of tests and applications from the 1990s through the 2000s. Actually, the two are not all that different. While control theory postulates that various bonds to society (attachment, commitment, belief, and involvement) control the individual and prevent delinquency, the general theory of crime proposes, simply, that individuals are born with and/or are raised to have different levels of self-control.

These authors propose that there are no real differences between serious and non-serious crimes, and disagree with the proposition that criminals are different from each other in their criminal orientation (i.e., career criminals versus occasional criminals). They propose that one variable explains all criminal offending and that variable is *self-control*. Gottfredson and Hirschi propose that people with low self-control commit criminal acts and a host of other dangerous and impulsive behaviors; people with more self-control do not. Low self-control types are also engaged in other activities indicative of low self-control, such as smoking, drinking, using drugs, gambling, having illegitimate children, and engaging in illicit sex.[46]

White-collar criminality is a problem for this theory. The authors explained that white-collar criminals, like embezzlers, simply have less self-control than their professional colleagues who do not commit crimes. However, their argument that white-collar crime by professionals is relatively rare flies in the face of evidence that graft, fraud, and other forms of corporate criminality are widespread.

The major cause of a lack of self-control, according to these authors, is ineffective parenting. They argue that the conditions necessary to teach self-control include monitoring behavior, recognizing deviant behavior, and punishing such behavior.[47] Applications and tests of this theory of crime typically explore associations between other indications of low self-control and criminality. Not surprisingly, such associations exist, although some researchers argue that self-control adds nothing new to existing facts that have identified the association between crime and impulsivity and risk-seeking.[48]

A major weakness of the theory is that it does not adequately explain the sex differential in crime unless one was to assume that women generally have more self-control than men.[49] Another criticism of the theory is that it does not include any concept of the meaning of actions and how personal meaning interacts with and influences self-control. Values, motivations, and meanings interact with individual self-control, explaining why some people show a great deal of self-control in some areas and none in others. Further, there is a qualitative difference, it seems, in the acts labeled "criminal" and those merely injurious to one's health. Many people drink and smoke but relatively few commit victim-harming crimes. In other words, there are many more "weak" people than there are "harming" people, thus, even if we find that most criminals have low self-control, it does not follow that most people with low self-control are criminals.

Sgt. Vincent Matranga, of the Sacramento City Unified School District, left, questions Lydia Ochoa, 15, right, and her boyfriend, Antonio, 17, center, about why the pair were not in school Jan. 30, 2007. Police had recently teamed up with school officials to start rounding up truants in an effort to cut crime as well as prevent kids from dropping out.

Robert Agnew[50] reformulated strain/opportunity theory (which was a social structure theory) into a social process theory by reinterpreting strain as an individual construct rather than an experience shared by the group or due to societal factors such as poverty. His **General Strain theory** proposes that individuals who commit crime experience strain from not getting what they want, losing something that was important, or in other ways being in a situation that is experienced as noxious. In this theory, negative relationships that generate negative emotions, such as disappointment, fear, depression, and anger cause delinquency and individuals commit delinquent acts in order to relieve the strain of the negative emotions.

4.3 Summary

Sociological theories are more common in criminology because the beginning of criminology in this country occurred with the Chicago School of the 1930s. These theories identify elements of society or the interaction of the individual with his or her environment as the reason people become criminal. These elements range from poverty and subcultures (in structural theories) to social bonds and negative emotions (in social process theories). While virtually none of these theories directly explains the sex or age differential in crime rates, later researchers have attempted to apply them in such a way as to explain these crime patterns. Some seem better able to explain these crime correlates than others.

5. INTEGRATED THEORIES OF CRIMINOLOGY

Integrated theories combine elements of psychological theories and sociological theories, and even accept some elements of biological criminology in a more complicated and comprehensive approach to explaining criminal choices. The methodology typically associated with integrated theories is the cohort study, also called longitudinal research because it involves following a sample of individuals for a long period.

One finding of the longitudinal research studies is that there seem to be two separate groups of delinquents/criminals. The first group begins committing delinquent acts very early and these individuals are chronic and serious criminal offenders; however, the second "late onset" group drifts into delinquency during their teenage years and matures out fairly quickly. Their delinquency seems to be episodic and peer-influenced.

The following traits or characteristics seem to be correlated with the group who begin delinquency very early: low intelligence; high impulsiveness; child abuse victimization; harsh and erratic parental discipline; cold and rejecting parents; poor parental supervision; parental disharmony, separation, and divorce; one-parent female-headed households; convicted parents or siblings; alcoholic or drug-using parents or siblings; non-white race membership, low occupational prestige of parents; low educational level of parents; low family income; large family size; poor housing; low educational attainment of the child; attendance at a high delinquency school; delinquent friends; and high-crime area of residence.[51]

Unfortunately, cohort samples for longitudinal studies often exclude women. This is especially unfortunate because the studies consistently identify correlates of delinquency such as Attention Deficit Disorder (ADD) and hyperactivity, which are more prevalent among boys. Sex/gender differences may also be present in other factors related to criminal choices, such as sensation-seeking, low physiological arousal, intelligence, poor supervision and erratic discipline, and delinquent peers. By excluding women from the cohort sample, these studies are unable to determine the relative effects of these factors on male and female delinquency and criminality.

Denno[52] utilized biological and sociological factors in an integrated explanation of criminality and delinquency. She identified predisposing factors (that increase the likelihood of criminality), facilitating variables (that, in combination with predisposing, increase the likelihood of delinquency), and inhibiting variables (that counteract predisposing factors and decrease the probability of delinquency). At birth, individuals are already affected by such factors as culture, gender, prenatal maternal conditions, pregnancy and delivery complications, socioeconomic status, and family stability. By age seven, other factors, such as cerebral dominance, intelligence, and physical and health development have influenced their predisposition to delinquency, and during the pre-teen and teen years, school behavior, achievement, and learning disabilities are affected by intelligence and influence, in turn, the likelihood of delinquency and, eventually, adult crime. In Box 3.2, Sampson and Laub's integrated theory is presented.

BOX 3.2

Sampson and Laub's Development Theory

A set of predisposing factors:

- ★ Structural and background factors
- ★ Low family SES
- ★ Family size
- ★ Family disruption
- ★ Residential mobility
- ★ Parent's deviance
- ★ Household crowding
- ★ Foreign-born
- ★ Mother's employment

Combined with individual constructs:

- ★ Difficult temperament
- ★ Persistent tantrums
- ★ Early conduct disorder

Which interact with social control processes:

- ★ Family
- ★ Lack of supervision
- ★ Threatening/erratic, harsh discipline
- ★ Parental rejection
- ★ School
- ★ Weak attachment
- ★ Poor performance
- ★ Delinquent influence
- ★ Peer delinquent attachment
- ★ Sibling delinquent attachment

That then leads to:

- ★ Delinquency
- ★ Length of incarceration

Which, in turn, influences:

- ★ Social bonds
- ★ Weak labor force attachment
- ★ Weak marital attachment

And, ultimately, creates the continuation of:

- ★ Crime and deviance

Source: Adapted from Sampson, R. and J. Laub (1993). *Crime in the Making: Pathways and Turning Points Through Life.* Cambridge, MA: Harvard University Press, p. 244.

Integrated studies are comprehensive in that they include precursors and facilitators of delinquency. In fact, most of the elements identified by all previous theories are incorporated into these integrated theories. While some may say that is the strength of these theories, others argue that it is a weakness because it makes the theory more complicated and by using every explanation, in effect, there is no explanation that easily explains crime choice. On the other hand, it is probably unrealistic to assume that there is a simple answer to criminal behavior—or any human behavior, for that matter.

6. CONCLUSION

Courses in criminology cover a multitude of theories that have been created and tested to attempt to answer the question, "Why do people commit crime?" This chapter barely skims the surface of this material, but it provides some general descriptions of the types of theories that have been developed. Any good theory should be able to explain the sex and age differential, as well as why minorities are overrepresented in street and violent crimes.

Generally the field of criminology has de-emphasized biological and psychological factors of crime causation and focused solely on sociological causes of crime. More recent theories, such as the general theory of crime and general strain theory, bring the focus back to the individual and, thus, one can argue that the pendulum of scientific/criminological thought has swung from the legal system (classical) to the individual (positivist), to the society and neighborhood (Chicago School), and back to the individual (General theory). Integrated theories incorporate aspects of all three types of theories—biological, psychological, and sociological—and, arguably, provide the most complete answer to why people commit crime. In Box 3.3, there are very brief descriptions of the theories discussed in this chapter.

The quest for reasons why people make criminal choices is ultimately for a practical purpose. We want them to stop. All criminology serves the practical purpose of developing policies and societal interventions that reduce crime. Thus, another way to discuss the theories presented in this chapter is to figure out the policy implications that follow from each theory. It seems clear that most theories support the idea of full employment and strengthening the family unit to ensure that all children grow up in stable homes where parents are able to discipline and monitor their behavior through strong, loving attachments. Whether this can ever be accomplished is a difficult question. The answer to why people commit crime and how we can reduce crime, in fact, goes far beyond the criminal justice system. But then we knew that, because the criminal justice system is the social control institution that steps in when others (family, church, school) fail. If those institutions could be made stronger, there would be less need for the criminal justice system components, because there would be less crime.

BOX 3.3

Theories of Crime

Biological

Non-genetic: idiopathic tumors, brain injuries, toxins

Genetic: testosterone, brain chemicals, neural conditionability, other inherited personality traits, such as impulsiveness

Psychological

Psychoanalytic: individual suffers trauma in childhood

Developmental: individual does not progress to mature social-interpersonal levels

Learning: individual is rewarded for criminal behavior

Sociological Theories

Social Structure Theories

Chicago School – individual lives in the mixed zone of a city where crime occurs

Cultural Deviance – individual is socialized to deviant norms

Strain – individual is blocked from achieving societal goals

Radical/Critical – individual is oppressed by capitalistic economic system

Social Support – individual lives in area with low social support

Social Disorganization – individual lives in area with indices of social disorganization

Social Process Theories

Differential Association – individual learns to be criminal

Labeling – individual is labeled a deviant and so lives up to the label

Rational choice – individual weighs options and chooses crime

Routine activities – crime occurs when there is motivated offender and opportunity

Control (bonds) – individual has few bonds to society

General theory of crime – individual has low self-control

General strain theory – individual suffers strain, which leads to crime

Integrated Theories

Different aspects of the theories above explain crime at different periods in the life course

REVIEW QUESTIONS

1. What are the three strongest correlates of crime?

2. Differentiate between the classical school and the positivists.

3. What would be a way to study the relative effects of genetics and socialization?

4. What personality traits have been associated with criminality?

5. Distinguish between developmental theories and learning theories.

6. Distinguish social structure theories from social process theories.

7. Provide some examples of social structure theories and their policy implications.

8. What are the elements of critical or radical criminology?

9. Provide some examples of social process theories and their policy implications.

10. What are integrated theories? Describe.

VOCABULARY

classical School – includes the contributions of Cesare Beccaria and Jeremy Bentham and the ideas that men were rational, operated with free will, and could be deterred from criminal acts

concordance – measure of genetic influence; if one twin has an affliction (i.e., alcoholism), then so does the other twin. Discordance means that the twins are different

control theory – Hirschi's theory that delinquents are not controlled by bonds to society, specifically attachment, commitment, involvement, and belief

criminology – the study of crime and criminal motivation

critical criminology – rejects definitions of crime and includes the idea that the legal system is a tool of the powerful

cultural deviance theory – identifies crime as occurring when cultures clash, i.e., when individuals migrate to a new culture

differential association theory – Sutherland's theory that delinquency develops because of an excess of definitions favorable to crime

eugenics – the idea of improving the human race through controlled procreation

General Strain theory – Agnew's theory that delinquency occurs because of strain from negative emotions that are caused by a number of "strains"

General Theory of crime – Gottfredson and Hirschi's theory that crime results from low self-control

"hedonistic calculus" – Bentham's idea that punishment should be adjusted to slightly outweigh the perceived pleasure or profit from crime in order to deter people

integrated theories – combine elements of psychological, biological, and sociological theories and explain crime over the life course

labeling theory – focuses attention on the official labeler as well as the deviant and assumes that labeling creates secondary deviance

mixed zones – zones where residential, commercial, and industrial activity are mixed and characterized by crime and other forms of disorder

modeling – form of behavior change that occurs when one desires to be like others, especially those whom one admires

positivism – "scientific method" or the search for causes using scientific method

psychopathy – an individual without a conscience or habits of law-abidingness that normally constrain antisocial impulses

rational choice theory – theory that criminals rationally choose criminal action because of immediate rewards

reinforcement – form of learning in which behaviors and beliefs that are rewarded continue and behaviors and beliefs that are punished disappear

routine activities theory – theory that for a crime to happen, there must be a motivated offender, suitable targets of criminal victimization, and the absence of guardians of persons or property

sociopathy – persons whose unsocialized character is due primarily to parental failures rather than to inherent peculiarities of temperament

social process theories – theories of crime that focus on the individual's interaction with the world around them

social disorganization theory – theory that crime occurs in neighborhoods where there is no cohesion, transitory populations, and few indices of social support

social support theory – theory that assumes crime occurs where social supports (both emotional and concrete) are absent

strain or opportunity theory – theory that assumes that lack of economic opportunity causes crime

subcultural theories – theory that deviant subcultures with different values and belief systems socialize individuals to crime

FOR FURTHER READING

Agnew, Robert (2007). *Pressured into Crime: An Overview of General Strain Theory*. New York, NY: Oxford University Press.

Andrews, Don and James Bonta (2006). *The Psychology of Criminal Conduct*, Fourth Edition. Newark, NJ: LexisNexis/Matthew Bender.

Brown, Stephen E., Finn-Aage Esbensen, and Gilbert Geis (2007). *Criminology: Explaining Crime and Its Context*, Sixth Edition. Newark, NJ: LexisNexis/Matthew Bender.

Tonry, Michael, Lloyd Ohlin, and David Farrington (1991). *Human Development and Criminal Behavior: New Ways of Advancing Knowledge*. New York, NY: Springer-Verlag.

Vold, George, Thomas Bernard, and Jeffrey Snipes (2002). *Theoretical Criminology*, Fifth Edition. New York, NY: Oxford University Press.

Walsh, Anthony (1995). *Biosociology: An Emerging Paradigm*. Westport, CT: Praeger.

---

[1] Bentham, J. (1843/1970). "The Rationale of Punishment." In R. Beck and J. Orr (eds.), *Ethical Choices: A Case Study Approach*. New York, NY: Free Press, pp. 326-340.

[2] Lombroso, C. & W. Ferrero (1895/1972). *The Criminal Man*. Montclair, NJ: Patterson Smith.

[3] Lombroso, C. & W. Ferrero (1894/1958. *The Female Offender*. New York, NY: Philosophical Library.

[4] Andrews, D. & J. Bonta. 2006. *The Psychology of Criminal Conduct*, Fourth Edition. Newark, NJ: LexisNexis/Matthew Bender, p. 128-129.

[5] Maccoby, E. & C. Jacklin (1974). *The Psychology of Sex Differences*. Stanford, CA: Stanford University Press. See also Tedeschi, J. & R. Felson (1994). *Violence, Aggression and Coercive Actions*. Washington, DC: American Psychological Association; Mednick, S. & K. Christiansen. 1977. *Biosocial Bases for Criminal Behavior*. New York, NY: Gardner; Mednick, S., T. Moffitt, & S. Stack (eds.) (1987). *The Causes of Crime*. New York, NY: Cambridge University Press; Walsh, A. (1991). *Intellectual Imbalance, Love Deprivation and Violent Delinquency: A Biosocial Perspective*. Springfield, IL: Charles C Thomas.

[6] Eysenck, H. & G. Gudjonsson (1989). *The Causes and Cures of Criminality*. New York, NY: Plenum, p. 135. See also Walsh, A. (1991). *Intellectual Imbalance, Love Deprivation and Violent Delinquency: A Biosocial Perspective*. Springfield, IL: Charles C Thomas, p. 140.

[7] Walsh, A. (1991). *Intellectual Imbalance, Love Deprivation and Violent Delinquency: A Biosocial Perspective*. Springfield, IL: Charles C Thomas, p. 127.

[8] Walsh, A. (1995). *Biosociology: An Emerging Paradigm*. Westport, CT: Praeger, p. 50-54. See also Ellis, L. (1991). "Monoamine Oxidase and Criminality: Identifying an Apparent Biological Marker for Antisocial Behavior." *Journal of Research in Crime and Delinquency* 28: 227-251.

[9] Caspi, A., T. Moffitt, P. Silva, M. Stouthamer-Loeber, R. Krueger, & P. Schmutte (1994). "Are Some People Crime Prone? Replications of the Personality-Crime Relationship across Countries, Genders, Races, and Methods." *Criminology* 32: 163-195.

[10] Raine, A. (1993). *The Psychopathology of Crime: Criminal Behavior as a Clinical Disorder*. San Diego, CA: Academic Press, p. 93.

[11] Eysenck, H. & G. Gudjonsson (1989). *The Causes and Cures of Criminality*. New York, NY: Plenum, p. 55.

[12] Wood, P., B. Pfefferbaum & B. Arneklev (1993). "Risk-Taking and Self-Control: Social Psychological Correlates of Delinquency." *Journal of Crime and Justice* 16, 1: 111-130.

[13] Eysenck, H. & G. Gudjonsson (1989). *The Causes and Cures of Criminality*. New York, NY: Plenum, p. 126.

[14] Sandhu, H. & H. Satterfield (1987). "Childhood Diagnostic and Neurophysiological Predictors of Teenage Arrest Rates." In S. Mednick, T. Moffitt and S. Stack (eds.), *The Causes of Crime*. New York, NY: Cambridge University Press, pp. 146-168.

[15] Denno, D. (1990). *Biology and Violence: From Birth to Adulthood*. New York, NY: Cambridge University Press, p. 15.

[16] Denno, D. (1990). *Biology and Violence: From Birth to Adulthood*. New York, NY: Cambridge University Press, p. 17.

[17] Moffitt, T. (1990). "The Neuropsychology of Juvenile Delinquency: A Critical Review." In M. Tonry & N. Morris, *Crime and Justice: A Review of Research*, Vol. 12. Chicago, IL: University of Chicago Press, pp. 99-171.

[18] See Moffitt (1990), "The Neuropsychology of Juvenile Delinquency: A Critical Review." In M. Tonry and N. Morris, *Crime and Justice: A Review of Research*, Vol. 12. Chicago, IL: University of Chicago Press, pp. 99-171, p. 112. See also Andrews, D. & J. Bonta (2006). *The Psychology of Criminal Conduct*, Fourth Edition. Newark, NJ: LexisNexis/Matthew Bender, p. 128-129; and Raine, A. (1993). *The Psychopathology of Crime: Criminal Behavior as a Clinical Disorder*. San Diego, CA: Academic Press.

[19] Andrews, D. and J. Bonta (2006). *The Psychology of Criminal Conduct*, Fourth Edition. Newark, NJ: LexisNexis/Matthew Bender.

[20] Andrews, D. and J. Bonta (2006). *The Psychology of Criminal Conduct*, Fourth Edition. Newark, NJ: LexisNexis/Matthew Bender.

[21] Holloway, J. (2003). *The Perils of Profiling for the Media*. Retrieved 5/24/07 from APA Online: http://www.apa.org/monitor/jan03/perils.html.

[22] Lykken, D. (1995). *The Antisocial Personalities*. Hillsdale, NJ: Lawrence Erlbaum, p. 6-7.

[23] Cowie, J., B. Cowie, & E. Slater (1968). *Delinquency in Girls*. London, England: Heinemann.

[24] Piaget, J. (1965). *The Moral Judgment of a Child*. New York, NY: Free Press.

[25] Kohlberg, L. (1981). *The Philosophy of Moral Judgment*. San Francisco, CA: Harper and Row.

[26] Gilligan, C. (1982). *In a Different Voice: Psychological Theory and Women's Development*. Cambridge, MA: Harvard University Press.

[27] For a review of research, see Pollock, J. (2007). *Ethics in Criminal Justice: Dilemmas and Decisions*, Fifth Edition. Belmont, CA: Wadsworth.

[28] Bandura, A. (1977). *Social Learning Theory*. Englewood Cliffs, NJ: Prentice-Hall.

[29] Andrews, D. & J. Bonta (1994). *The Psychology of Criminal Conduct*, Second Edition. Cincinnati, OH: Anderson, p. 111.

[30] See, for instance, Shaw, C. & H. McKay (1934/1972). *Juvenile Delinquency and Urban Areas*. Chicago, IL: University of Chicago Press.

[31] Pollock, J. (2002). *Women, Prison, and Crime*. Belmont, CA: Wadsworth.

[32] Merton, R. (1938). "Social Structure and Anomie." *American Sociological Review* 3, 6: 672-682.

[33] Cohen, A. (1955). *Delinquency in Boys: The Culture of the Gang*. New York, NY: Free Press. Also see Cloward, R. & L. Ohlin (1960). *Delinquency and Opportunity*. New York, NY: Free Press.

[34] See, for instance, Taylor, I., P. Walton & J. Young (1998). *The New Criminology*. New York, NY: Harper and Row; and, Quinney, R. (1973). *Critique of the Legal Order*. Boston, MA: Little, Brown.

[35] Bursik, R. & H. Grasmick (1993). *Neighborhoods and Crime: the Dimensions of Effective Community Control*. New York, NY: Lexington Books. See also Cullen, F. (1994). "Social Support as an Organizing Concept for Criminology." *Justice Quarterly* 11, 4: 528-559.

[36] Reiss, A. & M. Tonry (1986). *Communities and Crime*. Chicago, IL: University of Chicago Press. See also Sampson, R. & W. Groves (1989). "Community Structure and Crime: Testing Social Disorganization Theory." *American Journal of Sociology* 94: 774-802.

[37] Sutherland, E. & D. Cressey (1960/1966). *Principles of Criminology*. Philadelphia, PA: Lippincott.

[38] Akers, R. (1973). *Deviant Behavior: A Social Learning Approach*. Belmont, CA: Wadsworth. Burgess, R. & R. Akers. (1966). "A Differential Association-Reinforcement Theory of Criminal Behavior." *Social Problems* 14: 128-47.

[39] Burgess, R. & R. Akers (1966). "A Differential Association-Reinforcement Theory of Criminal Behavior." *Social Problems* 14: 142.

[40] See, for instance, Lemert, E. (1951). *Social Pathology: A Systematic Approach to the Theory of Sociopathic Behavior*. New York, NY: McGraw-Hill.

[41] Akers, R. (1973). *Deviant Behavior: A Social Learning Approach*. Belmont, CA: Wadsworth

[42] Cornish, D. and R. Clarke (1986). *The Reasoning Criminal: Rational Choice Perspectives on Offending*. New York, NY: Springer-Verlag.

[43] Cohen, L. and M. Felson (1979). "Social Change and Crime Trends: A Routine Activities Approach." *American Sociological Review* 44: 588-608.

[44] Hirschi, T. (1969). *Causes of Delinquency*. Berkeley, CA: University of California Press.

[45] Gottfredson, M. & T. Hirschi (1990). *A General Theory of Crime*. Stanford, CA: Stanford University Press.

[46] Gottfredson, M. &d T. Hirschi (1990). *A General Theory of Crime*. Stanford, CA: Stanford University Press, p. 90.

[47] Gottfredson, M. & T. Hirschi (1990). *A General Theory of Crime*. Stanford, CA: Stanford University Press, p. 97.

[48] Longshore, D., S. Turner, & J. Stein (1996). "Self Control in a Criminal Sample: An Examination of Construct Validity." *Criminology* 34, 2: 209-227.

[49] Miller, S. & C. Burack (1993). "A Critique of Gottfredson and Hirschi's General Theory of Crime: Selective (In)Attention to Gender and Power Positions." *Women & Criminal Justice* 4, 2: 115-134.

[50] Agnew, R. (2007). *Pressured into Crime: An Overview of General Strain Theory*. New York, NY: Oxford University Press.

[51] Tonry, M., L. Ohlin, & D. Farrington (1991). *Human Development and Criminal Behavior: New Ways of Advancing Knowledge*. New York, NY: Springer-Verlag, p. 142.

[52] Denno, D. (1990). *Biology and Violence: From Birth to Adulthood*. New York, NY: Cambridge University Press.

Chapter 4

Police in America

What You Need to Know

★ There are more than 20,000 different state and local police agencies.

★ There are about 1.5 officers for every 1,000 citizens.

★ Law enforcement includes many overlapping jurisdictional agencies. There are federal, state, county, and municipal law enforcement agencies.

★ The first municipal police department was begun by Sir Robert Peel in London, England in 1828.

★ The first municipal police department in the United States was created in Boston in 1838.

★ Two major functions of law enforcement are crime control and order maintenance.

Cops are our modern-day cowboys. Despite the existence of female officers, the image of a police officer continues to represent the masculine stereotype in our society. Marshall Dillon from the old *Gunsmoke* television series in the 1960s has been replaced by the stalwart heroes of the numerous cop shows on television today. If you think about it, the ideal police officer shares the traits of the "ideal man"—strong, courageous, and able to handle crises with calmness, authority, and integrity. On television, the image of policing is largely drawn from characters who are detectives rather than patrol officers. This gives viewers the false impression that most of the investigative work—indeed, most of the "real" police work—is conducted by plainclothes detectives. This is not the case. The vast majority of police officers are patrol officers, and, in reality, many crimes are solved by patrol officers, not detectives, either because the perpetrator is caught immediately or because the patrol officer acquires information that solves the crime.

Law enforcement in the United States is composed of a complex network of overlapping jurisdictions and agencies, all with the function of enforcing laws. There are federal, state, and local police agencies as well as special jurisdictional agencies. Increasingly, private police add to the numbers of individuals who enforce the law and protect the citizenry from crime and disorder.

Another major feature of policing is the existence of the dual goals of crime control and order maintenance. The image of policing emphasizes the crime control function, while the reality is that most police work is in the nature of **order maintenance**, meaning tasks associated with keeping peace and order in society beyond crime control. We consider our police to be the 24-hour one-stop-shop for problem solving. Think about the types of calls police are dispatched to:

- ★ traffic accidents
- ★ health emergencies
- ★ burglar alarms
- ★ crime reports
- ★ crimes-in-progress
- ★ domestic disputes
- ★ mentally disturbed citizens
- ★ noise violations
- ★ alcohol violations
- ★ abandoned vehicles
- ★ animal control issues
- ★ neighbor disputes
- ★ lost elderly
- ★ lost and runaway children

★ "public welfare checks" (where police are asked
   to check on someone who isn't answering their phone)

★ and cats in trees

Well, perhaps police dispatchers won't send officers out to the cat-in-a-tree call anymore, but that doesn't stop people from calling police for help in those situations. In fact, whenever we are in trouble, our first thought is probably to call 911. Police officers, then, have a day that may begin with a person suffering from Alzheimer's who has forgotten where they live or even what their name is, and end with an alligator in someone's backyard pool that has just eaten the family's Chihuahua. Crime calls happen too, but car chases and catching burglars is not the day-to-day routine of most police officers. In fact, one might say that there is no such thing as a day-to-day routine.

1. POLICE: JUST THE FACTS

It has been reported that there are more than 20,000 police agencies in the United States[1] and more than one million full-time state and local law enforcement personnel.[2] There are more than 451,737 full time sworn municipal officers and 174,251 sheriff's deputies.[3] This translates to about 1.5 officers for every 1,000 citizens.[4] One survey of police agencies in 2000 identified 12,666 local police agencies, 3,070 sheriff's agencies, 1,376 "special jurisdiction" agencies, 623 constables (unique to Texas), 171 tribal police agencies, and 52 county police agencies operating in the United States.[5] This figure does not include the numerous federal law enforcement agencies.

> To find numerous reports on police and policing, go to the Bureau of Justice Statistics Web site: http://www.ojp.usdoj.gov/bjs/ and look at the section called State and Local Law Enforcement.

1.1 Increasing Diversity in the Ranks

The first black police officer was hired in 1861,[6] however, the vast majority of officers from the late 1800s to mid-1900s were white. The recruitment and hiring of minority police officers increased in the 1960s and 1970s when there was a growing realization that departments needed to diversify their forces. During the 1960s, race riots gave the appearance of the police as "foreign" soldiers policing minority groups living in the city ghettos. A concerted effort was made to make police departments more accurately represent the city and community that they policed, and this effort has resulted in some cities having a greater percentage of minority representation than others. Large cities have more minority representation than cities under 10,000.

The majority of police officers are still white (77.4 percent), but 11.7 percent are black (only somewhat smaller than their percentage of the total population). Another 8.9 percent of police officers are Hispanic, with the remaining 2.6 percent from other minority groups.[7]

The first female police officer was hired in 1910 but her role was restricted to dealing with children and female prisoners. Early policewomen also performed clerical tasks. Policewomen were hired under a separate job category from male police officers, with separate hiring requirements. That all changed in the 1970s, when women were integrated into the patrol ranks. They joined women who, in increasing numbers, were entering other "nontraditional" professions, such as engineering, law, and construction.[8]

By 1997, women represented 10.6 percent of all police officers.[9] Not a huge percentage, to be sure, but more than perhaps some ever thought there would be, given the early cold reception they received from their male colleagues. Today, a female police officer does not raise eyebrows, but it hasn't been that long since the first woman was hired for patrol duties. The first women hired in their police departments have interesting stories of their early years when the public was skeptical of female officers, and some fellow officers were downright hostile to the idea of women joining their ranks. Some of the first female patrol officers experienced sexual harassment, some were the targets of hostile practical jokes, some found that back-up was slow and/or that male partners tried to protect them rather than let them do their job.

There seems to be residual doubt that women are as capable as men in meeting the requirements of the role. The IACP (International Association of Chiefs of Police) conducted a survey of its members, finding that 28 percent believed that women did not have the strength, capacity for confrontation, size, and ability to use force sufficient to be an effective police officer.[10] On the other hand, research studies indicate that in most measures, female officers are identical to their male counterparts. There are some interesting differences. For instance, women are less likely to use their firearm and they receive fewer citizen complaints.[11]

The Kobal Collection

Mariska Hargitay portrays a female police officer on television. Female police officers are no longer unusual in reality or on television, and almost every series about police officers has at least one female character.

Most police departments require officers to be citizens, and most have age restrictions—i.e., applicants must be between 21 and under 35-40 to be hired. Some departments now require 60 or 90 college hours. There are written, physical, and psychological tests during the selection process. No one has ever gotten rich as a police officer—although cities vary widely, the average starting salary is about $31,700.[12] Seniority and overtime can substantially increase the annual salary of an officer.

2. HISTORY OF POLICING

It may surprise you to know that police agencies are a relatively recent phenomenon in the history of social order, beginning less than 200 years ago.

Of course, there has always been a need to control crime and deviance, but that function was largely undertaken by the military, by private watchmen and guards, and by citizens themselves up until the 1800s.

We trace American policing back to the British "Bobbie" and the "shire reeve" (sheriff). Early England was divided into shires and each shire had an authority figure called the **shire reeve**, or sheriff, who was responsible for tax collection and enforcing the king's peace. Another authority figure in early shires was the constable, who was responsible for the administration of shire courts and carrying out the orders of the magistrate. The constable was also responsible for keeping the **gaol** (jail) where prisoners were kept before being punished. There was no organized police force and citizens themselves participated in a watch system.

By the 1800s, this informal system of crime control had become ineffective, especially in major cities like London. Henry Fielding, a magistrate in London, created the **Bow Street Runners** in 1748, which could be considered the first type of organized police force. Their first duties were to enforce warrants from the magistrate's court, but they eventually added crime detection and investigation. Eventually, their reach

> See the Web site of the London Metropolitan Police Force archives for pictures and more history: http://www.met.police.uk/history/archives.htm

extended all over England when pursuing criminals. They also provided protection in the Bow Street area of London, especially after a mounted patrol was established by Fielding's successor.

In 1829, Robert Peel, the Home Secretary of England, convinced Parliament to pass the Metropolitan Police Act, creating the first police force as we know it today. They eventually became known as "**Bobbies**," referencing Peel's role in their creation. By 1839, the Metropolitan Force had absorbed the Bow Street Runners, the Bow Street mounted patrol, and the Wapping Marine Police. The Force was initially based in Scotland Yard with five more watch houses and 17 districts. In 1831, the Special Constables Act was passed that added more officers to the force.

In the colonies, crime prevention was the responsibility of every citizen. Watch systems existed that were similar to those found in the early English shires. Boston holds the honor of having the first police department in this country, if one uses the date of origin of 1838 (when the first "day police" were hired), and not 1854 (when the police department was created as an agency separate from the constable's office).

New York City's police department was created in 1844. By the early 1800s, New York was overwhelmed with the dual problems of poverty and rising crime. The area of the Bowery, and espe-

The movie *Gangs of New York* is a fictional portrayal of a time when Irish gangs were prevalent in New York City.

BOX 4.1

Boston Police Department—A Brief Historical Chronology

1760s: First night watch established.

1788: The word "police" appeared for the first time, designating a specific office, "Inspector of Police."

1822: The Town of Boston became the City of Boston. Increases in the population and in the number of businesses operating created an increased demand for police patrol.

1838: Law passed permitting day patrol. City had a Day Police and a Night Watch, which by all accounts operated completely independently of one another.

1852: The metal badges were issued—a six-point star made of brass.

1854: Boston Police Department established, structured after the model developed by Sir Robert Peel for the London police force.

1858: Telegraph system completed, linking central office and police stations.

1861: White cotton gloves worn by the officers for the first time. Thereafter, "full uniform" included the wearing of such gloves.

1870: 180 "night walkers" were arrested; most were placed on probation and sent home.

1872: The Great Boston Fire of November 9 and 10, which destroyed 776 buildings. The fire was discovered by a patrolman who was chasing boys on Lincoln Street.

1873: First mounted patrol established.

1883: Department headquarters moved from City Hall to 37 Pemberton Square.

1889: Statute passed providing for right-of-way for patrol wagons and ambulances.

1903: First motor patrol wagon placed in service—a Stanley Streamer touring car operated by a chauffeur; the police officer sat on higher seat so that he could look over area's back fences.

Source: http://www.cityofboston.gov/police/glance.asp.

cially the "Five Points" neighborhood, were the center of the problems that threatened to overrun the city. The power of the immigrant Irish gangs is fancifully portrayed in the hit 2002 movie *Gangs of New York*. Although there was growing support for an organized police force, citizens were suspicious of allowing such a centralized power. Still, by 1845, the Mayor of New York had created a municipal police force with an initial staffing of 900 men.

For an interesting article that compares the movie to historians' descriptions of the "Five Points" area and the Irish gangs of the time period, see http://news.nationalgeographic.com/news/2003/03/0320_030320_oscars_gangs_2.html

New York's police force, like other city police departments, was very much influenced by politics. Police officers received appointments of several years, rather than being hired, and these appointments came through political patronage. Both the Democrats and Whigs fought over the police department, and in 1857 the Whigs had managed to get the state legislature to pass a bill creating the Metropolitan Police for the City of New York, Brooklyn, and Westchester County. The two police forces operated simultaneously and, at one point, even engaged in a large brawl in front of city hall as the Metropolitan Force sought to arrest the Mayor. The Metropolitan Force emerged as victor, but the police force was returned to municipal control in 1870.[13]

One of the early police commissioners was Theodore Roosevelt. Starting in 1895 he began a series of reforms that included:

★ hiring based on skill and aptitude rather than political patronage

★ the creation of disciplinary rules and enforcement

★ adopting an early form of fingerprinting

★ creating a bike squad

★ requiring officers to have pistol practice

★ instituting physical exams of officers

★ hiring the first female police matron to supervise female prisoners (Minnie Gertrude Kelly)

★ eliminating the practice of homeless people sleeping in the basements of the precinct offices in horribly unsanitary conditions[14]

City police departments were slower to emerge in the west and the marshal was often the only law enforcement officer in early Western towns. For instance, a

> For an interesting Web site that covers the history of the New York City Police Department, go to: http://www.nycpolicemuseum.org/html/museum-map.html

true city police department didn't emerge in Los Angeles until almost 1870. The precursor to the Los Angeles Police Department was the "Los Angeles Rangers," who were volunteers enlisted to help the county sheriff and marshal in the unruly times of the 1850s. Los Angeles was inundated with immigrants and others who were spurred by "gold fever" to come to the west coast to make a fortune. The Rangers wore a white ribbon that indicated they served under the authority of the Council of Los Angeles. The "Los Angeles City Guards" succeeded the Rangers and wore the first official uniform. Vigilante justice was commonplace and early authorities were unable to keep order. Evidently, during the 1860s, a group of residents were successful in their request to the French government for protection. For some period of time, French troops were deployed in the city to guard residents![15]

In 1869, six officers were formally hired and paid out of city funds. Led by the city marshal, who also acted as dog catcher and tax collector, this early force was the beginning of the LAPD of today. The mounted patrol began in 1875 and existed until 1916. In 1876, the Board of Police Commissioners was formed and a police chief was hired after the marshal was killed by one of his own men. In 1885, the chief of police commanded 18 men and earned $150 a month. In 1886, two black officers were hired.

For an interesting description of the early days of the LAPD, go to the official Web site: http://www.lapdonline.org/history_ of_the_lapd/content_basic_view/1107

In 1889, professional standards emerged with a new chief, John M. Glass, who instituted hiring standards and formalized training.[16]

As the 1800s gave way to the 1900s, cities and towns grew, and most eventually created their own police departments. That process continues today and small towns sometimes make the decision to create a municipal police force, even if it is only a chief and one or two officers, rather than depend on the county sheriff's office for police protection. Sheriff's deputies provide patrol protection and crime investigation to unincorporated areas and small towns that do not have their own police department.

2.1 Policing in the 20th Century

Early police departments continued to be very influenced by politics through the 1930s. Positions were awarded through political patronage, and sometimes police campaigned in their uniform for politicians running for re-election. Of course, if their candidate lost, they would have lost their jobs and so there may have been, in some situations, more than a hint of coercion and corruption in their involvement with the political process. Police were implicated in coercing votes and stuffing ballot boxes.[17]

Training was minimal, and police were paid very little. Some officers were corrupt and utilized their position for graft. While early police departments were involved in a range of community activities, such as running soup kitchens and pursuing moral reforms such as anti-alcohol campaigns, they were also involved in strike-busting and immigrant control, sometimes through extralegal and violent means.[18] In some cities with strong political machines, police might have been seen almost as a private security force serving only those in power. The control of the working and "immigrant classes" was not necessarily done with any degree of sensitivity or even legality.[19]

August Vollmer (1876-1955) is credited with beginning the process of professionalizing the police. He was elected marshal of Berkeley, California, in 1905 and later became its first police chief. During his long tenure with the Berkeley Police Department, he was instrumental in a large number of innovations in policing that spread across the country and led to police departments being considered more as professional crime fighters than "hired muscle" for political machines. Interestingly, he is also credited with beginning the first criminal justice department at the University of California at Berkeley, where he taught some of the emerging leaders in the field.

BOX 4.2

August Vollmer and the Berkeley Police Department

1906: Installed a basic records system

1906: Installed the first Modus Operandi (MO) System

1907: First use of scientific investigation (Kelinschmidt case—analysis of blood, fibers, and soil)

1907: First police academy was established

1911: Organized the first Police Motorcycle Patrol

1913: Changed to automobiles for patrolling

1916: Chief Vollmer established the first School of Criminology at University of California at Berkeley

1918: Began using intelligence tests in recruiting police officers

1920: The first lie detector instrument was developed at University of California and used by the police department

1921: Began using psychiatric screening in recruitment

1924: Established one of the first single fingerprint systems

1925: Established Crime Prevention Division and hired a policewoman

Source: Berkeley Police Department Web site: http://www.ci.berkeley.ca.us/police/history/history.html.

In effect, the "professionalization" of police resulted in a real, or at least perceived, shift of police loyalty from political bosses to the law itself.[20] Professionalization implied objectivity, professional expertise, and specialized training. The professionalization of police probably also led to the emphasis of the crime fighter role over order maintenance in the following decades. Professionalization led to more training, hiring standards, and standard operating procedures.

By the 1960s, police were seen as professional crime fighters, but certain factors had combined to drastically change their relationship with the community. They were isolated in patrol cars instead of meeting and interacting with citizens while walking beats, and they had layers of bureaucracy that reduced their discretion when handling community problems. Professionalization may have led to police officers in some cities being seen as well-trained crime fighters, but it also made them seem more like soldiers than public servants.

Then in the 1960s, police departments around the country were faced with civil protests that challenged their ability to maintain public order. When civil rights protests began in the south, police were seen on television news shows using dogs and high-pressure water hoses on peaceful demonstrators.

When race riots broke out in the cities of the north, police were seen by some as an all-white force oppressing an all-black ghetto. The antipathy one finds between police departments and urban minority communities today has its roots as far back as the late 1800s when police were used to control the immigrant classes, but the more immediate origin is the 1960s race riots. In 1992, after the acquittal of police officers accused of beating Rodney King, Los Angeles erupted in a riot similar to those of the 1960s, making it apparent that race relations is a topic that continues to be problematic for police departments. Not all departments are equally successful at balancing community relations with crime control strategies.

Because of the discord and conflict of the 1960s, police departments around the country sought to improve their relationships with minority communities through the recruitment and hiring of minority and female officers. They also created community relations and public information officers. Citizen advisory committees were started in some communities, and other attempts were made to make the relationship between the police department and the community it served more open and cooperative. These efforts continue today.

2.2 The Texas Rangers

In addition to municipal police departments, law enforcement agencies at the state level emerged in the early 1900s, but at least one police organization had a much earlier origin. While the Department of Public Safety in Texas was not created until 1935, the Texas Rangers, a unit of the state police, trace their origins back to 1823 when Stephen F. Austin hired 10 men to protect the frontier from Indians and bandits. In 1835, the provisional government of Texas created the first official Ranger force in preparation for the revolution against Mexico. By the 1880s, the Rangers had developed into a law enforcement agency rather than a paramilitary organization.[21]

Although associated with some darker periods of Texas history, especially after the Civil War, the Rangers have attained an almost iconic image. Through the late 1880s and early 1900s the Rangers were utilized as a statewide crime-fighting force, dispatched to quell marauding Indians, track down criminals, and protect citizens when local authorities could not. In 1935 when

> For more history on Texas Rangers stories, see the official Texas Ranger Museum site at: http://www.texasranger.org/today/rangerstoday.htm or one of the many books about the Rangers.

the Department of Public Safety was created, the Texas Rangers were absorbed into this larger agency. They are known as the oldest statewide law enforcement organization in the country.

Of course, today, many television viewers associate the Texas Rangers with martial arts star Chuck Norris from the *Walker, Texas Ranger* television series, but some of the real Texas Rangers, from all accounts, may have been even more "larger-than-life" than the television character.

★ Exercise: In the State of . . .

1. Choose a city in your state that has an official
   Web site for its police department, including the history of the department.

2. See when the department was created and review its early history.

3. Note hiring qualifications and starting salary if given.

4. Note the structure and organization of the department.

5. Repeat with the state police agency (state patrol or other name).

---

3. THE STRUCTURE AND ORGANIZATION OF POLICING

Local and state police agencies have adopted an organizational model based on the military, while federal agencies tend to have organizational structures more similar to other bureaucracies. The military command system found in state, county and local law enforcement often uses the same ranks as one would find in the military (Captain, Lieutenant, Sergeant). Information flows downward in a hierarchical pattern and span of control principles are similar to the military, with each officer responding to his or her own chain of command. Some argue, however, that the police organization is very different from the military, in that each officer has much more discretion and makes more decisions than the average soldier. This discussion of whether patrol officers are basically "foot soldiers" or whether they are autonomous decision makers is also present in the discussion of whether policing is a profession or an occupation. It seems clear that, whatever one wants to call them, police officers on the street must be comfortable with a large degree of discretion and authority to handle a wide range of different situations on the street.

3.1 Federal Law Enforcement

Unlike many countries, the United States has no national police force. Part of the reason for this is the vast area encompassed within the borders of this country, but another reason is that, since the American Revolution, there has been a cultural hostility and suspicion of centralized power. This does not mean, however, that there are no federal law enforcement officers. In fact, there are more than 93,000 federal employees who have the authority to make arrests and are considered law enforcement officers. Prior to 2003, the Immigration and Naturalization Service (INS) employed the largest number of federal officers (19,101), followed by the Federal Bureau of Prisons (14,305) and then the U.S. Customs Service (11,634). The Department of Homeland Security (DHS) has absorbed both INS and the U.S. Customs Service, making the DHS the largest federal law enforcement agency.

We are probably most familiar with the Federal Bureau of Investigation (FBI) and the Drug Enforcement Administration (DEA); however, there are numerous other federal agencies that employ law enforcement officers who have the power to make arrests and carry firearms. Box 4.3 shows some of these agencies.

As you might expect, these agencies have specific duties and missions. The U.S. Marshals Service, for instance, is responsible for seizing and maintaining property confiscated through civil and criminal forfeiture hearings, providing security for federal courtrooms and judicial officials, transporting federal prisoners, and protecting federal witnesses (some through the Federal Witness Protection Program).

BOX 4.3

Federal Agencies with Law Enforcement Officers

★ Department of Agriculture

★ Department of Commerce

★ Department of Defense

★ Department of Energy

★ Department of Health and Human Services

★ Department of the Interior

★ Department of State

★ Department of Transportation

★ Department of the Treasury

★ Department of Veterans' Affairs

★ U.S. Postal Service

★ Department of Justice:

  • Drug Enforcement Administration (employing about 4,020)

  • Federal Bureau of Investigation (employing about 11,248)

  • Federal Bureau of Prisons (employing about 14,305)

  • Alcohol, Tobacco, Firearms, and Explosives
    (law enforcement functions) (employing about 2,335).

★ U.S. Secret Service (now part of DHS, employing about 4,256)

★ Administrative Office of the U.S. Courts (employing about 2,855)

★ U.S. Postal Inspection Service (employing about 3,135)

★ Internal Revenue Service (employing about 2,855)

★ U.S. Marshals Service (employing about 2,646).

Source: Reaves, B. and L. Bauer (2003). *Federal Law Enforcement Officers*, 2002. Washington, DC: Bureau of Justice Statistics, p. 1.

The Department of Homeland Security (DHS), created in 2002, has absorbed a number of other agencies. As mentioned previously, the Immigration and Naturalization Service and U.S. Customs Service are now under DHS. The functions of these two agencies have been reorganized, and now the agency primarily responsible for border protection is called U.S. Customs and Border Protection, and another agency called U.S. Immigration and Customs Enforcement enforces immigration laws within the interior of the country. Other agencies absorbed by the Department of Homeland Security include the U.S. Coast Guard and the U.S. Secret Service. The Transportation Security Administration (TSA) is a new agency charged with providing protection at airports. The same Act

> For a list of federal agencies that employ law enforcement officers and their Web sites, see http://www.ojp.usdoj.gov/bjs/pub/pdf/fleo02.pdf

that created DHS also changed the Bureau of Alcohol, Tobacco and Firearms (ATF), which is now The Bureau of Alcohol, Tobacco, Firearms and Explosives, and the law enforcement functions of the agency have been transferred to the Justice Department while the revenue functions remain with the Department of the Treasury.[24]

Federal law enforcement agencies enforce federal laws. They share jurisdiction with state and local law enforcement agencies when an action is a violation of both federal and state law. The most common example of this is the sale of controlled substances. While smuggling drugs into the country is a federal crime, sales of controlled substances break both federal and state laws. That is the reason special task forces were created in the 1980s to investigate drug offenders. These task forces were staffed by federal and local officers so that their efforts would not be duplicated, or, worse, they would not get in the way of each other's investigations.

3.2 State Law Enforcement

State law enforcement agencies are typically called Highway Patrol, Department of Public Safety, or State Patrol, although their mission encompasses more than patrolling the state highways and issuing drivers' licenses. These statewide agencies usually have a state-of-the-art crime lab to assist smaller jurisdictions that have no analysis capabilities. They also provide assistance with investigation and detection to local agencies and carry out their own investigations when the criminal activity is statewide, especially if the criminal activity involves drugs or auto theft rings. The state agency may be the central repository for crime statistics, may have authority over gun registrations and investigations for licenses, and may have supervision over controlled substances registration. In Box 4.4, the Wisconsin State Patrol is described.

Many states also have limited jurisdiction law enforcement agencies. Examples include state agencies that enforce alcohol and tobacco laws, fish and game agencies that enforce hunting and other laws, and child support enforce-

BOX 4.4

Wisconsin State Patrol

The **Wisconsin State Patrol** (WSP) enforces traffic and criminal laws; helps motorists in need; inspects trucks, school buses, and ambulances; and helps local law enforcement agencies with natural disasters or civil disturbances.

★ The **Communications Bureau** provides the engineering, installation and technical maintenance for the statewide telecommunications network, including all radio tower sites and voice and data transmitting equipment, the Mobile Data Communications Network (MDCN), including equipment in cruisers, such as radios and mobile data computers. (608) 267-9763

★ The **Field Operations Bureau** enforces criminal and traffic laws, conducts criminal highway interdiction programs, and helps local law enforcement agencies with traffic safety, civil disturbances and disasters (natural and manmade). (608) 267-9522

★ The **Transportation Safety Bureau** provides a department-wide focus for safety program and safety policy analysis, carries out public outreach on safety issues, administers the statewide chemical testing program, oversees motor carrier safety and weight facilities (SWEFs), inspects and regulates motor carriers, school buses and ambulances. (608) 266-0402

★ The **State Patrol Academy Office** provides diverse training for State Patrol recruits, federal and local law enforcement officers, and state employees. The facility is used by other agencies for training programs as well.

Source: Wisconsin Department of Transportation: http://www.dot.wisconsin.gov/about/structure/dsp.htm.

ment agencies. State universities may have their own police departments (or they may use private security officers who are not police officers). Each state is slightly different in the type and number of these agencies.

3.3 County Law Enforcement

Recall that one of the earliest law enforcement officials was the shire reeve, who was responsible for collecting taxes for the king, and keeping the king's peace in the shires (or counties) of England. The modern-day shire reeve is the county sheriff. Sheriffs are elected officials, but sheriff's deputies are hired through civil service selection procedures in a similar manner to municipal law enforcement officers. Usually county sheriffs also have the responsibility of managing the county jail. In some jurisdictions, sheriff's deputies may be assigned either patrol duties or jail duties, but in other jurisdictions, the position of jailer is a different job from that of deputy. Sheriff's offices also serve warrants and civil documents, including eviction notices.

While sheriffs are elected, police chiefs are hired by the city manager and/or a city council and mayor. Both, however, have notoriously short average tenures, because both positions are lightning rods for public controversy. A few counties also have county police agencies separate from the sheriff's office. These agencies are more like a municipal police agency and the police chief of this agency is not an elected official.

3.4 Municipal Law Enforcement

When we think of police, we typically think of the municipal police department. Most towns and cities of any size have their own police department. Small towns may have a police department of only three or four officers, while cities such as New York have more than 38,000 officers. Most police *officers* work in the larger police departments, even though most police *departments* have fewer than 50 officers.[25] The majority of departments in the country are quite small; in fact, about 800 police departments have only one officer![26]

Larger police departments are typically broken into divisions, such as patrol and investigation. Under the investigation division, there may be further subdivisions, such as sex crimes, juvenile, and vice. Other departments exist as well, including community relations, internal affairs, training, and research and planning. Some police departments have created special domestic violence teams, police squads specially trained to respond to the mentally ill, and other specialized teams. In smaller departments, of course, patrol officers are expected to be generalists and handle a large variety of calls.

3.5 Special Jurisdiction Law Enforcement Agencies

In your community, there may also be special or limited jurisdiction law enforcement agencies. Some cities have park police, airport police, housing police, or transit police. These agencies have the power of arrest but their jurisdiction is limited to crimes that occur within or in relation to their specific jurisdiction.

Indian tribes may have their own tribal police that have exclusive jurisdiction on reservations. In fact, there is a completely separate justice system existing on some Indian reservations, complete with tribal police and a tribal court system. Even civil court matters are dealt with by tribal courts and a state district court does not have any authority once a matter is deemed under the jurisdiction of these tribal courts. The Oneida Indian Nation, for instance, has a police department. From its Web site, we learn that:

> Created in 1993, the Oneida Nation Police Department has become an integral part of Central New York's law enforcement community. Working closely with state, county, and local police agencies, the Oneida Nation's 39 sworn officers and six non-sworn employees

preserve the peace and protect the property of the Oneida Nation and its Members in Central New York's Madison and Oneida Counties. They also are responsible for the safety of the more than 3.4 million visitors each year to the Oneida Nation's Turning Stone Casino Resort, as well as the 3,000 employees who work at the Oneida Nation's businesses and government offices. . . . Commissioned as Bureau of Indian Affairs Deputy Special Officers under the U. S. Department of the Interior, the Oneida Nation's force is the third largest tribal police agency in the country. Officers investigate violations of the General Crimes Act and Major Crimes Act pursuant to Title 18 of the U.S. Code. Members of the Department's Bureau of Investigation also conduct criminal, non-criminal, and background employment investigations for the Oneida Nation's enterprises. In November 1998, the Oneida Nation Police Department was accredited by the Commission on Accreditation for Law Enforcement Agencies (CALEA), a group that sets standards for professionalism and assesses agency success in meeting or exceeding each individual standard. The department is the first tribal police force to be accredited in the United States and only the seventh police department to receive CALEA accreditation in New York State.[27]

3.6 Private Law Enforcement

Private security officers are not peace officers. They are paid with private funds rather than public dollars, and their primary duty is to provide protection and investigative services to the hiring entity, which might be a company, neighborhood or private individual. We mention private security officers here only because many people misunderstand their power and assume they have similar powers to those of public peace officers. The other reason that we must mention them is that there may be many more private security officers than police officers. There are probably more than 1.5 million individuals employed in private security and private security expenditures are on track to be almost double that of public expenditures.

It should also be noted that there is overlap between private and public policing because public police officers are often hired as private employees of security companies. Because police are certified peace officers who can carry a weapon and use their arrest powers even when off-duty, they carry those powers with them into the private position. Otherwise, private security officers have no greater powers of arrest or use of force than an average citizen.

The American Society for Industrial Security (now ASIS International) is the largest professional organization for security professionals. Its Web site states that it was founded in 1955 and has more than 35,000 members worldwide. ASIS administers three certification programs. The Certified Protection Professional (CPP™) designation indicates board certification in security management. The Physical Security Professional (PSP™) and the Professional Certified Investigator (PCI™) are also offered.[28]

4. THE FUNCTION OF POLICE IN SOCIETY

What is the function of police? You probably said crime control, but that is not a complete answer. Police officers are dispatched to many different types of calls and crime calls form only a portion of their workload. According to researchers, the majority of police work is divided among patrol, service calls, and paperwork. Further, only 13 percent of their time is taken up with potentially criminal matters according to these authors.[29]

It is common to identify crime control and order maintenance as the two major functions of law enforcement. Crime control includes all the tasks associated with preventing crime and enforcing the law. Patrol, responding to dispatched calls, investigating crimes, engaging in sting operations, arresting suspects, testifying in court, and all the other tasks associated with either preventing crime or catching criminals is included in the crime control function.

Order maintenance tasks include everything else police do. When police respond to a car accident and control traffic and see that the victims get medical treatment, this is order maintenance. When police are called by a worried mother to check on her college-age daughter because she hasn't answered her phone in three days, and they do so, this is order maintenance. When police drive slowly by a rowdy group of teenagers late at night, pull over, and watch until the teenagers disperse and go home, this is order maintenance. Police are present when there are medical emergencies, water rescues, traffic problems, public disturbances and organized protests, weather related and other natural disasters, and civil defense. You will recall that after Hurricane Katrina, New Orleans police officers were expected to ignore the needs of their own families and stay on duty over the days and weeks following the flooding to provide victim rescue, crime control, and public order. The subsequent criticism of their performance should only serve to illustrate how much was expected of them.[30] This incident also shows how both the law enforcement and order maintenance functions are expected of police. Police swung between being law enforcers (against looting) and service providers (when they broke into stores and distributed the goods to desperate citizens). Politicians ordered police to concentrate on lawbreaking, then they demanded that police emphasize saving lives even if it meant ignoring lawbreaking, and then, when the public attitudes toward looting became very negative, the politicians ordered police (and the National Guard soldiers who had arrived) to emphasize law enforcement again. However, individual police officers in the flooded streets were the ones who had to choose between those sometimes conflicting role responsibilities in every situation, over the exhausting days that stretched into months.

Order-maintenance and crime-control functions may overlap and even merge. When police are called to a neighbor dispute, this is order maintenance; but if they are unsuccessful in resolving the problem, it may turn into a crime when one neighbor decides to settle the argument with arson or a gun. A mentally ill person may complain to police that their brain is being scanned by an alien, which is obviously not a crime control issue; however, if they do not respond in an effective manner to this complaint, the delusional person may decide that an innocent bystander is the alien and assault or even kill the victim. When neighbors call police because there is a large group of "suspicious looking" people in a park late at night, not responding may result in nothing happening, or it may result in a series of vehicle burglaries or other crimes.

On the other hand, order-maintenance functions may be considered extralegal activities that exceed police authority. That group of people in the park late at night probably has every legal right to be there, at least until the official closing time. Do police use their coercive authority to "encourage" the people to disperse, satisfying the homeowners who are nervous, or do they allow the group to exercise their right to use a public park, satisfying the group members, but alienating the homeowners? These order-maintenance choices are sometimes difficult to make.

5. DISCRETION AND STYLES OF POLICING

Discretion can be defined as the power to make a decision between two or more choices. Patrol officers have a great deal of discretion in defining criminal behavior and deciding what to do about it. When police stop people for minor traffic violations, they can write tickets or give warnings. When they pick up teenagers for drinking or other delinquent acts, they can bring them in for formal processing or take them home. After stopping a fight on the street, they can arrest both parties or allow the combatants to work out their problems. One older study found that police do not make arrests in 43 percent of all felony cases and 52 percent of all misdemeanor cases.[31]

It appears that their discretion allows different styles of policing to emerge. That is, departments may emphasize crime control or order maintenance, or they may emphasize other goals or objectives. Similarly, individual police officers seem to approach their job in different ways, emphasizing certain functions over others. These styles influence the decisions that are made in situations encountered on the street.

James Q. Wilson[32] developed a typology of policing behavior in regard to the frequency and type of interchange with the citizenry. He perceived these types as departmental types and they occurred, in part, because of the type of community the police department served.

1. The *legalistic model* describes a department with frequent, but formal, exchanges with the public. This is a "by-the-book" type of department that has a strong emphasis on rules and proper procedures. Police officers are not encouraged to use discretion in decisionmaking. Relationships with the community are formal and legalistic. This type of model may be found in cities and larger towns.

2. The *service model* describes a department with frequent but informal exchanges with the public. Police officers are encouraged to use informal means of conflict resolution when appropriate and have stronger ties with the community. This model is common in small towns and suburban areas.

3. The *watchman model* is characterized by infrequent exchanges with the public. This department has less frequent interchanges with the public and makes distinctions between groups or types of individuals. Citizens who are deemed nonthreatening will be given a "pass" when caught doing something minor (like DUI or juvenile offenses), but utilize formal processing for those who are outsiders or identified as troublemakers.

Although Wilson's typology may appear to be dated today and not describe police departments very accurately, there do seem to be differences between departments. Some police departments are known to be more or less likely to use force; some have better or worse relationships with minority communities; some are known to be progressive, some reactionary. Just as with all organizations, city police departments' reputations may lag behind reality and a department that encounters bad press, for instance, may suffer a negative reputation for years after the problems have been dealt with.

Other authors describe individual officers and their different performance styles. William Muir[33] discussed four types of police officers and their willingness and acceptance of the use of force and coercion. According to Muir, the successful police officer is able to balance willingness to use coercion with an understanding of humankind, with empathy and sympathy toward the

BOX 4.5

Muir's Police Typology

1. *Enforcers* are willing to use force, but unable to empathize with citizens. They may use force too quickly and not understand when it is absolutely necessary and when it isn't.

2. *Professionals* are willing to use force, but able to empathize with citizens, therefore they are able to use other means when appropriate. When force is necessary, they are effective but are always reluctant to use force except as a last resort.

3. *Reciprocators* are unwilling to use force because they empathize and identify with citizens. These officers attempt to get cooperation through negotiation, bargaining, and persuasion, but, ultimately, are less effective when these methods do not work.

4. *Avoiders* are unwilling to use force, but not because they empathize with citizenry. Rather, they prefer to avoid situations that are dangerous or troublesome and do so by staying on simple calls longer than necessary, not responding to dispatches for all available officers and, in other ways, they avoid the potential for the use of force or coercion.

Source: Muir, W. (1977). Police: Streetcorner Politicians. Chicago: University of Chicago Press, p. 24.

weaknesses of human nature. If officers overemphasize coercion, they become cynical and brutal; if they overemphasize understanding, they become ineffective. Sometimes, a young police officer's response creates internal conflict and eventually the officer will tend to avoid situations that create the need to make these choices; this kind of officer became either a *reciprocator* or an *avoider.* Finally some young officers found ways to exercise coercion legitimately with care and competence; these officers became *professionals.*[34] Box 4.5 shows Muir's types.

Michael Brown[35] also described four types of police officers. Instead of the use of force, this typology focused on how each officer uses the discretion that comes with the role.

1. *Old style crime fighters* are concerned only with action that might be considered crime control, therefore they will ignore or slight calls that they do not consider "real" police work.

2. *Clean beat officers* seek to control all behavior in their jurisdiction and take ownership over everything that happens in the area. They may use extralegal or persuasive authority to get desired results.

3. *Service style officers* emphasize public order and peace officer tasks, perhaps over crime fighting. These individuals like the public service aspects of the job rather than the tasks that result in more antagonistic relationships with the public.

4. *Professional style officers* are the epitome of bureaucratic, by-the-book policing. They may enforce the law with little discretion and seldom give anyone "a break."

Of course, no police officer fits into these described types perfectly. These are descriptions of the different ways that people approach situations they encounter (or the way departments emphasize different goals). Research has explored interesting questions, such as whether race and gender affect one's style of policing, whether any of the styles are more associated with corruption, and many other issues related to performance issues. Most typologies incorporate the dual roles of crime control and order maintenance. A major change in policing that also addressed this issue occurred in the late 1980s and 1990s in the form of community policing.

6. COMMUNITY POLICING

Community policing is based on a belief that police should partner with communities to prevent and reduce crime. The idea of community policing evidently began around the early 1980s with the theory propounded by James Wilson and George Kelling called the **"broken windows" theory** of crime. These researchers argued that signs of neighborhood disintegration and deterioration indicated to criminals that no one cared and no one would intervene in criminal acts, therefore crime is higher in these types of neighborhoods. The more crime, the less community members invest in their neighborhoods, increasing the spiral of disorder, decay, and crime. Herman Goldstein argued that police had a role in strengthening the community, which would, in turn, increase the community's ability to prevent crime.[36] Box 4.6 shows some community policing strategies.

BOX 4.6

Community Policing Strategies

★ Direct engagement with the community with greater information about neighborhood problems;

★ Freeing community police officers from responding to dispatched crime calls so they could engage in proactive crime prevention;

★ More visible police operations;

★ Decentralized operations that lead to greater familiarity with specific neighborhoods;

★ Encouraging officers to see citizens as partners;

★ Moving decisionmaking and discretion downward to patrol officers;

★ Encouraging citizens to take more initiative in preventing and solving crimes.

Source: National Institute of Justice (1992). "Community Policing in the 1990s." *NIJ Research Bulletin*. Washington, DC: U.S. Department of Justice, p. 3.

The purpose of all such efforts was to increase the partnership between the community and police in crime prevention.[37] The programs loosely grouped under a community policing strategy attempted to get community members to assist in crime prevention efforts. These partnerships may have been as simple as "National Night Out," where neighborhood members were encouraged to go outside on a specified night and meet their neighbors, to more elaborate citizen-police partnerships that identified problems in the community and shared the responsibility to fix them. Community policing efforts have included the following:

★ increased foot and bike patrols

★ storefront police stations

★ bilingual crime hotlines

★ prevention newsletters and watch programs

★ meetings with community members

★ citizen police academies

★ D.A.R.E. and G.R.E.A.T. programs

In "Operation Night Light," probation and police jointly monitor conditions of probation; police assist in finding absconders and serving warrants; and both agencies work with community groups in obtaining treatment resources for offender-members.[38] The National Center on Institutions and Alternatives developed Operation Spotlight in 1995 in Maryland. This program also involved collaboration among probation, police, and citizens. Citizen volunteers work with teams of probation and police officers and small groups of offenders in high-crime areas. The program now exists in New York and Illinois.[39]

Community policing efforts also emphasize the decentralization of policing. Neighborhood storefront police stations were given greater autonomy in prioritizing and solving the problems of that particular neighborhood. The police role expanded to include helping citizens get the city to respond to abandoned cars, broken streetlights, overgrown empty lots, and dilapidated houses. Permanent assignments rather than rotating shifts help police officers develop working relationships with citizens and encourage a feeling of responsibility for their assigned community.

6.1 Criticisms of Community Policing

Critics of community policing programs argued that they were ineffective in crime prevention for a variety of reasons. One reason was that they mistakenly assumed "community" could be defined purely geographically. That is, community policing programs might have targeted a particular neighborhood, drawing boundaries by crime rates, voting districts, or through some other means of establishing the border of the "community." However, people may be affiliated more through activity than "place." For instance, a family may not know its neighbors but be very active in a church that is three miles away.[40] More police presence in a particular geographic neighborhood may have deterred some crime, but it may not have been successful in strengthening the community sufficiently to prevent criminal decisionmaking.

Community policing efforts may have failed because there was no "community" to join with, or because the partnership was nonexistent. Critics argued that some programs used the community as the "eyes and ears" of police, to gain political support, monetary assistance and moral support; but they did not involve the community in power sharing or decision making.[41] Further, in some communities, police are seen as the enemy and the antipathy felt toward police overwhelmed any attempts to gain trust. Residents may not have liked criminals, but they liked police even less. In these neighborhoods, any partnerships needed to overcome the residual distrust and dislike before becoming workable.

Generally, evaluations of community policing efforts have been mixed. It seems that public satisfaction increased when a police department adopted community policing programs, but whether such approaches reduced crime is difficult to say. Some researchers argue that findings indicate the central organization and service delivery of policing never changed that much anyway.[42] Ironically, one of the major hurdles of community policing efforts was that the community police officer emphasized order-maintenance tasks rather than crime-control tasks. This may have been a less desirable role for many officers who preferred to see themselves as "crime fighters," regardless of the effectiveness of community policing efforts.

7. CONCLUSION

Law enforcement in this country is a descendent of the London "Bobbie" from the late 1800s. Most people think of municipal police officers when they think of police, but we should be aware that there are federal, state, and local law enforcement agencies. Police hold special powers in society and have a great deal of discretion in how they resolve the situations they deal with every day. We see a great deal of criticism of police, and we expect the men and women who hold these positions to conform to high standards of behavior, both on and off duty. We expect police to pursue both goals of crime control and order maintenance. In fact, we want police to be supermen (and women).

The surprising thing is that they do so well at this impossible task. At least one study shows that a majority of respondents hold favorable attitudes toward police—

★ 79 percent agreed that police were responsive;

★ 75 percent agreed that they do a good job maintaining order,

★ 84 percent agreed that they care about the safety of residents, and

★ 82 percent agreed that they do a good job protecting people from crime.

REVIEW QUESTIONS

1. Describe the two functions or goals of the police and provide some examples of each. *Crime control & order matenance*

2. How many police agencies and police officers are there in the United States?

3. Describe early law enforcement in England.

4. Which cities began the first police departments in the United States? When? *1838 Boston and NY 1844*

5. Who is considered responsible for the "professionalization" of police and what does that term entail?

6. Describe the types of law enforcement agencies at the federal, state, county, and local levels. What are special jurisdiction agencies?

7. Describe Wilson's typology of police departments.

8. Describe Muir's and Brown's typologies of police officers.

9. What are the principles of community policing?

10. Provide some examples of community policing strategies.

VOCABULARY

"Bobbies" – older term for London's police, which refers to Robert Peel's role in creating the force in 1829

Bow Street Runners – begun in 1748 by Magistrate Henry Fielding in London and considered the first type of organized police force

"broken windows" theory – (of crime) states that crime occurs when there are signs of neighborhood disintegration and deterioration indicating to criminals that no one cares and no one will intervene

community policing – a model of policing based on a belief that police should join with communities to prevent and reduce crime; programs include community members assisting in crime prevention efforts

discretion – the power to make a decision between two or more choices

gaol – early English jail where prisoners were kept before being punished

order maintenance – tasks associated with keeping order and peace in society beyond crime control

shire reeve – or sheriff; was responsible for tax collection and enforcing the king's peace

FOR FURTHER READING

Crank, John (2004). *Understanding Police Culture*, Second Edition. Newark, NJ: LexisNexis/Matthew Bender.

Gaines, Larry and Victor E. Kappeler (2005). *Policing in America*, Fifth Edition. Newark, NJ: LexisNexis/Matthew Bender.

Goldstein, Herman (1990). *Problem Oriented Policing*. New York: McGraw-Hill.

Langworthy, Robert and Larry Travis (2003). *Policing in America: A Balance of Forces*, Third Edition. Englewood Cliffs, NJ: Prentice Hall.

Martin, Susan (1980). *Breaking and Entering: Policewomen in Patrol*. Berkeley, CA: University of California Press.

Muir, William (1977). *Police: Streetcorner Politicians*. Chicago: University of Chicago Press.

Wilson, James Q. (1968). *Varieties of Police Behavior*. Cambridge, MA: Harvard University Press.

[1] Langworthy, R. & L. Travis (2003). *Policing in America: A Balance of Forces*, Third Edition. Englewood Cliffs, NJ: Prentice Hall.

[2] Obtained 6/10/07 from official Bureau of Justice Statistics Web site: http://www.ojp.usdoj.gov/bjs/sandlle.html.

[3] Obtained 6/10/07 from official Bureau of Justice Statistics Web site: http://www.ojp.usdoj.gov/bjs/sandlle.html.

[4] Hickman, M. & B. Reaves (2003). *Local Police Departments, 2000*. Washington, DC: Bureau of Justice Statistics, National Institute of Justice.

[5] Hickman, M. & B. Reaves (2003). *Local Police Departments, 2000*. Washington, DC: Bureau of Justice Statistics.

[6] Kuykendall, J. & P. Burns (1980). "The Black Police Officer: A Historical Perspective." *Journal of Contemporary Criminal Justice* 1, 4: 103-113.

[7] Hickman, M. & B. Reaves (2003). *Local Police Departments, 2000*. Washington, DC: Bureau of Justice Statistics, p. 4.

[8] Martin, S. (1980). *Breaking and Entering: Policewomen in Patrol*. Berkeley, CA: University of California Press.

[9] Hickman, M. & B. Reaves (2003). *Local Police Departments, 2000*. Washington, DC: Bureau of Justice Statistics, p. 4.

[10] I.A.C.P. 1998. *The Future of Women in Policing: Mandates for Action*. Fairfax, VA: IACP.

[11] Gaines, L. & V. Kappeler (2003). *Policing in America*, Fourth Edition. Cincinnati, OH: Anderson Publishing.

[12] Hickman, M. & B. Reaves (2003). *Local Police Departments, 2000*. Washington, DC: Bureau of Justice Statistics.

[13] From Andrews, W. (2007). *The Early Years. The Challenge of Public Order, From 1845 to 1870*. Retrieved from: http://www.ci.nyc.ny.us/html/nypd/html/3100/retro.html.

[14] From Andrews, W. (2007). *An Era of Corruption and Reform: 1870 – 1900*. Retrieved from http://www.ci.nyc.ny.us/html/nypd/html/3100/retro.html.

[15] From the official Web site of the LAPD, retrieved 6/1/07 from: http://www.lapdonline.org/history_of_the_lapd/content_basic_view/1107.

[16] From the official website of the LAPD, retrieved 6/1/07 from: http://www.lapdonline.org/history_of_the_lapd/content_basic_view/1107.

[17] Crank, J. (2003). *Understanding Police Culture*. Cincinnati, OH: Anderson Publishing.

[18] Kappeler, V., R. Sluder, & G. Alpert (1994). *Forces of Deviance: Understanding the Dark Side of Policing*. Prospect Heights, IL: Waveland Press, p. 41.

[19] Walker, S. (1977). *A Critical History of Police Reform: the Emergence of Professionalism*. Lexington, MA; Lexington Books.

[20] Kappeler, V., R. Sluder, & G. Alpert (1994). *Forces of Deviance: Understanding the Dark Side of Policing*. Prospect Heights, IL: Waveland Press, p. 49.

[21] Texas Department of Public Safety, retrieved 6/1/07 from: http://www.txdps.state.tx.us/overview.

[22] Reaves, B. & L. Bauer (2003). *Federal Law Enforcement Officers, 2002*. Washington, DC: Bureau of Justice Statistics, p. 1.

[23] Reaves, B. & L. Bauer (2003). *Federal Law Enforcement Officers, 2002*. Washington, DC: Bureau of Justice Statistics, p. 1.

[24] Reaves, B. & L. Bauer (2003). *Federal Law Enforcement Officers, 2002*. Washington, DC: Bureau of Justice Statistics, p. 5.

[25] Hickman, M. & B. Reaves (2003). *Local Police Departments, 2000*. Washington, DC: Bureau of Justice Statistics, p. 2.

[26] Hickman, M. & B. Reaves (2003). *Local Police Departments, 2000*. Washington, DC: Bureau of Justice Statistics, p. 4.

[27] Oneida Indian Nation Police Department. Retrieved 6/10/07 from: http://oneida-nation.net/police.

[28] ASIS International. Retrieved 6/8/07 from: http://www.asisonline.org/about/faqs.xml.

[29] Mastrofski, S., R. Parks, A. Reiss, & R. Worden (1999). *Policing Neighborhoods: A Report from Indianapolis*. Washington, DC: National Institute of Justice.

[30] Drew, C. (2006). "Police Struggles in New Orleans Raise Old Fears." *New York Times Online* (6/13/2006). Retrieved 6/1/07 from: http://www.nytimes.com/2006/06/13/us/13orleans.html?ex=1307851200&en=b53088f98360e0d8&ei=5088&partner=rssnyt&emc=rss.

[31] Williams, G. (1984). *The Law and Politics of Police Discretion*. Westport, CT: Greenwood Press, p. 4.

[32] Wilson, J.Q. (1968). *Varieties of Police Behavior*. Cambridge, MA: Harvard University Press.

[33] Muir, W. (1977). *Police: Streetcorner Politicians*. Chicago: University of Chicago Press.

[34] Muir, W. (1977). *Police: Streetcorner Politicians*. Chicago: University of Chicago Press, p. 24.

[35] Brown, M. (1981). *Working the Street*. New York: Russell Sage Foundation, p. 224.

[36] Goldstein, H. (1990). *Problem Oriented Policing*. New York: McGraw-Hill.

[37] McCold, P. & B. Wachtel (2002). "Community is Not a Place: A New Look at Community Justice Initiatives." In J. Perry (ed.), *Repairing Communities Through Restorative Justice*. Lanham, MD: American Correctional Association, pp. 39-53, 47.

[38] Retrieved 6/10/07 from: http://www.bostonstrategy.com/programs/12_OpNiteLite.html.

[39] Wooten, H. & H. Hoelter (1998). "Operation Spotlight: the Community Probation-Community Police Team Process." *Federal Probation* 62, 2: 30-35.

[40] McCold, P. & B. Wachtel (2002). "Community is Not a Place: A New Look at Community Justice Initiatives." In J. Perry (ed.), *Repairing Communities Through Restorative Justice*. Lanham, MD: American Correctional Association, pp. 39-53, 40.

[41] McCold, P. & B. Wachtel (2002). "Community is Not a Place: A New Look at Community Justice Initiatives." In J. Perry (ed.), *Repairing Communities Through Restorative Justice*. Lanham, MD: American Correctional Association, pp. 39-53, 43.

[42] Zhao, J., N. He & N. Lovrich (2003). "Community Policing: Did it Change the Basic Functions of Policing in the 1990s? A National Follow-Up Study." *Justice Quarterly* 20, 4: 697-724.

[43] Cao, L., J. Frank & F. Cullen (1996). "Race, Community Context and Confidence in the Police." *American Journal of Policing* 15, 1: 3-22.

Chapter 5

Police Operations

What You Need to Know

★ Hiring qualifications for police departments typically include age restrictions, educational requirements, good credit histories, no criminal history, physical fitness, and psychological stability.

★ There is conflicting research, but it does not seem to be true that police officers experience more stress than other occupations.

★ Patrol is most effective when targeted to a problem, as in saturated patrol operations.

★ The police subculture includes a number of themes that run contrary to the formal mission of policing, including the "blue curtain of secrecy" which protects officers who commit acts of misconduct.

★ The police subculture is not as strong as it once might have been because of hiring diversity, the rise of unions, and the threat of civil litigation.

★ Research shows that blacks are stopped more frequently than whites, but that they are not more likely to experience disrespectful behavior, at least initially, from the officers.

★ Large police departments have experienced periodic scandals of corruption throughout the history of policing.

★ Three areas of corruption include: graft and gratuities, abuse of authority, and "noble cause" corruption.

★ Three explanations of police deviance are: individual explanations, organizational explanations, and societal explanations.

★ Suggestions to reduce police corruption include: better training, integrity testing, civilian review/complaint boards, and early warning or audit systems.

What makes a good police officer? In this chapter, we will discuss how police departments select, train, and supervise their police officers. In a few cases, selection, training, and supervision fail for some reason, and police corruption occurs. It is important to realize, however, that the majority of the public have positive opinions regarding the police and the vast majority of police officers perform their role with integrity and competence. Most of the discussion in this and the following chapter emphasizes law enforcement at the local municipal level.

1. SELECTION

What are the requirements for being hired by a police department? Typically, departments have only a few absolute requirements. One major department, for instance, requires that applicants have the following qualifications:

- ★ be 21-44 years old,

- ★ have 60 hours of college or possess an honorable discharge from the military,

- ★ be a U.S. citizen,

- ★ be height and weight proportionate,

- ★ have a valid driver's license,

- ★ have no more than 2 moving violations within last 18 months,

- ★ have no Felony or Class A misdemeanors,

- ★ have no Class B misdemeanors within the last 10 years, and

- ★ have a stable credit history.

Applicants who meet these qualifications then take a civil service test that they must pass with a score of 70 or higher. The next steps of the hiring process include a preliminary interview, physical agility test, polygraph test, criminal background check, interview, medical exam (including a drug test), and a psychological exam.[1]

The process of police trainee selection is described as a "screening out" process rather than a selection process. Police departments recruit from diverse groups in society, but other than some efforts to encourage applicants from minority groups, there is little attempt to identify and select a desired type of person. In other words, all applicants are accepted and then screened out when factors indicate they would be inappropriate for policing. Factors that would screen out applicants include a lack of intellectual ability (civil service exam), lack of responsibility (bad credit), lack of honesty (failing polygraph), lack of physical fitness (failing physical test), or lack of mental stability (failing psychological exam).

The psychological exam utilizes objective personality tests, such as the Minnesota Multiphasic Personality Inventory (MMPI), and a personal interview. The psychologist looks for personality characteristics such as aggressiveness, bias, or anxiety, which would indicate the candidate is a poor fit for the job. On the other hand, there is no desired personality profile that police departments use to look for candidates. Little research has been done to explore whether certain personality profiles are more or less successful in policing careers.

In the past, height and weight requirements excluded women and some minorities from being hired by police departments. Stringent height and weight requirements have been struck down as discriminatory by the courts, so today you may see very short police officers. It is still acceptable to require that applicants be in good physical shape, however, and requirements that applicants be height and weight proportionate have generally been upheld. Applicants are also typically required to pass some form of physical fitness test. Although these vary from department to department, they usually involve some form of cardiovascular fitness (running), strength, and agility. There is some concern that physical ability tests unfairly exclude women or others who might otherwise make good police officers.

It is also ironic that although physical fitness tests screen out applicants at the hiring stage, many, if not most, police departments do not require officers to maintain physical standards once hired. It is difficult to make the argument that certain physical requirements are necessary to policing if employed officers are not required to maintain any level of fitness. Many advocate that physical standards be adopted by police departments, much as the military does, with gradations of fitness based on age. Arguably, departments could save money in insurance costs and lost time due to sickness and injury if officers were required to maintain height and weight ratios and cardiovascular fitness. These demands would reduce heart attacks or injuries when carrying out police duties.

1.1 A Police Personality?

One interesting topic that has been explored by researchers is whether there is such a thing as a "police personality." A related question is whether the career attracts people with certain personality characteristics, or whether the career changes people so that they develop such characteristics after working in the field. The so-called police personality has been described as having the traits of cynicism, authoritarianism, and suspiciousness. Some researchers have found police officers to be generally cynical, isolated, alienated, defensive, distrustful, dogmatic, and authoritarian.[2] There is conflicting research as to the prevalence of these traits. Another question is whether the traits exist before being hired or are acquired on the job.

Some argue that the traits listed above are part of the culture of policing and new officers eventually acquire them.[3] If there is a personality type that is attracted to policing, we would see a pattern of these traits in psychological tests of applicants; but if the characteristics emerge after being exposed to the police subculture, then anyone who is hired may develop them as they are socialized to the subculture. It is far from clear whether any of these traits are more prevalent among police officers or applicants. Furthermore, it is not clear that any particular traits are associated with undesirable behaviors or less effective officers. These are important research questions and should be addressed.

2. TRAINING

Early officers had no training and were basically given a uniform and nightstick and told to go do their job. Training has expanded exponentially and today police departments require hundreds of hours of academy training. To be certified as a peace officer in most states, one must have graduated from a recognized academy and passed standardized tests that include academic subjects as well as skills training, such as firearms and driving.

Police officers receive training in departmental or regional academies. Smaller departments may prefer to hire individuals who have already received certification through attendance at a regional academy, but larger departments have their own academies and require all applicants to attend, even those who may already have certification. In-service training hours are required for all police officers to maintain their certification. This in-service training usually has content that is mandated by the state, and also optional training segments that can be selected by the department or individual officer. Departments train officers either by assigning them to required training at certain times during the year, or some departments allow the officer to choose training segments from a selection of course offerings, as long as they total the required number of hours.

Recruit Training includes law, operations, mental health assessments, communication skills, domestic violence, firearms, physical combat, and driving skills, among other topics. In-service training may cover updates on laws related to policing, communication skills, forensic analysis topics, testifying, and many other topics.

Field training officer programs started in 1972.[4] This last portion of training pairs the new recruit with a field training officer who supervises the trainee for a period that may range from weeks to months. Field training officers (**FTOs**) are expected to help the new academy graduate apply their academy training to the real-life problems of the street. Some FTOs and others convey the idea that what one learns in the academy is irrelevant and now they will teach the recruit the way "it really is." Because most academy instructors are better versed in current law and departmental policies, it is usually a problem when this approach is taken. FTOs should be, and usually are, chosen for their ability to teach recruits good practices that will prevent citizen complaints and lawsuits against the department.

3. SUPERVISION

Most police officers start as patrol officers, although they may quickly transfer to "desk jobs," such as community relations. During the probationary period, officers may be fired at will; however, once the probationary period is over, civil service protections require that if an officer is to be fired, it must be for cause and there is a hearing and appeals process. Promotions typically take place through civil service tests and interview boards and, typically, if an officer is promoted to sergeant, he or she must accept a transfer to whatever division has an empty sergeant position.

Sergeants are the front-line supervisors and are called whenever a police officer thinks it is necessary or required to seek the advice or authority of a supervisor. Sergeants are responsible for evaluating and contributing to performance reviews of officers. Sometimes sergeants experience personal challenges in supervising and disciplining officers who they patrolled and/or partnered with before being promoted. It has been said that sergeants are the foundation of the department, and if sergeants do their job well, the department is usually in good shape. However, if sergeants do not supervise, if they allow patrol officers to ignore policies, or if they make decisions based on favoritism, then the department will be weaker because of it.

3.1 Stress

Early research indicated that police officers experienced higher stress than most other occupations; however, this may not be the case. It is certainly true that policing has a few unique stressors not shared by most other occupations—i.e., using or being a target of lethal force is not present in most occupations. On the other hand, other types of stress, such as dealing with bureaucracy, or unfair supervisors, are similar to other occupations and professions. Some researchers have concluded that police officers do not experience more stress than others.[5]

Other researchers have found that individuals experience the stress of policing differently and factors such as gender, age, and ethnicity seem to affect the ability to cope with the stressors.[6] Stress is an important issue because it may lead to **burnout**, which is when officers merely "go through the motions" of their job and may be susceptible to corruption. It can also lead to turnover when officers quit or retire early because of stress. This is unfortunate for the officer and also presents a high cost to the public, because training is expensive. Departments have responded to the reality of stress by offering psychological services and other departmental policies that encourage good coping skills.

4. PATROL AND INVESTIGATION

In the last chapter we discussed the dual goals of crime control and order maintenance. **Reactive policing** describes activities that respond to crime when brought to the attention of the police through crime reports or complaints.

Proactive policing is when police engage in active behavior to seek out crime, including undercover work, the use of informants, and sting operations.

4.1 Patrol

Patrol can be considered both reactive and proactive. Typically patrol officers look for crime, but they also spend a great deal of time responding to dispatched calls for service. Responding to dispatched calls is obviously reactive crime control.

There has been interesting research that has focused on how effective patrolling really is. One of the most famous research projects in policing was the Kansas City Preventive Patrol Study. In this study, part of Kansas City, Missouri, was divided into three different areas. One area had no patrol at all—police only responded to dispatched calls. The second area had increased patrol, roughly five to six times the normal pattern. The third area was the control group, with normal patrols scheduled. Study authors found that no significant differences were found among the three areas in level of crime or citizen satisfaction.[7] This does not mean, of course, that police have no effect on crime; but it does call into question the effectiveness of normal patrols.

Police departments may at times initiate **saturated patrols**, meaning that a certain neighborhood or area of town is targeted for frequent, perhaps even a constant patrol presence. The "hot spot" is identified through crime reports and the saturated patrol continues for a set period or until the crime reports are reduced to an acceptable level. Research has indicated that saturated patrols do work in reducing crime; there is a **residual effect**, meaning reduced crime continues after the saturated patrol ends; and that there does not seem to be a **displacement effect**, meaning that crime merely moves to another area of the city.[8]

Most police officers are engaged in general patrol and respond to dispatched calls. However, it would be a mistake to think of policing only in this light. Many departments are constantly trying innovative methods to more effectively serve the public. For instance, there may be special units to deal with the mentally ill or domestic violence. One of the most difficult calls police respond to is when a mentally ill individual is threatening family members or other citizens. In some of these calls, police resort to using violent means to subdue the individual and then encounter criticism for doing so. Some police departments have responded to the challenge by training special officers to handle these calls. These officers are trained to identify the signs of mental illness. They also have received specific training in how to deal with the mentally ill, and what resources are available in the community to assist these individuals.

Some police departments also have special victim units, crisis teams, or domestic violence units that respond to calls that involve battered women, abused children, rape victims, and other specific types of calls. These specialized patrol units receive additional training and are sensitive to the needs of the targeted types of crime victims.

One of the most publicized new approaches to policing has been the CompStat program. This approach was developed in New York City during the tenure of Chief William Bratton. Basically it uses computer-generated crime statistics and daily or weekly meetings of division heads to hold these managers responsible for the crime in their districts. Immediate feedback, in the form of crime reports, allows higher-level administrators to see who is and who is not successful in reducing crime. Critics argue that the program is nothing more than what has always occurred in good departments and others suggest that the format may create pressure to "doctor" crime reports. However, advocates argue that it is an efficient, modern approach to policing that is based on management principles.[9]

4.2 Undercover Operations

Proactive policing is looking for crime before it happens, but without creating crime. There are a wide range of undercover activities engaged in by police. Some of these activities present opportunities for criminals to commit crimes so that they can be caught; other operations are designed to collect evidence once an investigation has centered on a particular suspect. Police officers may pretend to be drug dealers, prostitutes, "johns," crime bosses, friends, and perhaps even lovers, to catch criminals.

We can think of undercover operations as operating on a continuum of intimacy. The least personal relationships would be represented by a brief "buy–bust" incident in which the officer pretends to be a drug user and buys from a street dealer, and moments later an arrest is made. Similar set-ups are done to control street prostitution—policemen routinely pretend they are "johns," and policewomen dress up as prostitutes. At the other extreme would be a situation in which an undercover officer develops a long-term relationship with the suspect.

Some argue that undercover operations that go on for a long time, and where others besides the suspect are misled, should not occur.[10] It is also true that these operations are difficult for the officer. Undercover officers have difficulty, at times, separating themselves from their cover and feel that they have deceived innocent people (if they become close to the family members of the suspects).[11] Evidently, even other officers have difficulty seeing the undercover narcotics officer as an officer instead of drug dealer and it has been reported that undercover officers have trouble integrating back into the department after a long operation.[12]

In proactive investigations, the central question is: Who do police target and why? Members of Congress convicted of bribery in the Abscam operation in 1980 alleged improper conduct in the FBI's selection of targets. Marian Barry, the ex-Mayor of the District of Columbia, also alleged he was "set up" because of his race, after he was videotaped using drugs with a girlfriend in a hotel room in 1990. How targets are selected is a serious question; arguably, the selection should be based on reasonable suspicion.

Police operations that provide opportunities for crime change the police role from discovering who has committed a crime to one of discovering who might commit a crime if given the chance. Some examples of "set ups" include:

★   a fake deer placed by the side of the road, used to entice overeager hunters, who are then arrested for violating hunting laws;

★   police officer decoys dressed as drunks and "passed out" on sidewalks with money sticking out of their pocket to entice thieves

★   undercover officers, posing as criminals, entice doctors to prescribe unneeded medications that are controlled substances, such as Percoset and Oxycontin

★   police set up fencing operations to buy stolen goods from unsuspecting thieves and burglars.

Are only bad people tempted? If police cross a line in their undercover operations, it is called entrapment and we will discuss entrapment in the next chapter. Anything short of entrapment, however, is legally acceptable.

One type of sting operation is when police set up a fencing operation, receive stolen goods for a period of time, and then arrest all the burglars and thieves who brought the goods in to be sold. Some argue that this creates crime, but others counter by saying that the burglar would have taken their goods to another fence anyway. Some argue that, despite the effectiveness of stings, government deception appears unseemly; others argue that they are creative ways to catch criminals.

Informants are individuals who are not police officers, but who assist police by providing information about criminal activity, acting the part of a buyer in drug sales, or otherwise "setting up" a criminal act so that police may gather evidence against the target. Informants perform such services for some reward—money, to get charges dropped or reduced or, in some documented cases, for drugs supplied by an officer. They may do it to retaliate against the suspect for some wrong done to them. Informants typically are not middle-class, upstanding-citizen types.[13] They probably have engaged in criminal activities themselves, and they may even be currently committing crimes at the same time they are acting as informants.

Police use informants partly to avoid problems that undercover police officers would encounter if they attempted to accomplish the task, but also because informants are under fewer restrictions. Some observers question the use of civilians in dangerous operations, especially if they are threatened with prosecution if they do not cooperate. Another problem with informants is that sometimes their reliability is highly questionable. Their rewards, whatever those might be, are contingent upon delivering some evidence of crime to law enforcement. In some cases, this evidence may be purely manufactured.[14] Some officers openly admit that they could not do their job without informants. There are other arguments, however, that the perceived value of informants is overstated.[15] The Commission on Accreditation for Law Enforcement Agencies (CALEA) has developed standards for working with informants.

5. THE SUBCULTURE OF POLICING

A subculture exists when a group has a different set of values, beliefs, and even language from the dominant culture. In the case of the police subculture, there is research that indicates that in some departments there is a "subculture" of policing that is different from, and in conflict with, formal departmental mission statements.

Researchers argue that the reason this subculture exists is the special nature of policing, including the following characteristics:

★ police typically form a homogenous social group,

★ they have a uniquely stressful work environment, and

★ they participate in a basically closed social system.[16]

Police have tended to come from the same socioeconomic and ethnic groups; although diversity is more common today than in the past. Further, the work life of police officers is marked by shift work and special characteristics (such as dangerousness and stigma). Police officers' social lives tend to include other police officers. This can lead to closed viewpoints and groupthink (where no one feels free to offer competing viewpoints).[17]

The subculture of policing has been described by various researchers as including certain values or themes. This is a similar discussion to the one above about a police personality, but, instead of individuals with certain traits being attracted to policing or adopting traits afterward, the idea here is that the subculture is already established and individuals are socialized to the subculture. Socialization is adopting the values and beliefs of one's culture (or subculture). The police subculture has been described as including the following traits:

★ Stereotypical views of large numbers of citizens as troublemakers;[18]

★ Loyalty to colleagues over citizens or the department;

★ View that the use of force is acceptable even when not strictly legal;

★ View that police officer discretion should not be questioned;

★ View that the truth is relative and subject to protecting officers or crime control.[19]

Another researcher identified the three dominant characteristics of the police culture as cynicism or suspicion (of everyone); the acceptance of the use of force when their authority is threatened; and the perception that they are victims of public misunderstanding and scorn, low wages, and unfair administrators.[20]

In one interesting study of police values, the researchers found that police officers indicated value preferences that were similar across time (comparing 1961 to 1997), and across place (comparing two cities). In their study, they found police rated equality significantly lower than the general public and, in general, were more conservative in their viewpoint than the general public.

They also found that more educated officers rated freedom higher, and female officers rated happiness higher than male officers.[21] Other research has indicated that police officers place less emphasis on independence and more emphasis on obedience than the general public.[22]

Part of the police subculture involves the "**cop code**," a set of informal rules for police officers that are not necessarily the same as those taught in the academy. The code has been described as including the principles found in Box 5.1.

BOX 5.1.

The "Cop Code"

★ "You cover your men: don't let any officer take a job alone"

★ "Keep a cool head"

★ "Don't backdoor it" (a prohibition against certain gratuities)

★ Watch out for your partner first and then the rest of the guys working that shift

★ Don't give up another cop

★ Be aggressive when you have to, but don't be too eager

★ Don't get involved in anything in another guy's sector

★ Hold up your end of the work

★ If you get caught off base, don't implicate anybody else

★ Make sure the other guys know if another cop is dangerous or "crazy"

★ Don't trust a new guy until you have checked him out

★ Don't leave work for the next shift

★ Protect your ass

★ Don't give them too much activity

★ Don't do the bosses' work for them

★ Don't trust bosses to look out for your interest

Source: Muir, W. (1977). *Police: Streetcorner Politicians.* Chicago: University of Chicago Press, p. 191; Reuss-Ianni, E. (1983). *Two Cultures of Policing: Street Cops and Management Cops.* New Brunswick, NJ: Transaction, p. 14.

Some argue that the police subculture is merely a mix of a conservative political viewpoint and a work culture that is not that much different from many other workplaces.[23] It also seems to be true that the subculture may not be as prevalent or extreme as it once might have been. Several factors contribute to the possible weakening of the subculture.

1. *Increasing diversity:* Many diverse groups are now represented in police departments, including blacks, Hispanics, women, and the college-educated. These different groups bring their own value systems into the police environment.

2. *Police unions:* Unions formalize relationships between the line staff and the administration; thus, instead of subcultural (informal) methods for coping with perceived administrative unfairness, there are formal grievance procedures.

3. *Civil litigation:* Police officers face large monetary damages when gross negligence and perjury can be proven. They may be less likely to cover for a fellow police officer when faced with these possible sanctions.

More recently, researchers have found that there is substantial variation among officers and differences in their cultural views. Although there are some associations seen between certain values and gender and ethnicity, these associations are not strong. The researchers conclude that the police culture is less uniform and powerful today than it might have been in earlier decades.[24]

5.1 Race Relations and the Police Subculture

One of the most persistent criticisms of police is that they enforce the law in a discriminatory manner against minorities. This criticism persists despite the entry of minority officers in the ranks, and despite the attempts by police departments to improve relations with minority communities. Some argue that police officers enforce the law differentially or that they withhold the protections and benefits of the law from certain groups.[25] The groups that believe they experience discrimination by police include the poor, gays, and minorities, especially blacks.[26]

Some studies report that lower-class blacks have significantly more negative interactions with police. More than twice as many report disrespectful language or swearing by police officers in surveys.[27] Studies have indicated that blacks and Hispanics are most supportive of police reforms, such as racial diversification of police departments, enhanced mechanisms of accountability, and community policing. Minorities that live in metropolitan areas, have less education, less income, are younger, and report more bad experiences with the police, not surprisingly, perceive more police misconduct and exhibit the highest endorsement of police reforms.[28] Areas of concentrated disadvantage showed the least satisfaction with police, but race was still a predictor, even when controlling for neighborhood characteristics.[29]

The Project on Policing studies used 240 hours of observations of encounters with 3,130 suspects in Indianapolis and St. Petersburg in 1996-1997. In this study, trained observers noted characteristics of these encounters and the results were used to examine such things as police officers' use of force and disrespect. The authors provided a careful review of prior studies and noted that police disrespect had been linked in prior studies to those who were disrespectful or resistant, intoxicated, or mentally ill. In other words, the results tended to indicate that whether a police officer was disrespectful or not was associated with demeanor, rather than class or race.[30]

Observers in the Project on Policing study noted that suspects were disrespectful toward police in 15 percent of encounters, while police were *initially* disrespectful toward suspects in only five percent of encounters (this percentage does not include police disrespect after a suspect initiated disrespect). While only five percent of the citizens who did not initiate disrespect received it from the officers, 35 percent of those who did initiate disrespect received it in turn. Contrary to other studies and popular opinion, these researchers found that minority suspects experienced less "disrespect" than white citizens. The difference was more pronounced in St. Petersburg, arguably because a new police chief made race relations a priority in his administration.[31]

The authors also reported that blacks in both cities appeared in the pool of encounters at roughly one and one-half times their percentage of the general population. In other words, even though blacks were no more likely to receive disrespect than whites when stopped, they were stopped one and one-half times as often as their population percentage would have predicted.[32]

5.2 The Blue Curtain of Secrecy and the Police Subculture

The **blue curtain of secrecy** refers to the practice of police covering up the misdeeds of other officers and/or not testifying against them in administrative discipline hearings or legal proceedings. It should be noted that recent research indicates that this conspiracy of silence is breaking down.[33] There are interesting contradictions, however, because in a recent survey, while 80 percent of police officers did not think that the "code of silence" was essential for police trust and good policing, fully two-thirds reported that a "whistleblower" would suffer informal punishment from fellow officers. Further, more than half agreed that it was not unusual for police to ignore improper conduct on the part of other officers.[34]

One of the greatest harms of police cover-ups is the damage that is inflicted upon a police officer's credibility. Prosecutors can ordinarily rely on a jury to take police testimony as fact and believe police witnesses over non-police witnesses when there is contradictory testimony. When jury members believe that police officers lie, it is much more difficult for a prosecutor to obtain a conviction.

The "blue curtain of secrecy" may not exist in some departments, or may exist at varying levels in different police departments. If it does exist, it occurs for various reasons. Officers feel loyalty toward each other. They also may believe that the officer's wrongdoing is not as serious as the discipline he would receive or equal the loss of an experienced officer to the department. There may be egoistic reasons as well, because the officer may believe that he or she has also committed acts that could be disciplined. Even good officers who have not engaged in misconduct may experience great anguish and self-doubt over turning in or testifying against friends and colleagues, and that is understandable. Loyalty is perhaps stronger in law enforcement than in other professions because police depend on one another, sometimes in life-or-death situations. Loyalty to one's fellows is part of the *esprit de corps* of policing and is an absolutely essential element of a healthy department, but it seems that it can also cause some problems when there are officers who are "tarnishing the badge."

FOCUS ON ETHICS

You are a young police officer and still patrolling with your FTO. One day you and your FTO are called to assist in an altercation at a fraternity house. When you arrive, there are about 30 people outside the house and two other patrol cars are there. It seems that most of the people are watching several young men who are physically struggling with the four officers who are already there. Your FTO jumps out of the car and immediately grabs one of two men who appeared to be fighting with one of the officers. You also begin to wrestle with another man when he attempts to push you away from the others. After a short struggle, you manage to put handcuffs on him. Taking him to the car, you see that your FTO has a young man in the car and he is repeatedly hitting him in the face and head with his baton. The young man is trying to protect his face by squirming away and kicking at the officer, although he is handcuffed. Only when two other patrol cars arrive does your FTO stop hitting the man who, by that time, is bloody and almost unconscious. Later, there is an investigation into the incident spurred by reports that the police officers on the scene used excessive force. What, if anything, would you say to the investigating officers?

The informal practice of punishing individuals who come forward is an especially distressing aspect of loyalty. For the individual who tears the blue curtain of secrecy, subcultural sanctions can be extreme. This is not just true of law enforcement agencies, of course. In fact, sanctions against whistleblowers are so common that most states and the federal government now have laws designed to protect whistleblowers. In Box 5.2, two quotes show how the subcultural sanctions against whistleblowers remained virtually unchanged for more than 20 years in New York City.

6. POLICE CORRUPTION

The International Association of Chiefs of Police developed the Law Enforcement Code of Ethics and The Canons of Police Ethics, and many departments have used these or adapted them to their own situations. There are at least four major themes in the International Chiefs of Police Code. They are as follows:

1. The principle of justice or *fairness* is the single most dominant theme in the law enforcement code. Police officers must uphold the law regardless of the offender's identity. They must not single out special groups for different treatment.

2. A second theme is that of *service*. Police officers exist to serve the community and their role, appropriately and essentially, concerns this idea.

3. The third theme is the *importance of the law*. Police are protectors of the Constitution and must not go beyond it or substitute rules of their own. Because the law is so important, police not only must be concerned with lawbreakers, but also their own behavior must be totally within the bounds set for them by the law.

4. The final theme is one of *personal conduct*. Police, at all times, must uphold a standard of behavior consistent with their public position. This involves a higher standard of behavior in their professional and personal lives than that expected from the general public. "Conduct unbecoming" is one of the most often cited discipline infractions and can include everything from committing a crime to having an affair or being drunk in public.

Unfortunately, despite the code of ethics, and departmental efforts in selection, training, and supervision to minimize the occurrence of misdeeds on the part of officers, scandals do occur. Examples of widespread corruption have been uncovered by various committees and investigative bodies since the very beginnings of organized police departments.

New York City has experienced a series of police scandals that occurred in 1894, 1913, 1932 (the Wickersham Commission), 1949 (the Kefauver Commission), 1972 (the Knapp Commission), and 1993 (the Mollen Commission). But New York City is definitely not alone. The "Miami River Rats" also committed armed robberies of drug dealers, collecting cash and drugs. These robberies by a small group of police officers eventually led to at least one homicide.[35] A New Orleans police officer is in a federal prison today because he used a police radio to order a hit on a woman who was going to testify against him and others in a corruption trial. Luckily for her, he was being monitored by federal agents who decoded the thinly disguised murder solicitation.[36]

To read the International Chiefs of Police Law Enforcement Code, go to: http://www.lib.jjay.cuny.edu/cje/html/codes/codes-usa-organizational/lece-r.html

The movie *Training Day* may be partially based on the Rampart scandal in Los Angeles. In the real-life incident, it was discovered that a group of officers belonging to a narcotics task force were shockingly similar to the crooks they were pursuing. They engaged in intimidation, planted evidence and, in one instance, shot an unarmed suspect. They also vandalized houses they searched and once sprayed "L.A.P.D. Rules" on the wall of a house. The scandal came to light when one of the officers attempted to make a deal with prosecutors to get out of a drug prosecution and testified against the others, detailing all of their illegal activities.

Many other large cities have their own historical cycles of corruption and exposure. In 1998, 44 Cleveland cops were indicted for providing protection for

★ Exercise: In the State of . . .

Do a newspaper or Google search of your state to see if there have been any police corruption scandals. What city was the location of the scandal? What happened? What steps have been taken to respond to the problem?.

cocaine shipments. In 1996, seven Chicago cops were indicted for conspiracy to commit robbery and extortion for shaking down undercover agents they thought were drug dealers. Other Chicago police officers have been accused of shaking down Polish immigrants and robbing suspected drug dealers (who turned out to be FBI agents). This group of officers evidently joined forces with a street gang in order to control the cocaine trade. Brutality charges and other corruption charges have also been recently leveled against Chicago officers.[37]

It does seem to be the case that the most extreme cases of police corruption occur in large cities. Perhaps this is because there is more anonymity in large departments and it is more difficult to supervise all offices in all divisions and squads. Further, it is harder to develop a cohesive culture of integrity and service in larger departments with thousands of officers. We will discuss three areas of corruption: graft, abuse of authority, and "noble cause" corruption.

6.1 Graft and Gratuities

Graft refers to any exploitation of one's role, such as accepting bribes or protection money. Graft also occurs when officers receive kickbacks from tow truck drivers, defense attorneys, or bail bondsmen for recommending them. The Knapp Commission documented examples of a wide range of graft, including taking bribes for changing testimony or "forgetting," or phrasing answers in a way that would aid the defense.[38] Although there are some regional differences, bribery is considered one of the more serious forms of corruption by police officers. In one study, only theft from a crime scene was rated as more serious.[39]

Gratuities are items of value received by an individual because of his or her role or position, rather than because of a personal relationship with the giver. The widespread practice of free coffee in convenience stores, half-price or free meals in restaurants, half-price dry cleaning, and so on, are all examples of gratuities. Although the formal code of ethics prohibits accepting gratuities, many officers feel there is nothing wrong with businesses giving "freebies" to a police officer.

The police obviously have discretionary authority and make judgments that affect store owners and other gift givers. This may explain why some think it is wrong for police to accept gifts or favors. It also explains why so many people do not see anything wrong with some types of gratuities, because police officers may not make decisions affecting the giver and, instead, are simply providing a service, such as responding to a burglary or disturbance call. There are extensive arguments relating to the ethics of taking gratuities.[40] What is not in dispute, however, is that the rules of most police departments expressly prohibit accepting them; therefore, officers who do expose themselves to possible disciplinary sanctions.

6.2 Abuse of Authority

Police abuse of authority comes in three different areas: physical abuse (excessive force, sexual assault); psychological abuse (disrespect, harassment, intimidation), and legal abuse (unlawful searches or seizures or manufacturing evidence).[41]

The most famous case of physical abuse is probably the use of force against Rodney King in Los Angeles, but the most shocking case was that of Abner Louima. Justin Volpe, an NYPD officer, sodomized Louima, who was hand-cuffed, with the handle of a bathroom plunger in a police precinct. The officer ended up in prison, but the larger question is how could the incident have happened in the first place? The fact is that despite departments' best efforts, some individuals who enter policing are predisposed to abuse their position or cannot handle the stress of policing and succumb to unlawful uses of force, often in retaliation for suspects' actions against them.

The use of force may be perfectly legal—officers have the right to tackle a fleeing suspect, or hit back when they are defending themselves. Illegal or excessive force is when the officer goes beyond what is necessary to secure a lawful arrest, or has no lawful reason to use force at all. Excessive force appears to be more likely when victims challenge police authority—passing a patrol car, asking questions, challenging the stop, or intervening in the arrest of another.[42]

After reviewing the research on the use of force and excessive force, a few generalizations can be made:

★ Force is present in a small percentage of the total encounters between police and citizens.

★ A small percentage of officers seem to be responsible for a disproportionate percentage of the force incidents.

★ Some studies do find an association between force and race or socioeconomic status, but other factors, such as demeanor, seem to be even more influential.[43]

There is nothing more divisive in a minority community than a police shooting that appears to be unjustified. Cities are quite different in their shooting policies, and in their rates of civilian deaths. New York's shooting policy, for instance, involves an automatic investigation and multiple layers of reports and investigations before the shooting is cleared. Even New York, however, has had its share of deaths that have raised tensions.

It is a sad reality that a few police officers use their position of authority to extort sex from female citizens. The other category of sexual misconduct is sexual harassment of female police officers. Egregious cases in the United States include rapes by officers on duty, and by jailers in police lock-ups. In a few instances, several officers have been involved in sexual misconduct and protected by departmental supervisors.[44]

Peter Kraska and Victor Kappeler proposed a continuum of sexual invasion that ranges from some type of invasion of privacy to sexual assault. This range of behavior includes viewing victim's photos for prurient purposes to deception to gain sex, to sexual assault.[45] Sexual harassment of fellow officers also occurs. These same researchers found that 70 percent of female officers reported being sexually harassed by other police officers.[46] Although female officers do not encounter the virulent harassment and hostility that was present in the 1970s when women first entered patrol assignments, it is fair to say that similar incidents occur, though infrequently, in some departments even today.

6.3 "Noble Cause" Corruption

In the "**Dirty Harry problem**," the question is whether it is acceptable for a police officer to inflict pain on a suspect in order to acquire information that would save an innocent victim (from the *Dirty Harry* movies of Clint Eastwood).[47] This is a specific example of what is also called **noble cause corruption**, which is when officers employ unethical means to catch criminals because they believe it is right to do so. John Crank and Michael Caldero[48] argue that such practices as "**testilying**" (lying in affidavits or when giving testimony) and coercion occur because of **ends-oriented thinking**, which means that the person believes "the end justifies the means" regardless of how bad the means are.

Police officers behave this way when they place a high value on crime control, even over due process. The behaviors under the noble cause category are done by those who believe they are fulfilling their oath of protecting the public. Crime lab investigators and prosecutors may also engage in shortcuts and unethical acts in order to convict the perceived guilty. Prosecutors have been known to suppress evidence and allow perjured testimony, so it is not only police officers who feel compelled to break the law in order to further the noble cause of crime control.[49]

The trouble with these behaviors is that—first—they are against the law. "Testilying" is perjury and officers could get a prison sentence for committing this felony. These acts may not serve the goal of crime control in the long term either, because officers who are caught lying jeopardize all the prior convictions based on their testimony. Finally, such actions may start out for noble reasons, but eventually, those involved end up lying to keep themselves out of trouble. Covering up personal misdeeds and protecting oneself by subverting the justice process is not exactly noble.

6.4 Explanations for Corruption

Explanations of corruption can be described as:

★   individual

★   institutional (or organizational)

★   systemic (or societal)

Individual explanations assume that the individual officer has deviant inclinations before he or she even enters the police department and merely exploits the position. The most common explanation of police officer corruption is the **rotten-apple argument**—that the officer alone was deviant and that it was simply a mistake to hire him or her. Such explanations support better selection procedures and better supervision for reducing the possibility of corruption.

Institutional (or organizational) explanations point to organizational problems. Some argue that police scandals are due to rapid hiring without proper background checks, a lack of supervision from front-line sergeants, and other issues.[50] Others argue that administrators can breed corruption by ignoring certain types of rule-breaking and incompetence.[51]

The "noble cause" corruption discussed earlier is also a type of organizational explanation because officers lie or commit other unethical acts to catch criminals because of formal and/or subcultural support for such actions.[52] Organizational explanations are those that explain police corruption as being supported by the organizational culture, whether that be the "formal culture" or the "subculture."

A systemic (or societal) explanation of police deviance focuses on the relationship between the police and the public.[53] The public expects the police to enforce laws but sometimes believes that some people should be excused, while others should be investigated, caught, and punished. The result might be that some police decide that a hypocritical public won't mind a few gambling operations, or a certain number of prostitutes, or even a few drug dealers, so they might as well accept protection money. As long as the general public engages in illegal activities (like gambling, prostitution, and drug use), it is no surprise that some police officers are able to rationalize not enforcing the law. In another vein, as long as the public relays a message that crime control is more important than individual liberties and rights, then we should not be surprised when some police act on that message and violate the law.

BOX 5.3

Reduce Policing Corruption

★ Increase the salary of police,

★ Eliminate unenforceable laws,

★ Establish civilian review boards,

★ Improve training,

★ Improve leadership.

★ Set realistic goals and objectives for the department,

★ Provide a written code of ethics,

★ Provide a whistle-blowing procedure that ensures fair treatment of all parties.

Source: Malloy, E. (1982). *The Ethics of Law Enforcement and Criminal Punishment.* Lanham, NY: University Press, pp. 37–40; Pollock, J. (2007). *Ethical Dilemmas and Decisions in Criminal Justice.* Belmont, CA: Wadsworth/IT; Metz, H. (1990). "An Ethical Model for Law Enforcement Administrators." In F. Schmalleger (ed.), *Ethics in Criminal Justice.* Bristol, IN: Wyndam Hall, pp. 95-103.

6.5 Reducing Corruption

A wide range of suggestions has been offered that may reduce or minimize the chance of police corruption, including those found in Box 5.3.

Education has been offered as one suggestion to reduce police corruption, but education itself is certainly not a panacea. Ethics training in the academy, as well as part of in-service training, is common and recommended for all police departments today. There is also some doubt that these ethics training courses are successful. One author pointed out that after the Knapp Commission uncovered wide-ranging corruption in the NYPD, ethical awareness workshops were begun. Unfortunately, they have not stopped the periodic corruption scandals in the NYPD that have occurred since.[54]

The NYPD has also been known to use **integrity testing** since the late 1970s. Candidates are recruited straight from academies to investigate suspected officers.[55] This attempt to "police the police" involves setting up a situation in which the officer might commit a wrongful act. For instance, an officer responds to a report of an open door to an apartment, and when he checks it out, he sees money in plain sight. The scene is being monitored, however, to see if he takes the money. There are also tests whereby a wallet is turned in to see if officers would take money out of the wallet.[56]

All departments have some form of Internal Affairs division. Some departments also have **civilian review/complaint boards**. Civilian review boards have been created in several cities to monitor and review the investigation and discipline of officers who have complaints filed against them. Citizens not connected to the police department sit on these committees, commissions, or boards to monitor how police investigate citizen complaints. There are many models for the idea of civilian review, and no one model has been reported to be more effective or better than any other.[57]

BOX 5.4

Integrity Tests for Police

New Orleans police have staged car wrecks, left money in abandoned cars, and set up fake drug buys. New York has had undercover operators ask police officers for directions to see how polite they are. These are all integrity tests of officers. While some departments use such tests only when an officer is already under suspicion, others engage in random testing. A Baltimore police officer was caught in a sting where a bag of cocaine was left on a park bench and then an anonymous tip was placed with the police dispatcher. The officer who responded did bring the bag in, but he lied when he stated that he saw a burglary suspect place it on the bench, and then falsely arrested the suspect. He was suspended and is facing charges of perjury.

Source: O'Hagan, M. (2000). "Putting Police to Honesty Test." *Washington Post.* October 6: B1.

Another idea is an **early warning or audit system**. Because research shows that a small number of officers are responsible for a disproportionate share of excessive force complaints and other types of citizen complaints, the idea is to identify these officers early. Early warning systems have been used by New Orleans, Portland, and Pittsburgh.[58] The early warning systems utilize number of complaints, use of force reports, use of weapon reports, reprimands, and other indicators to identify officers. Intervention may include greater supervision, additional training, and/or counseling.

Employee behavior is directly influenced by superiors. A supervisor cannot promote ethical ideals, then act unethically, and expect employees to act ethically. Thus, regardless of formal ethical codes, police are influenced by the standards of behavior they observe in their superiors. One might note that the police corruption scandals have usually exposed very high-level officials. Alternatively, police departments that have remained relatively free of corruption have administrators who practice ethical behavior on a day-to-day basis.

Even if leaders are not involved in corruption directly, encouraging or participating in the harassment and ostracism that is directed toward whistle-blowers supports an organizational culture in which officers may be afraid to come forward when they know of wrongdoing. A different problem may be when certain people in the department do not receive punishment for behaviors that others would receive punishment for. This climate destroys the trust in police leadership that is essential to ensure good communication from the rank and file.

7. CONCLUSION

Police departments go through great efforts to hire individuals who do not have any obvious qualities that would prevent them from being good police officers. The screening tools include civil service tests, physical tests, and psychological tests. Then candidates are subjected to hundreds of hours of training in academies as well as annual in-service training. After selection and training, supervision is supposed to prevent officers from abusing their discretion and power. However, the discretion of policing creates opportunities and temptations to behave in unethical and even illegal ways.

The vast majority of police officers perform their job admirably, with a great deal of professionalism and integrity. Unfortunately, periodic scandals have occurred because of the actions of a few officers. There are types of corruption that are purely for self-interest, and then there is corruption that stems from the "noble cause" of crime control. Explanations for why some police officers engage in these practices can be categorized into individual explanations, organizational explanations, and societal explanations. Solutions to reduce or minimize corruption have included better training, and better supervision through such things as early warning systems. Perhaps the most important suggestion, however, is that police departments must strive to a make sure that police leadership promotes honesty and ethical behavior.

REVIEW QUESTIONS

1. What are the typical hiring requirements for policing?

   age, fitness, edu

2. Describe the characteristics of the police personality.

3. Describe the training curriculum for police.

4. Describe research findings on police stress.

   no more than other occupations

5. What were the findings of the Kansas City Preventive Patrol Study? Describe the research on saturated patrol efforts. *①No patrol ②↑patrol ③reg. patrol →not much diff*

6. What are the arguments for and against undercover operations?

   go on for too long — mislead

7. Describe the police subculture and cop code and why it may be breaking down today.

8. Describe the Project on Policing Study and its results.

9. What are the three areas of police corruption? Describe each.

   abuse of auth, violation of occup. | substantive law

10. Describe the three explanations for police deviance. Provide some suggestions for reducing or minimizing police corruption.

    indiv, organizational, societal

VOCABULARY

blue curtain of secrecy – the practice of police covering up the misdeeds of other officers and/or not testifying against them

burnout – when officers merely "go through the motions" of their job after experiencing prolonged stress

civilian review/complaint boards – citizen groups that monitor and review the investigation and discipline of officers who have complaints filed against them

"cop code" – a set of informal rules for police officers that are not necessarily the same as those taught in the academy

"Dirty Harry problem" – the question of whether it is acceptable for a police officer to inflict pain on a suspect in order to acquire information that would save an innocent victim (from the "Dirty Harry" movies of Clint Eastwood)

cisplacement effect – when crime merely moves from a heavily patrolled area to another area of the city

early warning or audit system – identification system for finding problem officers early through tracking citizen complaints, use-of-force reports, and other markers

ends-oriented thinking – the belief that "the end justifies the means"

FTOs – Field Training Officers

groupthink – the situation in a group of decisionmakers where no one feels free to offer competing viewpoints

integrity testing – setting up police officers with opportunities for lying or theft to see if they do so

noble-cause corruption – when officers employ unethical means to catch criminals because they believe it is right to do so

proactive policing – active behavior to seek out crime

reactive policing – activities that respond to crime when brought to the attention of the police through crime reports or complaints

residual effect – the effect of saturated police patrols when crime continues to be at low levels even after saturated patrol programs have ended

rotten-apple argument – the explanation that it is only the individual officer who is deviant

saturated patrols – when a certain neighborhood or area of town is targeted for frequent or constant patrol presence

socialization – adopting the cultural values and beliefs of one's culture

subculture – a different set of values, beliefs, and even language from the dominant culture.

"testilying" – lying in affidavits or when giving testimony to convict a criminal

FOR FURTHER READING

Baker, Mark (1985). *Cops*. New York: Pocket Books.

Conlon, Ed (2004). *Blue Blood*. New York: Riverhead.

Crank, John and Michael Caldero (2004). *Police Ethics: The Corruption of Noble Cause*, Second Edition. Newark, NJ: LexisNexis/Matthew Bender.

Kappeler, Victor, Richard Sluder, and Geoffrey Alpert (1998). *Forces of Deviance: Understanding the Dark Side of Policing*, Second Edition. Prospect Heights, IL: Waveland Press.

Klockars, Carl, Sanja Ivkovic' and Maria Haberfeld (2004). *The Contours of Police Integrity*. Thousand Oaks, CA: Sage.

Lersch, Kimberly (2002). *Policing and Misconduct*. Upper Saddle River, NJ: Prentice Hall.

Pollock, Joycelyn (2007). *Ethical Dilemmas and Decisions in Criminal Justice*. Belmont, CA: Wadsworth/ITP.

[1] Houston Police Department. Retrieved 6/1/07 from: www.houstontx.gov/police/img/hr_chart.jpg.

[2] Johnson, C. & G. Copus (1981). "Law Enforcement Ethics: A Theoretical Analysis." In F. Schmalleger & R. Gustafson (eds.), *The Social Basis of Criminal Justice: Ethical Issues for the 80s*. Washington, DC: University Press, p. 39-83.

[3] See the following section on police subculture.

[4] McCampbell, M. (1986). *Field Training for Police: State of the Art*. Washington, DC: National Institute of Justice.

[5] Storch, J. & R. Panzarella (1996). "Police Stress: State-Trait Anxiety in Relation to Occupational and Personal Stressors." *Journal of Criminal Justice* 24, 2: 99-103.

[6] Haar, R. & M. Morash (1999). "Gender, Race, and Strategies of Coping with Occupational Stress in Policing." *Justice Quarterly* 16, 2: 303-336.

[7] Kelling, G., T. Pate, D. Dieckman, & C. Brown (1974). *The Kansas City Preventive Patrol Experiment: A Summary Report*. Washington, DC: The Police Foundation.

[8] Sherman, L. & D. Weisburd (1995). "General Deterrent Effects of Police Patrol in Crime 'Hot Spots': A Randomized, Controlled Trial." *Justice Quarterly* 12, 4: 625-648. See also Weisburd, D. & L. Green (1995). "Policing Drug Hot Spots: the Jersey City Drug Market Analysis Experiment." *Justice Quarterly* 12, 4: 711-735.

[9] White, M. (2007). *Current Issues and Controversies in Policing*. Boston, MA: Allyn and Bacon.

[10] Schoeman, F. (1985). "Privacy and Police Undercover Work." In W. Heffernan & T. Stroup (eds.), *Police Ethics: Hard Choices in Law Enforcement*. New York: John Jay Press, p. 133-153.

[11] Marx, G. (1985). "Police Undercover Work: Ethical Deception or Deceptive Ethics?" In W. Heffernan & T. Stroup (eds.), *Police Ethics: Hard Choices in Law Enforcement*. New York: John Jay Press, p. 83-117; Mieczkowksi, T. (2002). "Drug Abuse, Corruption and Officer Drug Testing." In K. Lersch (ed.), *Policing and Misconduct*. Upper Saddle River, NJ: Prentice-Hall, p. 157-192; Baker, M. (1985). *Cops*. New York: Pocket Books, p. 139–140.

[12] Conlon, E. (2004). *Blue Blood*. New York: Riverhead.

[13] South, N. (2001). "Police, Security and Information: The Use of Informants and Agents in a Liberal Democracy." In S. Einstein & M. Amir (eds.), *Policing, Security and Democracy: Special Aspects of Democratic Policing*. Huntsville, TX: Office of International Criminal Justice (OICJ), Sam Houston State University, pp. 87-105.

[14] Curry, M. (2002). "Faulty Drug Cases Draw Police Inquiry." *Dallas Morning News*, February 21: 25A.

[15] Dunningham, C. & C. Norris (1999). "The Detective, the Snout, and the Audit Commission: The Real Costs in Using Informants." *Howard Journal of Criminal Justice* 38, 1: 67-87.

[16] Scheingold, S. (1984). *The Politics of Law and Order*. New York: Longman.

[17] Scheingold, S. (1984). *The Politics of Law and Order*. New York: Longman, p. 97-100.

[18] Van Maanen, J. (1978). "The Asshole." In P. Manning & J. Van Maanen (eds.), *Policing: A View From the Street*. Santa Monica, CA: Goodyear, pp. 221-240. Herbert, S. (1996). "Morality in Law Enforcement: Chasing 'Bad Guys' with the Los Angeles Police Department." *Law and Society Review* 30, 4: 799-818.

[19] Sherman, L. (1982). "Learning Police Ethics." *Criminal Justice Ethics* 1, 1: 10–19.

[20] Scheingold, S. (1984). *The Politics of Law and Order*. New York: Longman, p. 100–104.

[21] Zhao, J., N. He & N. Lovrich (1998). "Individual Value Preferences Among American Police Officers." *Policing: An International Journal of Police Strategies and Management*, 21, 1: 22-37.

[22] Crank, J. & M. Caldero (2000/2005). *Police Ethics: The Corruption of Noble Cause*. Cincinnati, OH: Anderson Publishing.

[23] Scheingold, S. (1984). *The Politics of Law and Order*. New York: Longman, p. 97.

[24] Paoline, E., S. Myers & R. Worden (2000). "Police Culture, Individualism, and Community Policing: Evidence From Two Police Departments." *Justice Quarterly* 17, 3: 575-605.

[25] Kappeler, V., R. Sluder & G. Alpert (1994). *Forces of Deviance: Understanding the Dark Side of Policing*. Prospect Heights, IL: Waveland Press, p. 175; Cole, D. (1999). *No Equal Justice*. New York: Free Press; Walker, S., C. Spohn & M. DeLone (2000). *The Color of Justice*. Belmont, CA: Wadsworth; Crank, J. 1998. *Understanding Police Culture*. Cincinnati, OH: Anderson.

[26] Kappeler, V., R. Sluder, & G. Alpert (1994). *Forces of Deviance: Understanding the Dark Side of Policing*. Prospect Heights, IL: Waveland Press, p. 176-184.

[27] Weitzer, R. (1999). "Citizens' Perceptions of Police Misconduct: Race and Neighborhood Context." *Justice Quarterly* 16, 4: 819-846.

[28] Weitzer, R. & S. Tuch (2000). "Reforming the Police: Racial Differences in Public Support for Change." *Criminology* 40, 2: 435-456.

[29] Reisig, M. & R. Parks (2000). "Experience, Quality of Life, and Neighborhood Context: A Hierarchical Analysis of Satisfaction with Police." *Justice Quarterly* 17, 3: 607-630.

[30] Mastrofski, S., M. Reisig & D. McCluskey (2002). "Police Disrespect toward the Public: An Encounter Based Analysis." *Criminology* 40, 3: 519-551.

[31] Mastrofski, S., M. Reisig & D. McCluskey (2002). "Police Disrespect toward the Public: An Encounter Based Analysis." *Criminology* 40, 3: 519-551, p. 534.

[32] Mastrofski, S., M. Reisig & D. McCluskey (2002). "Police Disrespect toward the Public: An Encounter Based Analysis." *Criminology* 40, 3: 519-551, p. 543.

[33] Barker, T. (2002). "Ethical Police Behavior." In K. Lersch (ed), *Policing and Misconduct*. Upper Saddle River, NJ: Prentice Hall, p. 1-25.

[34] Weiburd, D. & R. Greenspan (2000). *Police Attitudes Toward Abuse of Authority: Findings from a National Study*. Washington, DC: U.S. Department of Justice.

[35] Dorschner, J.(1989). "The Dark Side of the Force." In R. Dunham & G. Alpert (eds.), *Critical Issues in Policing*, 2d Ed., Prospect Heights, IL: Waveland Press, pp. 254-274; Crank, J. & M. Caldero (2000/2005). *Police Ethics: The Corruption of Noble Cause*. Cincinnati, OH: Anderson Publishing, p. 162.

[36] Human Rights Watch (1998). *Shielded From Justice: Police Brutality and Accountability in the U.S.* New York: Human Rights Watch.

[37] Kappeler, V., R. Sluder, & G. Alpert (1994). *Forces of Deviance: Understanding the Dark Side of Policing*. Prospect Heights, IL: Waveland Press, p. 197; Babwin, D. (2001). "In Chicago, Allegations Plague Police Department." *Austin American-Statesman*, April 22: A26; Fountain, J. (2001). "Former Top Chicago Detective Admits to Leading Theft Ring." *New York Times*, October 26: A16. Crank, J. & M. Caldero (2000/2005). *Police Ethics: The Corruption of Noble Cause*. Cincinnati: Anderson.

[38] Manning, P. & L. Redlinger (1991). "Invitational Edges." In C. Klockars & S. Mastrofski (eds.), *Thinking about Police: Contemporary Readings*. New York: McGraw-Hill, p. 398-413.

[39] Klockars, C. S. Ivkovic' & M. Haberfeld (2004). *The Contours of Police Integrity*. Thousand Oaks, CA: Sage.

[40] Pollock, J. (2007). *Ethical Dilemmas and Decisions in Criminal Justice*. Belmont, CA: Wadsworth/ITP.

[41] Barker, T. & D. Carter (1994). *Police Deviance*, Third Edition. Cincinnati, OH: Anderson Publishing.

[42] Kappeler, V., R. Sluder, & G. Alpert (1994). *Forces of Deviance: Understanding the Dark Side of Policing*. Prospect Heights, IL: Waveland Press, p. 159.

[43] Pollock, J. (2007). *Ethical Dilemmas and Decisions in Criminal Justice*. Belmont, CA: Wadsworth/ITP.

[44] McGurrin, D. & V. Kappeler (2002). "Media Accounts of Police Sexual Violence." In K. Lersch, *Policing and Misconduct*. Upper Saddle River, NJ: Prentice-Hall, pp. 121-142, 133.

[45] Kraska, P. & V. Kappeler (1995). "To Serve and Pursue: Exploring Police Sexual Violence Against Women." *Justice Quarterly* 12, 1: 85-111, p. 93.

[46] Kraska, P. & V. Kappeler (1995). "To Serve and Pursue: Exploring Police Sexual Violence Against Women." *Justice Quarterly* 12, 1: 85-111, p. 92.

[47] Klockars, C. (1983). "The Dirty Harry Problem." In C. Klockars & S. Mastrofski (eds.), *Thinking about Police: Contemporary Readings*, pp. 428-438. New York: McGraw Hill.

[48] Crank, J. & M. Caldero (2000/2005). *Police Ethics: The Corruption of Noble Cause*. Cincinnati, OH: Anderson Publishing.

[49] Crank, J. & M. Caldero (2000/2005). *Police Ethics: The Corruption of Noble Cause*. Cincinnati, OH: Anderson Publishing.

[50] Dorschner, J. (1989). "The Dark Side of the Force." In G. Alpert (ed.), *Critical Issues in Policing*, Second Edition. Prospect Heights, IL: Waveland, pp. 254-274.

[51] Murphy, P. & D. Caplan (1989). "Conditions That Breed Corruption." In R. Dunham & G. Alpert (eds.), *Critical Issues in Policing*. Prospect Heights, IL: Waveland Press, pp. 304-324.

[52] Crank, J. & M. Caldero (2000/2005). *Police Ethics: The Corruption of Noble Cause*. Cincinnati: Anderson.

[53] Johnston, M. (1995). "Police Corruption." In D. Close & N. Meier (eds.), *Ethics in Criminal Justice*. Belmont, CA: Wadsworth; Pollock, J. (2007). *Ethical Dilemmas and Decisions in Criminal Justice*. Belmont, CA: Wadsworth/ITP

[54] Reuss-Ianni, E. (1983). *Two Cultures of Policing: Street Cops and Management Cops*. New Brunswick, NJ: Transaction.

[55] Reuss-Ianni, E. (1983). *Two Cultures of Policing: Street Cops and Management Cops*. New Brunswick, NJ: Transaction, p. 80.

[56] Marx, G. (1991). "The New Police Undercover Work." In C. Klockars & S. Mastrofski (eds.), *Thinking about Police: Contemporary Readings*. New York: McGraw-Hill, pp. 240-258.

[57] Prenzler, T. & C. Ronken (2001). "Models of Police Oversight: A Critique." *Policing and Society* 11: 151-180.

[58] Barker, T. (2002). "Ethical Police Behavior." In *Policing and Misconduct*, In K. Lersch, *Policing and Misconduct*. Upper Saddle River, NJ: Prentice-Hall, pp. 1-25; Walker, S. & G. Alpert (2002). "Early Warning Systems as Risk Management for Police." In K. Lersch, *Policing and Misconduct*. Upper Saddle River, NJ: Prentice-Hall, pp. 219-230, 224.

Chapter 6

Policing and the Legal Process

What You Need to Know

★ Four types of police-citizen interactions are: consent stops, fixed checkpoints, investigatory detentions, and arrest.

★ Racial profiling is when police stop motorists or pedestrians based solely on their race. Some evidence does indicate that minorities are stopped more often than whites.

★ The Fourth Amendment protects us against unreasonable searches and seizures of our home, person, or papers by law enforcement officers.

★ The types of searches include: pat-downs, searches incident to arrest, exigent circumstance searches, auto searches, inventory searches, consent searches, and border searches. Plain view seizures are not searches.

★ The Fifth Amendment gives us the right to be silent when accused of a crime. The *Miranda* warnings are judicially created procedures to ensure that everyone knows of this and other rights.

★ The three types of identifications are: showups, photo arrays, and lineups.

★ Entrapment occurs when someone who did not have a predisposition to commit a crime does so because of police actions.

★ The Exclusionary Rule is the punishment imposed when police violate the rights of the accused; however, there are at least three exceptions: the good faith exception, the inevitable discovery exception, and the public safety exception.

Much of the training that police officers receive in recruit training as well as in-service classes relates to the law. The authority of the police officer derives from the law, but the law also sets limits on the powers of police. Most of the case holdings that will be discussed in this chapter have set restraints on the power of police to stop, detain, search, or question. Some argue that these court decisions have "handcuffed" the police from doing their job. Actually, there is no research to indicate that many cases have been lost or arrests have not been made because of the due process protections recognized and/or created by the Supreme Court.

1. STOPS AND ARRESTS (SEIZURES)

When can police stop and question someone? One answer is any time the person consents to stop and answer their questions. However, the more important question is when can they stop and question someone who doesn't want to be stopped? The answer to that question is when they have reasonable suspicion that a crime has been or is about to be committed. We can distinguish four types of situations in which police stop citizens:

★   **Consent stops** – individual doesn't have to but consents to stay and talk to police officers

★   **Fixed Checkpoints** – everyone, or some random selection of individuals, are stopped for a very brief check of driver's license and registration and to check for intoxication or other impairment

★   **Investigatory Detentions** – police have *reasonable suspicion* that a person is engaged in or about to commit a crime, police can stop that person, ask for identification, and conduct a superficial search for weapons

★   **Arrest** – police have *probable cause* that the person committed a crime or traffic violation; search may be conducted for weapons and evidence of crime if an arrest occurs

1.1 Consent Stops

A large number of police-citizen interactions occur because the citizen agrees to stop and talk to police officers. When police stop someone on the street and ask what they are doing, it is a consent stop unless the individual is not free to leave. Similarly, if a police officer asks someone if they can look into their bag, it is a consent search unless the person says no and the officer does it anyway. When police ask someone to accompany them down to the station for questioning, it is a consent visit unless they make it clear that the person would be arrested if they don't come. Police do not need any level of suspicion or probable cause to ask citizens to talk to them or ask to search, but a citizen can also refuse to comply with such requests.

On the other hand, some courts have held that police can't stop automobile drivers and say it is a consent stop. The situation of stopping a moving car is different because it affects a person's movement more completely than a pedestrian stop. Therefore, police need at least reasonable suspicion before they stop a moving automobile (unless it is at a fixed checkpoint). In many cases, they stop a car only after they have seen a traffic violation, however minor. Once the driver has committed a traffic violation, police have probable cause of a crime (even if only a traffic offense), and can stop the car.

1.2 Fixed Checkpoints

Despite the discussion above, courts have also allowed police departments to engage in "fixed checkpoints" set up to check for DWI offenders. The rationale for allowing such stops is that the inconvenience to the public is minor, the governmental interest in stopping drunk drivers is high, and the stops are not conducted with individual officer discretion that can be abused. Every driver must be stopped or police must use some random system for stopping some drivers, if not all drivers. Further, the checkpoints can only occur with supervisory approval.

So far, fixed checkpoints have been acceptable only when the goal is to stop drunk drivers. Courts have not allowed such checkpoints to be used to find drug smugglers (away from border areas) or criminal suspects.[1]

1.3 Investigatory Detentions

One of the earliest cases that set the boundaries of the police power to stop was *Terry v. Ohio*[2] in 1968. In this case, a police officer observed Mr. Terry walking around a bank several times and peering in the window. While the officer did not have probable cause to arrest, he did have a reasonable suspicion that Terry was "casing" the building for a robbery or burglary. The officer stopped and searched Terry, and found a gun. He was convicted of an unlawful weapons charge. He appealed the conviction, arguing that the gun should have been excluded because the stop and search was unlawful in that there was no probable cause that he had committed a crime. The Supreme Court held that the search was lawful because the stop was lawful. According to the Court, police officers can stop and detain someone briefly to investigate a potential crime if they have reasonable suspicion that a crime had been, or was going to be, committed. Furthermore, police officers had a right to search for weapons to protect themselves while they were conducting a brief investigation.

The case clearly supported the right of police officers to detain individuals for short periods of time, and to question and even search them for weapons, if there were enough facts to support reasonable suspicion. The stop must be brief and not unduly inconvenience the citizen. Furthermore, a police officer's "hunch," without any factual basis, that an individual was going to commit a crime would not be sufficient to justify such a stop. Interestingly, however, the Supreme Court stopped short in this case of requiring the individual to answer the officer's questions. Justice White said, in his concurring opinion, that the person stopped is not obliged to answer questions and his refusal cannot be used to justify an arrest.

However, 36 years later, in *Hiibel v. Nevada*,[3] the Supreme Court upheld a Nevada statute that made it illegal to refuse to give police officers one's name, when they had reasonable suspicion the detainee was involved in a crime. The Court held that this law did not violate the Fourth or Fifth Amendments of the federal Constitution. In the *Hiibel* case, the detainee was stopped by police responding to a report that a woman had been assaulted. It turned out that Mr. Hiibel had been in an argument with his daughter who had gotten out of his car and walked home. When police arrived, he refused to give his name even after they threatened him with arrest. He was subsequently arrested and fined $250 and appealed the conviction all the way to the Supreme Court, arguing that citizens shouldn't have to give their name to police when they have not been arrested. The Supreme Court did not agree. The Court held that as long as police have a reasonable suspicion to stop someone, a state statute that requires an individual to simply give their name does not violate the Fourth or Fifth Amendments to the Constitution. You should understand, though, that some state statutes only require an individual to give identification when there is *probable* cause that a crime has been committed—in other words, when police have enough evidence to arrest the suspect.

★ Exercise: In the State of . . .

Look in the penal code for your state and find out if there is a statute that requires a person to give their name to police officers when asked. Do police need *reasonable suspicion* or *probable cause* if there is such a statute?

1.4 Racial Profiling

Racial profiling occurs when the decision to stop a driver (or pedestrian) is based on a "profile," and the major element of this profile is race. Profiling began when federal agents developed a profile of drug smugglers to assist border patrol and customs agents in airports. The list of indicators included behavior as well as demographic indices, including race. Behaviors such as nervousness, traveling with a one-way ticket, traveling without baggage, and so on, were combined with race to create the "drug smuggler profile." The profile was adapted to highway drivers by state patrol officers who were attempting to stem the flow of drugs up through the interstates in Florida, Georgia, Texas, and other southern states.[4] Eventually, the term "racial profile" was coined because, at least for some officers and some departments, race became the predominant element in deciding which drivers to stop.

Eventually, the practice of police officers stopping, detaining, and searching minority motorists disproportionately to their population was believed to be so prevalent that advocates argued that a new "crime" had been created called DWB (Driving While Black). There was a strong enough public backlash that in 1999 President Clinton condemned the practice and Congressional hearings were held to investigate how widespread the practice was. The result of federal attention was that many states passed legislation that required police departments to collect demographic information on police stops in order to determine whether they were done in a discriminatory manner that violated state and federal Constitutional rights.

It cannot be ignored that there is a widespread perception that police stop minorities more often than whites. In a 1999 police public contact survey, it was found that blacks reported more stops (12.3 percent) than Hispanics (10.44 percent) or whites (8.8 percent); and 81 percent of blacks, but only 60 percent of whites thought the practice was widespread. Further, blacks were about three times as likely to have unfavorable opinions of their local police and four times more likely to have unfavorable opinions of their state police. The authors found that race and personal experience with racial profiling were the strongest predictors of attitudes toward the police.[5]

There are difficult methodological problems involved in analyzing the extent of racial profiling. Just because certain groups may be stopped more often does not necessarily mean they are being targeted: there may be more individuals in that group; they may drive more; they may commit more traffic offenses, they may be more likely to drive in high-crime areas, and so on. If one is comparing the rate of stops with population figures, it is important to know how many stops were of residents, as opposed to drivers passing through the area. Alternatively, if one is using agency information on stops, the information may not be complete because it may count only stops that resulted in tickets or searches.

The Supreme Court has upheld the right of police officers to stop individuals when they use profiles that utilize race as *one factor* of several that, together, may establish reasonable suspicion for a brief investigatory detention.[6] It is also important to note that most traffic stops occur after a traffic violation has been observed, so police have a legal right to stop the driver. Opponents argued, however, that police engage in **pretextual stops**, which refers to the practice of using a minor traffic violation to stop the individual and, in the course of the traffic stop; look for other evidence of wrongdoing, specifically by a search, usually a consent search. According to some research, minorities are more likely to be stopped with "pretextual stops." When this practice was the basis of a court challenge, however, the Supreme Court upheld the right of officers to stop for minor traffic violations, even if the main reason for the stop was the officer's desire to search based on a racial profile.[7]

By 2000, public opinion had solidified against the practice and police were heavily criticized for racial profiling. Some researchers argued that it was an inefficient use of police resources anyway because the "hit rate" for finding drugs was lower for blacks than for other groups.[8] The main argument against racial profiling, however, is that it violates the civil liberties of those who are stopped *only* because of their color.

Ironically, about the time that law enforcement began developing formal policies against racial profiling and public opinion has shifted against it, the tragedy of September 11, 2001, occurred. After the terrorist attacks, those who looked like they were Middle Eastern were subject to increased scrutiny before they boarded airplanes. In some cases, individuals were denied entry when other passengers complained that they would not fly with men who looked like they might be suicide bombers. Many people who objected to racial profiling, when the targets were blacks suspected of drug smuggling, believe that it is acceptable toward those of Middle Eastern extraction, especially when they are flying on commercial airliners. We will discuss the challenges of policing in the age of terrorism in Chapter 15.

1.5 Arrest

Police officers have the legal authority to arrest individuals when they have probable cause to believe that the person has committed a crime. In some states, the crime must be a felony and misdemeanor arrests must be based on an arrest warrant supported by a criminal complaint, filed by a victim or a police officer. However, usually if the misdemeanor is committed in the presence of an officer, the police officer can arrest the suspect without a criminal complaint having been filed. Generally, if officers need to enter a private dwelling to arrest the suspect, they must first obtain an arrest warrant.

Arrest is the power to hold someone against their will. Police officers may be guilty of unlawful arrest only when there is evidence of maliciousness. Otherwise, if the arrest turns out to be invalid or in error, the officer can use a "good faith" defense.

An interesting fact is that police officers don't necessarily have a legal obligation to arrest. In fact, the decision to arrest is one of the least studied areas of criminal justice. Generally, police officers use their discretion, and in many cases where there is legal authority to arrest, officers choose not to. Most of us have not received a traffic ticket when we deserved one; this is an example of police discretion. Even when more serious offenses occur, police may choose not to arrest, unless there is a specific law that compels arrest. For instance, some states have passed "mandatory arrest" laws in domestic violence cases that require police officers to arrest when there is probable cause that future violence will occur.

When has an arrest occurred? If a reasonable person would not feel free to leave, then an arrest has occurred. There are no "magic words" that are required to create the arrest. If a police officer puts handcuffs on an individual and places him or her in a patrol car, that person is under arrest without having to hear the words "you are under arrest." On the other hand, if someone is asked to come in to the police station to talk about a crime, they are not under arrest unless a reasonable person would not feel free to leave.

You may not realize that a traffic ticket is an alternative to a custodial arrest. You have committed a crime and the officer may arrest you and take you into custody; however, in all states, there is enabling legislation that allows the officer, instead, to give you a citation or "ticket to appear," which operates in lieu of a custodial arrest. You still have to appear in court (or admit guilt by paying the fine). The Supreme Court has upheld the right of police officers to utilize full custodial arrests in minor traffic violations, even when the maximum penalty involved is only a fine.[9]

Police are authorized to use force to accomplish an arrest and it is unlawful to resist an arrest (which would be a crime in addition to the original crime). Police cannot, however, use lethal force to subdue a suspect if there is no reason to believe the suspect poses a danger to the officer or others. The case of *Tennessee v. Garner*[10] involved the police shooting of an unarmed teenager who was running away from them after being caught burglarizing a home. The Court held that it was a violation of the Fourth and Fourteenth Amendments to shoot at a fleeing suspect if the only reason for the shooting was to stop him or her from escaping and there was no evidence that the suspect would be dangerous to others.

2. SEARCHES

The **Fourth Amendment** protects citizens against the unreasonable intrusion by government agents into one's private home or papers. The Fourth Amendment states:

The right of the people to be secure in their persons, houses, papers, and effects, against unreasonable searches and seizures, shall not be violated, and no Warrants shall issue, but upon probable cause, supported by Oath or affirmation, and particularly describing the place to be searched, and the persons or things to be seized.

In all Fourth Amendment cases, the guideline for the Court's reasoning is whether there is a reasonable expectation of privacy on the part of the individual. Additionally, the court balances the individual's right to privacy against the state's right to investigate and prevent crimes.

When it was written, the Fourth Amendment protected citizens from un-lawful searches by federal agents. Indeed, the **Bill of Rights** (the first 10 Amendments to the Constitution) only protects us against violations by federal officers, but not by state or local agents of the law. The Fourteenth Amendment was ratified in 1868 after the Civil War. It states:

> *. . . all persons are citizens of the United States and of the state wherein they reside. No state shall make or enforce any law which shall abridge the privileges or immunities of citizens of the United States; nor shall any state deprive any person of life, liberty, or property, without due process of law . . .*

The **due process clause** tells states they cannot: "deprive any person of life, liberty or property without due process of law." What constitutes due process of law depends on what is at stake, but it basically means that when-ever the government seeks to deprive an individual of life, liberty or property, there must be procedural protections.

The Fourteenth Amendment was the basis for the **incorporation** of some of the protections from the First, Fourth, Fifth, Sixth and Eighth Amendments to citizens who may be faced with actions by state or local government agents. In other words, through a sequence of court cases, the Supreme Court held that although, when written, the protections only applied to actions by the federal government, the Fourteenth Amendment created due process rights that created fundamental protections against local police actions as well. For instance, Fourth Amendment protections now apply when a search is being conducted by city police officers (not just federal law enforcement agents), and the Sixth Amendment right to counsel now applies when the prosecution is by a state rather than the federal government, but they weren't recognized before the court cases that "incorporated" the rights to individuals against state action. Most of the Bill of Rights now applies to us as state citizens as well as federal citizens. In *Mapp v. Ohio*,[11] for instance, the Supreme Court held that the Fourth Amend-ment protections against governmental searches and seizures without probable cause applied to the actions of state and local law enforcement.

In practice, law enforcement agencies cannot search your house or papers without probable cause. In many cases probable cause is assured through the issuance of a warrant. A **magistrate** (any judicial figure authorized to issue a warrant) must evaluate the evidence brought to him or her by police officers and conclude that there is probable cause to search. The search warrant is the legal authority to do so. On the other hand, there are many exceptions to the warrant requirement, which will be discussed below. The standard is always probable cause, however, and even if police officers do not need a warrant to search for evidence, they always need to show probable cause that evidence or instrumentalities of the crime will be at the location they want to search.

BOX 6.1

Sample Search Warrant

State of Ohio, _____ County, ss:

To the sheriff (or other officer) of said County, greeting:

Whereas there has been filed with me an affidavit, of which the following is a copy (here copy the affidavit).

These are, therefore, to command you in the name of the State of Ohio, with the necessary and proper assistance, to enter, in the daytime (or in the nighttime) into (here describe the house or place as in the affidavit) of the said _____ of the township of _____ in the County aforesaid, and there diligently search for the said goods and chattels, or articles, to wit:

(here describe the articles as in the affidavit) and that you bring the same or any part thereof, found on such search, and also the body of ____, forthwith before me, or some other judge or magistrate of the county having cognizance thereof to be disposed of and dealt with according to law.

Given under my hand this _____ day of _____, 2008 _____ , Judge, County Court

---

Source: Ohio Revised Code Annotated § 2933.25. Form of search warrant. Copyright © 2007 by Matthew Bender & Company, Inc., a member of the LexisNexis Group.

2.1 Surveillance, Wiretaps, and Other Electronics

One typically thinks of only physical searches as being protected by the Fourth Amendment, but wiretaps and some forms of electronic surveillance are also treated as searches because they also intrude upon the privacy of citizens. Arguably, before police "bug" your house, tap your phone, or record your actions, they should have some justification for doing so. Crimes against wiretapping by private citizens go back as far as the telegraph in the late 1800s, and restrictions on police using such devices have been in place for decades.[12]

Although there are some exceptions, states generally follow federal law in allowing some wiretapping and eavesdropping; specifically, when there is consent by at least one party, and when law enforcement has the proper authorization from the court. Cases involving wiretapping, as in all Fourth Amendment cases, involve one's reasonable expectation of privacy. One of the earliest cases was *Katz v. United States*.[13] In this case, the Supreme Court held that police officers must have a warrant before placing a wiretap on a public telephone because people using public phone booths had a reasonable expectation of privacy. On the other hand, individuals talking in a public park do not have a reasonable expectation of privacy if police officers sitting close by can hear without the aid of any electronic listening devices, but officers must obtain a warrant before using any electronic equipment that amplifies sound from distances.[14] Individuals in jails have no reasonable expectation of privacy when they use jail phones, especially when there are signs that say calls may be monitored and recorded.[15] The USA PATRIOT Act and federal laws governing law enforcement investigations of terrorists expand regular law enforcement guidelines and will be covered in Chapter 15.

Police, like criminals, have embraced technology. In all cases where police use increasingly sophisticated devices for listening, recording, and surveilling citizens, courts use the basic guidelines of "expectation of privacy" and "reasonableness." In *Kyllo v. United States*,[16] for instance, the Supreme Court held that a thermal-imaging device that was able to measure the amount of heat coming from a house was a "search" and required a warrant. The Court held that individuals had a reasonable expectation of privacy in their own home and a right to expect that police are not using electronics not available to the general public to measure sound, heat, or anything else coming out of their private home. Note that police can use such equipment, but they must develop probable cause first and seek a warrant from a magistrate before "searching" using the equipment. While state agents must comply with both the federal minimum standards and any additional restrictions imposed by their state, federal investigators are governed by federal regulations and laws.[17]

2.2 Physical Searches

The law on searches and when warrants are required is somewhat complicated, but the first thing to understand is the type of searches that exist. In Box 6.2, there are descriptions of some types of searches and the legal justification for each type of search. The basic type of searches without warrants are pat downs during a *Terry* stop, searches incident to arrests, and "exigent circumstances" searches.

2.3 Requirements for a Warrant and Informants

When police officers need a warrant to search a house, person, or business, they need probable cause that they will find contraband or evidence of a crime. They must state what they expect to find and where they expect to find it with

BOX 6.2

Searches

1. *Search for weapons to protect officers during investigative stops—"pat downs"*

When an officer stops an individual who is acting suspiciously, the officer must have a reasonable suspicion that criminal activity has or is about to take place. If the stop is justified and the officer has a reasonable suspicion that the suspect may have a weapon, then the officer has a right to "pat down" the subject for his or her own protection. The search is limited to a tactile search for weapons. If something feels like a weapon, the officer can remove it from a pocket and if other contraband is found during the search, that evidence can be used against the suspect. (*Terry v. Ohio*[18])

2. *Search for weapons and evidence upon lawful arrest*

When a suspect has been placed under a lawful arrest, officers have the right to search the person and immediate vicinity of the person for weapons and contraband and evidence of the crime. This is to ensure that evidence is not destroyed by the suspect or others. This search is more intrusive than the pat-down search, but is justified by the arrest. (*Chimel v. California*[19])

3. *Exigent circumstances*

All exigent circumstance exceptions are based on logic and reasonableness. Basically, the exception recognizes that there are some circumstances where getting a warrant is impossible because the suspect will flee, the evidence will be destroyed, or there is some other good reason to allow the officer to search without a warrant. Note that it is *not* an exception to probable cause. The officer must still have probable cause that the suspect has engaged in a crime, but it provides an exception to the requirement to obtain a warrant before undertaking a search.

The **hot pursuit exception** is a type of exigent circumstances search. It refers to situations where police officers are following a suspect who has just committed a crime or they have probable cause to believe he has just committed a crime. If waiting for a warrant will result in the escape of the suspect or the destruction of evidence, they may pursue the suspect into a dwelling and search for him or her. If they see contraband or the fruits of the crime during the course of the search for the suspect, they may seize that evidence as well. (*Warden v. Hayden*[20])

Another exigent circumstance is when police have cause to believe someone is in danger. If police officers hear screaming from inside the home, they can enter the home without permission and without a warrant to protect the suspected victim. Even if they turn out to be wrong (i.e., the screaming was coming from the television), the entry is legal, therefore any contraband seen by the police is subject to seizure and use as evidence against the homeowner. As soon as they are aware that there is no danger to anyone, however, they must stop the search. Only evidence that is seen during the course of the legitimate entry can be used in any subsequent prosecution.

BOX 6.2 — *continued*

4. *Automobile Searches*

Automobile searches are a type of exigent circumstance search, but the line of court cases became so complicated that they require a separate discussion. Recall that exigent circumstances exist when there is a real danger that the suspect will flee or the evidence will be destroyed. Both of these circumstances exist when an automobile driver is stopped and there is probable cause to believe that there is evidence of a crime or contraband inside the car. Earlier cases distinguished between a car and the trunk, and a car and any containers in the car, but finally, in *United States v. Ross*, the Supreme Court held that when a police officer had probable cause to believe a crime had been committed using or within the automobile, then that auto could be searched, along with any containers found inside, including containers (such as purses) owned by passengers. Later, another case holding expanded that provision to when the probable cause applied only to a container that happened to be in a car.[21] Therefore, when a police officer stops a car because of a minor traffic violation and smells marijuana, or observes any other evidence of a crime that rises to probable cause, he or she may search the car and any bags, purses, or backpacks found in the car (*United States v. Ross*[22]).

5. *Inventory Searches*

An inventory search is not a search for evidence—it is simply a search to identify and record any possessions, especially valuables, found inside a car or other vehicle that is impounded by a law enforcement agency. If contraband or evidence is found during a routine inventory search, it can be used against the suspect. On the other hand, an inventory search does not include taking the panels off the inside of the car or deconstructing it in any way. If police choose to do this type of search, they should obtain a warrant.

6. *Consent Searches*

Probably most searches are conducted because the individual has given the law officer consent to search. Even without probable cause, if a police officer asks to look into a driver's trunk, and the driver opens it, then the search is legal because the driver has given consent. Similarly, if a police officer asks someone to empty their pockets and they agree to do so, the officer doesn't need probable cause for this type of consent search. Only if the consent is clearly coerced would any contraband or evidence be excluded in this type of situation.

7. *Plain View Seizures (These are not searches!)*

When an officer has legal authority to be in a particular place, then anything that can be seen with the aided or unaided eye is subject to seizure. This is not considered a search and, therefore, requires no legal justification other than the legal right to be there. For instance, when an officer responds to a domestic disturbance call and is allowed into a home, then anything he or she sees in the home, i.e., drugs on the table, is subject to seizure and used for prosecution. When an officer is in a public hallway in an apartment building and peers through an uncurtained

BOX 6.2 — *continued*

front window and sees narcotics, this is a plain view situation and he may use this information to get a search warrant. However, if a police officer comes into a yard with "no trespassing" signs posted and comes onto the porch and stands on a box to peer into a window, that is considered a search and any evidence or "fruits" of the evidence obtained from such a "search" will be excluded.

8. *Border Searches*

There are greater police powers to search at the borders of this country. The argument, of course, is that there is a great need to protect the country's borders and people choose to go across a border, therefore, they choose to be subject to the greater powers of search by border agents. We are all familiar today with the metal detectors and even pat downs by TSA officers when traveling through airports. These pat downs are done without probable cause or even reasonable suspicion because flying isn't a right and one implicitly consents to such searches by choosing to fly. Our bags are sniffed by drug dogs and we may be asked to open our luggage to be searched by customs or border agents.

In cases where officers have reasonable suspicion, they may detain an individual in an airport or a border for a reasonable period to determine if a crime is being committed. When individuals are suspected of smuggling drugs, they may be detained and asked for consent to an ultrasound of their stomach and, if they refuse, be monitored when they go to the bathroom to see if drugs are being carried in their body. These invasions of privacy are done without warrants only because airports are considered similar to borders and we all have a reduced expectation of privacy when crossing the border.

specificity. In other words, they cannot make application to a magistrate for a search warrant based on a hunch, a suspicion, or state that they need to look but don't know exactly what might connect the individual to a crime. If they are looking for drugs, they must say so; if they are looking for particular papers, they must say so, and so on. They must prove to the magistrate that they have credible evidence that rises to probable cause to believe that they will find the target of the warrant where they say it will be.

In *Illinois v. Gates*,[23] the Supreme Court addressed the question of whether the police could use the information provided by an anonymous informant in order to secure a search warrant. In this case, the officers learned from an anonymous informant that a couple would be driving back from Florida. The information provided the travel dates, the description of the car, and the fact that they would be carrying a large amount of drugs. All turned out to be true. Before this case, police were required to show the credibility of the informant through either the content of the information (i.e., how detailed it was) or the credibility of the informant (i.e., how many times he or she had told the truth in the past). In the *Illinois v. Gates* case, the court created a "totality of circumstance" test, which basically means that if the totality of the informant's tip, even an anonymous tip, indicates the information is likely to be true, then police will be able to obtain a search warrant.

3. INTERROGATION

The Fifth Amendment to the United States Constitution states, in part:

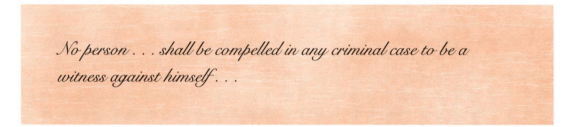

No person . . . shall be compelled in any criminal case to be a witness against himself . . .

The Fifth Amendment was added by our founding fathers to prevent courts from using evidence obtained by force, coercion, and torture. Throughout the eighteenth and nineteenth centuries, the Fifth Amendment was interpreted to mean the right not to be forced to speak. Then, in the twentieth century the Supreme Court developed a broader interpretation of the Fifth Amendment that included the right of the individual to remain silent, with their choice to remain silent not being used against them. As with the Fourth Amendment, the Fifth Amendment protects citizens (from being compelled to give testimony against themselves) in *federal* prosecutions, and the right had to be "incorporated" to us as state citizens in state prosecutions.

The Supreme Court in *Miranda v. Arizona*[24] implemented a requirement that procedural safeguards should exist that ensured that all suspects knew their privilege against self-incrimination. The procedural safeguards developed in *Miranda* meant that an individual subject to custodial interrogation must first be warned of his rights, including his right to remain silent, before the commencement of any type of questioning; thus, the famous *Miranda* warning, as set out in Box 6.3.

BOX 6.3

Miranda Warning

You have the right to remain silent. If you give up this right, anything you say can and will be used against you in a court of law. You have the right to an attorney during questioning. If you cannot afford an attorney, one will be appointed for you by the court. Do you understand these rights?

What this means for police is that the *Miranda* warning must be given before they can conduct an interrogation of a suspect held in custody. The requirement of police to give *Miranda* warnings is widely misunderstood, however, and in many situations where police are interacting with the public, there is no requirement for the warnings to be given. For instance,

★ When police arrive after receiving a crime report, they will question a number of people to get information about the alleged crime. No warnings are required because no one is a suspect and no one is in custody.

★ When police ask someone to come into the station house to talk to them about a crime, but the person is not officially in custody (is free to leave), warnings are not required.

★ When a suspect is arrested but police do not question him or her, and the suspect volunteers information about the crime, no warnings are required (but are recommended).

Interrogations occur when the investigation has narrowed to one or a few suspects and the questioning is directed specifically at uncovering evidence or obtaining a confession. Interrogations can occur even if the officer is not asking the suspect specific questions. In *Brewer v. Williams*,[25] officers were transporting a suspect and engaged in a conversation about the body of the girl he was suspected of killing. They commented to each other about how hard it would be to find the body since snow had started to fall even if the defendant did tell them where he dumped it and how sad it was that she would not receive a "Christian burial." The suspect did confess and showed the officers where the body was buried. The officers admitted that the "Christian burial" speech was designed to elicit the location of the body and, therefore, the conversation was deemed to be an interrogation; and because the suspect had already invoked his right to counsel and been appointed an attorney, his attorney should have been present at this "interrogation."

In more recent cases, the Supreme Court has upheld the use of deception and other mental tricks used by police on suspects in order to get them to confess or provide evidence. The use of the "father confessor" approach (a sympathetic paternal figure for the defendant to confide in) or "Mutt and Jeff" partners (a "nice guy" and a seemingly brutal, threatening officer) are other ways to induce confessions or obtain information.[26]

These methods do not violate the suspect's rights; however, once the right to an attorney is invoked, the interrogation should cease until an attorney is present. It should be noted that, after indictment, the right to an attorney comes from the Sixth Amendment and is part of the defendant's "trial rights," but the right to an attorney during a pre-indictment interrogation stems from the Fifth Amendment. The right to an attorney during interrogation is largely to protect the defendant from coercive methods that overcome his or her Fifth Amendment right to remain silent. It is called a "prophylactic" right, meaning that it is largely to prevent the violation of another right—in this case, the right not to be forced to incriminate oneself.

4. LINEUPS

A lineup is when the suspect is placed with other individuals in order for the victim to identify him or her. In *United States v. Wade*,[27] the Supreme Court held that the defendant's attorney must be present at a lineup in order to make sure that it was not biased against the defendant. On the other hand, if it is an earlier phase of the investigation and the suspect has not been indicted, then there is no requirement for an attorney to be present.[28]

Other forms of identification procedures include **showups** and **photo arrays**. Showups are frowned upon and should only occur when circumstances are such that it is unlikely that the victim-witness would make a mistake in identifying the suspect. In the most common example, a victim calls the police and provides a description, the suspect is found nearby and is immediately brought to the victim for identification, i.e., "Did this guy take your purse?" Showups have the potential for biasing the witness and, therefore, are not used except in circumstances similar to the example given above. In the photo array, a suspect's picture is placed on a page with other pictures of similar-looking men or women. The photo array is, perhaps, the best method of identification to assure admission of the identification because the array can be admitted into trial as evidence and jury members can see for themselves that the array was not biased and did not unfairly target the suspect as the potential offender.

5. SEIZURES OF BLOOD, TISSUE, HAIR, SALIVA, AND HANDWRITING SAMPLES

The popular *CSI* television series indicates that police agencies are increasingly using sophisticated crime analysis of physical evidence to prosecute criminals. This may or may not be true, but it does raise interesting new questions regarding seizures. Can police obtain one's blood, hair, saliva, or handwriting for forensic examination? These are searches and seizures of a sort; therefore, the Fourth Amendment applies. It has also been argued that this is a Fifth Amendment issue because giving one's blood, for instance, may be akin to giving testimony against oneself. The courts have disagreed with the latter presumption, however, distinguishing physical evidence (such as blood or DNA) from testimonial evidence (confession). One cannot be compelled to confess, but one can be compelled to give a DNA sample.

If the collection of body evidence is not intrusive (i.e., picture, handwriting or voice exemplar, fingerprint), then police merely need the legal justification to hold the person (it can be reasonable suspicion if the collection can be done without taking the individual to the police station). Even blood samples may be taken in DWI cases without consent and without a warrant when there is no time to obtain one and the blood is taken following standard medical procedures. However, generally police must obtain a court order to collect body fluids. Courts give approval for these seizures when the government successfully argues that their need for the evidence outweighs the individual's right to privacy over their own body.[29] This argument is easy to make when it is for a swab for DNA or a blood sample, but it is much harder to argue that the government's interest outweighs the individual's when the request is for surgery to recover a bullet.

In the television shows, the actors frequently obtain DNA from discarded soda cans or coffee cups. Although it is questionable that such tricks always will result in usable DNA, the practice does not violate any rights. The analogy would be when someone discards garbage and then police pick up the garbage and find evidence. The Supreme Court has held that there is no reasonable expectation of privacy over one's discarded garbage and, by analogy, none over a discarded soda can.

Crime labs have recently been the targets of investigations because of alleged shoddy laboratory procedures and possible bias in testimony.[30] The Houston Police Department crime lab, for instance, has been the center of an investigation that has forced the District Attorney's office to reexamine more than 100 cases. An independent investigation by the Justice Department discovered that untrained workers were conducting DNA analysis, there was evidence contamination from a leaky roof, "drylabbing" (making up scientific results), no quality control, and other problems. There were more than 2,000 cases that required review because of potentially tainted testimony from the police lab. Two men have had their sentences overturned or been granted new trials because of the findings concerning the lab.[31] But Houston is not alone. Other labs across the country have also been the subject of news reports. While sometimes the criticism has been simple incompetence and shoddy work practices, in other allegations, it appears that the lab examiners, who are sometimes employees of the police or sheriff's departments, and sometimes employees of independent labs, are engaged in "noble cause" corruption by working with police departments to arrive at desired results. Because juries place a great deal of faith in laboratory findings, it is imperative that the highest standards of competence and ethics be applied to crime laboratories that test forensic evidence.

6. ENTRAPMENT

As discussed in the last chapter, some police work involves proactively searching out crime before it happens. In one type of undercover operation, police offer opportunities for individuals to commit crimes rather than wait for them to do so. Bribery, drug sales, prostitution, and obscenity laws are areas that are particularly prone to the use of undercover officers offering the opportunity to commit the crime to unsuspecting individuals.

In legal terms, **entrapment** occurs when an otherwise innocent person commits an illegal act *because of* police encouragement or enticement. In the early 1980s, members of Congress were caught in the ABSCAM scandal. Police investigators, posing as representatives of an Arab sheik, told the defendants that the sheik was interested in building a hotel in Philadelphia, but that he wanted to make sure of having friends in high places to take care of any problems that might develop. Several politicians were convicted of bribery, but argued that they were entrapped. The court did not agree.[32]

The entrapment defense argues that even if the defendant *committed* the crime, he or she should not be punished because government agents *created* the crime. Two approaches have been used to determine whether entrapment has occurred. The **objective approach** examines the government's participation and whether it has exceeded accepted legal standards. For instance, if the state provided an "essential element" that made the crime possible, or if there was extensive and coercive pressure on the defendant to engage in the actions, then a court might rule that entrapment had occurred. The **subjective approach** looks at the defendant's background, character, and predisposition toward crime. If the offender is believed to have a predisposition to commit crime, then the police actions cannot be said to have entrapped the individual.

The defense of entrapment was first recognized by the U.S. Supreme Court in *Sorrells v. United States* in 1932.[33] The Court held that when the "criminal design originates with the officials of the government" and they give the idea of the crime to the defendant, then the defendant has a legitimate defense. In early cases, if police played too large a role in the crime, for instance, by providing essential ingredients or creating the idea of the crime and providing all the materials for it, then it was held that they "entrapped" the defendant. This was the so-called objective test of entrapment.

This objective test was replaced by the subjective test in *United States v. Russell*.[34] In *Russell*, the Supreme Court changed the focus of the test from government actions to the "predisposition" of the offender. If the offender was predisposed to commit the crime, then it did not matter what the government did. Only when the offender was a true innocent, who had no predisposition to commit the crime, could entrapment serve as a defense under this new test of entrapment.

Entrapment is an affirmative defense, which means that the defendant must raise the defense and offer some level of proof before the state is required

---

BOX 6.4

Colo. Rev. Stat. § 18-1-709[36]

The commission of acts which would otherwise constitute an offense is not criminal if the defendant engaged in the proscribed conduct because he was induced to do so by a law enforcement official or other person acting under his direction, seeking to obtain that evidence for the purpose of prosecution, and the methods used to obtain that evidence were such as to create a substantial risk that the acts would be committed by a person who, but for such inducement, would not have conceived or engaged in conduct of the sort induced. Merely affording a person an opportunity to commit an offense is not entrapment even though representations or inducements calculated to overcome the offender's fear of detection are used.

---

to argue and offer evidence that the police actions did not constitute entrapment.[35] Some states have codified the defense in their penal codes, such as Colorado's Criminal Code, as shown in Box 6.4.

The federal government and most states follow some version of the subjective predisposition test. However a minority of states continue to apply the objective test and a few combine the tests and require that the defendant prove both elements (government activity and lack of predisposition) and at least one state (New Mexico) requires the defendant to prove either one or the other.[37]

The line between police conduct that amounts to entrapment and merely affording an opportunity for the defendant to commit the offense is often a fine one. In drug cases, the general rule is that if the defendant has been involved in drug crimes in the past, then he or she is predisposed to such crimes and is not entrapped when he or she buys or sells to an undercover officer or informant.

Of course, providing the standard does not necessarily make the determination easy. Sometimes there is legitimate disagreement about whether the actions of law enforcement officers constituted entrapment. In one case, the Supreme Court held that a man who had ordered two magazines (*Bare Boys I* and *Bare Boys II*) was not predisposed to purchase child pornography and was entrapped by federal agents because they had been sending mailings to him for *three years* under several fictitious company names.[38] The dissent argued that his magazine orders indicated a predisposition, but the majority of the court held that the fact that it took three years to finally get him to order something was evidence that he did not have a predisposition to unlawfully obscene materials.

Police engage in a wide variety of situations where they provide the opportunity to commit a crime. They may pretend to be:

★ Individuals offering public officials a bribe in return for special treatment,

★ Drug sellers (or buyers),

★ Prostitutes (or "Johns"),

★ Children in Internet chat rooms offering to meet a predator for sex,

★ Fences encouraging the theft of certain types of automobiles,

★ Hit men who are willing to kill for money (or an individual wanting to hire someone to kill),

★ Someone who can provide cable service for free; and

★ A drunk on the street with money sticking out of his pocket.

The guideline for which of these situations constitutes entrapment is whether the person who succumbs to the temptation had a "predisposition" to commit the crime.

7. EXCLUSIONARY RULE

What happens when an officer violates the rights of a citizen by ignoring a warrant requirement, putting the individual in a biased lineup, or using physically coercive or other illegal interrogation tactics? The Supreme Court has held that the court's response to such violations will be to exclude the evidence obtained from the illegal action.

In the 1914 case of *Weeks v. United States*,[39] the Supreme Court excluded evidence obtained in violation of the Fourth Amendment by federal officers, but the ruling did not bar state or local police from using illegal evidence. Then in 1961, in *Mapp v. Ohio*,[40] the Court extended the ruling to state and local police as well. In the *Mapp* case, Dolree Mapp's home was searched by officers looking for explosives or other evidence of revolutionary activity. They said they had a warrant, but they didn't. The officers found no explosives but did find some pornography in her basement and they arrested her for that. In the subsequent court trial and appeal, she argued that the evidence should have been excluded because it was obtained through an illegal search. The Supreme Court agreed, and eliminated the **silver platter doctrine**, whereby state and local officers, who were not bound by the *Weeks* decision, obtained evidence illegally and handed it to federal officers "on a silver platter." The *Mapp* decision extended the exclusionary rule to all law enforcement officers, whether they are federal, state, or local.

This decision, along with the *Miranda* decision, is heavily criticized by those who argue that they "handcuff" the police from doing their job and that criminals should not go free because of police mistakes or errors in judgment. On the other hand, there is no credible evidence that these decisions have affected criminal investigations and court processing to any great degree. Furthermore, the Supreme Court has recognized several exceptions to the exclusionary rule that allow evidence to be admitted when police actions are reasonable.

7.1 Exceptions to the Exclusionary Rule

There are times when evidence is obtained unlawfully but admitted anyway. In several cases, the Supreme Court held that there was either minimal harm in the violation or the exclusion would generate more harm than letting in the evidence. In all of these cases, the evidence was admitted despite a constitutional violation.

1. The "Good Faith" Exception

In 1984, the Supreme Court decided in *United States v. Leon*[41] that if the officer relied in good faith on a warrant, and that warrant turned out to be faulty, then evidence obtained under the warrant would still be admitted. In this case, the warrant was faulty because it was granted without meeting the probable cause standard. Therefore, the warrant issued by the magistrate was without legal authority. On the other hand, the court stated that the police officer should not be punished because the magistrate erred, and therefore, the evidence would be admitted under this "good faith" exception.

2. The "Inevitable Discovery" Exception

Under this exception, if the state can show that the evidence would have been found anyway, without using the illegally obtained eveidence, then the information may be admitted as evidence. Basically the argument here is that the evidence shouldn't be excluded because it would have been discovered inevitably anyway.[42]

3. "Public Safety" Exception

Even though interrogations are supposed to be prefaced by a *Miranda* warning, in some situations when police officers do not give the warning, the information obtained from questioning can be used as evidence anyway. In *New York v. Quarles*,[43] police officers had cornered a suspect in a grocery store. They demanded to know where he had hidden a gun he had been seen carrying and they argued that they did so because they were afraid that citizens in the store might find the weapon and be hurt. He pointed out where he had hidden the gun and it was used as evidence against him. When he appealed, arguing that the question was an interrogation for evidence and therefore the gun should be excluded, the Supreme Court held that the officers' question was for public safety reasons, not for evidence collection, and the evidence could be admitted.

Arguably, these cases and others show that police and the courts don't have to be adversaries. Law enforcement is ultimately all about law. Generally, case decisions are made by balancing the needs of crime control against individual due process protections. If police officers don't believe in the law or only think it should apply to some and not others, then it is difficult to see how this approach cannot but hurt the process of justice.

8. CONCLUSION

In this chapter, we have examined a number of different legal principles as applied to police practices. In general, the government's intrusion into one's personal privacy is restricted. The Fourth Amendment requires police officers to have probable cause before they search a person's private papers or home. This provision has been held to include searches made by technology. Police do not necessarily need a warrant, but they do need probable cause. There are times when no warrant is needed, such as when evidence is in plain view or when there are exigent circumstances. The Fifth Amendment gives individuals the right not to incriminate themselves during the court process and also during the police investigation, but it does not cover physical evidence, such as blood or DNA.

Courts have also held that individuals should not be enticed to commit a crime and then be arrested for it. If it is shown that the suspect had no predisposition to commit the crime and it was only the police action that caused him or her to violate the law, then the defense of entrapment can be used.

If police overstep their authority and ignore the rights recognized by the courts, then evidence obtained can be excluded from any court proceeding against the defendant. However, courts have recognized several exceptions to the rule, including the good faith exception, the inevitable discovery exception, and the public safety exception.

REVIEW QUESTIONS

1. Describe the four types of stops or seizures and the legal justifications required for each type. *Consent stops, fixed VRTs, investigatory detentions, arrest*

2. What are the methodological problems in studying racial profiling? *more stops, ± targeted indiv, drive more in risk areas*

3. What is the Bill of Rights? What does the Fourth Amendment say? *unreasonable intrusion*

4. Do police need search warrants to wiretap? Can they use thermal-imaging equipment against a homeowner without a warrant? Can they do the following without a warrant: Obtain blood samples from a suspect? Get a picture of a suspect? Require handwriting samples? Hair samples? Fingernail scrapings?

5. What are the types of searches and what legal justification is necessary for each? *pat downs, auto, inventory, consent, border, exigent, lawful arrest*

6. When can police use anonymous informants to support an affidavit for a search warrant? *Totality of circumstance test*

7. When must the *Miranda* warning be given and when is it not needed?

8. What are the three procedures used for victims to identify suspects? *showups, photo arrays, lineups*

9. What two tests are used to determine if entrapment has occurred? *objective (exam govt part), subjective (defendent exam)*

10. What is the exclusionary rule? Describe the three exceptions recognized by the Supreme Court. *violates accused right? ① good faith ② inevitable discovery ③ public safety*

VOCABULARY

arrest – custodial seizure when police have *probable cause* that person committed crime

Bill of Rights – the first 10 amendments to the Constitution; as written, they only protected citizens against violations by federal officers, but not by state or local agents of the law

consent stops – interactions when the individual doesn't have to, but consents to stay and talk to police officers

due process clause – appears in the Fifth and the Fourteenth Amendments to the Constitution; states that no person shall be deprived of life, liberty, or property without due process of law

entrapment – when a person, who is not predisposed to commit crime, commits an illegal act because of police encouragement or enticement

fixed checkpoints – police stop everyone or employ random stops of individuals for a very brief license and registration check (usually for deterring DWI)

Fourth Amendment – protects citizens against intrusion by government agents into one's private home or papers.

hot pursuit exception – exception to the warrant requirement when police chase a suspect into a home

incorporation – approach of the Supreme Court to apply our Bill of Rights protections from the First, Fourth, Fifth, Sixth, and Eighth Amendments to citizens who may be faced with actions by state or local government agents

investigatory detentions – when police officers have a *reasonable suspicion* that an individual has or is about to commit a crime, they can stop the person, ask for identification; and conduct a pat-down search for weapons

magistrate – any judicial figure authorized to issue a warrant

objective approach – defines entrapment by examining the government's participation in the crime and whether it has exceeded accepted legal standards

photo arrays – suspect's picture is placed with others for victim identification

pretextual stops – the practice of using a minor traffic violation to stop the individual and, in the course of the traffic stop; look for other evidence of wrongdoing

racial profiling – occurs when reasonable suspicion to stop a driver (or pedestrian) is based on a "profile" with the major element of this profile being race

showups – type of identification where officers bring suspect to victim and ask victim to identify the offender

silver platter doctrine – referred to situation when state and local officers, who were not bound by the Fourth Amendment, would hand evidence to federal officers "on a silver platter"

subjective approach – definition of entrapment that looks at the defendant's background, character, and predisposition toward crime; those with a predisposition cannot be entrapped

FOR FURTHER READING

del Carmen, Rolando and Jeffery T. Walker (2006). *Briefs of Leading Cases in Law Enforcement*, Sixth Edition. Newark, NJ: LexisNexis/Matthew Bender.

Harris, D. (2004). "Review Essay/Profiling: Theory and Practice." *Criminal Justice Ethics* 23, 2: 51-57.

Hemmens, C. (2007). *Current Legal Issues in Criminal Justice*. Los Angeles, CA: Roxbury.

Kanovitz, J. and M. Kanovitz (2005). *Constitutional Law*, Tenth Edition. Newark, NJ: LexisNexis/Matthew Bender.

---

[1] Kanovitz, J. & M. Kanovitz (2005). *Constitutional Law*, Tenth Edition. Newark, NJ: LexisNexis/Matthew Bender.
[2] 392 U.S. 1 (1968).
[3] 124 S. Ct. 2451 (2004).
[4] Harris, D. (2004). "Review Essay/Profiling: Theory and Practice." *Criminal Justice Ethics* 23, 2: 51-57.
[5] Weitzer, R. & S. Tuch (2002). "Perceptions of Racial Profiling: Race, Class, and Personal Experience." *Criminology* 40, 2: 435-456, 436, 443.
[6] *United States v. Martinez-Fuerte*, 425 U.S. 931 (1976).
[7] *Wren v. United States*, 517 U.S. 806 (1996).
[8] Cole, D., & J. Lamberth (2001). "The Fallacy of Racial Profiling." *New York Times,* May 13: A19.
[9] *Atwater v. City of Lago Vista*, 532 U.S. 318 (2001).
[10] 471 U.S. 1 (1985).
[11] *Mapp v. Ohio*, 367 U.S. 643 (1961).
[12] *Berger v. New York*, 388 U.S. 41, 87 S. Ct. 1873, 18 L. Ed. 2d 1040 (1967).
[13] 389 U.S. 347 (1967).
[14] *Malpas v. State*, 16 Md. App. 69, 695 A.2d 588 (1997).
[15] *United States v. Friedman*, 300 F.3d 111 (2d Cir. 2002).
[16] 533 U.S. 27 (2001).
[17] *United States v. Pratt*, 913 F.2d 983 (1st Cir. 1990), *cert. denied*, 408 U.S. 1028, 111 S. Ct. 681, 112 L. Ed. 2d 673 (1990).
[18] 392 U.S. 1 (1968).
[19] 395 U.S. 752 (1969).
[20] 387 U.S. 294 (1967).
[21] *Acevedo v. California*, 500 US 565 (1991).
[22] 456 U.S. 798 (1982).
[23] 462 U.S. 213 (1983).
[24] *Miranda v. Arizona*, 384 U.S. 436 (1966).
[25] 430 U.S. 387 (1977).

[26] Pollock, J. (2007). *Ethical Dilemmas and Decisions in Criminal Justice*. Belmont, CA: Wadsworth/ITP.

[27] 388 U.S. 218 (1967).

[28] *Kirby v. Illinois*, 406 U.S. 682 (1972).

[29] *Schmerber v. California*, 384 U.S. 757 (1966).

[30] Axtman, K. (2003). "Bungles in Texas Crime Lab Stir Doubt Over DNA." *Christian Science Monitor*, April 18, 2003. Retrieved April 21, 2003 from: http://www.csmonitor.com/2003/0418/p03s01-usgn.html.

[31] Hays, K. (2005). "Report: Houston Crime Lab Was Long Neglected." *Austin American-Statesman*, July 1: B7.

[32] *United States v. Jannotti*, 673 F.2d 578 (3d Cir. 1982).

[33] 287 U.S. 435 (1932).

[34] 411 U.S. 423 (1973).

[35] *McGowan v. State*, 671 N.E.2d 872 (Ind. 1996).

[36] Colo. Rev. Stat. § 18-1-709 (2002). See also § 18-1-710, which provides that entrapment is an affirmative defense.

[37] See *State v. Little*, 435 A.2d 517 (N.H. 1981); *England v. State*, 887 S.W.2d 902 (Tex. Crim. App. 1994). *State v. Vallegjos*, 945 P.2d 957 (N.M. 1997).

[38] *Jacobsen v. United States*, 503 U.S. 540 (1992).

[39] 232 U.S. 383 (1914).

[40] 367 U.S. 643 (1961).

[41] 484 U.S. 897 (1984).

[42] *Nix v. Williams*, 467 U.S. 431 (1984).

[43] 467 U.S. 649 (1984).

Chapter 7

Law and Society

What You Need to Know

★ The purpose of law is to define and enforce the norms of society. It is declarative as well as purposive.

★ Criminal law and civil law used to be combined, but today they have separate purposes and objectives.

★ The three types of harm law protects us from are harm to self, harm to others, and harm to society's morals.

★ The three paradigms of law are: the *consensus*, the *conflict*, and the *pluralist* paradigms.

★ Common law has been largely supplanted by statutory law.

★ Laws must not violate constitutional rights, specifically those rights specified in the Bill of Rights.

★ Crimes can be classified as felonies, misdemeanors, and treason.

★ Crimes must include an *actus reus* and a *mens rea*.

We take the law for granted, but it is important to take a moment to think about the purpose and origins of law. What is the purpose of law? How are laws created? Why are certain behaviors defined as crimes? In this chapter, we will answer these questions and others before moving on to describe in more detail the American court system.

1. THE DEFINITION AND PURPOSE OF LAW

The law serves as a written embodiment of society's norms and morals. It is said to be declarative as well as purposive. That is, it declares the correct behavior in a society, but it also serves as a tool for enforcement. It cautions against certain types of behavior and warns of the consequences of ignoring the warning.

Natural law refers to the belief that some law exists in the natural world and can be discovered by reason. For instance, some behavior is believed to be intrinsically wrong (**mala in se**), such as murdering an innocent. Other behaviors are prohibited in certain societies, but are not inherently wrong. They are called **mala prohibita**.[1]

We can trace the history of law back to very early codes, such as the Code of Hammurabi (c. 2000 B.C.), which mixed secular and religious rules of behavior. These codes also standardized punishments. Early codes of law did not differentiate between what we might call public wrongs and private wrongs. Today we have criminal law and civil law.

Criminal law is the branch or division of law that defines crimes and provides for their punishment. In a criminal case, the state pursues justice to preserve the public peace. On the other hand, in **civil law** one person is wronged by another, and that person seeks a remedy against the wrongdoer by bringing a civil, or *tort*, action. **Torts** are personal wrongs. Some examples of torts are assault, defamation, intentional infliction of emotional distress, and arson. *Torts* and *crime* are not synonyms. While there is a great deal of overlap between crimes and torts, some crimes are not torts, and some torts are not crimes.

With torts, the emphasis is on adjusting the conflicting interests of individuals to achieve a desirable social result. The aggrieved party is the plaintiff and he or she must pay for the cost of the trial, although, if he or she wins, the court may order the defendant to reimburse the plaintiff for costs incurred. For example, if Ann hits Bob, causing him bodily injury, Bob may bring an action in court for recovery of expenses and for compensation for losses incurred. The state may also initiate an action against Ann for assault and battery and prosecute the case in criminal court. The most famous example of this dual response to a tort/crime was the successful civil suit against O.J. Simpson for wrongful death *after* his acquittal in criminal court. It is entirely possible for a defendant to "win" in one court and "lose" in the other, partially because of the different burdens of proof in civil versus criminal court. In earlier times, however, these two different legal systems were combined. The remainder of our discussion in this chapter refers to criminal law, not civil law.

1.1 The Purpose of Criminal Law

Why are some acts defined as crimes and punished? Blackstone, a famous English jurist, defined crime as "an act committed or omitted in violation of public law, either forbidding or commanding it."[2] Specifically, the objectives of criminal law in a free society are to:

★ make it possible for individuals to coexist in society,

★ define the wrongs that are considered necessary to protect the individuals,

★ define the method of determining guilt or innocence, and

★ designate the type of punishment or treatment following conviction for violating the laws of society.[3]

The purpose of criminal law is to protect society so that members of that society can be reasonably secure. There is always a balance to be achieved between the rights of the individual and the protection of society. The **social contract**, a concept originating with Thomas Hobbes and John Locke in the age of the Enlightenment, describes how individuals give up certain liberties in return for being protected by society. We give up the "right" to steal what we want in return for society's protection against our being victimized by others. We agree to follow the law but, in return, society should impose laws that are minimally intrusive to our individual liberties.

There are three forms of harm that criminal law protects against:

★ protection from the harm caused by others;

★ protection from the harm caused by ourselves;

★ protection of societal morals.

The most obvious protection that the criminal law provides is protection against harm caused by others. Laws against homicide, rape, theft, and arson offer obvious protections. If we are harmed, these laws ensure that the offender will be punished if caught. The second form of protection that the law provides is protection against harm caused by ourselves. So-called **paternalistic laws** protect us against our own foolish behavior. Seat belt laws are one example of a paternalistic law. Although you may prefer to drive your car without such a restraint, you will be punished with a fine if you do so.

The third form of protection the law provides is protection of societal morals. We used to have many more laws that protected societal morals. Laws against businesses operating on Sunday, blasphemy, and adultery may all be relics of the past, but some of our current laws (gambling, pornography, prostitution) still have the major purpose of enforcing society's morals.

When a Georgia state law prohibiting sodomy (homosexual intercourse) was upheld by the Supreme Court in 1986 in *Bowers v. Hardwick*,[4] the rationale was protection of society's morals. The Supreme Court upheld the right of the state to criminalize such behavior because they found that general societal morals condemned such behavior. However, in *Lawrence v. Texas*[5] in 2003, the Supreme Court overturned the earlier case. The majority held that the Texas law that criminalized homosexuality was unconstitutional. Evidently, just 17 years later, society's morals had changed to the extent that the law did not reflect societal morals. More recently, there has been a great debate about whether the law ought to recognize and legitimize same-sex marriages. The underlying justification that both sides employ is the protection of society's morals, or legal moralism. Obscenity laws are also justified by this rationale. Regardless of whether or not obscenity harms individuals, society may rationalize laws outlawing obscene pornography based on protecting society's morals.

It is clear that privacy rights may conflict with the government's right to enforce morality, and it should also be noted that whether an action is moral or immoral is a different question from whether there should be laws and governmental sanctions regarding the behavior. In some cases, individuals may agree that a particular action is immoral; but, at the same time, believe that the government should not have the power to restrict an individual's choice. For instance, some who advocate decriminalization of drugs do so because of cost effectiveness or libertarian reasons, not necessarily because they approve of drug use. Also, it seems fairly obvious that the state loses its moral authority to condemn gambling, for instance, when there is a state lottery. Laws that are based on the rationale of moral harm are usually the most controversial of all laws, and they have been, and continue to be, subject to shifts in public opinion and concern.

2. PARADIGMS OF LAW

A **paradigm** is a "fundamental image of the subject matter within a science. . . . It subsumes, defines, and interrelates the exemplars, theories, and methods/tools that exist within it."[6] In other words, a paradigm is a way of organizing knowledge. It is a broad perspective that shapes the way we process information. There are at least three paradigms (or perspectives) of law that can be identified: the consensus paradigm, the conflict paradigm, and the pluralist paradigm.

The **consensus paradigm** views society as a community consisting of like-minded individuals who agree on goals that are important for ultimate survival. This view sees the law as an aid to the growth and survival of society. Emile Durkheim (1858–1917), one of the first sociologists, wrote that criminal law represents the consensus of citizens.[7] We define an action as criminal because the majority of the populace holds the opinion that the behavior is wrong. An alternative view would be that the law is educational, and teaches us what is wrong. In either case, the function of criminal law is the maintenance of social cohesion. Law defines who is "normal" and who is deviant.

The consensus view would point to evidence that we all agree, for the most part, on what behaviors are wrong and the relative seriousness of different types of wrongful behavior. In criminology, the consensus view is represented by classical thinkers such as Bentham and Beccaria, who relied on the accepted definitions of crime in their day. In fact, most criminologists (except radical or conflict criminologists) accept the legal definitions of crime, without questioning why some behaviors are defined as criminal.

In the consensus paradigm, we all pretty much agree with what is defined as wrong. Law reinforces social cohesion. It is also seen as value-neutral and objective; in other words, it is not used against any particular group for the benefit of another.

The **conflict paradigm** views society as being made up of those who have power and those who don't. Rather than perceiving law as representative, this perspective sees law as a tool of power holders that they use for their own purposes, which are to maintain and control the status quo. The law is seen as an instrument of special interests.

In this paradigm, it is believed that laws are written by power holders and tend to be against the interests of those who have no power.[8] Advocates of the conflict paradigm would point to laws against only certain types of gambling, or against the use of only certain types of drugs, as evidence that the ruling class punishes only the activities of other classes.

One example of differential definitions and enforcement that would support the conflict view is that federal drug laws impose more severe sanctions on crack cocaine than on powder cocaine. Many believe it is not merely a coincidence that crack cocaine, which is more likely to be the drug of choice for minorities (being cheaper), is punished at a rate 100 times more than powder cocaine, which is typically associated with Caucasians and social elites.

The **pluralist paradigm** shares the perception that society is made up of competing interests; however, pluralism describes more than two basic interest groups. Power may also shift when interest groups form or coalitions emerge. These power shifts occur as part of the dynamics of societal change. Thus, Mothers Against Drunk Driving, for instance, was a grassroots group that amassed enough political power to change DWI laws. In the ever-changing political landscape, small groups may create power by forming coalitions or aligning themselves with more powerful groups. In this view, determining who has the power to create law is much more complicated that the simple "powerful versus powerless" scenario described by the conflict view.

Paradigms are subtly powerful in that they influence and shape the way we process information. If we hold a consensus perspective, we accept laws as they are passed and handed down to us from our representatives, with the assumption that they must be fair if they were the result of the legislative process. Conflict theorists are more critical of existing legislation and are able to see that some laws are passed because of hidden agendas, but their perspective that all law is the product of the powerful "pulling the strings" of government is probably not as realistic as the pluralist paradigm.

3. THE CREATION OF LAW

Recall that our system of laws in the United States is especially complex, because the criminal law is derived from English common law, statutory law, and our own case law tradition, split into 50 different state jurisdictions and the federal system.

Most of the present-day crimes in the various states have their origins in the so-called **common law** of England. This was the law that developed in the early English case decisions. William the Conquerer (1066) and his son, Henry I (1100-1135), are generally credited with the development of a national court system that involved judges who traveled across England and provided guidance to local magistrates. The effect was a gradual consistency in court decisions that led to the establishment of similar decisions in similar cases, which became known as the "common law." Eventually, judges decided the cases that came before them according to established principles from prior cases. In 1765, William Blackstone published *Commentaries on the Laws of England*. This work was the most comprehensive written source of the common law at the time, and is still cited as a legal source.

Common law became the starting point for American criminal law. Gradually, states passed their own criminal codes that supplanted the common law, but if a particular code was silent on an issue, many courts would fall back to common law principles. For instance, in the 1970 case of *Keeler v. Superior Court*, the defendant was prosecuted for intentionally killing his wife's unborn child by kicking her in the stomach. However, because the California statute in question defined homicide as the killing of a "person," and the common law definition of person did not include the unborn, Keeler could not be prosecuted for the death of the fetus.[9] This led to California and other states changing their criminal code by redefining "person" to include a fetus, or creating the new crime of feticide. However, the decision in the *Keeler* case had to be made based on common law definitions because the California Penal Code was silent on the issue.

Today, almost all crimes in all states are "statutory crimes," meaning that the state criminal code defines it as a crime. When a legislative body (federal or state) determines that certain conduct is undesirable and should be forbidden, a bill is prepared describing what conduct should be prohibited. This is introduced in the House of Representatives or the Senate, and is voted upon by the elected members of the legislative body. If both houses of the legislature approve the bill, it then goes to the governor or president for consideration and approval. If the chief executive officer signs the legislation, it then becomes a law to be enforced by those involved in the justice process. Even if the chief executive officer refuses to sign (in other words, vetoes the bill), the bill may become law if enough members of the legislative body approve it, overriding the veto. The legislature is permitted to define criminal offenses in any way it chooses, as long as the law is not arbitrary and does not violate the state or federal Constitution.

As discussed in the first chapter, states have primary **police power**, which is the authority to enact and enforce legislation to protect the health, welfare, morals, and safety of the people of the state. Recall that the Tenth Amendment to the Constitution was added to make clear that the powers not delegated to the United States by the Constitution would remain in the states, respectively, and the people. The Tenth Amendment states:

> *The powers not delegated to the United States by the Constitution, nor prohibited by it to the States, are reserved to the States respectively, or to the people.*

The federal government, supposedly, has no inherent police power. In the federal system, there have also never been common law crimes, because the federal government only has the power that is delegated to it by the Constitution. However, Congress may pass laws that are related to one of the express powers granted to the federal government by the Constitution. The enumerated powers granted to the federal government are found primarily in Article I, Section 8 of the Constitution. Certain crimes, such as treason, are federal crimes because the Constitution grants to the federal government the right to define and prosecute such a crime. Other crimes are consistent with other powers. For example, under the power to regulate interstate and foreign commerce, Congress has created federal crimes such as transporting stolen vehicles (interstate), kidnapping (with the element of interstate transport). Federal laws against drug smuggling come from the federal power to protect our borders.

Cities, counties, townships, and municipal corporations also have limited authority to make and enforce rules and regulations. State legislatures have given these units of government the power to create laws as long as the regulations and ordinances do not conflict with the U.S. Constitution, the state constitution, or the laws of the state. The state may withhold, grant, or withdraw powers and privileges as it sees fit.

It should become clear by now that "law" in this country is a complex system of overlapping jurisdictions. There is the United States Criminal Code, which describes all federal criminal laws; the criminal codes of the 50 states; and thousands of city and county codes. Another code of law is the Model Penal Code, which was created by the American Law Institute. It is not the law in any state, but rather serves as a guide to state lawmakers. The American Law Institute is an association of judges, lawyers, and law professors and they created the **Model Penal Code** in 1962 with revisions and commentary being added through 1985. The MPC is helpful as a general outline of criminal law because it is impossible to have a discussion about the laws of the 50 states and the federal government.

4. CONSTITUTIONAL CHALLENGES TO THE CREATION OF LAWS

The federal government, states, and municipalities do not have the power to pass a law that violates one of the rights granted by the United States Constitution. Specifically, protections are found in the first 10 amendments, which make up the **Bill of Rights**. We are protected against laws that are vague, that punish behavior after the fact (**ex post facto laws**), or that infringe upon our freedom of expression, association, or religion. Furthermore, laws that treat people in a discriminatory manner or that infringe upon individual privacy rights are prohibited. A summary of the rights granted in the Bill of Rights appears in Box 7.1.

4.1 Vagueness Challenges

It is a fundamental principle of criminal law that the legislation must not be vague, meaning that there is some reasonable doubt as to the meaning of the law. In vagueness challenges, the law is criticized as being so unclear as to what is prohibited that reasonable people would not have proper notification that some act was wrong.

BOX 7.1

Bill of Rights

First Amendment – freedom of religion, expression, association

Second Amendment – right to bear arms as a civilian militia

Third Amendment – right not to have soldiers quartered in peoples' homes

Fourth Amendment – right to be free from unreasonable governmental search and seizure

Fifth Amendment – right to be free from compulsory self-incrimination, federal right to grand jury, protection against double jeopardy, due process

Sixth Amendment – right to an impartial jury trial that is speedy and public, with specified due process elements

Seventh Amendment – right to trial in suit at common law, jury to be trier of fact

Eighth Amendment – right against excessive bail, right to be free from cruel and unusual punishment

Ninth Amendment – states "The enumeration in the Constitution, of certain rights, shall not be construed to deny or disparage others retained by the people."

Tenth Amendment – reserves all other powers not specifically delegated in the Constitution to the states

In *City of Chicago v. Morales*, the Supreme Court struck down an anti-gang law passed by the Chicago City Council in order to control gang activity. The law/ordinance prohibited those "believed to be criminal street gang members" from "loitering in any public place." Criticisms of this law centered on the vague nature of identifying who were street gang members, and the vagueness of the term "loitering" and "public place."[10] The majority of the court, however, objected to the fact that it was solely within the police officer's discretion to define when loitering was occurring. The Supreme Court, in this case, indicated that there may be anti-gang laws that could pass the vagueness test, but they needed to be written in a way that definitely stated what actions would be defined as criminal.

Basically, the right to be free from vague and overbroad laws comes from the Fifth and Fourteenth Amendments. Both amendments provide that an individual should receive "due process of law" before being deprived of life, liberty, or property. The Fifth Amendment provision has been interpreted to provide protection against due process violations by federal actors (such as the FBI), and the Fourteenth Amendment provision protects us from due process violations by state governmental actors (such as your municipal police). **Due process** has been defined as the procedures designed to protect against error in the governmental deprivation of life, liberty, and property. Due process includes the right to notice (to know what we are being accused of). Obviously, in order to have notice, a law must be clear and not subject to arbitrary definitions.

4.2 Equal Protection Challenges

Laws that treat "similarly situated" people differently also violate the Fourteenth Amendment's "equal protection" clause. The government must have a very good reason for treating different racial, ethnic, or religious groups differently under the law. If a law that is neutral on its face differentially affects only one group of people, it would also be scrutinized.

In 1967, the Supreme Court struck down Virginia's **miscegenation laws**, which made it a crime to marry someone of a different race.[11] The groups at issue were those who wished to marry a person from the same race compared to those who wished to marry someone of a different race. The Court held that the state did not have a reason that was sufficiently important to justify treating these groups differently and the holding invalidated all miscegenation laws in not only Virginia, but also the other states that had them.

In the case *In re Michael M.*, a California statutory rape law was challenged. The argument was that the law violated equal protection because it treated male and female actions differently by defining the crime in such a way that only men could be perpetrators and only girls could be victims.[12] In this case, the Supreme Court upheld the law because the parties were *not* considered similarly situated, in that only female victims could become pregnant, and the law's imputed purpose was to prevent teenage pregnancy.

4.3 Ex Post Facto Challenges

The U.S. Constitution and state constitutions specifically prohibit ex post facto laws. The two sections of the federal Constitution that relate to ex post facto laws are Article I, Section 9, which provides that "no bill of attainder or ex post facto law shall be passed," and Section 10, which provides that "[n]o state shall . . . pass any ex post facto law."

These provisions were added to the Constitution of the United States and similar provisions have been added to the constitutions of the respective states to prohibit legislative bodies from punishing a person for an act that was neither a crime nor punishable when the act was committed, or from increasing the punishment after the fact. Two critical elements are necessary to establish an ex post facto claim:

★   The law must be retrospective—that is, it must apply to events occurring before its enactment.

★   It must disadvantage the offender affected by it.[14]

A mere procedural change in the law, not increasing punishment, or not changing the elements of the offense, does not result in an ex post facto violation. A law may be invalid as ex post facto toward a particular person who committed an act before its enactment, but that does not affect its validity generally. Such legislation would be ex post facto in relation to persons who committed the act prior to the enactment of the legislation, but would be upheld when applied to persons who commit the same act after the legislation.

4.4 First Amendment Challenges

Neither the states nor the federal government can pass a law that limits First Amendment rights. As you know, the First Amendment protects our freedoms of speech, association, and religion. The government has a right to pass laws that do not unduly interfere with these rights. Thus, for instance, if our speech creates an imminent danger to others, it can be prohibited and even punished. One does not have the right to incite a riot. On the other hand, an ordinance that makes it criminal to simply *verbally* (not physically) object to the arrest of another has been ruled as unconstitutional in that it infringes upon free speech.[15]

In *Texas v. Johnson*, an individual was arrested and punished under a Texas statute that made flag burning illegal. The Supreme Court ruled that the state could not create a crime that punished flag burning.[16] This case decision is still controversial and a large number of people believe that burning the American flag, even if done as a protest, should be criminalized. However, the Supreme Court found that the act was protected speech and, thus, could not be punished. In response, Congress has considered a proposal for a constitutional amendment that would criminalize flag burning. Such a constitutional amendment would ultimately be challenged in court again, and it is possible that, because the composition of the Supreme Court has changed, the new justices may over-rule the earlier decision.

Other constitutional challenges may involve the First Amendments protec-tions of religion, speech, or association. Generally, one has the right to speak, associate freely, and practice one's religion without state interference. How-ever, laws can be passed if the behavior in question harms others or intrudes unduly on governmental interests in safety and order. These areas can raise interesting questions in how to balance individual freedoms and societal inter-ests. Should worshipers, for instance, be allowed to sacrifice goats as part of their religion, or should they be bound by animal cruelty laws? Should follow-ers of certain religions be allowed to have multiple wives, or be subject, as everyone else, to bigamy laws? If your religion uses peyote, as do some Native American groups, are you exempt from state and federal drug laws that crimi-nalize the use and possession of this controlled substance? These challenges to created laws are always difficult and will continue to exist as long as legisla-tures pass laws regulating citizen behavior.

4.5 Privacy Challenges

The right to privacy is not identified specifically in the Constitution, but has been recognized by the Supreme Court in various case decisions. Basically, their position has been that the framers of the Constitution meant that privacy rights should exist, based upon their language in certain amendments, such as the Fourth Amendment. One of the most important cases that established the protected right of privacy against governmental interference was *Griswold v. Connecticut*.[17] In that case, the Supreme Court struck down Connecticut's criminal law that punished the distribution of information regarding birth con-trol and contraceptives to married couples. According to Justice Douglas, the First, Third, Fourth, Fifth, Ninth, and Fourteenth Amendments can be read to construe a privacy right that restricts the government from interfering with private decisions of procreation by a married couple.

The balance between individual liberty and governmental interest in these cases is typically the right to privacy versus protection of society's morals. Laws against drugs, pornography, gambling, and prostitution have been challenged under the privacy rationale, but generally have lost to the argument that the government interest in societal safety justifies such laws. Laws against sodomy (same-sex sexual intercourse), however, have been abolished. As discussed above, in *Lawrence v. Texas*, the Supreme Court struck down the sodomy law of Texas as unconstitutionally infringing on the individual's right to privacy.

5. THE ELEMENTS OF A CRIME

If a law is not struck down because it violates one or more constitutional rights, it is enforceable as a crime. All crimes are classified as felonies, misde-meanors, or treason. These classifications are important not only in determining the degree of punishment, but also when determining the authority of justice personnel to take action. For example, in some states, law enforcement officers may not make misdemeanor arrests unless the offense was committed in their presence (or they had an arrest warrant).

According to most authorities, crimes punishable by death or by imprisonment in a state prison or penitentiary are **felonies**. A crime may be made a felony by reference to the punishment attached, or it may be made a felony by a statute that specifically says that it is a felony. When an offense is not designated by statute as either a felony or a misdemeanor, but a specific punishment is prescribed, then the grade, or class, of the offense is determined by the punishment. Generally, felonies are punishable by at least one year in prison.

Misdemeanors are offenses for which the punishment is other than death or imprisonment in a state prison or that have not been designated felonies by statute. A person convicted of a misdemeanor will ordinarily be incarcerated in a local jail or be required to pay a fine, but will not be sent to a state penitentiary. What is defined as a felony in one state may be a misdemeanor in another, except for the most serious crimes, such as murder, robbery, and rape, which are always felonies.

Treason is the only crime that is described in the Constitution. Because those who commit treason threaten the very existence of the nation, it is given a higher classification than a felony. According to the Constitution:

> *Treason against the United States shall consist only in levying war against them, or in adhering to their enemies, giving them aid and comfort.*

Also, the Constitution provides that no person shall be convicted of treason unless on the testimony of two witnesses to the same overt act, or on confession in open court.

Each crime, as defined in a criminal code, must include a specific prohibited act (or omission). This principle is referred to as the **actus reus**. The law does not punish mere criminal thoughts, nor does it punish a person for who he or she is. Each crime's definition includes a physical act or, in some instances, a failure to act. The physical act must be voluntary, such as pulling the trigger of a gun or breaking into a house to commit theft. There have been a few cases in criminal law in which the act was deemed to be not "volitional" or voluntary on the part of the perpetrator. Examples of acts that are not considered voluntary include actions taken during epileptic seizures or spasms, reflexive actions, or actions taken while sleepwalking or in some other form of "unconscious" state.

In some cases, the crime consists of a failure to act, such as a failure to register for the draft or failure to prepare income tax returns. An omission to act can only constitute a crime when there is also a legal duty. Legal duties are created by either:

★ Statute

★ Relationship

★ Contract

★ Voluntary assumption of care

Examples of statutory duties are, for instance, the duty to file tax returns and the duty (of convicted sex offenders) to register in sex-offender registries. Failure to perform these duties is a crime in itself. Other statutory duties include:

★ The duty to stop and render assistance if involved in a traffic accident; and

★ The duty of "mandated reporters" to report child abuse to law enforcement;

Certain relationships also carry duties. The most obvious and common is the duty of a parent to care for a minor child. Care includes not only feeding and housing your child, but also providing medical care and ensuring that school age children receive an education. In about 28 states, "filial responsibility" laws exist. These statutes create a duty for adult children to financially provide for one's aged and infirm parents if one is able to do so. In some states, a defense can be offered that the parent abandoned the child before the age of majority. Despite the fact that these state statutes exist, they are rarely enforced; in 11 of these states, *no one* has ever been prosecuted.[18]

Contractual duties arise when one person receives something of value in exchange for a duty to care for others. If they are negligent in that duty, criminal culpability may be created. Examples of contractual duties exist between the following actors:

★ Lifeguards to swimmers

★ Child care provider to those in their care

★ Police officer to citizen

★ Doctor to patient

If a person who has no statutory, relationship, or contractual obligation to render aid but chooses to begin administering assistance, then they may create a duty for themselves. For instance, unless a state has a Good Samaritan law, there is no statutory duty to stop and render assistance if one sees a traffic accident (unless one is involved in the accident). However, if a driver does stop and begins to help, then they must not abandon their effort if it would leave the victim in a worse condition than before. If one sees a person in distress on the street, there is no duty to render aid; however, if the passerby helps the person in distress to a park bench or helps them to a doorway, or in any other way moves them away from where they might have received assistance from others, then the duty to continue care has been created. The rationale is that abandoning one's effort would leave the victim in a worse condition than before.

Another element of every crime, in addition to the *actus reus*, is a criminal state of mind, or **mens rea**. Under common law, each crime possessed a *mens rea*, but the language used in old English cases and early state statutes and cases in this country was not uniform; thus, for instance, the necessary intent for homicide was defined as malicious, premeditated, depraved indifference, depraved heart, or wanton disregard. The Model Penal Code condensed all the myriad definitions of *mens rea* into only four enumerated mental states. In all states that have adopted the Model Penal Code, statutes clearly specify that the actor must have acted *purposely, knowingly, recklessly,* or *negligently.* Further, the definitions of these terms do not vary state by state; they always mean the same thing. The definitions of these terms are as follows:

- ★ *Purposely:* when the actor intends the act and intends to cause the result.

- ★ *Knowingly:* when the actor is aware of the nature of his conduct and is aware of the practical certainty of the result of his conduct.

- ★ *Recklessly:* when the actor knows of, but consciously disregards, an unjustifiable risk (and the action involves a gross deviation from a reasonable standard of conduct).

- ★ *Negligently:* when the actor is unaware of, but *should have been* aware of, an unjustifiable risk (and the action involves a gross deviation from a reasonable standard of conduct)

★ Exercise: In the State of . . .

Find the criminal code for your state and determine the following:

1. Has the code completely replaced common law, or does it "supplement" common law (meaning that common law would be applied if any particular issue was not contained in the code).

2. Is there a law prohibiting sodomy? As it is written, does it conflict with the Supreme Court's holding in *Lawrence v. Texas*?

3. When is theft/larceny a misdemeanor and when is it a felony?

4. What are the *actus reus* and *mens rea* of the crime of burglary, according to your criminal code?

One other concept important to criminal *mens rea* is the principle of **transferred intent**. This can be remembered as "bad aim" intent because the classic example is that if Defendant intends to kill Victim A, but misses and kills Victim B instead, he will be guilty of First Degree Murder (for B's death) and Attempted Murder (for trying to kill A). The intent to kill was transferred to the actual victim.

If you examined any crime in your state's criminal code, you should be able to identify the specific *actus reus* and the *mens rea* required for criminal culpability. If the *mens rea* is not specifically stated, case law usually assumes the legislators meant "knowingly."

6. RECENT ISSUES IN CRIMINAL LAW

Controversies concerning the law and its implementation occur all the time. Abortion has continued to be a divisive issue for the country and for the Supreme Court. Although *Roe v. Wade*[19] ruled that the Texas law against abortion unconstitutionally infringed upon a woman's right to choose; subsequent cases refined and restricted the "right" to abortion. Today's Supreme Court may very well overturn the *Roe* decision completely. In *Gonzales v. Carhart*, [20] decided in April 2007, the Supreme Court upheld the Partial Birth Abortion Ban Act of 2003. In this decision, the justices held that prohibiting this type of abortion did not unduly interfere with a woman's right to privacy. In addition to their stated reasons for upholding the federal law, the holding was probably also due to the fact that Samuel Alito and Chief Justice Roberts, both very conservative justices, were added to the court. Legal analysts predict more court holdings in this area of law.

The issue of whether abortion should be a crime is a *substantive* legal issue, meaning that the substance of the law is the issue or what is being challenged, i.e., *should* abortion be considered a crime? There are also *procedural* legal issues, typically concerning the nature and extent of due process. For instance, the Supreme Court will hear, in the 2007 term, whether the United States' prisoners in Guantánamo Bay should be held without access to federal courts. This has nothing to do with their guilt or the particular crime they might be determined to be guilty of; but, rather, it is an issue of procedure. Specifically, the legal issue is whether they have due process rights that include access to federal courts.

One need only look in the newspaper to see current legal controversies. Should hate crimes be extended to gender? Should same-sex marriages be legal? Should Congress pass laws that make it a federal crime to give aid to foreign organizations defined as terrorist (even if some other activities are philanthropic)? After the Virginia Tech tragedy, laws banning firearms on college campuses were re-evaluated in some states, in light of the argument that pistol-packing students might have reduced the death toll. Should there be a crime that holds owners of dogs who maul victims criminally culpable? DWI laws have gotten progressively harsher, both in the punishment prescribed, and in the definition of intoxication (by states reducing the limit at which one is considered to be legally intoxicated). The point is that the law affects you every day and it is a dynamic entity. It constantly changes in response to current events and political and social influences.

7. CONCLUSION

Society has law in order to protect the citizenry from harm. Criminal law is the branch or division of law that defines crimes, their elements, and provides for their punishment. In a criminal case, the state (or federal government) is the plaintiff, and the purpose of the prosecution is to preserve the public peace or address an injury to the public at-large. It can be distinguished from civil law.

The protections of law fall into the three areas of: protection from harm from others; protection from harm from oneself; and protection of society's morals. Paradigms of law are descriptions of one's perspective concerning the basic function in society and include the consensus, conflict, and pluralist paradigms.

Most of the present-day crimes in the various states had their origins in the common law of England. This was the law developed in the early English court decisions and modified by English legislative bodies. This became the starting point for our criminal law, but has now largely been supplanted by statutory law as found in state and federal criminal codes.

Once the legislative or judicial branch of government decides that certain conduct is prohibited or required, criminal justice personnel are charged with enforcing those laws, and have the responsibility to do so until the laws are repealed or declared unconstitutional. Constitutional challenges fall into the areas of: vagueness, equal protection, ex post facto, First Amendment, and privacy challenges.

Crimes are also classified as felonies, misdemeanors, and treason. According to most authorities, crimes punishable by death or imprisonment in a state prison are felonies, while crimes not amounting to felonies are classified as misdemeanors. Each crime's definition includes a prohibited action (the *actus reus*) and the requisite state of mind (*mens rea*).

Law is dynamic and changes depending on public opinion and shifting public morals. On any given day, one could identify numerous legal issues in the daily newspaper or from an analysis of current events. Without law, there would be no crime.

REVIEW QUESTIONS

1. What is the purpose of law? What three types of harms does law protect us from?

2. Distinguish between criminal and civil law.

3. What is a paradigm? Describe the three paradigms of law.

4. Distinguish between common law and statutory law.

5. What are the most common constitutional challenges? Describe them.

6. When can government define private behavior as criminal without violating freedom of speech, association, or religion?

7. Distinguish felonies, misdemeanors, and treason.

8. What are the two elements of a crime? When does a failure to act constitute the *actus reus* of a crime?

9. What are the four different criminal states of mind?

10. Describe some current legal issues in your state.

VOCABULARY

actus reus – the specific prohibited act (or omission) that constitutes a crime

Bill of Rights – the first 10 amendments to the Constitution

civil law – the branch of law that seeks to resolve differences between individuals and repair damages or compensate victims

common law – early case law of England

conflict paradigm – views society as being made up of competing and conflicting interests

consensus paradigm – views society as a community consisting of like-minded individuals who agree on what is a crime

crime – an act committed or omitted in violation of public law, either forbidding or commanding it

criminal law – the branch or division of law that defines crimes and provides for their punishment

due process – the procedures designed to protect against error in the governmental deprivation of life, liberty, and property

ex post facto laws – laws that punish behavior after the fact

felonies – crimes punishable by death or by imprisonment in a state prison or penitentiary

mala in se – behavior that is intrinsically wrong

mala prohibita – behavior that is prohibited in certain societies but not inherently wrong

mens rea – criminal state of mind (purposive, knowing, reckless, negligent)

miscegenation laws – laws that made it a crime to marry someone of a different race

misdemeanors – offenses for which the punishment is other than death or imprisonment in a state prison

Model Penal Code – created by the American Law Institute, it is a guide or model code but does not have any legal authority

natural law – refers to the belief that some law is inherent in the natural world and can be discovered by reason

paradigm – a fundamental perspective of a subject matter

paternalistic laws – laws that protect us against our own behavior, i.e., seat belt laws

pluralist paradigm – view that society is made up of many competing interests that ultimately control the definition of laws

police power – the authority to enact and enforce legislation to protect the health, welfare, morals, and safety of the people of the state

social contract – a concept originating with Thomas Hobbes and John Locke in the age of the Enlightenment that describes how individuals give up certain liberties in return for being protected by society

torts – personal wrongs

transferred intent – "bad aim" intent; the intent is transferred from what the perpetrator meant to do to what he actually did do

FOR FURTHER READING

Hemmens, Craig (2007). *Current Legal Issues in Criminal Justice*. Los Angeles, CA: Roxbury Press.

Kanovitz, Jacqueline and Michael Kanovitz (2005). *Constitutional Law*, Tenth Edition Newark, NJ: LexisNexis/Matthew Bender.

Klotter, John and Joycelyn Pollock (2007). *Criminal Law*, Eighth Edition. Newark, NJ: LexisNexis/Matthew Bender.

[1] Mackie, J. (1977). *Ethics: Inventing Right and Wrong*. New York: Penguin, p. 232.

[2] Blackstone, W. (1769). *Commentaries*. Volume 4, p. 15, as cited in Klotter, J. & J. Pollock (2007), Criminal Law. Newark, NJ: LexisNexis/Matthew Bender.

[3] Klotter, J. & J. Pollock (2007). *Criminal Law*. Newark, NJ: LexisNexis/Matthew Bender, p. 3.

[4] 106 S. Ct. 2841 (1986).

[5] 539 U.S. 558 (2003).

[6] Rich, R. (1978). *Essays on the Theory and Practice of Criminal Justice*. Washington, DC: University Press, p. 1.

[7] Durkheim, E. (1969). "Types of Law in Relation to Types of Social Solidarity." In V. Aubert (ed.), *Sociology of Law*, p. 17-29, p. 21. London: Penguin Press.

[8] Sheley, J. (1985). *Exploring Crime*. Belmont, CA: Wadsworth, p. 1. Quinney, R. 1974. *Critique of the Legal Order*. New York: Little, Brown, p. 15–16.

[9] *Keeler v. Superior Court*, 470 P.2d 617 (Cal. 1970).

[10] 119 S. Ct. 1849 (1999).

[11] *Loving v. Virginia*, 388 U.S. 1 (1967).

[12] 450 U.S. 464 (1981).

[13] U.S. Const. Art. I, §§ 9 and 10, Cl. 1.

[14] *United States v. Abbington*, 144 F.3d 1003 (6th Cir. 1998); *Myers v. Ridge*, 712 A.2d 791 (Pa. 1998).

[15] *City of Houston v. Hill*, 482 U.S. 451 (1987).

[16] 491 U.S. 397 (1989).

[17] 381 U.S. 479 (1965).

[18] See Anonymous (2001). "Caring for Our Parents in an Aging World: Sharing Public and Private Responsibility for the Elderly," *N.Y.U. Journal of Legislative and Public Policy* 5: 563-595.

[19] 410 U.S. 113, 93 S. Ct. 705, 35 L. Ed. 147 (1973).

[20] 550 U.S. _____ (2007).

Chapter 8

Courts in America

What You Need to Know

★ Each state generally has trial courts, intermediate appellate courts, and a supreme or highest court.

★ Trial courts are separated into courts of general jurisdiction and courts of limited jurisdiction. Courts of general jurisdiction may include special courts such as community courts, domestic violence courts, or drug courts.

★ Appeals allege legal errors in the proceedings leading to conviction.

★ Appeals may end up in the federal court system when there is a federal constitutional issue at stake.

★ Defense attorneys for indigents are provided through a public defender system, an appointment system, or by contract attorneys.

★ Judges may be either elected officials or appointed. The Missouri Plan, or some version of it, is the most common method of appointment.

★ The Federal System also has trial courts (Federal District Courts), appellate courts (Circuit or Courts of Appeals) and a court of last resort (Supreme Court).

★ The Supreme Court hears only a small fraction of the cases that are appealed to it. When they choose to hear a case, they issue a writ of certiorari.

1. COURT SYSTEMS

There are 50 states and 50 different court systems in this country (not to mention Puerto Rico and the federal court system!). Generally, each state has trial courts, intermediate appellate courts, and a supreme court or court of last resort that hears final appeals. Trial courts can be further separated into courts of general jurisdiction and courts of limited jurisdiction. Box 8.1 shows the basic outline of the court systems in most states.

The names of each level of the court system can vary considerably from state to state. "Supreme" may refer to the court of last resort, or, in some states, this term refers to trial courts. "Circuits" may refer to the intermediate appellate courts or the trial courts. That is why it is best to become familiar simply with the general categories of:

★ Trial Courts (Limited Jurisdiction and General Jurisdiction),

★ Intermediate Appellate Courts, and

★ Courts of Last Resort.

BOX 8.1

State Court Systems

COURT OF LAST RESORT

⬆

INTERMEDIATE APPELLATE COURT(S)

⬆

TRIAL COURTS (GENERAL JURISDICTION)
Specialized caseload courts, i.e., Drug, Juvenile, Family

⬆

TRIAL COURTS (LIMITED JURISDICTION)
Municipal, Justice of the Peace, Traffic

General jurisdiction courts are the courtrooms of television and movies, and they are what most people think of when they think of courts. These courts typically try felonies and have the power to sentence to state prison. General jurisdiction courts also try civil cases, although the courts are usually divided, so that there are Civil Trial Courts and Criminal Trial Courts. These general jurisdiction courts may be called district courts, superior courts, or some other name.

Courts of limited jurisdiction can be found in all but six states.[1] Their jurisdiction is limited to specific types of cases. For instance, municipal courts may only adjudicate city ordinances and misdemeanors. There may be special traffic courts that only hear traffic violations up to a certain level of seriousness. Justices of the peace exist in some states and may hear minor misdemeanors and ordinance violations as well as civil cases. The judges/magistrates in such courts may also hold first appearances and arraignments for felony cases. Civil cases are usually limited to low-dollar claims (Small Claims Courts). The powers of such courts are set by legislation, and their jurisdiction may be limited to a county, part of a county, city, or municipality.

1.1 Specialized Courts

Juvenile and/or Family Courts may exist in your state and are typically courts of general jurisdiction, only with a specialized caseload. Probate courts (handling matters of estates and wills) may also exist in your state. In states without such specialized courts, such cases are heard in regular trial courts (courts of general jurisdiction). There are also a growing number of **community courts**, which may be courts of limited jurisdiction, but more often are courts of general jurisdiction, meaning that they may handle up to and including felony criminal matters. The focus of such courts tends to be on juvenile and minor criminal cases. These courts are part of the **restorative justice** movement and the defining feature of this type of court is a focus is "problem solving." The goal of the restorative justice approach is to resolve each situation by meeting the needs of victims and offenders alike.[2] Restorative justice models are not interested simply in assessing guilt or innocence and determining punishment—the goal is to address underlying issues that might have led to the offense and also to make sure the victim is "made whole" again and fully recovered from the offense. Community courts fit well with community policing because both are interested in strengthening the community's ability to respond to such problems as delinquency and crime. Typically, community courts use alternative sentencing models to achieve the restorative justice goals.

Relatively new to the scene are **drug courts**, which are typically courts of general jurisdiction, but with a specialized caseload of drug cases. Drug offenses form a huge portion of the workload of criminal courts. What is also true, it seems, is that drug offenders are repeat customers of the justice system, returning again and again on probation revocations. By 2000, more than 400

drug courts were established in most of the 50 states. The judges in these alternative courts identify first-time drug offenders, sentence them to drug testing
and treatment programs, and then monitor the offender's progress through the
program. If the offender successfully completes the program, he or she may be
diverted from incarceration and their conviction may also be erased.[3] In other
jurisdictions, offenders may be sentenced to regular probation, but they receive
specialized prosecution and monitoring.

Drug courts have undergone dramatic growth since the first one was developed in Dade County, Florida, in 1989. They are described as an outgrowth of
community-based justice programs and the system's response to the criticism that
our nation's prisons and jails are filled with non-violent drug users who need treatment, not punishment.[4] One of the distinguishing characteristics of drug courts is
that the judge stays involved with the offender through the period of supervision,
which usually includes drug treatment. The major goal of drug courts is to break
the cycle of drug use rather than simply administer punishment.

Some studies have shown that offenders who go through drug courts are
more likely to complete drug treatment programs and have lower recidivism
rates than offenders who are sentenced through regular court processes.[5] However, at this point, the research is mixed, with just as many evaluations showing
no difference as those that find that drug courts reduce recidivism, as compared to regular court processing.[6] In a study of a Cincinnati drug court, researchers found that drug court participants were more likely to get probation
than a comparison group, and the comparison group was more likely to receive
intensive supervision probation.[7] While there was no difference in drug arrests
between the drug court participants and the control group (30.8 percent versus
37.4 percent were rearrested), there was a significant difference in theft/prop-
erty arrests (18.4 percent versus 31.7 percent).[8]

Another study looked at whether biweekly review sessions with the judge
had an effect on recidivism. In some drug courts, there is minimal interaction
between the offender and the judge, but this study looked at a program where
the judge met much more frequently with the offenders. The findings indicated
that biweekly hearings reduced recidivism among high-risk offenders, but not
low-risk offenders.[9]

In one review of several drug court evaluations, the authors concluded that
effectiveness would be increased if the courts:

★   used objective risk and need instruments,

★   used behavioral and cognitive treatment strategies,

★   made sure the level of treatment was matched to the offender

★   provided aftercare, and

★   maintained quality control over treatment options.[10]

In the same way that drug courts siphon away drug offenders for specialized
prosecution and seek to break the cycle of drug addiction, domestic violence

courts have been created to do the same thing with domestic violence offenders. Domestic violence refers to assaults that occur between intimates, either in a spousal (husband-wife), familial (parent/caregiver-child/dependent), or intimate (boyfriend-girlfriend or same-sex partners) relationship.

These courts have developed because of the growing awareness of the problem of domestic violence and the system's reaction to it. Mandatory arrest policies, for instance, have led to an increase in prosecutions for domestic assaulters, taxing the courts and filling jails and prisons with offenders. The impetus for domestic violence courts came from the Violence Against Women Act, which created federal funding for the implementation of the courts. Domestic violence courts increase coordination among the courts, police, and social service agencies, and adopt a "therapeutic approach" to justice.[11] In 1998, there were more than 300 domestic violence courts or specialized processes for handling domestic violence cases across the country.[12] The concept of a specialized court recognizes the unique interpersonal issues involved in domestic violence and emphasizes treatment for the batterer and services for the victim. These courts employ both sanctions (punishment) and services for greater effect.

In the few studies that have been undertaken, domestic violence courts were found to reduce recidivism over traditional court processing. In one study, recidivism in the domestic violence court sample was six percent compared to a control sample of 14 percent.[13] On the other hand, another study showed that the creation of a domestic violence court increased the number of arrests for domestic violence. This was explained as the result of law enforcement becoming sensitized to the issue, as well as being more likely to arrest, knowing that the domestic violence court was available as a resource. The study also found that participants in the domestic violence court were significantly less likely to recidivate than those who went through traditional court processing. The conclusion of the study described above was that a "coordinated community response" to domestic violence, involving the police, courts, and social services, reduces recidivism.[14]

1.2 Jurisdiction

Courts have subject matter jurisdiction and geographic jurisdiction. **Subject matter jurisdiction** refers to the type of case that can be heard in each type of court; this is defined by legislation. Courts must also have **geographic jurisdiction** over the case. In criminal cases, this means that the crime must have taken place in the court's geographic jurisdiction. If the prosecutor does not prove this essential fact, the defendant must be acquitted. In California and many other states, the geographic boundary for each court is the county; however, in some states, a district or circuit may encompass more than one county.[15] In larger jurisdictions, there may be many judges, each with their own courtroom, for that jurisdiction. Each of the courts receives incoming cases on a random or rotating basis.

1.3 State Trial Courts

Trial courts may not bear much resemblance to television courtroom dramas on a day-to-day basis. If one were to enter a trial court in most states, it would be easy to identify the judge, the prosecutor(s), and perhaps the defense attorney(s). One could also identify the bailiff, who may be either a sheriff's deputy or a court employee. Typically, there is also a court administrator who handles the non-judicial aspects of the court, including scheduling and caseload processing. The court clerk handles legal filing of court orders, may collect court fees, and schedules the trial docket. In larger jurisdictions where there are many judges, one of the trial judges also serves as a presiding or administrative judge and handles the managerial and budgetary aspects of the court system in that jurisdiction.

What may surprise a person who visits one of these courtrooms is the amount of time when "nothing is happening." Of course, something may be happening, but it is not recognizable as a trial. The judge may be meeting in chambers with attorneys, or conducting a pretrial motion hearing to determine if certain evidence should be allowed. Other activities that take place in trial courts are first appearances, preliminary hearings, and arraignments. You might, for instance, see a large number of individuals marched in, wearing jail uniforms, for the judge to arraign. Judges may also "take pleas," meaning that the defendant, his or her attorney, and prosecutor stand before the judge and submit the documentation of a plea bargain. This affidavit includes a confession and the prosecutor's recommendation for sentencing and serves as the sole evidence supporting the conviction. In busy courtrooms, defense attorneys may be conducting business in the back of the courtroom, or going inside "the bar" (the area in front of the defense and prosecutor's tables) to talk to the court clerk about court orders or other business. This may be happening even while the judge is on the bench and involved in a proceeding. Some judges run a very formal courtroom, but others have more relaxed rules.

The combined state and federal trial courts convict hundreds of thousands of offenders each year. In 2002, more than one million adults were convicted of a felony in state trial courts, and 69 percent were sentenced to jail or prison.[16] There is a tremendous variation between judges, however, in how many trials are conducted each year, even within the same jurisdiction. While some judges may clear up to a dozen cases off their **docket** (cases assigned to their court) each month, others take a more leisurely pace.

Many states now allow cameras and audio equipment in the courtroom, but jury deliberations continue to be held in private. Despite the presence of cameras and news footage, most people's perception of what happens in a courtroom is derived from the countless television shows and movies that find courtroom drama so compelling.

1.4 Appellate Courts

As you know, defendants who are convicted may appeal only if there has been some error in the proceedings. In some states, there are several intermediate courts of appeal, distributed geographically across the state. While the court of last resort in any state is usually a very old institution, probably dating back to the beginning of statehood and the state constitution, intermediate appellate courts are more recent additions and serve to reduce the highest court's caseload. About 40 states have these intermediate courts.[17] California has the largest number of intermediate courts, divided into nine divisions with more than 100 judges. Most of the time cases are heard by a panel of three judges, rather than the total number of judges in each division.

The highest court in the state, or court of last resort, is often called the state supreme court. Texas and Oklahoma are the only two states that split their court of last resort into two courts, one that hears criminal appeals (Court of Criminal Appeals), and one that hears civil appeals (Supreme Court).[18] In most states, there are seven justices that sit on the court of last resort (28 states), although some states have nine (five states), and others only five (16 states).[19]

A good rule of thumb is that trial courts decide upon facts, and appellate courts rule on points of law. However, this is not completely accurate because trial courts also make rulings on interpretations of law. The most important thing to remember is that an appeal can only be filed because of an error of law. Appellate courts never retry facts. Thus, the guilt or innocence of a defendant is never the issue, only whether there was some legal procedural error, or violation of a state or federal constitutional right, during the proceedings. Further, even when an error exists, an appellate court may rule that it is "harmless" and did not affect the outcome of the case.

In most states, the intermediate appellate court must review all appeals filed from trial courts (at least in criminal cases). That does not necessarily mean that there is any type of hearing. The court may review the appellate brief and find it is without merit and deny a full hearing. If an intermediate appellate court denies review or an appellant loses their appeal at this level, they can appeal to the court of last resort. In many states, the court of last resort has discretion to review or not review the many appeals filed. In these situations, appeals are reviewed by panels of the full court and there must be a certain number of justices who vote to hear the case before it receives attention from the full court. Capital cases, however, carry a mandatory appeal and review process.

When an intermediate appellate or court of last resort hears an appeal, oral arguments will be scheduled. In these proceedings, the petitioner's attorney (the one who filed the appeal) and the respondent's attorney (typically the state is the respondent) will present their arguments to the appellate judges and answer questions from them. There are no witnesses or evidence presented because the only issues are points of law.

When a petitioner loses in a court of last resort, there is a possibility that he or she may file a further appeal in the federal court system. This is the case if there is a federal constitutional issue that the state's ruling has not addressed or ruled against. Petitioners must exhaust all state remedies before turning to federal courts. After exhausting state appeals, the appellate attorney may begin again by filing the appeal in federal court. The ultimate court of last resort, of course, is the Supreme Court. Box 8.2 illustrates one state's court system.

BOX 8.2

Florida Court Structure

Florida
(Court structure as of Fiscal Year 2007)

Supreme Court   COLR
7 justices sit en banc   A

CPS Case Types:
★ Mandatory jurisdiction in civil, capital criminal, criminal administrative agency, juvenile, disciplinary, advisory opinion cases.
★ Discretionary jurisdiction in civil, noncapital criminal, administrative agency, juvenile, advisory opinion, original proceeding, interlocutory decision cases.

District Court of Appeals (5 courts)   IAC
62 judges sit in 3-judge panels   A

CPS Case Types:
★ Mandatory jurisdiction in civil, noncapital criminal, administrative agency, juvenile, original proceeding, interlocutory decision cases..
★ Discretionary jurisdiction in civil, noncapital criminal, juvenile, original proceeding, interlocutory decision cases.

Circuit Court (20 circuits)   GJC
599 judges
Jury trials except in appeals

CPS Case Types:
★ Tort, contract, real property ($15,001 – no maximum), miscellaneous civil. Exclusive mental health, probate/estate, civil appeals
★ Exclusive domestic relations.
★ Exclusive felony, criminal appeals.
★ Juvenile.

County Court (67 counties)   LJC
322 judges

CPS Case Types:
★ Tort contract, real property ($5,001 - $15,000), miscellaneous civil. Exclusive small claims (up to $5,000).
★ Exclusive misdemeanor. Preliminary hearings.
★ Exclusive traffic/other violations, except parking (which is handled administratively).

COLR = Court of Last Resort   LJC = Limited Jurisdiction Court   ☐ = Appellate Level
IAC = Intermediate Appellate Court   A = Appeal from Admin. Agency   ☐ = Trial Level
GJC = General Jurisdiction Court   → = Route of Appeal

Source: National Center for State Courts Web site. http://www.ncsconline.org/D_Research/Ct_Struct/state_inc.asp?STATE=FL. Accessed January 2, 2008.

One other thing to note is that there are also tribal courts in many states that are independent of the state in which they reside. These courts adjudicate offenses that take place on Indian reservations and/or that involve members of the tribe. The following is a list of the only states that do not have formally recognized tribes and tribal courts: Arkansas, Delaware, Georgia, Hawaii, Illinois, Indiana, Kentucky, Maryland, Missouri, New Hampshire, New Jersey, Ohio, Pennsylvania, Tennessee, Vermont, Virginia, and West Virginia.

★ Exercise: In the State of . . .

1. Go to **http://www.ojp.usdoj.gov/bjs/pub/pdf/sco04.pdf**
   This is a report titled State Court Organization 2004 by the Bureau of Justice Statistics.

2. Find your state's page in the state-by-state section. Describe your state's court structure.

3. What is the trial court called? How many trial courts are there? How many appellate judges are there in your state? What is the court of last resort called?

4. Another source that provides similar information is: **http://www.ncsconline. org/D_Research/Ct_Struct/Index.html.**

---

2. PROSECUTORS

A district attorney (prosecutor) is usually an elected official (except in Alaska, Connecticut, the District of Columbia, and New Jersey).[20] In all but the smallest jurisdictions, there are also assistant prosecutors who also try cases but are hired, and not elected. In larger jurisdictions, they may number in the hundreds, and the elected district attorney never actually prosecutes a case, but, rather, acts as the policy director and CEO of the office.

There are about 2,344 state court prosecutors' offices, employing 78,000 attorneys, investigators, and support staff. This does not include county or city prosecutors who prosecute in courts of limited jurisdiction. Our conception of prosecutors' offices is probably shaped by television and movies, which tends to portray large jurisdictions such as New York City and Los Angeles. In reality, most offices are quite small. In 2005, most prosecutors' offices nationwide employed 10 or fewer people. In some offices, prosecutors served on a part-time basis, maintaining their own private law practice as well. Most prosecutors' offices receive both state and county funding.[21] Box 8.3 provides some information on prosecutors' offices.

In very rare cases, special prosecutors are appointed by the governor or attorney general when it is believed that a local prosecutor has a conflict of interest or the prosecution involves a case that crosses jurisdictional lines. Such special prosecutors can also be found at the federal level. (You may recall that one special prosecutor was U.S. Attorney Patrick Fitzgerald, who prosecuted and obtained a conviction against I. Lewis "Scooter" Libby for lying in the congressional investigation into the exposure of Valerie Plame as a CIA agent.

BOX 8.3

State Court Prosecutors' Offices, 2005

	Full-Time Offices (Population Served)				Part-time offices
	All offices	1,000,000 or more	250,000 to 999,999	Under 250,000	
Number of Offices	2,344	42	213	1,515	574
Median: 2004 population served	36,515	1,475,488	449,685	42,263	12,764
Total staff size	9	419	105	10	3
Salary of chief prosecutor	$85,000	$149,000	$125,000	$95,000	$42,000
Budget for prosecution	$354,755	$33,231,705	$6,034,575	$388,544	$132,586

Source: Rottman, D. and S. Strickland (2006). *State Court Organization.* Washington, DC: Bureau of Justice Statistics.

In some larger jurisdictions, the prosecutor's office is divided into divisions. The most common divisions are the misdemeanor division and the felony division. There may also be specialized caseloads, such as sexual assault or domestic violence caseloads. Prosecutors may be attached to a specific court and always appear before the same judge in the same courtroom, following a case from first appearance through sentencing. Alternatively, prosecutors may be assigned different stages of the process, so that they may deal with only preliminary hearings or only first appearances and pass the case on to those who specialize in litigation for the trial portion.

Prosecutors in the smallest towns may have a part-time law practice as well. There may be conflicts of interest when the duty to prosecute an alleged offender conflicts with the prosecutor's duty to clients or social and business contacts. The role of a part-time prosecutor in a small town is very different from the district attorneys in large cities like New York, Chicago, or Houston, which have hundreds of assistant prosecutors.

The role of any prosecutor is quite different from that of the defense attorney. While the defense attorney's role is to protect the rights of the accused, the prosecutor has the ethical duty to "seek justice"; and this does not necessarily translate into "get a conviction." Prosecutors must balance office resources, the relative seriousness of the crime, and the desires/needs of the victim and community when making decisions about whether and how to prosecute. Not all cases that begin with arrest are prosecuted. In fact, prosecutors drop many cases without prosecution and this decision-making ability is one of the least studied areas of the criminal justice system.

Why would a prosecutor choose not to pursue prosecution? In most cases, it is because he or she believes there is not enough evidence to obtain a conviction. In other cases, evidence may be present, but the offense is considered not very serious and there is no public pressure for prosecution. The prosecutor has legal discretion to prosecute or not. It is important to remember that not all crimes are always prosecuted "to the fullest extent of the law."

Prosecutors do not typically make as much money as attorneys in private civil practice; their salaries are closer to those of criminal defense attorneys. The largest prosecutors' offices often have graduates of the finest law schools willing to be hired for much less than they might earn in private practice because of the opportunity to practice their litigation skills. An assistant prosecutor in a city such as Houston, New York, or Chicago may try more cases in a year than an average civil attorney tries in a lifetime. The career path of prosecutors is often to spend several years in the prosecutor's office, then use the skills developed there in a lucrative private litigation practice. Some prosecutors go on to political careers, such as Rudolph Giuliani, a presidential contender in the 2008 election.

Republican presidential hopeful, former New York City Mayor Rudy Giuliani, left, listens as Republican presidential hopeful, former Sen. Fred Thompson, R-Tenn., speaks during a Republican debate Wednesday, Nov. 28, 2007 at the Mahaffey Theater in St. Petersburg, FL. While only Fred Thompson portrayed a prosecutor on television, both Thompson and Giuliani have served as prosecutors in real life.

AP Photo/Chris O'Meara

3. DEFENSE ATTORNEYS

Defense attorneys are favorite characters for television and movie script writers. They are portrayed as tireless crusaders for the downtrodden or sleazy "hacks" willing to do anything to help their clients avoid their just punishment. The reality, of course, resembles neither of these two extremes. Defense attorneys, for the most part, help the system work by helping individual defendants navigate the complex and confusing world of the justice system. Clients are more likely to receive due process because of defense attorneys.

Most defense attorneys are not superstars who appear in the newspaper frequently, although there are a few of these celebrities, such as Alan Dershowitz, who is also a professor at Harvard Law School. Defense attorneys tend to be on the lower rungs of earning ladders for graduates of law schools. Criminal law is not a favored specialty of lawyers; less than 10 percent of all lawyers have a full-time criminal practice. Most attorneys who do take criminal cases also carry a general law practice.

The Supreme Court holding in *Gideon v. Wainwright* (1963)[22] recognized a Sixth Amendment right to an attorney when a defendant was facing a felony conviction, and later, in *Argersinger v. Hamlin* (1972),[23] the Court held that all indigent offenders facing incarceration had a Sixth Amendment right to counsel (an attorney). This requirement meant that states needed to develop ways of providing defense counsel to all defendants facing jail or prison. The two most common ways are appointed counsel systems and public defender offices.

Appointed counsel systems occur when each trial court judge (or the jurisdiction as a whole) holds a list of those attorneys approved to be appointed to indigent defendants. Assignments are given on a rotating or other basis. Attorneys get on this list by volunteering, or in fewer cases, all attorneys in the jurisdiction are on the list. These attorneys are in private practice and have private clients as well as court appointments.

In public defender systems, the defense attorneys are full-time employees of a public defender office. They may be either county or state employees, or employees of a private non-profit agency that holds a contract from the state for indigent defense. Public defender systems are more common in urban areas, while appointed counsel systems are more common in suburban and rural areas.

A third form of indigent defense is the contract attorney model. This is similar to the appointed counsel model, except that, instead of distributing cases to all the attorneys on a list, one or two attorneys take all of the indigent cases for a set contract amount. These attorneys may or may not also have a separate private practice, depending on how many cases are part of the indigent caseload. This model has proven to be attractive to some jurisdictions because it may be less expensive than the appointed counsel model and is useful in jurisdictions that do not have enough indigent cases to justify a public defender office.

The general thought is that individuals who are defended by a public defender or appointed counsel do not receive the same quality of legal assistance as those who are able to hire their own private attorneys. While the findings of researchers are mixed, it seems to be the case that indigents are more likely to receive a sentence to jail or prison and are more likely to plead guilty when they have counsel provided to them, but they receive shorter terms than those with privately retained attorneys.[24]

More recent research indicates that, at least in the federal system, appointed attorneys perform considerably worse than public defenders. They

FOCUS ON ETHICS

You are a recently graduated attorney and feel very lucky to have been hired as one of three contract attorneys for the district court in your hometown. While you didn't necessarily think you would ever work as a criminal defense attorney, you know that the experience in the courtroom will be very valuable when you move on and start a practice of your own. One of the indigent defendants assigned to your caseload is a guy who has already had two prison terms. He is being prosecuted for "indecency with a child." After interviewing him and reading the police reports, you believe that there are some problems with the prosecution's case. For one thing, the child belonged to the defendant's ex-girlfriend and witnesses are available that will testify that she said she was going to "get even" with him for their break-up. Furthermore, it appears that he was held and questioned by the police without being informed of his *Miranda* warnings. Obviously, as a two-time convict, he knew his rights, but it was possible that this fact alone might be enough to exclude his comments made to police about when he was alone with the child. On the other hand, you don't necessarily believe that he didn't do it, especially because of his history. Also, the judge has indicated that he wants the guy to go away for a long time. In effect, the judge let you know that he doesn't want you to put up a strong defense that might stand in the way of a conviction. What should you do?

evidently bill for more hours per case, are less qualified, and achieve worse results for their clients. They cost the public, in the aggregate, about $61 million more than if public defenders had taken the cases. Suggested reasons for the difference between appointed attorneys and public defenders are that public defenders have more experience in criminal law and have a better relationship with prosecutors.[25]

Defendants also have the right to defend themselves. A **pro se defense** is when the defendant chooses to defend himself (or herself). This is very rare, and often the judge will insist that an attorney sit with the defendant to provide legal advice anyway. Judges must balance the right of the individual to use a pro se defense and the need for competent counsel, if for no other reason than to forestall an appeal based on incompetent counsel.

4. JUDGES

As described above, judges may be either trial judges in courts of general jurisdiction or courts of limited jurisdiction, or they may be appellate judges in intermediate courts or the court of last resort in the state (the state supreme court). In this court, they might be called justices instead of judges.

Judges may be either elected or appointed. They typically serve fixed terms, although in a few states their terms are for life or at least until retirement age. The **Missouri Plan** is a method of appointing judges that substitutes a nominating process by state-wide (for appellate) and local (for trial judges) nominating committees. These committees send the nominees' names to the governor, who makes the appointment. The appointee then faces an election after one year, running against his or her own record. While 37 states use some form of nomination process, the remaining states still use general elections. In some of those states, the elections are partisan (with judges running as Democratic, Republican or Independent), and in others the elections are non-partisan.

Typically, the constitution and statutes of a state specify residency, age, and legal credentials as requirements to serve as a judge. Many states require judges to receive continuing legal education beyond that necessary for all lawyers in the state. Nineteen states have formal procedures for evaluating the performance of judges.

4.1 Trial Judges

Trial judges may preside over courts of general jurisdiction or limited jurisdiction. They may be family court judges, juvenile judges, criminal judges, or civil judges or, in other jurisdictions, they may try all these kinds of cases in the same courtroom. Judges of limited jurisdiction (county courts, municipal courts, justices of the peace) may sit only part time. Some of these magistrates may not even need to be lawyers to hold the judicial position (although this is rare). Some jurisdictions may occasionally hire retired judges to help with overloaded dockets.

As mentioned before, judges may be elected or appointed. About a third of all state trial judges receive their position through a general non-partisan election (33.3 percent). Roughly another third (31.4 percent) are chosen through some form of merit selection process (such as the Missouri Plan). Another 17.6 percent are elected through partisan elections. The rest obtain their judgeships through legislative appointments, gubernatorial selection, or other means.[26]

Trial judges are basically like umpires in the justice process. They make decisions on rules of evidence and procedure. If a defendant decides to plead guilty (as the vast majority of defendants do), the judge must ensure that the confession is voluntary and that there is other evidence, in addition to the confession, upon which to convict the defendant. The judge, in these cases, must decide whether to agree with the prosecutor's recommendation for sentencing. Most pleas come after a **plea bargain** in which the defendant agrees to plead guilty in return for a favorable sentencing recommendation.

In cases that go to trial, the defendant may choose to have a **bench trial**, which means that there is no jury and the case is tried solely to the judge. The judge not only ensures that rules are followed, but also determines guilt or innocence in these trials. Most felony trials, however, include a jury. Judges carry great weight with the jury and jurors may be influenced by any obvious bias the judge displays toward either the defense or the prosecution. The ideal of a judge is someone who is neutral and objective and makes decisions based on law, rather than favoritism.

The judge may be called upon to rule on any pretrial motions, such as a motion for a **change of venue**, which is a request that the case be moved because the defendant would not get a fair trial in the local jurisdiction. Another pretrial motion would be a motion to exclude evidence, typically based on the allegation that the police violated one or more of the offender's rights in obtaining such evidence. Another pretrial motion is a **motion in limine**, which is a motion to bar the mention of something that might be prejudicial during the trial, but has no bearing on guilt or innocence in the case, such as a prior prison term. It may be the case that one of the attorneys files a motion for **recusal**, asking the judge to step out of the case and assign it to another judge because he or she has a conflict of interest or cannot make an objective decision about the case. Interestingly, it is the judge who gets to rule on his or her own bias in this hearing, although if the attorney loses the motion, and the defendant is convicted, the decision may be appealed.

During the trial, judges rule on objections, based on rules of procedure in that jurisdiction. Some of the more common objections made during a trial are that the evidence does not have a proper foundation (meaning that the attorney has not obtained, through questioning witnesses, the proper level of proof that the item is what it is purported to be), that the question asks something that is irrelevant or prejudicial, or that the attorney was "leading" the witness (meaning that they were answering the question or suggesting the answer to the witness).

Although the jury determines guilt or innocence, the judge does have the power to throw out a guilty verdict if he or she finds that there is not sufficient evidence to support a judgment of guilt, as a matter of law. If a guilty verdict occurs, the judge may also be obliged to sentence the offender, although in some states juries have this function. Judges (or juries) must sentence within the statutory guidelines for sentencing.

If an offender is sentenced to probation, the judge maintains control over the defendant. Probation officers periodically submit progress reports to the court. The sentencing judge will ultimately be the one to close the case, either by revoking probation and sending the person to prison, by agreeing to an early release, or by recognizing that the offender has served the full term of probation.

4.2 Appellate Judges

There are about 1,335 appellate judges in the country. Their terms range from four to 16 years, but Rhode Island judges have a term for life, and judges in Massachusetts and Puerto Rico have terms that last until age 70 (the mandatory retirement age).[27]

Appellate judges may not be as newsworthy as their brethren in trial courts, but their decisions are, in some ways, much more powerful. Appellate courts overturn trial verdicts when they recognize errors of law and/or constitutional violations. Much of their caseload consists of civil appeals, but they also hear criminal appeals. One of the issues, in fact, when appointing or electing a judge, is whether or not they have any experience in civil and/or criminal law. While civil procedure and criminal procedure rules have many similarities, there are differences and, thus, a civil judge who aspires to become an appellate judge may have had no experience trying or judging criminal law cases, or vice versa.

Typically, appeals are heard by three-judge panels, and, if the three-judge panel denies relief, the petitioner may appeal to have the case heard **en banc**, meaning with the full number of appellate judges, or, in a state with more than one appellate jurisdiction, with all of the justices in that jurisdiction. It is typically from the ranks of state appellate judges that federal justices are selected.

5. THE FEDERAL SYSTEM

The discussion up to this point has been a description of state court systems, but there is also a parallel federal court system. Recall that federal crimes are listed in the United States Criminal Code. There are federal law enforcement agencies, such as the DEA and FBI, assigned to enforce these laws. When someone is arrested for a federal crime, they will be prosecuted in a federal court. The federal court system is similar to the state court system in that there are trial courts (Magistrates' courts and U.S. District Courts), intermediate appellate courts (Courts of Appeals), and, finally, the court of last resort, the Supreme Court.

The United States military has its own judicial system. Each of the branches of the military has their own Court of Military Review. Military law is set out in the Uniform Code of Military Justice. Decisions may be appealed to the United States Court of Military Appeals and, ultimately, to the Supreme Court. Procedures, rules of evidence, and even crimes are different in the military justice system. One of the interesting differences is that the defense and prosecutor for a case are assigned out of the same office (the Adjutant General's office).

Recently there has been a lot of controversy about the procedural justice for those held in Guantánamo Bay. The Bush administration's position is that because they are not soldiers, the Geneva Convention does not apply to them; and because they are not U.S. citizens, the procedural protections in place granting due process and access to courts does not apply either. The individuals are being adjudicated in military tribunals, with military attorneys serving as counsel and prosecutors. However, the Supreme Court has agreed to hear an appeal concerning the jurisdiction of federal courts over these prisoners and we should expect a decision sometime during the 2007 term of the Court.

The United States Attorney is the federal equivalent of a district attorney or state prosecutor. There are about 94 U.S. attorneys,[28] attached to the 94 U.S. Federal District Courts, which are the federal trial courts. There are also specialized courts that have limited jurisdiction over matters such as tax and patent law.

In 2006-2007, a controversy arose about the firing of several U.S. Attorneys that eventually led to the resignation of Attorney General Alberto Gonzales. The firings were investigated by Congress because of allegations that they were politically motivated. The Attorney General certainly has the power to fire U.S. Attorneys, and some presidential administrations have, at the beginning of their term in office, removed U.S. Attorneys as well as the Attorney General and replaced them with party loyalists. However, it is unusual to fire U.S. Attorneys for prosecutorial decisions while they are in office, because such decisions must be insulated from politics. If it appears that firings are based on their decisions to prosecute or not to prosecute friends and/or enemies of the administration, then the justice system itself is suspect.

In 2004, U.S. attorneys supervised cases against 141,212 suspects. Most cases are drug offenses (27 percent), followed by immigration offenses (26 percent). Other types of cases prosecuted in federal courts include property of-

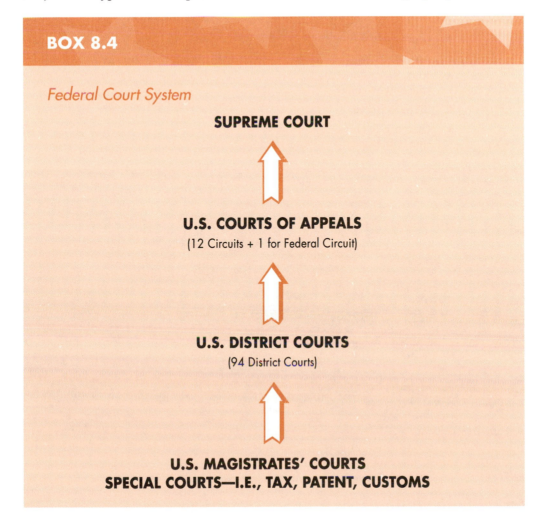

BOX 8.4

Federal Court System

SUPREME COURT

⬆

U.S. COURTS OF APPEALS
(12 Circuits + 1 for Federal Circuit)

⬆

U.S. DISTRICT COURTS
(94 District Courts)

⬆

U.S. MAGISTRATES' COURTS
SPECIAL COURTS—I.E., TAX, PATENT, CUSTOMS

fenses (18 percent), weapons offenses (10 percent), and regulatory offenses (9 percent).[29] Only about four percent were violent crimes such as murder, rape, assault, and robbery, but this is because these crimes are almost always state crimes, rather than federal crimes. About 96 percent of federal defendants submitted guilty or no-contest pleas.[30] Box 8.4 describes the federal court system.

A federal case can be appealed to the Court of Appeals. The country is divided into 12 circuits, each with its own Court of Appeals. Box 8.5 shows the circuit courts of the United States. These justices hear appeals from the Federal District Courts, as well as state cases that allege a violation of constitutional rights.

All federal judges are nominated by the President after receiving recommendations from the U.S. Senators in that jurisdiction. The nominees must go through a confirmation process by the United States Senate. Once confirmed, they may hold their position for life, unless they are impeached by Congress.

The United States Supreme Court is the highest court in the land. The nine Justices on the Supreme Court hold their position for life. The current members of the court are:

* Chief Justice John Roberts
* Samuel Alito
* Ruth Bader Ginsburg (the only woman)
* Stephen Breyer
* Clarence Thomas (the only black)

* David Hackett Souter
* Anthony Kennedy
* Antonin Scalia
* John Paul Stevens

Collection, The Supreme Court Historical Society. Photographed by Steve Petteway, Supreme Court.

Members of the Supreme Court sit for a group portrait at the Supreme Court in Washington. Seated in the front row, from left to right are: Associate Justice Anthony M. Kennedy, Associate Justice John Paul Stevens, Chief Justice of the United States John G. Roberts, Associate Justice Antonin Scalia, and Associate Justice David Souter. Standing, from left to right, in the top row, are: Associate Justice Stephen Breyer, Associate Justice Clarence Thomas, Associate Justice Ruth Bader Ginsburg, and Associate Justice Samuel Alito Jr.

BOX 8.5

Federal Judicial Circuits

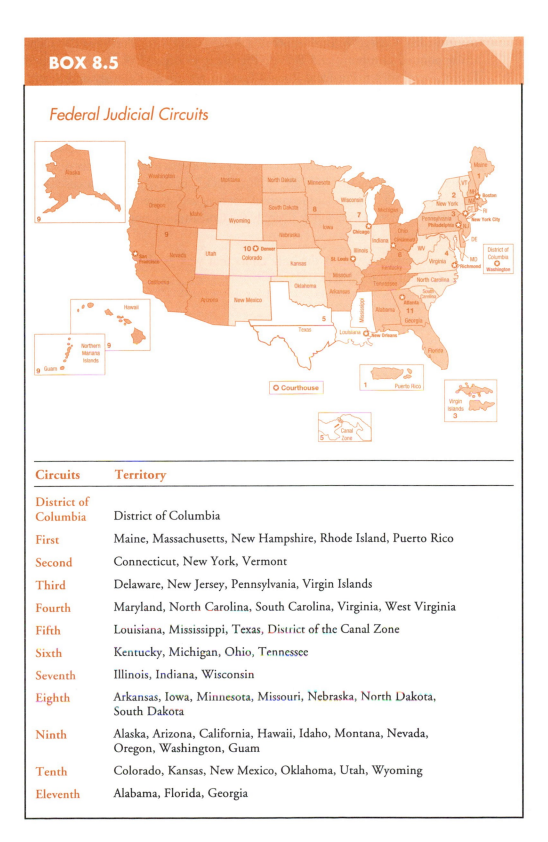

Circuits	Territory
District of Columbia	District of Columbia
First	Maine, Massachusetts, New Hampshire, Rhode Island, Puerto Rico
Second	Connecticut, New York, Vermont
Third	Delaware, New Jersey, Pennsylvania, Virgin Islands
Fourth	Maryland, North Carolina, South Carolina, Virginia, West Virginia
Fifth	Louisiana, Mississippi, Texas, District of the Canal Zone
Sixth	Kentucky, Michigan, Ohio, Tennessee
Seventh	Illinois, Indiana, Wisconsin
Eighth	Arkansas, Iowa, Minnesota, Missouri, Nebraska, North Dakota, South Dakota
Ninth	Alaska, Arizona, California, Hawaii, Idaho, Montana, Nevada, Oregon, Washington, Guam
Tenth	Colorado, Kansas, New Mexico, Oklahoma, Utah, Wyoming
Eleventh	Alabama, Florida, Georgia

President George W. Bush appointed Roberts and Alito. President Bill Clinton appointed Ginsburg, and Breyer. President George H.W. Bush appointed Thomas and Souter. President Ronald Reagan appointed Kennedy and Scalia. The longest-serving member of the Court is John Paul Stevens, appointed by President Gerald Ford. It is clear to all legal analysts that today's Supreme Court is "conservative," meaning that its decisions do not uphold attempts to "interpret" the Constitution to expand civil liberties. Recent decisions have struck down voluntary school integration and denied relief to employees alleging gender discrimination. Critics argue that they are "rolling back" the civil rights era case decisions. Proponents argue that the current court is self-correcting a judicial body that went far beyond its mandate to apply the Constitution, not rewrite it for modern sensibilities.

The Supreme Court is the only court that was established by the United States Constitution. Article II states:

The judicial Power of the United States, shall be vested in one supreme Court, and in such inferior Courts as the Congress may from time to time ordain and establish. The Judges, both of the supreme and inferior Courts, shall hold their Offices during good Behavior; and shall, at stated Times, receive for their Services a Compensation which shall not be diminished during their Continuance in Office.

Article III specifies the jurisdiction of the court.

The judicial Power shall extend to all Cases, in Law and Equity, arising under this Constitution, the Laws of the United States, and Treaties made, or which shall be made, under their Authority; — to all Cases affecting Ambassadors, other public Ministers and Consuls; — to all Cases of admiralty and maritime Jurisdiction; — to Controversies to which the United States shall be a Party; — to Controversies between two or more States; — between a State and Citizens of another State;—between Citizens of different States; — between Citizens of the same State claiming Lands under Grants of different States, and between a State, or the Citizens thereof, and foreign States, Citizens or Subjects.

Article III goes on to specify that, in some cases, the jurisdiction of the Supreme Court shall be original (meaning that the case can be brought directly), but in other cases, the jurisdiction is appellate (meaning that the Court can only hear appeals after the case has been litigated in a lower court).

In all Cases affecting Ambassadors, other public ministers and Consuls, and those in which a State shall be Party, the supreme Court shall have original Jurisdiction. In all the other Cases before mentioned, the supreme Court shall have appellate jurisdiction, both as to Law and Fact, with such Exceptions, and under such Regulations as the Congress shall make.

The Court rarely exercises original jurisdiction and almost all case decisions are those that occur when the Court issues a **writ of certiorari**, which means to bring the case forward. Because most of the cases appealed to the Supreme Court fall into the area of discretionary review, the Court does not have to hear them. When four or more justices agree to hear a case, the Court issues the writ of certiorari. Typically, the Court will only hear cases when there is a split in Federal Circuit Courts over a particular legal issue.

The Term of the Court begins on the first Monday in October and lasts until October of the next year. Approximately 8,000 petitions are filed with the Court in the course of a Term. In addition, some 1,200 applications of various kinds are filed each year that can be acted upon by a single Justice.[31] Of all these cases, the Court issues written opinions in only about a hundred or so cases.

It is important to note that only decisions of the Supreme Court are clearly and absolutely "the law of the land." In all other legal questions or issues, you cannot assume that you know the law in your state and jurisdiction unless you research case decisions in your particular jurisdiction. In textbooks, for instance, you may read cases from a court opinion from a federal circuit that does not encompass your state, or the supreme court of another state, or from a state intermediate court of appeals from a jurisdiction in your state, but one that does not include your city or town. In these cases, the holding or principle of law that is set by the court may or may not be the law in your jurisdiction. The holdings in other jurisdictions are only "persuasive," not "authoritative" when the same legal issue comes up. The Supreme Court's opinions, however, apply instantly and absolutely to all jurisdictions in the country. For this reason, these nine individuals on the court are sometimes called the most powerful people in the country.

6. CONCLUSION

In this chapter we have described the court systems of the states and federal government. State systems typically involve state trial courts of general and limited jurisdiction, intermediate appellate courts, and state courts of last resort. These last courts are the state equivalent of the U.S. Supreme Court. Specialized courts exist, such as family or juvenile court, community courts, drug courts, and domestic violence courts. District attorneys (prosecutors) are usually elected, but their assistant prosecutors are not. Most prosecutors' offices employ less than 10 people, but some large cities have hundreds of prosecutors. Judges may be elected or appointed. If appointed, typically a form of the Missouri Plan is utilized.

The federal court system operates in parallel to state systems and federal crimes (and civil matters relevant to federal laws or that cross state lines in jurisdiction) are prosecuted in these courts. There are 94 federal districts, each with their own trial court and a U.S. Attorney (and assistants) to prosecute federal crimes. Federal cases (and some state cases that allege constitutional issues) can be appealed to federal Courts of Appeals, and, ultimately, to the Supreme Court.

REVIEW QUESTIONS

1. Describe the three layers of courts in each state. Describe the two types of trial courts and give examples. *①Trial ②appellate ③supreme ・general & limited Juris.*

2. Describe three specialized courts. *Comm. drug, domestic violence*

3. Describe subject matter and geographic jurisdiction. *Type of case in type of court — crime will also*

4. How does the restorative justice approach change the traditional mission of the court system? *resolve by meeting needs of both offenders & victims "problem solving"*

5. What are the findings of the effectiveness of drug courts? *No effect*

6. When can you appeal a case? Give examples. *If there has been an error in proceedings*

7. What are the three methods for providing defense to indigents? What are the two cases that established the right to counsel for indigents? *②①appointed counsel ②public defender ③contract attorney model — Gideon v. Wainwright, Argersinger v. Hamlin 6th ← misdemeanor felony ← all offenders facing incarc. right to attor.*

8. About how many states still elect their judges? What is the Missouri Plan? *13 → appt judges subs. nominating process*

9. Describe the federal court system. *Similar to state court system → federal offenses*

10. Explain the origin and powers of the Supreme Court. *Judicial power — established by constitution.*

VOCABULARY

bench trial – a trial in which there is no jury and the case is tried solely to the judge

change of venue – motion asking that the case be moved because the defendant would not get a fair trial in the local jurisdiction

community courts – may be a court of limited or general jurisdiction and address juvenile and minor criminal cases in a more "restorative" way by trying to solve problems rather than assess guilt and punishment

courts of limited jurisdiction – handle specific and limited types of cases, such as municipal ordinances and traffic violations

docket – the cases assigned to a particular court

drug courts – are typically courts of general jurisdiction, but with a specialized caseload of drug cases

en banc – the full number of appellate judges in the jurisdiction

general jurisdiction courts – have broad subject matter jurisdiction and typically try felonies and have the power to sentence to state prison

geographic jurisdiction – the civil case or crime must have taken place within the geographic boundaries of the court's power

Missouri Plan – a method of appointing judges that substitutes a nominating process by nominating committees and appointment by the governor

motion in limine – motion asking that something not be mentioned during the trial because it would prejudice the jury

plea bargain – when the defendant agrees to plead guilty in return for a favorable sentencing recommendation

pro se defense – when the defendant chooses to defend himself or herself

recusal – when a judge steps out of a case and assigns it to another judge because he or she may be biased

restorative justice – focus is "problem solving" and involves a range of innovations in the justice system, including alternative sentencing such as restitution and the like

subject matter jurisdiction – refers to the type of case that can be heard in each type of court; this is defined by legislation

writ of certiorari – "to bring the case forward," is an order to provide the U.S. Supreme Court with the case in order for it to be heard

FOR FURTHER READING

Hancock, Barry and Paul Sharp (2004). *Criminal Justice in America: Theory, Practice and Policy*. Upper Saddle River, NJ: Prentice-Hall.

Kanovitz, Jacqueline and Michael Kanovitz (2005). *Constitutional Law*, Tenth Edition. Newark, NJ: LexisNexis/Matthew Bender.

Meyer, Jon'a and Diana Grant (2002). *The Courts in our Criminal Justice System*. Upper Saddle River, NJ: Prentice-Hall.

Neubauer, David (2007). *America's Courts and the Criminal Justice System*. Belmont, CA: ITP.

Bazemore Gordon, and Mara Schiff (2001). *Restorative Community Justice*. Cincinnati, OH: Anderson Publishing Co.

Van Ness, Daniel W., and Karen Heetderks Strong (2006). *Restoring Justice: An Introduction to Restorative Justice*, Third Edition. Newark, NJ: Lexis-Nexis/Matthew Bender.

---

[1] Rottman, D. & S. Strickland (2006). *State Court Organization*. Washington DC: Bureau of Justice Statistics, p. 4.

[2] Casey, P. & D. Rottman (2003). *Problem Solving Courts: Models and Trends*. Washington DC: National Center for State Courts.

[3] Petersilia, J. (2002). *Reforming Probation and Parole*. Lanham, MD: American Correctional Association, p. 4.

[4] Listwan, S., J. Sundt, A. Holsinger & E. Latessa (2003). "The Effect of Drug Court Programming on Recidivism: The Cincinnati Experience." *Crime & Delinquency* 49, 3: 389-411.

[5] Petersilia, J. (2002). *Reforming Probation and Parole*. Lanham, MD: American Correctional Association, p. 5

[6] Listwan, S., J. Sundt, A. Holsinger & E. Latessa (2003). "The Effect of Drug Court Programming on Recidivism: The Cincinnati Experience." *Crime & Delinquency* 49, 3: 389-411.

[7] Listwan, S., J. Sundt, A. Holsinger & E. Latessa (2003). "The Effect of Drug Court Programming on Recidivism: The Cincinnati Experience." *Crime & Delinquency* 49, 3: 389-411.

[8] Listwan, S., J. Sundt, A. Holsinger & E. Latessa (2003). "The Effect of Drug Court Programming on Recidivism: The Cincinnati Experience." *Crime & Delinquency* 49, 3: 389-411, p. 400.

[9] Marlow, D., D. Festinger, P. Lee, K. Dugosh & K. Benasutti (2006). "Matching Judicial Supervision to Clients' Risk Status in Drug Court." *Crime & Delinquency* 52, 1: 52-76.

[10] Johnson, S., D. Hubbard & E. Latessa (2000). "Drug Courts and Treatment: Lessons to be Learned from the 'What Works' Literature." *Corrections Quarterly Management* 4, 4: 70-77.

[11] Gover, A., J. MacDonald & G. Alpert (2003). "Combating Domestic Violence: Findings from an Evaluation of a Local Domestic Violence Court." *Criminology and Public Policy* 3, 1: 109-132.

[12] Levy, L, M. Steketee & S. Keilitz (2001). *Lessons Learned in Implementing an Integrated Domestic Violence Court*. Williamsburg, VA: National Center for State Courts.

[13] Gover, A., J. MacDonald & G. Alpert (2003). "Combating Domestic Violence: Findings from an Evaluation of a Local Domestic Violence Court." *Criminology and Public Policy* 3, 1: 109-132, p.111.

[14] Gover, A., J. MacDonald & G. Alpert (2003). "Combating Domestic Violence: Findings from an Evaluation of a Local Domestic Violence Court." *Criminology and Public Policy* 3, 1: 109-132, p. 119.

[15] Rottman, D. & S. Strickland (2006). *State Court Organization*. Washington DC: Bureau of Justice Statistics, p. 4

[16] Bureau of Justice Statistics. Retrieved 6/1/2007 from: http://www.ojp.usdoj.gov/bjs/.

[17] Bureau of Justice Statistics. Retrieved 6/1/2007 from: http://www.ojp.usdoj.gov/bjs/.

[18] Rottman, D. & S. Strickland (2006). *State Court Organization*. Washington DC: Bureau of Justice Statistics.

[19] Rottman, D. & S. Strickland (2006). *State Court Organization*. Washington DC: Bureau of Justice Statistics.

[20] DeFrances, C. (2001). *Prosecutors in State Courts, 2001*. Washington DC: Bureau of Justice Statistics.

[21] Rottman, D. & S. Strickland (2006). *State Court Organization*. Washington DC: Bureau of Justice Statistics.

[22] 373 U.S. 335 (1963).

[23] 407 U.S. 321 (1972).

[24] Harlow, C. (2000). *Defense Counsel in Criminal Cases*. Washington DC: Bureau of Justice Statistics.

[25] Liptak, A. (2007). "Study Reveals Gap in Performance of Public Defenders." *Austin American-Statesman*, July 14: A9.

[26] American Judicature Society (2004). *Judicial Selection in the States*. Des Moines: American Judicature Society.

[27] Bureau of Justice Statistics. Retrieved 6/1/2007 from: http://www.ojp.usdoj.gov/bjs/.

[28] Obtained 6/1/2007 from: http://www.usdoj.gov/usao/offices/usa_listings2.html#n.

[29] Bureau of Justice Statistics. Retrieved 6/1/2007 from:http://www.ojp.usdoj.gov/bjs/.

[30] Bureau of Justice Statistics. Retrieved 6/1/2007 from: http://www.ojp.usdoj.gov/bjs/.

[31] Retrieved 6/1/2207 from: http://www.supremecourtus.gov/about/briefoverview.pdf.

Chapter 9

Due Process: Arrest through Sentencing

What You Need to Know

★ Due process refers to the protections designed to protect you against governmental error in the deprivation of life, liberty, or property.

★ Due process rights are created by the Fifth and Fourteenth Amendments to the Constitution.

★ The steps of the criminal justice system include: arrest, booking, first appearance, preliminary hearing, arraignment, trial, and sentencing.

★ Bail is solely to ensure presence at trial. We have no constitutional right to bail.

★ An indictment is the charging document used by grand juries, while the information is the charging document of prosecutors.

★ Plea bargaining occurs in more than 90 percent of all cases.

★ A trial includes: pretrial motions, jury voir dire, opening statements, direct examinations, cross-examinations, rebuttal witnesses, and closing statements.

★ The sentencing hearing has been determined to be a "critical stage" of the proceeding, and therefore a Sixth Amendment right to an attorney exists.

★ The goals of sentencing include: punishment, incapacitation, rehabilitation, and deterrence.

1. DUE PROCESS

What is the purpose of the court process? Obviously we expect the courts to determine guilt or innocence and assess punishment, but the most important function of the court is to minimize or avoid errors in identifying and punishing offenders. Many people are impatient with the "slow wheels" of justice and the many rules and appeals that must be adhered to before punishment can commence. There is a very good reason for such procedures, however, and the reason is to prevent error. Recall that the concept of **due process** refers to procedural protections that guard against errors when the government seeks to deprive anyone of life, liberty, or property.

Due process is perhaps the most important civil right guaranteed to us by our Constitution. We have certain protections when governmental actors want to take something from us, whether it is life, liberty, or property. These protections don't stop the deprivation, but they do make it more likely that government actors make these decisions in a fair, unbiased, and non-arbitrary manner. Before being punished, for instance, criminal defendants deserve a fair trial that is designed to minimize any chance that the defendant is innocent. Even after conviction, offenders have some due process rights that remain before further deprivations can be imposed upon them during the correctional process.

The Fifth Amendment guarantees due process rights to us, as citizens of the United States, against any deprivations that occur through the actions of the federal government. Similar due process rights are incorporated through the Fourteenth Amendment to us as state citizens, guarding against actions by state actors (which includes local municipal police).

Due process is not a static concept. What is considered appropriate due process depends on the nature of the deprivation. First, something must be

BOX 9.1

Due Process Amendments to the United States Constitution

Fifth Amendment: *No person shall . . . be deprived of life, liberty, or property, without due process of law . . .*

Fourteenth Amendment: *. . . No State shall make or enforce any law which shall abridge the privileges or immunities of citizens of the United States; nor shall any State deprive any person of life, liberty, or property, without due process of law; nor deny to any person within its jurisdiction the equal protection of the laws.*

identified as a "protected liberty interest." This means that whatever the state or federal government wants to take away or do to a person must affect a protected interest. One's life is always a protected liberty interest, as is one's liberty. Any deprivation of these will always deserve some due process. However, some things are not protected. If it is not a protected liberty interest, then no due process is necessary. For example, prisoners have no right to be in any particular prison, so they have no procedural protections when prison authorities decide to transfer them, even if it is to a harsher prison.[1] On the other hand, if officials want to quarantine a citizen because of an infectious disease, the law allowing such confinement also specifies the process due before such a deprivation of liberty can occur. The process is designed to minimize any errors that this deprivation of liberty will occur for no good reason.

Once it is decided that the object of the deprivation is a protected liberty interest, the question becomes: "What process is due?" The chart below is a visual explanation of the idea that due process is a continuum and the greater the deprivation, the more process is due, while the less serious the deprivation, the less due process is required. So, for instance, when the government at-

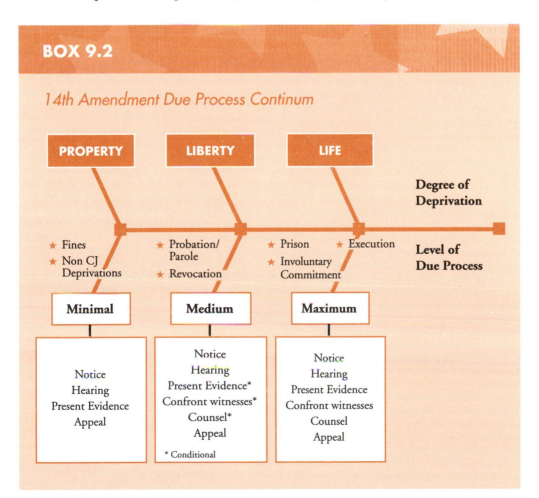

BOX 9.2

14th Amendment Due Process Continuum

PROPERTY	LIBERTY	LIFE

Degree of Deprivation

★ Fines
★ Non CJ Deprivations

★ Probation/ Parole
★ Revocation

★ Prison   ★ Execution
★ Involuntary Commitment

Level of Due Process

Minimal	**Medium**	**Maximum**
Notice Hearing Present Evidence Appeal	Notice Hearing Present Evidence* Confront witnesses* Counsel* Appeal * Conditional	Notice Hearing Present Evidence Confront witnesses Counsel Appeal

tempts to take away your property, as in an IRS action, or when you are denied Social Security benefits, then some due process applies, but it is much less than that required before the government can take away your life with a death sentence. The reason is obvious—the more serious the deprivation, the more important it is to make sure that no errors are made. Therefore, more steps exist to make sure the decision is accurate. Box 9.2 presents a display showing how due process rights are tied to the level of the deprivation at stake.

Due process never protects you against governmental deprivations. The purpose is to protect *against errors* in the decision to deprive. Thus, the steps before a long prison sentence or an execution are taken to ensure that the guilty verdict is accurate and the punishment just. Due process is not limited to criminal justice applications. Eminent domain, for instance, is a procedure whereby the government has the power to take away one's land; however, there are due process requirements, including a public hearing and finding that the public benefit outweighs the loss to the individual. The landowner must receive a fair market value before his land is taken.

★ Exercise: In the State of . . .

Find your state Constitution. Compare your state constitutional rights, as they exist in either the Constitution, amendments, or related statutes, to those described in the Bill of Rights. Are there differences?

Obviously, when a person is punished by the criminal justice system, the government must meet the demands of due process. In Box 9.2, showing the continuum of due process, we see that punishments range from the most serious (execution) to the least serious (fines). Criminal defendants have certain rights to a fair trial guaranteed by the Sixth Amendment. The Sixth Amendment states that the accused deserves a speedy and public trial, by an impartial jury. Further, each defendant has a right to be informed of the nature of the charges, to have the opportunity to confront and cross-examine the accusers and witnesses, and to have the assistance of counsel. Sentencing has been determined to be part of the trial process; therefore, the right to counsel continues through the sentencing hearing.

It should be understood, however, that the Sixth Amendment "trial rights" are only an example of due process. Indeed, the criminal justice system is only one example of due process. Any time the government interferes with the life, liberty, or property of an individual, due process applies. The rights provided by the Sixth Amendment end at the point of sentencing; however, due process protections (from the Fourteenth and Fifth Amendments) apply even after sentencing. In the due process diagram above, the rights of probationers, parolees, and others are illustrated as determined by the nature of the deprivation. In a series of

BOX 9.3

Sixth Amendment to the U.S. Constitution

In all criminal prosecutions, the accused shall enjoy the right to a speedy and public trial, by an impartial jury of the State and district wherein the crime shall have been committed, which district shall have been previously ascertained by law, and to be informed of the nature and cause of the accusation; to be confronted with the witnesses against him; to have compulsory process for obtaining witnesses in his favor, and to have the Assistance of Counsel for his defence.

court cases, the Supreme Court has dealt with a variety of issues regarding how much process is due when the government seeks to deprive a criminal offender of some form of liberty interest *after* sentencing, such as being moved to punitive segregation, having their probation or parole revoked, or losing "good time."

Due process also applies before the trial. Pretrial diversion, being held before booking, and being arrested implicate due process rights because they involve various types of deprivation. In this chapter, we will examine the steps of the criminal justice process from arrest through sentencing, but with an eye to these steps as they represent deprivations, and the due process rights attached to each step to protect us from governmental error.

2. ARREST TO TRIAL

An arrest is a deprivation of liberty, therefore due process applies. What process is due? Before an arrest can be made, there must be **probable cause** that the suspect has committed a specific crime. Arrests can be made with or without a warrant, but both types of arrest require probable cause. What is probable cause? The answer has been the focus of many law school discussions and courtroom speeches, but generally, probable cause means that there is enough evidence to indicate that the offender is "probably" guilty.

Recall that police officers can also temporarily detain individuals as **investigative detentions**. These brief deprivations of liberty only require reasonable suspicion. The reason the level of proof is less is because the level of deprivation is lower. What is a reasonable length of detention? Legislators don't specify what a reasonably short period of detention is; however, case decisions have drawn the parameters of what is considered reasonable. For instance, is being held for two hours on the side of the road while the police officer waits for a drug dog to inspect the car for drugs a reasonably short period of time or an unreasonable deprivation of liberty? To know the answer to that question, you would have to do legal research in your jurisdiction. If the length of the detention becomes unreasonable, and the person is not free to leave, then the deprivation becomes a de facto arrest. If the police officer does not meet the probable cause standard, then the arrest is an illegal deprivation of liberty.

The legal remedy for an improper arrest is that any evidence obtained directly from that arrest can be excluded under the exclusionary rule. If maliciousness can be proven, an individual subject to a false arrest may also pursue a civil judgment against the individual officer, and even the department, if there was complicity on the part of superiors.

2.1 Booking

Booking typically involves transporting the suspect to the lockup or county jail and filling out appropriate paperwork before the individual enters the facility. Booking is a due process step only in the sense that some errors of identity may be discovered at this point when fingerprints are taken. In rare cases, individuals are arrested because of outstanding warrants for others with the same name and birthdate. If fingerprints are on file for the true offender, the booking process may be instrumental in discovering this mistake. Generally, however, booking is an administrative procedure to accommodate the needs of the jail or confinement facility. Individuals may also be kept in **lockups** for a short period. These temporary holding cells are in police stations.

2.2 Initial Appearance

As mentioned earlier, every person taken into custody must see a magistrate within a reasonable period, usually within 48 hours. In *Riverside v. McLaughlin*,[2] the Supreme Court ruled that, unless there were special circumstances, the initial hearing must take place within 48 hours of arrest. This is in order to assure that the detention of the individual is legal, i.e., the charging documents are in order, there is probable cause for the arrest, and there is no clear abuse of power. Generally, this hearing is a fairly *pro forma* experience.

One of the major functions of the initial appearance is to notify the accused of the charges against him or her. One of the first elements of due process is notice. It is impossible to defend yourself unless you know what it is you are being accused of. The accused is usually provided with a copy of the complaint or charging document at this point. The magistrate also recites the *Miranda* warnings again to make sure that the defendant understands them.

The hearing magistrate, who may be a judge of any level from municipal court to state district court, will begin to assess whether the accused is indigent and will need an attorney provided by the state. Jurisdictions typically use some form of a questionnaire that asks the defendant to show assets and debts in order to determine **indigency**, which simply means without appreciable assets. The other major function of the hearing is to assess bail or offer some other form of pretrial release.

2.3 Bail or Release on Recognizance (ROR)

The adjudicatory process sometimes takes months or even years to complete. Until it is over, it is obviously important that the suspect/defendant remain in the jurisdiction. For this reason, many are kept in jail until a conviction, dismissal, or acquittal occurs. However, if other means are sufficient to ensure that the individual does not disappear, then pretrial detention is unnecessary. The bail hearing is the due process designed to minimize error in the decision regarding this deprivation of liberty. The judge determines how likely it is that the defendant will **abscond** (escape the jurisdiction), and then determines whether to offer a pretrial release option, and/or what level of bail is the lowest necessary to ensure presence at trial.

It must be understood that bail is merely a way to ensure presence at trial. The individual pledges money and/or property that is forfeited if they do not appear. Bail is supposed to be set based on the threat of escape. More serious crimes carry with them more serious punishments; therefore, bail is set higher because it is assumed that defendants have more reason to run when facing more serious punishments. Although bail is not guaranteed in the Bill of Rights, the Eighth Amendment orders that no individual shall be forced to post "excessive bail."

The amount of bail for each suspect is determined not only by the seriousness of the crime, but also by the characteristics of the defendant. Homeownership, employment, and residential stability indicate that the suspect is a low risk for flight (unless the crime is very serious); however, if the offender is unemployed, has no family in the area and has no place to stay prior to trial, there is a high probability that he or she will flee. Of course there is also the high probability that they can not afford bail either, and so these individuals would probably remain in jail.

There are a variety of bail/surety alternatives involving the courts and/or private bail bonds providers:

1. Direct/full bail

2. Private bail bonds—secured (requiring collateral) or unsecured

3. Court surety programs—secured (requiring collateral) or unsecured

4. Release on recognizance

Some defendants may be able to post the full amount of bail; however, most do not have the ability to offer that amount of cash. Most often, defendants or their families contract with bail bonds agents who often demand collateral from the defendant (i.e., house, car, money) in return for the bond agent signing a promissory note to the court. If the defendant does not appear, the bond agent must pay the full amount of the bail. Bond agents receive a fee even if the defendant appears; thus, even if the defendant is acquitted of all charges or the charges are dropped, they still have to pay the bond agent for the right to be released prior to court proceedings. In other instances, bond agents do not require collateral; they take on the risk of having to pay the court the full amount if the defendant absconds. In return for their assumption of this risk, the bond fee may be higher.

In some jurisdictions, the court cuts out the private bond agents and allows the defendant to offer the collateral directly to the court, along with a percentage (typically 10 percent), of the full amount of bail. If the defendant does not appear, then the deposit and the property are forfeited. In a very few jurisdictions, courts offer an unsecured bond option where the defendant promises to pay the full amount but it is unsecured by collateral. In both types of these court surety programs, if the defendant does appear, he or she pays only a small administrative fee. These programs, where they exist, save defendants quite a bit of money. Even in the areas where there are court surety programs, private bail bonds agents still have a role because defendants typically must meet fairly stringent background characteristics in order to be eligible for the **court surety program**, and all others must resort to the private vendor if they want to be released prior to trial.

The problem is that many defendants do not have any collateral at all. They do not have financial resources to equal the bail amount and, therefore, are not eligible for programs that require collateral. Thus, it is argued that the poor spend pretrial time in jail while those who have money do not, regardless of their risk of flight. That does not seem fair and, so, back in the 1960s, the Vera Institute of Justice funded the Manhattan Bail Project. This was the first formal **Release on Recognizance program** (ROR). Defendants who could not afford bail but who seemed to be good risks were identified. In the course of one study period (1961-1964), the project evaluated 10,000 defendants for release; 4,000 were recommended for release; 2,195 were released; and only 15 did not show up for a court appearance. In general, ROR programs find that the failure-to-appear rates for those in the program are similar to those on bail.[3]

In a government study of large urban counties, only seven percent of all felony defendants were denied bail. However, only 62 percent were released prior to trial or final adjudication.[4] Most were released under bail secured through a bail bonds agent. Roughly a third of all offenders were released through some form of financial bond; a third were released through some form of release on recognizance with no financial bond; and a third remained in jail (because only seven percent were denied bail, the rest evidently couldn't or wouldn't make bail or did not qualify for the recognizance programs). The median bail amount for those using bail bonds agents was $7,500, with a mean of $13,800.[5]

In 1984, Congress passed the Federal Bail Reform Act.[6] This bill allowed for the preventive detention of federal defendants. **Preventive detention** is when the individual is incarcerated before trial, not because of a fear that they will abscond, but because of a perceived risk to the public if they are in the community. With the federal preventive detention measure, judges can consider the offense, the weight of the evidence, the history and character of the defendant, ties to the community, drug history, and the nature and seriousness of danger to the community. They may determine that the risk to the public is too great to allow the offender to remain in the community prior to trial, and the offender will be held without bail. This seems to be contrary to the due process concept of "innocent until proven guilty," but there is at least some due process in that there is a separate preventive detention hearing where the magistrate weighs the risk and makes the determination.

The power to deny bail and hold under the preventive detention bill was challenged in *United States v. Salerno*.[7] The Supreme Court upheld the right of the federal government to hold individuals without bail, finding that, although the Eighth Amendment prohibited excessive bail, it did not prohibit a determination that no bail would be offered. The federal preventive detention power is held by federal judges and used for federal defendants. Your state probably has similar legislation allowing for the preventive detention of suspects in state prosecutions.

2.4 Preliminary Hearing

The preliminary hearing may also be called the preliminary examination, probable cause hearing, bindover hearing, or some other term. This type of hearing is sometimes combined with the initial hearing, but more often it takes place several days later. While defendants would not necessarily have an attorney at the initial appearance, they must have one at the preliminary hearing.

As stated before, the initial appearance is a due process step to identify if any clear abuse of power has occurred and to establish bail so that the accused might have the opportunity to remain free during the adjudication process. In the preliminary hearing, a judge or magistrate rules on the strength of evidence by determining whether the prosecutor has shown that there is probable cause the defendant did commit the crimes charged. The defense is not obligated to do anything at a preliminary hearing. If they choose, they can present evidence or witnesses, and they may cross-examine prosecution witnesses, but it is solely the prosecutor's burden to prove that there is enough evidence to go forward with the prosecution.

Defense attorneys utilize the preliminary hearing as a tool of discovery. Discovery involves finding out about the evidence the prosecutor plans to use at trial. Unlike a civil trial, there are fewer means in a criminal trial for either side to find out what the other side has as evidence if the case goes to trial. The preliminary hearing gives the defense a brief introduction to the evidence the prosecutor has, whether that be forensic evidence, witness testimony, or expert reports. On the other hand, prosecutors tend to provide only enough of their evidence in order to convince the judge that there is probable cause.

If the charges are dismissed at this point, the prosecutor is free to continue to try to make a case. **Double jeopardy**—the right not to be tried for the same offense—does not "attach" or become an issue until a jury is empaneled. About half of cases are dismissed before trial, although some are refiled when there is more evidence.[8]

2.5 Information or Grand Jury Indictment

Many people are confused about the difference between a grand jury and a petit jury. A petit jury is the type of jury you see in the courtroom determining guilt or innocence. You will not usually ever see a grand jury. These individuals are selected by the presiding or administrative judge and tend to be "good citizens known to the court." They sit for a month, six months, or even a year, for one day or afternoon a week. The grand jury listens to cases brought before them by the prosecutor. The prosecutor may bring in witnesses to question, or just describe the evidence in the case, and then they determine whether there is probable cause to go forward.

If a grand jury decides that there is probable cause, they return an **indictment**. It is the charging instrument of the grand jury. If they do not believe that the prosecutor has proven probable cause, they will **no bill** the case, meaning that there is no indictment. Not all states have grand juries. The Fifth Amendment guarantees the right of grand jury review to federal defendants, but the right has not been "incorporated" to state citizens (those facing prosecution by states). Only about half of the states use grand juries. In some of these states, the right, at least for felony defendants, is guaranteed by the state constitution (New York, Ohio, and Texas). In other states, there is an option to go to the grand jury for indictment, otherwise the prosecutor will issue the charging instrument.

The other method of charging is an **information**. An information is the charging instrument issued by the prosecutor when a grand jury indictment is not used. There is still due process because the prosecutor has had to show probable cause to a magistrate or judge in the preliminary hearing. If the prosecutor is successful in proving probable cause at the preliminary hearing, he or she will issue an information charging the defendant and setting the stage for trial.

Fifth Amendment

No person shall be held to answer for a capital, or other infamous crime, unless on a presentment or indictment at a grand jury.

2.6 Arraignment and Plea Bargaining

The next step in the proceedings is the arraignment. Here, the defendant is formally notified of the charges against him or her and asked for a plea. If the defendant accepts a plea bargain, the arraignment may become the end of the process with the judge accepting the plea and setting punishment. As you probably know, more than 90 percent of criminal defendants plead guilty. Most do so in return for a recommendation for a reduced sentence. Judges are not bound to accept the prosecutor's recommendation for sentencing, but they do so in the vast majority of cases. If a judge takes a plea, typically, the only evidence is an affidavit of the defendant admitting guilt. Attached to this legal document is the prosecutor's recommendation for sentencing. If the judge does not agree to the recommendation, the defendant has a right to withdraw the confession. The prosecutor is also barred from agreeing to a sentence and then retracting the agreement once he or she has obtained a confession. On the other hand, the Supreme Court has generally upheld cases where the defendant was forced to choose between a plea bargain and the possibility of the death penalty.

Although plea bargaining has been widely criticized, the interesting thing is that it is criticized by both sides of the political spectrum. Conservatives criticize plea bargaining as resulting in lenient sentences, while liberals criticize it as violating the presumption of "innocent until proven guilty," and creating pressure for innocent suspects to plead guilty. Most research shows, however, that, in general, both prosecutors and defense attorneys know and even agree on the basic range of sentences for crimes, and the plea bargaining procedure allows the system to dispose of a tremendous number of cases without the expense of further adjudication.

2.7 Pretrial Motions

Typically, after the arraignment, but before the beginning of the trial, there may be a number of pretrial motions. A **motion** is simply a request that the judge order something to be done or not done. For instance, the defense may file a motion to exclude evidence. The defense attorney would have to show either that the evidence was obtained illegally and should be excluded, or that the evidence is more prejudicial than probative (meaning helpful to prove). Generally, prior prison sentences or prior accusations are excluded because they are highly prejudicial and don't prove that the defendant did this particular crime; although, in some cases, such evidence might come in as evidence of a pattern of criminal behavior.

Another pretrial motion is a **change of venue**, which is a request for the trial to be moved to another jurisdiction because of a belief that any jurors from the locale where the crime took place would be too biased to render a fair verdict. This is also a motion typically filed by the defense.

Either side might, but rarely does, file a motion for the judge to **recuse** him- or herself. This motion basically argues that the judge is not able to conduct the trial in a fair and unbiased manner because of some conflict of interest. The attorney who files a recusal motion hopes that the judge will grant it and remove him- or herself from the case and give it to another judge.

3. TRIAL

In a criminal case, the state has the burden of proving the guilt of the accused beyond a reasonable doubt. That means that the prosecution has the responsibility to prove each of the elements of the crime with which the accused is charged.

For example, the crime of burglary generally has these elements: breaking and entering, the dwelling, of another, with intent to commit a felony therein.

If the prosecution fails to prove any element of the crime beyond a reasonable doubt, but proves the other elements, the accused may sometimes be found guilty of a lesser crime. But ordinarily, if the prosecutor is unable to prove all elements beyond a reasonable doubt, the person charged cannot be convicted of the crime. Also, recall that the prosecutor must also prove that the offense took place within the geographic jurisdiction of the court.

In a civil case the degree of proof is a "preponderance of the evidence;" but in a criminal case, the degree of proof is "beyond a reasonable doubt." In some states, the exact wording of the charge to the jury dealing with the standard of proof is stated by statute. In other states, there is no such requirement, and in fact, the judge does not have to explain the term at all.

The "beyond a reasonable doubt" standard is a constitutional requirement. In 1970, the Supreme Court left no doubt about the requirement in the holding of In *re Winship*:

> Lest there remain any doubt about the constitutional stature of the reasonable-doubt standard, we explicitly hold that the Due Process Clause protects the accused against conviction except on proof beyond a reasonable doubt of every fact necessary to constitute the crime with which he is charged.[9]

In most cases, the defense has no burden of proof at all, and can merely sit silent and argue that the prosecutor has not proven beyond a reasonable doubt that the defendant committed the crime. In certain cases, however, the defense may argue an **affirmative defense**, such as coercion, self-defense, entrapment, mistake, alibi, or insanity. In these cases, the defendant's attorney must offer a certain level of proof before the jury can consider the defense.[10] Unlike the burden on the prosecutor in a criminal case, the burden to prove an affirmative defense such as insanity or self-defense is by a preponderance of the evidence and not by evidence beyond a reasonable doubt. Legislative bodies may enact legislation modifying the burden of proof where this does not violate constitutional principles, and some states have increased the level of proof necessary for an insanity defense to "clear and convincing."

Insanity is an affirmative defense. In most states, the matter of the defendant's insanity must be put in issue by the defendant, and then the prosecution has the ultimate burden of disproving insanity. In 1984, as part of the Comprehensive Crime Control Act, Congress enacted legislation titled the Insanity Defense Reform Act of 1984. This section of the Code shifts the burden of proof to the defendant and sets the level at *clear and convincing*, a level of proof higher than preponderance, but lower than beyond a reasonable doubt.[11]

In other situations in which the defendant claims an affirmative defense, the state may require that the defense be proven by either a preponderance or clear and convincing evidence. The Supreme Court in 1987 upheld an Ohio law that required the defendant to prove self-defense by a preponderance of evidence.[12]

Although the defendant may be required to meet the preponderance or clear and convincing burden to submit the defense to the jury, it is still up to the prosecutor to prove beyond a reasonable doubt that the defendant is guilty of each element.

3.1 Jury Panels and Voir Dire

As you know, the Sixth Amendment gives criminal defendants the right to a trial by a jury of their peers. This has been interpreted by a line of court cases to mean that the jury pool must be pulled in such a way as to not clearly exclude any particular group, not necessarily that the jury panel represent the demographic characteristics of the defendant.

You may have been called to jury duty. Typically, jurisdictions use voter registration, driver's licenses, or motor vehicle registration lists to pull jury panels. Once called to perform jury duty, you may or may not actually serve on a jury. Depending on the jurisdiction, you may be on call for a day or a week (perhaps having the option to call in each morning to check to see if you are needed). If a judge in that jurisdiction is starting a trial, he or she will call for a jury panel of up to 50 people (depending on the case, the number of peremptory challenges, and the size of the jury in that jurisdiction).

Most jurisdictions allow for certain exemptions from jury duty. If one has minor children at home, is a full-time student, or is past a certain age, they are generally exempt. Some states have automatic occupation exemptions, some don't. Typically, jury members must be citizens, not have a criminal record, and be of "sound mind."

We tend to think that juries must be 12 individuals who vote unanimously to convict the defendant, but there is no constitutional right to a 12-person jury.[13] States may require only eight people to be on a jury (Arizona and Utah), or six (Connecticut and Florida), at least in non-capital cases. There is also no constitutional right to have a unanimous verdict.[14] Some states do not require unanimous jury verdicts (Louisiana and Oregon).

After the jury panel has been seated, the defense and prosecuting attorneys have a chance to examine the jury cards that jury panel members have filled out. These provide quite a bit of information about each panel member, includ-

★ Exercise: In the State of . . .

Find out how many jurors are required for your state. Also, check to see if your state requires a unanimous jury verdict. Finally, find out how many peremptory challenges are allowed for both the defense and the prosecution. You can find out this information in your state's rules of criminal procedure, which may be online. If not, see if there is a copy in your library. You can also use a BJS publication titled *State Court Organization — 2004*, available at: www.ojp.usdoj.gov/bjs/pub/pdf/sco04.pdf.

ing marital status, age, occupation, income, number of children, and so on. A translation of **voir dire** is something like "to see to say," but it basically means to speak the truth and it is the process by which attorneys quiz prospective jurors to find out if their biases prevent them from judging the evidence fairly. The first question that is asked is if jury members know any of the principal players in the trial, such as the victim, the offender, either attorney, or the judge. Then attorneys ask questions relevant to the particular case. For instance, if the defendant was charged with negligent manslaughter because he killed someone in an accident after a night of drinking, the defense attorney is going to want to know the drinking habits of the prospective jurors and whether any of them had a relative who had been killed by a drunken driver.

State statutes set the number of **peremptory challenges** for the prosecutor and the defense attorney. Peremptory challenges allow the attorney to reject the juror without having to show a particular reason. Although the attorney cannot use race, or any other factor prohibited by law or the Constitution, to strike (reject) jurors with his or her peremptory challenges, any other reason or no reason at all is allowed. **Challenges for cause** are unlimited, but there must be a reason why the juror would be biased in the trial. The attorney has to state what the objection is, and the judge will consider the challenge and agree and dismiss the juror, or disagree and allow the juror to remain.

After each attorney has identified the jurors he or she has rejected under the peremptory challenges, and the judge has dealt with any requests to strike jurors for cause, the remaining jurors are called up one at a time to the jury box until it is filled with the appropriate number and, in some instances, alternates. Once the jury is seated, the trial can begin.

3.2 Opening Statements

The opening statements are the attorneys' opportunity to address the jury as to what they should be looking for in the presentation of evidence. Each attorney seeks to educate the jury as to his or her version of the events. They need to convince the jury of their version through evidence that consists either of witnesses who testify to what they have seen, heard, or experienced, and/or expert witnesses who can offer opinions and judgments, at least within the confines of their expertise. The opening statement gives the attorney a chance to talk directly to the jury and tell them what they are going to hear. The defense often asks that their opening be deferred to the beginning of the defense's case.

3.3 Presentation of Evidence

You have probably seen innumerable trials on television shows and movies. Some are fairly accurate and some are not. Generally, you know that the prosecution presents the state's case first. Witnesses are put on the stand, the prosecutor goes through a **direct examination**, which is the questioning of your own witness. The questions cannot be leading (telling the witness the answer or making a statement); they cannot ask for an opinion, they cannot ask for **hearsay** (something that the witness did not hear, see, experience directly), although there are many exceptions to this rule; and they cannot ask for something that would be unduly prejudicial or otherwise not be allowed into evidence.

After the prosecutor has finished questioning the witness, the defense may cross-examine the witness. These questions have pretty much the same rules, but there is the opportunity to ask leading questions, such as, "Isn't it true that on the night of July 15, you had so much to drink that you were not able to see the defendant clearly across the parking lot of the bar?"

After the defense has finished the cross examination, the prosecutor has the opportunity to question again. This process continues until all the witnesses have been examined. Then the prosecutor has the chance to present any rebuttal witnesses that might be appropriate. This might occur if the defense has elicited some information from one of the witnesses that the prosecutor can show is irrelevant or untrue or just to shed additional light on the information. Rebuttal witnesses respond directly to the facts already in evidence.

The presentation of the defense's case comes next, beginning with the opening statement if the attorney reserved the right to give one. The direct examination, cross-examination, and rebuttal witnesses occur in the same order. After all witnesses are finished testifying, there are closing arguments.

An instance where the prosecutor has an advantage over the defense is that they are allowed to have the first closing statement and then are able to speak to the jury again after the defense's closing statement. This is because prosecutors have the burden of proof in a trial. In the closing, each side summarizes the evidence in a way that supports their version of the case. They emphasize certain portions of the evidence, and they comment on the weight of the evidence. Attorneys cannot mention any facts not in evidence.

After the closing, the judge reads the jury an instruction. The instruction to the jury is a product of both attorneys contributing suggested text, and the judge's determination of what instructions the jury should have. It may include definitions of legal terms. It may ask them to choose between two or more different levels of culpability. The rules for instructions are different among the states, but it is basically the guidelines or rules for the jury to follow in their deliberation.

If the jury cannot reach a verdict, it is called a "hung jury" and the prosecutor may decide to try the case again. This would not be double jeopardy because the trial is not officially over yet. If the jury comes back with an acquittal, it does not mean the jury members necessarily believe the defendant is innocent, it means that they did not believe the prosecutor proved the case beyond a reasonable doubt. If the jury comes back with a guilty verdict, the next step is sentencing.

4. SENTENCING HEARING

Depending on the state, judges or juries may sentence convicted felons and misdemeanants. In both cases, statutory guidelines limit the discretion of the judge or jury in what type of sentence can be imposed, and how long the sentence may last. A sentencing hearing is a "critical stage" of the trial process, meaning that the courts have held that a defendant must have an attorney present if they are facing the possibility of a jail or prison sentence. There are, however, relaxed rules of evidence. Hearsay may be admitted, as when people testify about the character of the offender. Victim statements may be read, which allow the victim or the victim's family to state how the crime has affected them.

In most states, presentence reports are also used in order to give the judge or jury more information about the offender before a sentence decision is made. A presentence division in a probation agency conducts presentence investigations and they provide information on the offenders' criminal, educational, family, and work history. In Box 9.4, a presentence report is described.

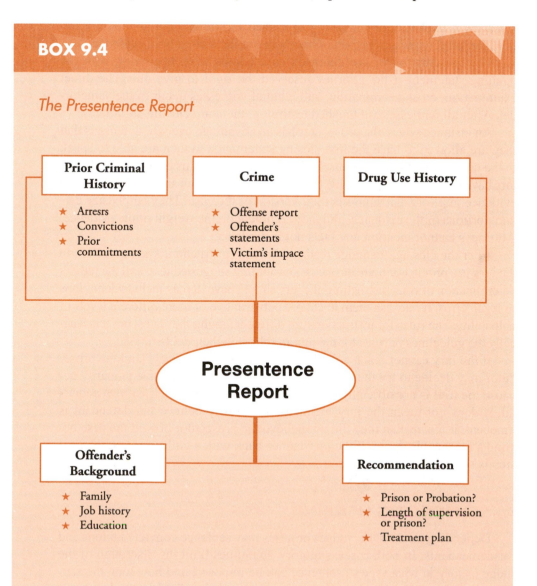

BOX 9.4

The Presentence Report

Prior Criminal History
★ Arresrs
★ Convictions
★ Prior commitments

Crime
★ Offense report
★ Offender's statements
★ Victim's impace statement

Drug Use History

Presentence Report

Offender's Background
★ Family
★ Job history
★ Education

Recommendation
★ Prison or Probation?
★ Length of supervision or prison?
★ Treatment plan

We have a system in which there are several concurrent goals of sentencing. They include:

★ punishment: we believe that criminals must be punished because they deserve it

★ deterrence: we believe that what we do to offenders will make others decide not to commit crime and also will encourage that offender not to commit additional crime

★ rehabilitation: we believe that programs and what is done to the offender in the system may create some internal change that will make him or her become more law-abiding

★ incapacitation: if nothing else, we believe that we should hold the offender in a manner that will prevent him or her from committing any crimes, at least for that period of time

Theoretically any sentence, or every sentence, should achieve one or more of these goals. An offender who is sent to prison is certainly incapacitated and each of the other goals is possible—especially, of course, punishment.

4.1 Types of Sentences

The most important sentencing decision is whether the offender is sent to prison or receives probation. This "in or out" decision is governed by state statute. The decision may come about through a plea agreement or it can be the decision of a judge or, in a few states, a jury. Besides the "in or out" (of prison) decision, sentencing decisions can include other forms of confinement or supervision. Box 9.5 illustrates some types of sentences.

BOX 9.5

Sentence Alternatives

1. **Split Sentence**—a short period in jail followed by probation supervision (also called "shock probation").

2. **Halfway house placement**—either as a condition of probation or as a stand-alone sentence.

3. **Boot camps**—military-style camps utilizing physical fitness and discipline.

4. **House arrest with electronic monitoring**—usually as a condition of probation but sometimes may be a stand-alone sentence.

5. **Fines**—either a stand-alone sentence or as a condition of probation.

It should also be remembered that a community corrections placement might result in additional or different sanctions during the course of the supervision period. For instance, if an offender is sentenced to probation, and one of the conditions is to submit to drug tests, a failed test may result in a judge adding a residential treatment center stay to the conditions of probation. Weekend jail may be added to a probationer's sentence if he or she has violated the terms of the probation, but the judge doesn't think it is serious enough to warrant revocation and a prison sentence. At any time during the probation sentence, a court proceeding to change the conditions may be initiated. Although the probation officer does not have the power to change the conditions or revoke probation, he or she can file a violation report and ask the prosecutor for a Motion to Revoke Probation hearing. The judge is the only person who can revoke or change the conditions.

4.2 Indeterminate, Determinate, and "Structured Sentencing"

An *indeterminate sentence* is one where the release date is unknown. The judge sets a period as provided for by statute, i.e., five to 15 years. How much of that is served depends on another agency, typically a paroling authority. This group of decisionmakers looks at the offender's behavior in prison. An offender may serve a small portion or the majority of the range of years, depending on the parole board (or paroling authority) decision.

A *determinate sentence* is when the release date is fixed. Determinate sentencing systems typically also set the amount of punishment for each crime by statute. The judge has little flexibility and, once there is a conviction and decision to send to prison, the judge must use the sentence specified by the statute. There is often a very small range for the judge to adjust the sentence by making it shorter or longer.

Indeterminate sentences have been around since the early reformatories in the late 1800s and early 1900s. They were the most prevalent sentencing structure in the 1960s and 1970s. However, critics argued that indeterminate sentences were unfair; either because offenders were getting out of prison too early, or because there was no accountability or predictability in who was getting out in what amount of time. Beginning in the late 1970s and 1980s, various forms of determinate or structured sentencing have taken the place of indeterminate sentencing in many states. The goals of structured sentencing have been listed as:

★ increase fairness in sentencing

★ reduce unwarranted disparity in decision to imprison or sentence length

★ establish truth in sentencing

★ balance sentencing policy with limited correctional resources[15]

In Box 9.6, there is a map of the United States showing which states have eliminated parole and instituted determinate sentencing.

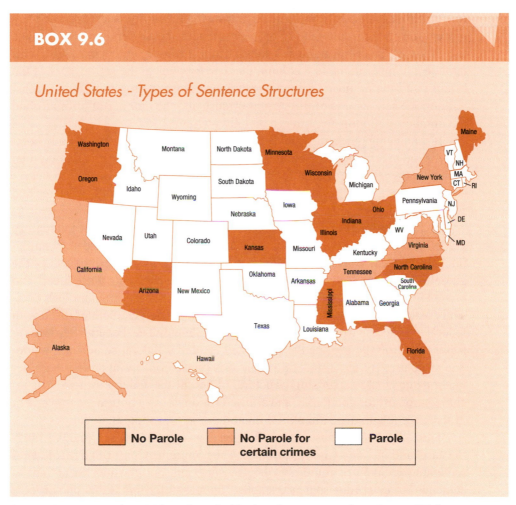

BOX 9.6

United States - Types of Sentence Structures

■ **No Parole**	■ **No Parole for certain crimes**	□ **Parole**

Source: P. Ditton and D. Wilson (1999). *Truth in Sentencing in State Prisons.* Washington, DC: Bureau of Justice Statistics.

Mandatory sentences are often embedded in a state's indeterminate sentencing structure. They are passed to control the sentencing discretion for certain specific crimes, usually because the crimes are heinous or have captured public attention. For instance, in a state that has an otherwise indeterminate sentencing system, there may be a mandatory jail sentence for third-conviction DUIs, or there may be a mandatory prison term for violent felonies that involve the use of a weapon. All 50 states have at least one type of mandatory sentence.[16] Along with these types of sentences, some states have three-strikes legislation that allow a prosecutor to prosecute repeat offenders as three-strike (or second-strike) offenders with much longer prison terms attached. About half of all states have some form of three-strikes (habitual felon) sentencing statutes.[17]

4.3 Sentencing Guidelines

Sentencing guidelines were introduced in the early 1980s as a measure to reduce sentence disparity. Guidelines may be mandatory or discretionary. They present the presumed amount of time an offender should serve in prison given the nature of the crime and a risk factor score. Federal Sentencing Guidelines include a number in the first column that corresponds to the seriousness of the offense and the number of prior convictions across the top row. Judges must look up the seriousness of the current offense and the number of priors to find the number of months to sentence an individual.

If sentencing guidelines are discretionary, the guidelines are only advisory, and the judge or sentencing body may ignore them. If they are mandatory, then typically, there is a provision for the sentencing authority to enter into the record the reason why they depart from the guidelines. As of 1998, 17 states had some form of sentencing guidelines.[18]

In 2005, the Supreme Court called into question the legality of mandatory guidelines. The first case dealt with the state of Washington's mandatory guidelines. In 2004, in *Blakely v. Washington*,[19] the Court invalidated the use of the guidelines to determine sentence length when elements not introduced and proven in court were used, i.e., number of priors or use of a weapon. This decision created doubt that the U.S. Sentencing Commission Guidelines, used with federal offenders, would be upheld in a challenge. The Federal Sentencing Reform Act of 1984 (effective 1987) had created a federal sentencing guideline structure. By 1992, federal parole was phased out in favor of the guidelines' determinate sentencing structure, although the federal system still included time off for good time, and allowed for downward or upward movement in sentence length depending on mitigating or aggravating factors.

The federal guidelines were challenged in an appeal similar to the Washington case, and in *United States v. Booker*,[20] the Supreme Court ruled that federal sentencing guidelines could only be advisory, and not consider facts "not in evidence" to determine sentence length. The reason for this is that due process rights require the government to prove the elements it uses to determine a sentence. Many of the elements in a sentencing guidelines structure are not entered into the record, the defendant does not get a chance to refute them, and they do not have to meet any burden of proof. Consequently, the Supreme Court decided that the due process rights of an offender were violated when the sentences in the guidelines were considered to be mandatory rather than advisory.

4.4 Split Sentencing

In the 1980s a new type of sentencing came onto the scene that allowed judges to use imprisonment and also keep control of the offender. Variously called split sentencing, shock probation, shock incarceration, or other terms, the idea was to be able to sentence the offender to a short period in jail or prison, and then put them on probation, thereby allowing the judge to keep control over the offender through the entire period of supervision. Joan Petersilia[21] reports that probation is combined with jail or a prison sentence in 27 percent of felony cases. In this type of sentence, the average jail sentence length is six months and the probation supervision length is 40 months.

4.5 Probation versus Prison

There is a widespread belief that most criminal offenders get a slap on the wrist in the sentencing process. However, according to national statistics, 78 percent of those convicted in 2004 were sentenced to incarceration, either alone or with a sentence to probation. Only 15 percent received probation, and only four percent received a fine as the sole method of punishment. Of those sentenced to some form of incarceration, the average sentence was 60 months, with drug offenders serving, on average, 84 months.[22] In the last several decades, probation has been surpassed by prison as the most frequent sentence handed down in felony courts.

4.6 Sentence Disparity

There seems to be good evidence that young, black males are not only more likely to engage in some types of crime (street crime such as robbery and homicide), but that they are also more likely to be sentenced harshly because of a perception that they are more dangerous, whether they are or not.

Studies that examine the interaction between race, age and gender find that the combination of these variables affects sentencing patterns more than any one individually. For instance, older black men are less likely to receive disproportionately severe sentences than young black men. Women, on the other hand, are sentenced fairly uniformly regardless of age. Race is less important as a factor in sentencing older rather than younger offenders, and for men rather than women. Darrell Steffensmeier and his colleagues have examined the interplay of these variables in several studies and find that race does seem to affect sentencing, but it influences sentencing mostly for young men.[23]

There has also been a lot of research on whether or not women receive leniency in sentencing. The so-called "chivalry effect" refers to the perceived practice of giving women lighter sentences than men who commit similar crimes. The research that has been directed to this question has had mixed findings, but, generally, it seems that for some women, and for some crimes, there might be a tendency to assess shorter sentences, but, the practice is not uniform. For some women, especially young women, minority women, and those who commit violent crimes, sentencing may actually be harsher than for men.[24]

5. CONCLUSION

In this chapter, we more fully described how the criminal justice system is a series of steps designed to protect against error in the court process. Due process protections come to us through the Fifth and Fourteenth Amendments. Our right to a criminal trial by a jury of peers comes to us from the Sixth Amendment, but our due process rights go far beyond the Sixth Amendment, and are implicated any time the government attempts to deprive us of life, liberty, or property.

The steps of the criminal process begin with arrest and booking, continue through initial appearance, preliminary hearing, indictment or information, arraignment, and trial and sentencing. At each step, the process is designed to minimize or eliminate any errors that the government may make.

REVIEW QUESTIONS

1. What is due process and what is the source of due process protections?

2. What are the steps from arrest to trial? (Describe each step.)

3. What are the four kinds of bail or surety programs?

4. What is the difference between an information and an indictment?

5. What are some examples of pretrial motions?

6. What are the steps of a trial?

7. What is an affirmative defense? Give some examples.

8. What is included in the PSR?

9. What are at least six different types of sentences? Describe sentencing guidelines and split sentencing.

10. What are indeterminate and determinate sentencing structures? Give examples of states that have indeterminate systems and states that have determinate systems.

VOCABULARY

abscond – escape the jurisdiction, leave without permission

affirmative defense – defenses where the defense must provide evidence to reach a certain level of proof (typically preponderance) before a jury can consider it; examples include: self-defense, entrapment, and insanity

challenges for cause – unlimited number of challenges either by defense or prosecution if they can prove that a prospective juror is not able to assess the evidence fairly at trial

change of venue – a request for the trial to be moved to another jurisdiction because of a belief that any jurors from the locale where the crime took place would be too biased to render a fair verdict

court surety programs – alternative to bail where the court administers a secured or unsecured bond in lieu of private bail

cross-examination – the questioning of the other side's witness

direct examination – the questioning of your own side's witness

double jeopardy – the right not to be tried or punished twice for the same offense

due process – procedural protections that guard against errors when the government seeks to deprive anyone of life, liberty, or property

hearsay – something that you did not hear, see, or experience directly

indictment – the charging instrument of the grand jury

indigency – without appreciable assets

investigative detentions – brief deprivations of liberty when police officers have a reasonable suspicion that a crime has occurred, or is about to occur

information – the charging instrument issued by the prosecutor

lockups –temporary holding cells, usually in a police station

motion – a request that the judge order something to be done or not done

no bill – the finding of the grand jury when the prosecutor has not proven probable cause

peremptory challenges – statutory number of challenges to prospective jurors without having to identify any specific bias

preventive detention – pretrial detention because of a perceived risk to the public

probable cause – when there is enough evidence to indicate guilt is more probable than not

recuse(al) – when the judge is not able to conduct the trial in a fair and unbiased manner because of some conflict of interest

release on recognizance program (ROR) – pre-release without bond for good risk defendants in lieu of bail

voir dire – to say the truth; the process by which attorneys question prospective jurors to determine their ability to be fair and unbiased during trial

FOR FURTHER READING

Bogira, Steve (2006). *Courtroom 302: A Year Behind the Scenes in an American Criminal Courthouse*. New York: Vintage Books.

Burnett, D. Graham (2003). *A Trial By Jury*. New York: Bloomsbury Publishers.

Davis, Kevin (2007). *Defending the Damned: Inside Chicago's Cook County Public Defender's Office*. New York: Atria/Simon and Schuster.

Moskovitz, Myron (2000). *Cases and Problems in Criminal Procedure: The Courtroom*. Cincinnati, OH: Anderson Publishing Co.

[1] *Meachum v. Fano*, 427 U.S. 215 (1976).

[2] 500 U.S. 44 (1991).

[3] Maxwell, S. (1999). "Examining the Congruence Between Predictors of ROR and Failures to Appear." *Journal of Criminal Justice* 27, 2: 127-141.

[4] Rainville, G. & B. Reaves (2003). *Felony Defendants in Large Urban Counties, 2000*. Washington, DC: Bureau of Justice Statistics.

[5] Rainville, G. & B. Reaves (2003). *Felony Defendants in Large Urban Counties, 2000*. Washington, DC: Bureau of Justice Statistics, p. 17.

[6] 18 U.S.C.A. § 3141 *et seq.* [1996].

[7] 481 U.S. 739 (1987).

[8] Boland, B., P. Mahanna & R. Sones (1992). *The Prosecution of Felony Arrests*, 1988. Washington DC: BJS.

[9] *In re Winship*, 397 U.S. 358, 90 S. Ct. 1068, 25 L. Ed. 2d 368 (1970).

[10] *State v. Babers*, 514 N.W.2d 79 (Iowa 1994).

[11] Title 18 U.S.C. § 17.

[12] *Martin v. Ohio*, 480 U.S. 228, 107 S. Ct. 1098, 94 L. Ed. 2d 267 (1987).

[13] *Williams v. Florida*, 399 U.S. 78 (1970).

[14] *Apodaca v. Oregon*, 406 U.S. 404 (1972).

[15] NCCD (1989). *National Assessment of Structured Sentencing*. Washington DC: Bureau of Justice Assistance.

[16] Travis, J. & J. Petersilia (2001). "Reentry Reconsidered: A New Look at an Old Question." *Crime and Delinquency* 47, 3: 291-313, p. 294.

[17] Travis, J. & J. Petersilia (2001). "Reentry Reconsidered: A New Look at an Old Question." *Crime and Delinquency* 47, 3: 291-313, p. 294.

[18] Travis, J. & J. Petersilia (2001). "Reentry Reconsidered: A New Look at an Old Question." *Crime and Delinquency* 47, 3: 291-313, p. 294.

[19] 542 U.S. 296 (2004).

[20] 543 U.S. 220 (2005).

[21] Petersilia, J. (2002). *Reforming Probation and Parole*. Lanham, MD: American Correctional Association, p. 29.

[22] Bureau of Justice Statistics. Retrieved 7/1/2007 from: http://www.ojp.usdoj.gov/bjs/.

[23] Steffensmeier, D., J. Ulmer & J. Kramer (1998). "The Interaction of Race, Gender, and Age in Criminal Sentencing: The Punishment Cost of Being Young, Black and Male." *Criminology* 36, 4: 763-797.

[24] For a review of this literature, see Pollock, J. (2002). *Women, Prison and Crime*. Belmont, CA: Wadsworth.

Chapter 10

Juvenile Justice and Corrections

(with Dr. Gini Deibert, Texas State University-San Marcos)

What You Need to Know

★ The juvenile justice system has a different origin and mission from the adult criminal court system and follows the model of *parens patriae* (it takes the place of a parent).

★ A series of Supreme Court cases in the 1970s established a variety of due process rights for juveniles, including the requirement of proof beyond a reasonable doubt.

★ Juvenile crime has been declining, and violent crime is now half that of its peak in the 1990s.

★ There are many differences in the terminology between the juvenile and adult system that are reflective of a more rehabilitative mission.

★ The three means by which juveniles end up in criminal court are waiver, concurrent jurisdiction (direct file), and statutory exclusion.

★ Probation is the most frequent sentence given for juvenile offenders.

★ In *Roper v. Simmons*, the Supreme Court disallowed the execution of youth who committed their crime when they were under the age of 18.

★ Recidivism of juvenile offenders is roughly 50 percent.

Nathaniel Brazill brought a gun to school and shot a well-liked teacher in the face, killing him. He was 13. The jury was asked to decide if he committed premeditated murder. Is a 13-year-old capable of "cold-blooded murder?" Throughout most of this country's history, we have excused juveniles from their crimes because of a belief that their immaturity prevented them from engaging in the calm, rational deliberation that is required for criminal (and moral) culpability. It is the same reasoning that supports laws that prevent juveniles from drinking alcohol or buying cigarettes, voting, or serving in the military. Others argue that 13-year-olds know right from wrong and should be held accountable for their actions. Brazill's jury found him guilty of second-degree murder, and he was sentenced to serve 28 years in prison. His earliest release date will be when he is 41.

The juvenile justice system is a separate and parallel justice system to the adult criminal system. Many police departments have specialized juvenile divisions; many states have specialized juvenile courts; and the juvenile corrections system is separate from the adult corrections system. The terminology in the juvenile justice system is different, as is the origin, history, and mission. A fundamental difference between the two systems is the emphasis placed upon the culpability of the offender and the system's role in changing behavior. Children are believed to be less responsible for their actions than adults. In this chapter, we will review the juvenile justice system with special attention to how it differs from the adult system.

1. CULPABILITY AND VIOLENT CRIME BY JUVENILES

If you believe that a 13-year-old murderer is responsible enough for his or her own behavior to serve a life sentence or even be executed, would you also agree that a 13-year-old is old enough to know whether to smoke or drink? Quit school if he feels like it? Serve in the military? If you answered "yes" to the life sentence, but "no" to the smoking or military, how do you explain the contradiction?

Lionel Tate was 12 years old when he killed a six-year-old by breaking her neck, imitating what he saw while watching pro wrestlers. His attorneys argued that he had not meant to hurt her and was just playing. It seems very possible that he did not mean to hurt the girl, and prosecutors must have thought so too, because they offered him a sentence of three years in a juvenile facility, one year of house arrest, and 10 years of probation. However, because he was a juvenile, his mother made the decision for him to refuse the plea bargain and go to trial, evidently assuming the jury would acquit him or find him guilty of a lesser crime. Instead, the jury found him guilty of first-degree murder, and he was sentenced to a mandatory term of life without parole.[1]

Lionel Tate has now become the poster child for a reexamination of how we treat juvenile offenders. Even the prosecutor in that case is now advocating a less harsh sentence for juveniles convicted of murder.[2] On January 29, 2004, after an appeal seeking a re-trial, the prosecutor and defense reached a plea agreement whereby Tate pleaded guilty to second-degree murder, with a sentence of three years in juvenile custody and one year of house arrest. Because he had already served that amount of time, he was released. In 2006 Tate was accused of committing armed robbery and is now back in prison for a probation violation.

In the 1990s, many states enacted new laws or changed existing laws to increase the controls and sanctions over juveniles. These laws included the following:

- ★ curfew laws
- ★ parental responsibility laws
- ★ anti-gang laws
- ★ juvenile boot camps
- ★ gun laws
- ★ removing laws that seal juvenile records
- ★ waiver laws (allowing waiver to adult courts)
- ★ concurrent jurisdiction laws (extending criminal court jurisdiction to more crimes)

The move to treat juvenile criminals more harshly has been fueled by the Columbine High School shooting and others, by the serious crimes committed by gang members, and by the pervasive view that juvenile crime is growing and the juvenile justice system is too lenient.

Part of the impetus for this harsher treatment of juveniles has been a public perception that juvenile crime is increasing and is becoming more violent. Because lawmakers respond to public pressure, public perceptions affect laws. For instance, the public perceives that there is a growing risk of violence in schools; therefore, we have seen an incredible escalation of security procedures and zero-tolerance treatment of juveniles who express hostile feelings.

In some cases the zero-tolerance approach toward expressions of violence has reached extreme levels that many believe are counterproductive. A 10-year-old girl who whispered "I could kill her" after she wet her pants because her teacher refused to let her go to the bathroom, a 10-year-old who said "I oughtta murder his face" when a classmate messed up his desk, a classmate who uttered a threat after he was pushed, a nine-year-old boy who shot a wad of toilet paper, and a kid in the school cafeteria line who warned his classmates if they ate all the potatoes he would "get them" were all suspended for these "threats of violence." Many of these children now have criminal records for such acts. In all, 50 suspensions in six weeks occurred in one school district after the county prosecutor met with school officials and told them they had no discretion in reporting threats to authorities.[3] Some parents and other observers believe that this response is unwarranted. The American Bar Association has passed a resolution condemning zero-tolerance policies that allow no discretion in defining children's acts as criminal.[4]

Observers note that there have been cycles of swinging back and forth between repressive and treatment-oriented approaches for juveniles from the beginning of our nation's court systems. What distinguishes the juvenile system from the adult legal system is that it supposedly addresses the needs of those who are abused or neglected, as well as those who have committed acts that would be crimes if committed by adults. Many juveniles, of course, fit into both groups.

There are many who believe that juvenile crime is becoming increasingly violent and that kids are literally "getting away with murder." This perception has been nurtured by the media's attention to a few notorious cases, the emphasis on gang activity in both fiction and news, and the idea that juvenile crime is increasing. According to 1998 crime figures, however, violent crime arrests of juveniles decreased by eight percent and property crime arrests decreased by 11 percent between 1994 and 1998.[5] Juvenile crime has continued to decrease since 1998, and in 2001 it was reported that the murder rate was at a 15-year low, and the burglary and robbery rates were at 20-year lows.[6] The Bureau of Justice Statistics indicates that between 1993 and 2005, the number of serious violent offenses committed by persons ages 12 to 17 declined 61 percent, while those committed by persons older than 17 fell 58 percent.[7] Thus, we are in a strange situation where the majority of the public believe that juvenile crime is increasing and becoming more violent, and legislation and public responses to juvenile crime are becoming increasingly harsher; while, in reality, the rate of juvenile crime continues to decline at dramatic levels.

2. THE HISTORY OF THE JUVENILE JUSTICE SYSTEM

As most people know, juveniles are dealt with in a separate judicial and correctional system than adults, operating under the legal concept of **parens patriae** (in the place of the parent). While there are many parallels between the juvenile justice systems and the adult criminal justice system, most characterize the juvenile system as more lenient, forgiving, and more oriented toward rehabilitation than the adult justice system. The spirit of the juvenile justice system is based on the notion that young people are more malleable than adults and can be reformed; further, that the culpability of very young offenders is less than that of adults.

The juvenile system handles both **delinquents** (those who commit an act that is defined as a crime by the penal code), and **status offenders** (whose behavior is prohibited only because they are juveniles, such as running away, breaking curfew, or being "incorrigible"). In some cases, juveniles who are taken into state custody have done nothing wrong. They have been declared either neglected or abused and the state takes the child away from the parent for their own protection. There is an idea that youth who lack supervision and/or who are difficult to control will graduate to more serious forms of delinquency; thus, most states have created the authority to intervene upon a finding that the juvenile fits the description of CHINS, PINS, or MINS (children in need of supervision, persons in need of supervision, minors in need of supervision).

Before the 1800s, children received very little protection or special treatment from society or the legal system. Only children under the age of seven were presumed to be incapable of criminal culpability, all others were punished similarly to adults. In the early jails of this country, children and adults were housed together.

Gradually, there came recognition that children should receive greater protections and that the state should step in when parents either could not or would not provide a safe and nurturing environment. The **Child Saver movement**, as described by Anthony Platt, involved upper-middle-class women who took on, as a reform project, the terrible living conditions of immigrant children in Northeastern cities.[8] These orphaned and/or poverty-stricken children roamed the streets as beggars and engaged in petty crimes to survive. In the late 1800s and early 1900s, the child saver movement resulted in states creating solutions such as foster care, orphanages, houses of refuge and, eventually, the juvenile justice system.

The first juvenile court was established in Chicago in 1899, and, by 1919, almost all states had created a separate judicial system for youth.[9] Very soon afterward, juvenile probation was established. The concept of a separate system for juveniles was based on the idea that children were different from adults—in their culpability and in their vulnerability. Originally, the differences between children who committed crimes and children who were neglected or abused by their parents were de-emphasized because of the idea that all were in need of care.

Status offenders, who might not have done anything other than run away from an intolerable home life, were housed with juvenile delinquents, who could have been serious offenders. In the 1970s, many recognized the injustice of this situation. The 1974 Juvenile Justice and Delinquency Prevention Act mandated, among other things, that neglected/abused children and status offenders needed to be removed from secure detention facilities. Further, if there was a determination that a status offender be sent to a residential placement, then there had to be a sight and sound separation between status offenders and juvenile delinquents if housed in the same facility. This led to a substantial decrease in the number of status offenders housed in secure detention, and the incentive to find community placements for those who posed no threat to the community.

The other major development was the Supreme Court holding that, even though the mission of the juvenile court system was benign, juveniles deserved some due process. A sequence of cases established due process rights for juveniles that led to a greater formalization of the court process. These cases are described in Box 10.1. Other due process rights have not been accorded to juveniles, however, including the right to a trial by jury.

BOX 10.1

Supreme Court Cases on Juvenile Rights

Kent v. United States
383 U.S. 541 (1966)
Required a hearing before waiver to adult court

In re Gault
387 U.S. 1 (1967)
Required some due process in juvenile proceedings

In re Winship
397 U.S. 358 (1970)
Required juvenile courts be held to the "beyond a reasonable doubt" standard in finding of guilt, instead of the preponderance standard

An increase in juvenile crime in the 1980s and early 1990s led to a "toughening" of the system, with more institutional placements and more judicial waivers to adult court. Depending on the state, the juvenile who is adjudicated in adult court may serve their sentence in an adult facility; thus, we have come almost full circle back to where we were before the child saver movement more than a century ago.

3. JUVENILE CRIME

Juvenile arrests have declined quite dramatically. Box 10.2 shows juvenile arrests as a percentage of total arrests. One can see that, in most crime categories, their share of total arrests has gone down over the 10-year period reported. In motor vehicle theft, for example, their percentage of the total number of arrests is almost half what it was 10 years ago. Thus, not only have the number of juvenile arrests declined, their *share* of arrests has also declined in most crime categories. There are some crimes where the share of arrests of juveniles has increased. For instance, "other assaults," shows an increase in the number of arrests, and juveniles' share of arrests has also increased from 18 percent of all arrests to 19 percent. However, some argue that this category of crime is subject to greater discretion on the part of law enforcement. It might be argued that the "greater formalization" of intervention in school misbehavior is partly the cause of this increase. In other words, a fight on the playground in years past might have been handled by the principal, but today it is more likely to be handled by the school safety officer or police officer assigned to the school, and formal charges are filed against both students. This might increase the recorded number of assaults. In types of crimes where there is less discretion in defining it as a crime, the juveniles' share of crime has decreased.

BOX 10.2

Juvenile Arrests (Selected) as a Percentage of Total Arrests

Crime	1996	2005
Total	19%	15%
Murder/Manslaughter	14.5%	9%
Forcible rape	17%	15.8%
Robbery	31%	24.7%
Aggravated assault	14.6%	13%
Burglary	38.6%	26%
Larceny-theft	35%	26%
MVT	42.8%	24%
Violent Crime	17.9%	15.2%
Property Crime	36%	26.4%

Source: *Uniform Crime Reports.* Adapted from Table 32: Ten-Year Arrest Trends. Retrieved 3/1/07 from: http://www.fbi.gov/ucr/05cius/data/table_32.html.

BOX 10.3

Juvenile Arrest Rates for All Crimes, 1980-2005

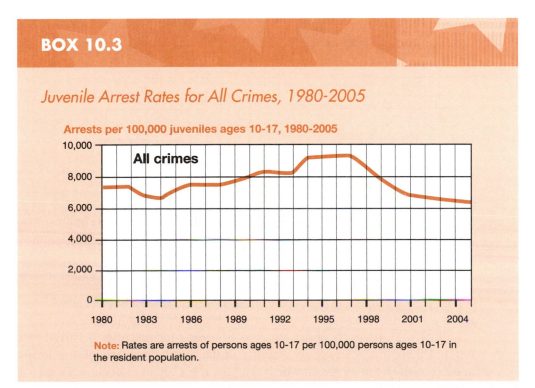

Arrests per 100,000 juveniles ages 10-17, 1980-2005

Note: Rates are arrests of persons ages 10-17 per 100,000 persons ages 10-17 in the resident population.

Source: Office of Juvenile Justice and Delinquency Prevention (March 19, 2007). OJJDP *Statistical Briefing Book.* Available at: http://ojjdp.ncjrs.org/ojstatbb/crime/JAR_Display.asp?ID=qa05200.

Juvenile arrests for violent crime fell proportionately more than adult arrest rates between 1994 and 2003. During this 10-year period, the percent decline in the number of arrests was greater for juveniles than for adults for each violent index offense.[10] The most serious charge in nearly half of all juvenile arrests in 2003 was larceny-theft, followed by simple assaults, drug abuse, disorderly conduct, or a liquor law violation.[11]

Box 10.3 shows the pattern of criminal arrests for all crimes over the years. We can see very clearly that arrest rates for juveniles have decreased from their peak in 1996-1998. In 2005, there were 6,350 arrests for every 100,000 youths ages 10 through 17. The overall juvenile arrest rate was lower in 2005 than in 1980.[12]

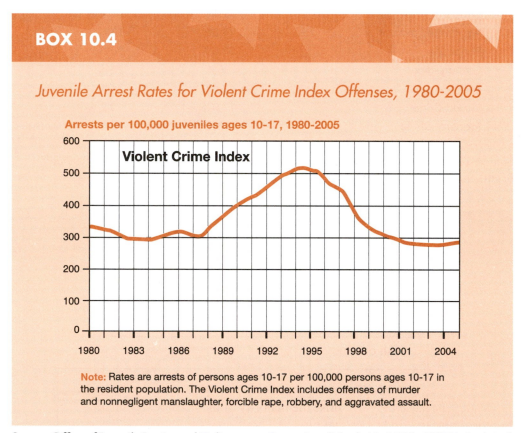

BOX 10.4

Juvenile Arrest Rates for Violent Crime Index Offenses, 1980-2005

Arrests per 100,000 juveniles ages 10-17, 1980-2005

Violent Crime Index

Note: Rates are arrests of persons ages 10-17 per 100,000 persons ages 10-17 in the resident population. The Violent Crime Index includes offenses of murder and nonnegligent manslaughter, forcible rape, robbery, and aggravated assault.

Source: Office of Juvenile Justice and Delinquency Prevention (March 19, 2007). OJJDP *Statistical Briefing Book.* Available at: http://ojjdp.ncjrs.org/ojstatbb/crime/JAR_Display.asp?ID=qa05200.

As for violent crime, the peak came about 1995 and the decline occurred more rapidly. Box 10.4 shows the violent crime arrest pattern for juveniles.

Finally, for property crime, the peak of arrests for juveniles occurred earlier and there has been greater stability in the arrest rates through the 1980s and first half of the 1990s, at which time the rates began to decline. Box 10.5 shows that the juvenile arrest rate for Property Crime Index offenses declined by 51 percent between 1980 and 2005.

BOX 10.5

Juvenile Arrest Rates for Property Crime Index Offenses, 1980-2005

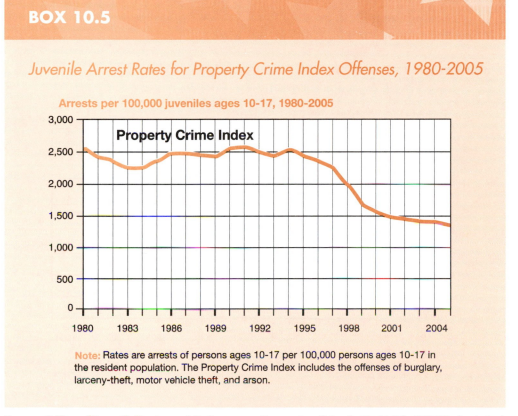

Arrests per 100,000 juveniles ages 10-17, 1980-2005

Property Crime Index

Note: Rates are arrests of persons ages 10-17 per 100,000 persons ages 10-17 in the resident population. The Property Crime Index includes the offenses of burglary, larceny-theft, motor vehicle theft, and arson.

Source: Office of Juvenile Justice and Delinquency Prevention (March 19, 2007). OJJDP *Statistical Briefing Book*. Available at: http://ojjdp.ncjrs.org/ojstatbb/crime/JAR_Display.asp?ID=qa05200.

3.1 Female Juvenile Offenders

Although some researchers have long been associated with identifying and calling attention to the issue of female juvenile offenders,[13] this small population has been largely ignored. Programming has been aimed at male juvenile offenders because they comprise the majority of the offender population. Theoretical research indicates that girls and boys may come to delinquency from different paths. Girls are less likely to be involved in delinquency and those that are may be using drugs and acting out as a coping strategy for victimization. Girls involved in the juvenile justice system are very likely to have experienced physical abuse (about 61 percent) and sexual abuse (about 54 percent). More than half have attempted suicide. A substantial number have been diagnosed with one or more psychiatric disorders.[14] Even more so than boys, delinquent girls come from dysfunctional backgrounds. In one study, it was found that girls involved as wards of the state in the child protective services system were four times more likely to be subsequently delinquent while boys who had been in care were only twice as likely to be adjudicated as delinquent.[15]

BOX 10.6

Juvenile Arrest Rates for All Crimes by Sex, 1980-2005

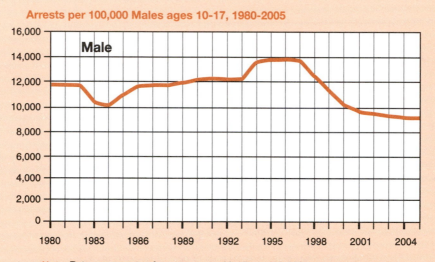

Arrests per 100,000 Males ages 10-17, 1980-2005

Note: Rates are arrests of persons ages 10-17 per 100,000 persons ages 10-17 in the resident population.

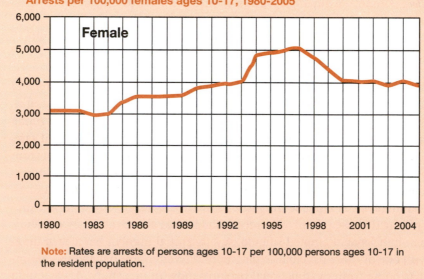

Arrests per 100,000 females ages 10-17, 1980-2005

Note: Rates are arrests of persons ages 10-17 per 100,000 persons ages 10-17 in the resident population.

Source: Office of Juvenile Justice and Delinquency Prevention (March 19, 2007). OJJDP *Statistical Briefing Book.* Available at: http://ojjdp.ncjrs.org/ojstatbb/crime/JAR_Display.asp?ID=qa05230.

According to the tables in Box 10.6, girls' arrest rates followed generally the same pattern of increase and decline over the last 20 years, but at a substantially different level (note the arrest rates along the left side of the tables). Those who argue that girls are becoming more criminal do so by referring to the fact that girls arrests' did not decline as dramatically as did boys' arrests. While boys' arrest rates for all crimes are the lowest they have been in two decades, the arrest rate for girls is still above that of 1980 rates.

A percentage increase (or decrease) is a statistic that shows how much of an increase or decrease occurred over a given period. During the period when juvenile arrests increased, the percentage increase for girls was higher than boys because their base numbers were much lower. Now, when juvenile crime is decreasing, their percentage decreases are lower than boys and some interpret this as girls are becoming more criminal. For instance, girls' arrest rates decreased between 1996 and 2005. While 445,332 girls were arrested in 1996, 381,643 were arrested in 2005. This is a percentage decrease of 14.3 percent.[16] However, the percentage decrease for boys was larger, meaning that their rate declined by a greater percentage.

It is also true that, in recent years, there are some crime categories that show percentage increases for girls and not for boys. For example, in 2005, there was a 59 percent increase in the number of girls arrested for prostitution from the previous year.[17] While that statistic seems alarming, the number of girls who were arrested is still relatively low for both years. In 2004, 420 female juveniles were detained for prostitution, and in 2005, 668 girls were arrested. So while the percentage change is very high, that statistic is not meaningful on its own without knowing the real numbers of arrests that are being represented. It should also be noted that prostitution is a crime that is highly subject to enforcement policy changes. The number arrested, in fact, may have more to do with policy shifts regarding enforcement rather than a reflection of the number of juveniles involved.

Many argue that girls are becoming more violent, pointing to an increase in the assault and aggravated assault rates of girls over the last several decades. Their rates have increased although, again, part of the reason that the percentage increases are high are the low base rates. Another explanation is the "greater formalization" of the way we treat juvenile misbehavior. With "school safety officers" in schools and an increasing tendency to arrest in any domestic violence incident, it is possible that the increase in assaults by girls is reflecting a greater tendency for formal adjudication. For instance, girls have always gotten into fights, but now they are more likely to be taken into custody for it. A few girls have always hit their mothers, but now they are much more likely to be formally processed. Ironically, the girls who are in most need of support because of dysfunctional families and victimization may be those who are most likely to be sent to secure detention.[18]

There has been long-standing and consistent evidence that girls are likely to be locked up for less serious acts than boys. Throughout the 1960s and 1970s, girls were more likely to be incarcerated in secure facilities for status offenses, while boys in the same facilities were likely to have committed delinquent acts. Even today, after a concerted effort to deinstitutionalize status offenders, current research finds that girls in detention facilities are still more likely to be less serious offenders than boys. What happens today is that judges place female status offenders or less serious delinquents on probation with conditions. Then the girl who violates a court order to not run away or skip school is found in contempt of court, which is a delinquent act and, with that finding, the girl is detained in a secure facility.[19] About 20 percent of girls who are locked up in secure facilities are status offenders, but only about three percent of boys locked up are there for status offenses. Twice as many girls as boys are locked up for violations of probation.[20] In many cases, these girls have babies and are mothers before their age of majority. More research is needed to understand the type of youth who receives secure detention, and what programs might be beneficial in breaking the cycle of state intervention.

3.2 Minority Juvenile Offenders

There are also serious concerns by observers that the juvenile justice system discriminates on the basis of race. Black and other minority youth are much more likely to be formally processed and end up in juvenile or adult facilities than whites. Poor kids are also more likely to be taken into the system. Part of this is due to lack of family support. Juveniles who have supportive families who are willing and likely to work with justice officials are more likely to be referred to community programs rather than institutionalized.

In 1997, black youth made up about 15 percent of the population, about 26 percent of juvenile arrests, about 30 percent of delinquency referrals, and about 40 percent of juveniles in long-term incarceration facilities. Minority youth are increasingly overrepresented at each successive phase of the system. Further, they are more likely to be found in public facilities, while white youth are more likely to be found in private "treatment" facilities.[21]

The increased punitiveness of the juvenile justice system has affected minority youth more dramatically than white youth. The violent crime rate of black young men in the mid-1980s and early 1990s provided the impetus to "toughen up" the juvenile system and de-emphasize the social work approach that had characterized juvenile corrections. Part of this get-tough movement included the increased use of the waiver to adult court. Black youth have been disproportionately subject to this option.[22]

Barry Feld argues that the economic changes that took place in the 1970s, which eliminated manufacturing jobs that had been the basis of a minority middle class, created an urban underclass. The poverty and hopelessness of inner-city minority neighborhoods were a fertile ground for the crack epidemic that swept these communities in the 1980s, and the crack trade was the primary cause of the spike in violent crime by young black men. Consequently, the changes that have taken place in the juvenile justice system have targeted minorities more than whites. Juvenile court judges are more likely to transfer minority delinquents to adult court than white delinquents, even after controlling for seriousness of crime.[23]

Black youth are also more likely to receive some form of detention rather than probation. In 1997, only about 19 percent of all juvenile delinquent referrals resulted in detention, but black youth made up 47 percent of those who were detained.[24] In 2002, 70 percent of all probation orders were to white youth, 27 percent involved blacks and only three percent involved other minorities.[25] In 2002, 36 percent of delinquency cases resulting in detention were blacks, substantially greater than their percentage of the juvenile population (16 percent). Further, the percent of black youth detained was also greater than their percent of the total number of delinquency cases (29 percent). The overrepresentation of black juveniles in the detention caseload was greater among personal offenses (41 percent) than other offenses. Studies indicate that race does play a factor in judicial decisions to detain, even after controlling for legal factors of the case, such as seriousness.[26]

Across offenses, for males and females, the black proportion of detained cases was in the 30 to 40 percent range. The one exception was among detained girls referred for drug offenses. Black girls accounted for just 19 percent of this group—close to their representation in the juvenile population (16 percent). Black girls constitute about half of all youth detained in public detention centers and Latinas comprise about 13 percent of the population. While the number of black girls increased by 123 percent between 1988 and 1997, the increase for white girls was only about 41 percent. While 7 of every 10 cases involving white girls are dismissed, only three of every 10 cases involving black girls is dismissed.[27]

4. THE PROCESSING OF JUVENILE OFFENDERS

Several key differences exist between the juvenile and adult justice systems in the United States. Unlike the criminal justice system, the juvenile justice system can consider extralegal factors in deciding how to handle cases. The juvenile court system can bypass all formal sanctions and judicial action, opting instead to handle matters informally.[28]

The language of juvenile corrections is different from adult corrections, as shown in Box 10.7. For instance, juveniles are not *sentenced* to jail, nor are they incarcerated. Instead juveniles are *adjudicated* with dispositions ranging from a variety of probations to *secure confinement* in *training schools*. Training schools are juvenile incarceration facilities that serve as a residential placement for the most serious juvenile offenders. The juveniles often live in *dorms* instead of prison *cells*, and are considered *students*, not *inmates*. Hopefully, these subtle differences in language are not euphemisms, but instead reflect the different mission of juvenile justice. These differences include diminished due process rights afforded to minors and a distinctly rehabilitative philosophy based on the idea that youth are more malleable than adults.

BOX 10.7

Terminology Differences for Juvenile and Criminal Justice Systems

Juvenile Justice Terminology	Criminal Justice Terminology
Respondent Detain	Defendant Arrest
Petition Intake	Indictment Prosecution
Hearing Adjudication Hearing Finding	Arraignment Trial Verdict
Secure Detention	Pretrial detention
Disposition Commitment	Sentencing Imprisonment
Aftercare	Parole
Secure Confinement	Imprisoned
Training School, State School, or Residential Placement	Jail/Prison

Sources: Austin, J., K.D. Johnson, and R. Weitzer (2005). *Alternatives to the Secure Detention and Confinement of Juvenile Offenders.* Washington, DC: Office of Juvenile Justice and Delinquency Prevention; del Carmen, R.V. and C.R. Trulson (2006). *Juvenile Justice: The System, Process, and Law.* Belmont, CA: Thompson-Wadsworth.

The process from offense through adjudication (conviction) for juveniles has several similarities as shown in Box 10.8. First, juveniles suspected of wrongdoing come into contact with the police. During this initial contact, law enforcement officers investigate a delinquent act and decide whether to proceed with informal or formal sanctions. Just as with adult criminals, an officer's reactions are based primarily on the seriousness of the offense committed. Informal sanctions include ignoring the behavior, admonishing the juvenile and consulting his or her parents, referring the family to a social service agency, or detaining the juvenile with a "station adjustment."[29] If the officer decides to officially respond to juvenile delinquency, the officer will detain the juvenile, meaning arrest the suspect.[30]

BOX 10.8

Flowchart of the Juvenile Justice System

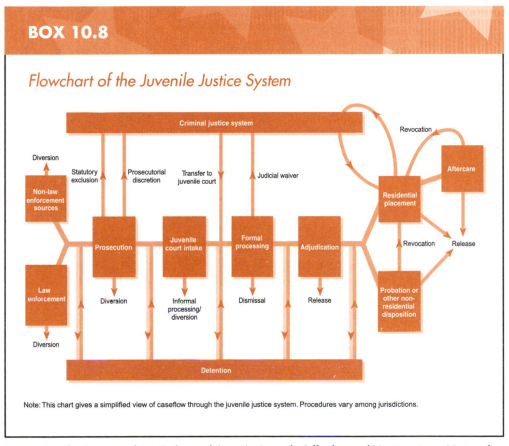

Note: This chart gives a simplified view of caseflow through the juvenile justice system. Procedures vary among jurisdictions.

Source: Snyder, H.N. and M. Sickmund (1999). *Juvenile Offenders and Victims: 1999 National Report.* Washington, DC: Office of Juvenile Justice and Delinquency Prevention, p. 98.

4.1 Arrest and Interrogation

Although some states require that juveniles have counsel or parents present when being interrogated by police, other states have no such requirement, or the juvenile is allowed to waive that right. Advocates for juveniles argue that they are simply unable to protect their own interests and are vulnerable to manipulation and intimidation by police officers. This danger can be illustrated by the 1989 Central Park jogger rape case. The juveniles who pled guilty have since been exonerated by the confession of another serial rapist and DNA evidence that linked him alone to the crime. Lawyers for the boys (now men) argue that their confessions were coerced by police through threats of the death penalty. Juvenile advocates argued that 14-year-olds were easily manipulated into confessing. Even though the prosecutor's office has declined to retry the case and they have won their freedom, they all served prison time for this crime.[31]

The intake process is comparable to the prosecution process in the criminal justice system; however, significant differences do exist in the juvenile system. Intake is the first step toward prosecution, but it is also a step toward returning the juvenile to the community. Once brought to a juvenile detention facility, the juvenile meets with an intake officer. These officers are typically probation officers. The probation/intake officer can decide to divert the youth from the formal juvenile justice system at any point. Frequently, an intake/probation officer can request that the case be placed on deferred prosecution or informal probation, during which time the juvenile must stay out of trouble so that all the charges will be discharged. If the case moves forward toward prosecution, the intake officer files a petition for an adjudication hearing with the juvenile court.[32]

4.2 Adjudication

The adjudication hearing is the juvenile version of a trial in a criminal court.[33] During this hearing a judge reviews the charges and evidence, and renders a decision about the juvenile. These hearings are less formal than criminal trials and are conducted in closed courtrooms to protect the anonymity of the youthful suspect. Rarely are adjudication hearings heard by juries, because states are not required to provide jury trials for juvenile processing.

During 2002, nearly 6 in 10 juvenile delinquency cases were handled formally through an adjudication hearing. Of those cases, nearly 7 in 10 resulted in a conviction or a disposition.[34] In 2003, in 1 in 5 delinquency cases, the juvenile was detained between the initial intake and the adjudication hearing.[35]

Drug courts exist in the juvenile system as well as the adult system. Several hundred of these courts exist across the country. In these special courts, juveniles who are identified as drug abusers are provided with specialized services. Cases are assigned to a specialized caseload and juveniles may be provided with mental health counseling, as well as family counseling and other services, in addition to drug treatment.[36] In a 2000 survey, 56 percent of male juvenile detainees and 40 percent of girls tested positive for drug use at the time of their arrest.[37] The number of juvenile court cases involving drug offenses more than doubled between 1993 and 1998, and 116,781 adolescents under the age of 18 were arrested for drug violations in 2002.[38] Therefore, it is clear that drug courts might be an appropriate response to a large segment of juvenile cases.

Waiver refers to when a juvenile court transfers a case over to adult court. Only four states do not have enabling statutes for waivers. The type of crime and the age of the youth eligible for waiver is set by state statute. Before waiver to adult court, juveniles must be determined to be **competent**. This legal concept means that juveniles are mature enough to know what is happening, to be able to judge the consequences of the decisions they make, and be able to assist in their defense. This determination requires that juveniles understand right from wrong, but it does not require that juveniles understand why they did what they did, or that they be able to control their actions.

Judicial waivers increased 73 percent between 1988 and 1994, but decreased 28 percent between 1994 and 1997. They comprise only about one percent of all juvenile cases.[39] The Office of Juvenile Justice and Delinquency Prevention publishes information on waivers, but the latest report only covers the period from 1989 to 1998. In that time period, it was reported that 1994 was the peak of juvenile waivers (with 12,100) and since 1994, the percent of juvenile cases waived to adult court has declined. In 1998 there were 8,100 cases waived to adult court.[40]

Other information indicates that this decline in the use of waiver does not mean there are fewer juveniles in the adult system, because states are increasingly using other methods such as "direct file" and "*statutory exclusion*." Statutory exclusion is when a certain crime is statutorily excluded from juvenile jurisdiction, regardless of who commits the crime, so that the juvenile is automatically tried as an adult. In some states, and for certain crimes, both adult and juvenile jurisdictions exist concurrently. In this situation, a prosecutor may choose to file charges on the juvenile in the adult system (**direct file**). It appears that the majority of cases where juveniles end up in the adult system now are not through waiver, but rather through either direct filing by the prosecutor or statutory exclusion.[41]

4.3 Sentencing

When the court finds that a juvenile committed the offense charged, the youth will appear at a disposition hearing. This disposition hearing is equivalent to a sentencing hearing in a criminal court. The key difference is that there

BOX 10.9

Disposition of delinquency Cases, 1985-2003

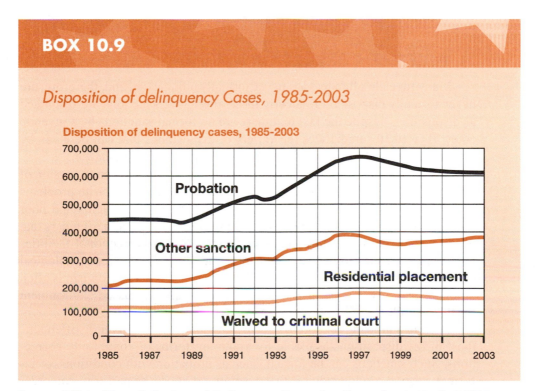

Source: Office of Juvenile Justice and Delinquency Prevention (September 8, 2006). OJJDP *Statistical Briefing Book*. Retrieved December 1, 2006 from: http://ojjdp.ncjrs.gov/ojstatbb/court/qu06501.asp?qaDate=2004.

are more options available for youthful offenders than for adults, including everything from informal sanctions to incarceration in an adult prison.[42]

Box 10.9 shows the trends in dispositions for juveniles from 1985 to 2003. In 2003, approximately 607,100 delinquent cases resulted in a disposition of probation, which is 43 percent higher than in 1985. In addition, adjudicated juvenile offenders represented 62 percent (376,100) of all cases placed on probation in 2003. In the remaining cases, the youth agreed to some form of informal probation.[43]

★ Exercise: In the State of . . .

The National Center for Juvenile Justice is an organization dedicated to research on the juvenile justice system. Through the Web site for this organization, you can research your own state's juvenile justice system. Go to **http://www.ncjj.org/stateprofiles/asp/using.asp** and find your state's description. What is the waiver policy of your state? What are the statutory exclusions, if any, to juvenile jurisdiction? Does your state allow executions of juveniles under the age of 21 and, if so, what is the statutory age?

5. JUVENILE CORRECTIONS

Many juvenile offenders are never formally adjudicated and, therefore, are never formally disposed. Frequently these alternative sanctions are discussed as dispositions despite the fact that there are no formal sanctions by a juvenile court. Box 10.10 summarizes the variety of dispositions that can be given by juvenile courts and also administered in lieu of a formal adjudication.

The most serious disposition is secure confinement, the juvenile version of jail or prison. Residential facilities are frequently characterized with problems such as overcrowding. Overcrowding is related to safety problems and poor service delivery. Obviously, there are some very violent juvenile offenders that need to be securely confined; however, in some cases, correctional facilities may cause juveniles to become more delinquent or exacerbate psychological problems.[44] Studies consistently show that, at the very least, recidivism is often no better than it would be in a less restrictive community-based environment for the juvenile.[45]

Despite a growing reliance on secure confinements for juvenile offenders, most of the dispositions available for youth are forms of community corrections. Such sanctions can be formal, such as probation with conditions, or informal, when the judge requires that a certain set of acts be performed in order for the case to be disposed of. Some of the more common sanctions are described in Box 10.10.

BOX 10.10

Types of Dispositions for Juvenile Offenders

Disposition	Definition
Dismissal of case	The case is dismissed and the juvenile is released.
Restitution/Fines	Restitution and/or damages are ordered by the court. This includes formal or informal supervision by probation officer.
Therapy	The juvenile must attend group and/or individual counseling sessions to address specific mental health concerns; formal or informal supervision by probation officer.
Mental Hospitalization	The juvenile is committed to a mental health facility to treat a specific mental illness.
Group Home Placements	The juvenile is sent to a group home or residential treatment facility, sometimes targeted to address specific problem. Outward Bound or wilderness programs or camps also are possible placements.
House Arrest/ Electronic Monitoring	The juvenile is required to be confined to home, except for school and court appearances, with or without electronic monitoring.
Probation	The juvenile is supervised in the community and required to meet set rules such as curfew, school attendance, and clean drug tests to stay out of a training school/state school facility.
Day Treatment/ Day Reporting Centers	The juvenile is supervised in the community and required to attend special classes or check-ins at set times at day centers. These centers usually have mental health services, vocational training, and other services to meet the needs of the juveniles.
Secure Confinement	The juvenile is sent to a placement in a state school or training school where he or she is expected to attend classes and rehabilitate. This sanction is the most serious for juvenile offenders who are not certified as adults.
Adult Prison	The juvenile is certified as an adult and a trial is conducted in a criminal (not juvenile) court. The juvenile is then sentenced to serve time in a prison and/or can be sentenced to death. The juvenile may serve part of the sentence in a juvenile facility until he/she is old enough to be placed in an adult prison.

Sources: Austin, J., K.D. Johnson, and R. Weitzer (2005). "Alternatives to the Secure Detention and Confinement of Juvenile Offenders." Washington, DC: Office of Juvenile Justice and Delinquency Prevention; Bartollas, C. and S.J. Miller (2005). *Juvenile Justice in America*, Fourth Edition. Upper Saddle River, NJ: Pearson/Prentice Hall; del Carmen, R.V. and C.R. Trulson (2006). *Juvenile Justice: The System, Process, and Law.* Belmont, CA: Thompson-Wadsworth.

5.1 Community Corrections

An alternative placement to secure, institutional confinement is a variety of problem-oriented residential facilities in which juveniles' specific issues are targeted in a therapeutic environment. These facilities have several different names, including group homes and residential treatment facilities, but they are usually in the juvenile's own community rather than in a rural location. Typically, each facility targets a particular issue such as substance abuse or sex offending. Mandatory completion of programs provided in these residential facilities is usually required to avoid secure confinement. The effectiveness of these programs varies according to each facility's mission. Boot camps, for example, are not particularly effective in reducing recidivism, but some sex-offender treatment facilities show success in reducing recidivism.[46]

Restorative justice programs attempt to meet the needs of the community and the offender. They are typically community based and involve the participation of the offender, the offender's family, the victim, and other community members. Restorative justice sentencing alternatives are most common with juvenile offenders. The concept of restorative justice is that it is best for the offender, victim, and community for the offender to remain in the community. Such programs, which usually include victim participation, work better with juvenile offenders who have not committed serious crimes.

One restorative justice sentencing option is family group conferencing, which began in New Zealand and Australia. In this alternative to traditional juvenile court dispositions, a group conference is held among the youth, victim, family members of both victim and offender, and other interested parties. The group determines the appropriate response to the offense and can order the youth to pay restitution, perform community service, or a range of other possibilities. In evaluations of such programs, it has been found that victims feel more satisfied after such an experience, as do the families of the offender. However, in one evaluation, about 26 percent of the youth in one such program recidivated, which was no better than a control sample who had received regular probation.[47]

5.2 Probation

Probation is the oldest and most widely used model of community-based corrections. All states have had juvenile probation since the 1930s, and probation is used for all types of juvenile offenders including first time, low-risk, and serious offenders.[48] This community-based supervision allows the juvenile to remain in a community while following a set of rules that are specifically tailored to the individual's circumstances.

Probation can be revoked if the juvenile violates the prescribed conditions, which may result in secure confinement for the juvenile offender. Probation was used in 62 percent of formal juvenile dispositions in 2002 and is more likely to be given to a juvenile offender than a residential placement.[49]

Failure on probation is distressingly common. The factors that have been

BOX 10.11

What Do Kids Think?

Six adjudicated juvenile delinquents who live in a residential placement were asked about their experiences while on probation. All of the juvenile offenders interviewed were asked about the requirements of probation, the relationship with their probation officer, and what might keep them and other juveniles out of trouble.

Jordan (15-year-old girl) said, "I think the requirements [for probation] can be hard and easy at the same time. Why I think that [is] because I mean [for] me, I have to report two times a week and its kind of hard because I mean I have a lot of things to do, like watch my daughter. Also the curfew is kind of hard to cope with because I mean 8:00, it's kind of hard to be in at that time, but it could be easy at the same time because it helps me stay on track."

Jordan also offered advice on preventing delinquency and crime. She stated, "I think the best way to prevent crime would be to like have more people willing to help people because mainly it's people in stress or having trouble. Also if they had family that really cared."

Most of the juveniles interviewed thought that family who cared and other adults who checked in with young people would prevent crime. Bryan (16) believes that young people "have someone checking up on them and talking to them to prevent [crime] from happening." Cassy (14) added, "Hang with the right people and don't let [any]body bring you down because they [are] down."

Another common theme was that despite the infrequency in which they would meet with their probation officers, most of the juveniles believed that the officers were helpful. Harris (14-year-old boy), said that her probation officer, "really helps me [to] be in a better situation." Natalie (15) agreed, adding, "My probation officer has made a difference in my life. She believed in me when others didn't."

---

associated with failure include: adjudication for a delinquent act before age 13 and several prior police contacts.[50] Intensive probation programs have been offered as a solution to the failure of regular probation to prevent juveniles from violating probation. Such programs have been evaluated and findings indicate that, similar to adult intensive probation, no significant difference exists between recidivism rates for intensive supervision caseloads and regular probation supervision.[51]

Other innovations have included enriched programming, offering adjudicated youths a range of counseling and educational services. In one such integrated program in Los Angeles, program youth were exposed to self-esteem building, educational tutoring, individual and group counseling, mental health services, substance abuse education and treatment, gang prevention alternatives, crisis intervention, family preservation services, education in parenting skills, housing and financial aid information, career development planning and employment services. In a careful quasi-experimental design, youth were assigned randomly to a treatment group or a control group who experienced regular probation. Although the treatment group performed better in school, and received fewer violations; after the initial six-month reporting period, there were no statistically significant differences found between the two groups.[52]

Arguably, the program did not result in significant differences in outcome because both groups had fairly high success rates (about 80 percent in both groups did not violate their probation). Critics argue that the evaluation did not take into account the high **attrition** (dropout) rate, especially in the treatment group, where twice as many youth were removed to secure facilities for more intensive counseling or treatment. Who were left, perhaps, were those who might have performed successfully with or without such enriched services.[53]

5.3 Institutionalization

The number of juveniles held in adult prisons has been declining over the years. In 2005, there were 2,266 inmates under age 18 in adult prisons and 6,759 juveniles in jails. Connecticut had the largest number (382), although it should be noted that they have a combined (jail and prison) correctional system; followed by New York (223), Florida (185), and North Carolina (169).[54] A much larger number of juvenile offenders are incarcerated in training schools or youth detention facilities. In 2003, there were about 109,225 juveniles in secure placements (training schools or youth detention facilities). About two-thirds of the youth were housed in public facilities, with the remaining in private facilities. Only about 12 percent were status offenders.

Experts in juvenile justice agree that secure confinement in "training schools," correctional schools, or detention centers should be used only as a last resort and reserved for serious, violent offenders.[55] Juvenile secure detention and confinement institutions are overcrowded, which is not only dangerous but limits programming options.[56]

These juvenile prisons and jails sometimes resemble their adult counterparts with high walls and razor wire. Most, however, have cottage-style architecture instead of cellblocks and they have enriched educational programming. Many youth facilities operate under a token or phase system that requires juveniles to work toward release. Even in states with determinate sentencing for adults, youth offenders typically have indeterminate sentences, so that facility staff may have a great deal of input into when the juveniles are released. Youth earn points or move through phases by following rules and participating in programming.

While these facilities for juveniles generally offer more educational and vocational programming than adult institutions, there seem to be as many scandals and problems associated with their management as with the adult prisons. In 2006-2007, the Texas Youth Commission, the state agency responsible for managing the network of secure and community placements for juve-

BOX 10.12

One-Day Count of Juveniles in Residential Placement Facilities, 1997-2003

	Number				Percent			
	1997	**1999**	**2001**	**2003**	**1997**	**1999**	**2001**	**2003**
All facilities								
All residents	116,701	120,996	118,008	109,225	100%	100%	100%	100%
Juvenile offenders	105,055	107,856	104,413	96,655	90	89	88	88
Other residents*	11,646	13,140	13,595	12,570	10	11	12	12
Juvenile offenders in								
Public facilities	75,600	76,379	73,328	66,210	65	63	62	61
State facilities	46,516	47,504	43,669	37,335	40	39	37	34
Local facilities	29,084	28,875	29,659	28,875	25	24	25	26
Private facilities	29,455	31,303	30,891	30,321	25	26	26	28
Tribal facilities	n/a	174	194	124	0	0	0	0

* Other residents include youth age 21 or older and those held in the facility but not charged with or adjudicated for an offense.

Notes: The census reference dates were 10/29/1997, 10/27/1999, 10/24/2001, and 10/22/2003.

Source: Office of Juvenile Justice and Delinquency Prevention (March 27, 2006). *OJJDP Statistical Briefing Book.* Available at: http://ojjdp.ncjrs.gov/ojstatbb/corrections/qa08201.asp?qaDate=2003. Adapted from Snyder, H. & M. Sickmund (2006). *Juvenile Offenders and Victims: 2006 National Report,* Chapter 7. Washington, DC: Office of Juvenile Justice and Delinquency Prevention.

nile offenders, was rocked by a scandal that eventually led to the resignation of several top administrators, the assignment of a governor-appointed special master, a threat to place the agency in receivership, and the indictments of several former staff. The scandal began with a series of news stories that detailed the investigation of supervision staff at one detention center for allegedly sexually abusing juvenile inmates of the facility. Despite a report from the Texas Rangers, and reports from the agency's own staff at the facility, no action was taken, by the agency or the local prosecutor, for several years. After the story broke, indictments were finally handed down for the two staff members allegedly involved, but the news stories led to a wholesale investigation of other charges and alleged cover-ups and mismanagement of agency officials. It was alleged that children in custody were being supervised by convicted felons, that they were held longer than their legal sentence, and that they were sexually and physically abused.[57]

The scandal points out the problems of monitoring and responding to abuses in youth detention facilities. Typically the facilities are far away from the youth's home and family, therefore local officials do not feel that they are part of their constituency. Staff members may believe that if they come forward with complaints, they will be retaliated against, especially if the perpetrators of such abuses are favored by higher administrators. The result is that, periodically, states experience scandals where evidence of sexual and physical abuse are reported in the press, and legislators call for the resignation of top administrators. After the furor dies down, the public generally never thinks about such facilities until the next scandal.

5.4 Capital Punishment

Only recently has the United States joined the majority of nations in banning the execution of juveniles. In *Roper v. Simmons* (May 7, 2005), the Supreme Court, in a 5 to 4 decision, held that the Eighth and Fourteenth Amendments barred the execution of anyone who committed their crime before the age of 18. At the time, 20 states allowed the execution of offenders who committed their crimes when they were 16 or 17. Texas had 29 of these offenders on death row when the Court reached its holding in the *Roper* case. In 2004, 59 individuals were executed who committed their crime before the age of 18.[58]

5.5 Recidivism

Approximately 100,000 juvenile offenders are released each year from secure correctional placements, including state schools, residential treatment facilities, and adult jails and prisons.[59] However, once released, most juvenile offenders will recidivate. Data show that recidivism rates for juvenile offenders released from correctional facilities are 55 percent or higher.[60] Juvenile offenders who are released from adult facilities have equal or higher rates of recidivism as youth released from juvenile facilities.

Juvenile offenders who are confined to a secure facility are likely to function well below their age-appropriate grade level in school, and a significant proportion of these offenders are functionally illiterate. Schools are reluctant to welcome back the re-entering juveniles and often juveniles are forced to start mid-year, which puts them even further behind. As a result, many of these youths never go back to high school and have excessive free time when they return to the community.[61]

In addition, many mental and physical health conditions go untreated or under-treated while juveniles are confined. Research estimates that at least one out of every five youth in the juvenile justice system has serious mental health problems.[62] Deteriorating mental health can affect a juvenile's ability to stay out of trouble. Substance abuse problems are often also left untreated while confined. Approximately half of all juvenile offenders who are confined have substance abuse problems. Yet many of these juveniles never receive any treatment for abuse and addiction problems. Once these offenders are released, their substance abuse problems frequently lead to other acts of delinquency.[63]

One example of a successful program was a specialized juvenile aftercare program in California. This 13-week course emphasized positive social skills, covered drug and alcohol abuse, education, and employment opportunities. After 90 days, the control group was twice as likely as the aftercare group to recidivate and use drugs or alcohol, and three times as likely to have returned to old peer networks. After one year, the recidivism rate of the control group was 53 percent compared to 32 percent of the treatment group.[64]

In an analysis of 40 promising programs, it was found that the elements associated with successful reduction of recidivism included systematic assessment, appropriate styles of service, and treatment "fidelity," which is the extent to which the program sticks to the original program elements.[65]

6. CONCLUSION

The juvenile justice system began with the mission to treat juveniles differently from adult offenders and to recognize their reduced culpability and greater ability to change. With a series of court cases in the 1970s, the juvenile system lost much of its informality and juvenile offenders were granted greater due process rights. During the 1990s, a variety of legislative and procedural changes were enacted in response to a spike in juvenile offending. The consequence has been that more juveniles are processed in the adult court system.

While juvenile offense rates have decreased since the 1990s, the use of correctional institutions for youthful offenders, both secure confinement and adult prisons, continues to increase.[66] The lack of treatment available to juveniles while they are confined is considered to be the biggest obstacle to effective reentry.[67]

Serious juvenile justice debates remain unresolved, including:

★ The use of adult courts to adjudicate youthful offenders

★ The perceived bias of the system toward minorities

★ The use of a variety of zero-tolerance measures in schools to address violence

★ The identification of successful programming for juveniles

Public policy remains committed to changing the delinquent ways of juvenile offenders and preventing these youth from becoming chronic criminal offenders. Community-based programs such as probation, group homes, and day reporting centers should be utilized for all offenders who do not pose serious risks to the public because there is evidence that these are more effective at reducing recidivism and improving community adjustment than secure confinements.[68]

REVIEW QUESTIONS

1. Describe the child saver movement. When were the first juvenile courts established?

2. What are the differences between status offenders and delinquents?

3. Identify the rights established in the *Kent v. United States*, *In re Winship, In re Gault*, and *Roper v. Simmons* cases.

4. Describe the pattern of juvenile arrests over the last 20 years.

5. Describe the arrest pattern of female juveniles compared to male juvenile offenders.

6. Describe the evidence used to show that minority youth are incarcerated disproportionately.

7. What are the differences in the terminology between the adult and juvenile systems?

8. Describe waivers and other means by which juveniles are prosecuted in criminal court.

9. Describe some of the sanctions used for youthful offenders.

10. How many juveniles are incarcerated in adult facilities? How many in juvenile facilities? Discuss the findings regarding the recidivism of juvenile offenders.

VOCABULARY

attrition – the number who drop out or quit

Child Saver movement – involved upper-middle-class women in the late 1800s who took on as a reform project the terrible living conditions of immigrant children

competent – able to understand right and wrong, understand the proceedings, and be able to assist in one's defense

delinquents – those who commit an act that is defined as a crime by the penal code

direct file – when the prosecutor and juvenile prosecutor both have jurisdiction to pursue a case, and the prosecutor in adult criminal court prosecutes the juvenile

parens patriae – the idea that the state will take the place of the parent

restorative justice – programs that are typically community based and involve the participation of the offender, offender's family, victim, and other community members

status offenders – juveniles who commit behavior that is punished only because they are juveniles, such as running away, breaking curfew, or being "incorrigible"

statutory exclusion – when a certain crime is statutorily excluded from juvenile jurisdiction, and the juvenile is automatically tried as an adult

waiver – when a juvenile court transfers a case to be adjudicated in adult court

FOR FURTHER READING

Chance, Randall (2004). *Raped by the State*. Bloomington, IN: Authorhouse. Available as an ebook at: http://www.authorhouse.com/BookStore/ItemDetail. aspx?bookid=21956.

del Carmen, R. and C. Trulson (2006). *Juvenile Justice: The System, Process, and Law*. Belmont, CA: Thompson-Wadsworth.

Platt, Anthony (1977). *The Child Savers*. Chicago, IL: University of Chicago Press.

Whitehead, John and Steven P. Lab (2006). *Juvenile Justice: An Introduction, Fifth Edition*. Newark, NJ: LexisNexis/Matthew Bender.

[1] Cable News Network (February 23, 2001). "Florida Judge Hears Motions in Child Murder Case." Retrieved 2/6/03 from: http://www.cnn.com/2001/la/02/23/child.killer.hearing.

[2] Riddle, A. (2001) "Recent Murder Trial Sparks Debate." ABC News. Retrieved 5/2001 from: http://dailynews.yahoo.com/h/ap/20010518/vs/young_killers/http.

[3] Zernike, K. (2001). "Crackdown on Threats in Schools Fails a Test." *New York Times*. Retrieved 5/17/01 from: www.nytimes.com/2001/05/17/nyregion/17THRE.html.

[4] Zernike, K. (2001). "Crackdown on Threats in Schools Fails a Test." *New York Times*. Retrieved 5/17/01 from: www.nytimes.com/2001/05/17/nyregion/17THRE.html.

[5] Federal Bureau of Investigation (1998). Uniform Crime Reports. 1998. Washington, DC: U.S. Department of Justice.

[6] Office of Juvenile Justice and Delinquency Prevention (2001). *OJJDP Statistical Briefing Book: Law Enforcement and Juvenile Crime*. Retrieved 8/7/07 from: http://ojjdp.ncjrs.org/ojstatbb/crime/JAR.asp.

[7] Bureau of Justice Statistics (2007). *Criminal Offenders*. Retrieved 7/30/07 from: http://ojp.usdoj.gov/bjs/.

[8] Platt, A. (1977). *The Child Savers: The Invention of Delinquency*. Chicago, IL: University of Chicago Press.

[9] Platt, A. (1977). *The Child Savers: The Invention of Delinquency*. Chicago, IL: University of Chicago Press.

[10] Snyder, H. & M. Sickmund (2006). *Juvenile Offenders and Victims: 2006 National Report*. Washington, DC: Office of Juvenile Justice and Delinquency Prevention, p. 127.

[11] Snyder, H. & M. Sickmund (2006). *Juvenile Offenders and Victims: 2006 National Report*. Washington, DC: Office of Juvenile Justice and Delinquency Prevention, p. 127.

[12] Office of Juvenile Justice and Delinquency Prevention (March 19, 2007). *OJJDP Statistical Briefing Book*. Available at: http://ojjdp.ncjrs.org/ojstatbb/crime/JAR_Display.asp?ID=qa05200.

[13] Chesney-Lind, M. (2006). *The Female Offender: Girls, Women, and Crime*. Thousand Oaks, CA: Sage; Chesney-Lind, M. & R. Sheldon (1998). *Girls, Delinquency, and Juvenile Justice*, Second Edition. Belmont, CA: West/Wadsworth.

[14] Dohrn, B. (2004). "All Ellas: Girls Locked Up." *Feminist Studies* 30, 2: 302-324, p. 307.

[15] Dohrn, B. (2004). "All Ellas: Girls Locked Up." *Feminist Studies* 30, 2: 302-324, p. 308.

[16] See the *Uniform Crime Reports*. Retrieved from: http://www.fbi.gov/ucr/05cius/data/table_33.html.

[17] See the *Uniform Crime Reports*. Retrieved from: http://www.fbi.gov/ucr/05cius/data/table_33.html.

[18] Chesney-Lind, M. (2006). *The Female Offender: Girls, Women, and Crime*. Thousand Oaks, CA: Sage. Dohrn, B. (2004). "All Ellas: Girls Locked Up." *Feminist Studies* 30, 2: 302-324, p. 313.

[19] Chesney-Lind, M. (1977). "Judicial Paternalism and the Female Status Offender." *Crime and Delinquency* 23: 121-130. Chesney-Lind, M. (2006). *The Female Offender: Girls, Women, and Crime*. Thousand Oaks, CA: Sage; Dohrn, B. (2004). "All Ellas: Girls Locked Up." *Feminist Studies* 30, 2: 302-324.

[20] Dohrn, B. (2004). "All Ellas: Girls Locked Up." *Feminist Studies* 30, 2: 302-324, p. 311.

[21] Feld, B. (2003). "The Politics of Race and Juvenile Justice: The 'Due Process Revolution' and the Conservative Reaction." *Justice Quarterly* 20, 4: 765-800, p. 794.

[22] Feld, B. (2003). "The Politics of Race and Juvenile Justice: The 'Due Process Revolution' and the Conservative Reaction." *Justice Quarterly* 20, 4: 765-800.

[23] Feld, B. (2003). "The Politics of Race and Juvenile Justice: The 'Due Process Revolution' and the Conservative Reaction." *Justice Quarterly* 20, 4: 765-800, p. 792.

[24] Leiber, M. & K. Fox (2005). "Race and the Impact of Detention on Juvenile Justice Decision Making." *Crime and Delinquency* 51, 4: 470-497.

[25] Livesey, S. (2006). *Juvenile Delinquency Probation Caseload, 1985-2002*. Washington, DC: Office of Juvenile Justice and Delinquency Prevention.

[26] Leiber, M. & K. Fox (2005). "Race and the Impact of Detention on Juvenile Justice Decision Making." *Crime and Delinquency* 51, 4: 470-497.

[27] Dohrn, B. (2004). All Ellas: Girls Locked Up. *Feminist Studies* 30, 2: 302-324, p. 309.

[28] Snyder, H., & M. Sickmund (2006). *Juvenile Offenders and Victims: 2006 National Report*. Washington, DC: Office of Juvenile Justice and Delinquency Prevention.

[29] del Carmen, R. & C. Trulson (2006). *Juvenile Justice: The System, Process, and Law*. Belmont, CA: Thomson-Wadsworth, p. 21.

[30] del Carmen, R. & C. Trulson (2006). *Juvenile Justice: The System, Process, and Law*. Belmont, CA: Thomson-Wadsworth.

[31] Schanberg, S. (2002). "A Journey through the Tangled Case of the Central Park Jogger." *Village Voice*. Retrieved 9/5/05 from: www.villagevoice.com/generic/show_print.php?id=39999&page=schanberg&issue=0.

[32] Bartollas, C. & S. Miller (2005). *Juvenile Justice in America*, Fourth Edition. Upper Saddle River, NJ: Pearson/Prentice Hall; del Carmen, R. & C. Trulson (2006). *Juvenile Justice: The System, Process, and Law*. Belmont, CA: Thomson-Wadsworth.

[33] Bartollas, C. & S. Miller (2005). *Juvenile Justice in America*, Fourth Edition. Upper Saddle River, NJ: Pearson/Prentice Hall.

[34] Snyder, H. & M. Sickmund (2006). *Juvenile Offenders and Victims: 2006 National Report*. Washington, DC: Office of Juvenile Justice and Delinquency Prevention, p. 173.

[35] Snyder, H. & M. Sickmund (2006). *Juvenile Offenders and Victims: 2006 National Report*. Washington, DC: Office of Juvenile Justice and Delinquency Prevention, p. 169.

[36] Office of Juvenile Justice and Delinquency Prevention (2001). *Juvenile Drug Court Programs*. Retrieved from: http://www.ncjrs.org/pdffiles1/ojjdp/184744.pdf. Washington, DC: OJJDP.

[37] National Institute on Drug Abuse (2006). *Principles of Drug Abuse Treatment for Criminal Justice Populations: A Research-Based Guide*. Washington DC: National Institutes of Health.

[38] National Institute on Drug Abuse (2006). *Principles of Drug Abuse Treatment for Criminal Justice Populations: A Research-Based Guide*. Washington DC: National Institutes of Health, p. 28.

[39] Petersilia, J. (2002). *Reforming Probation and Parole*. Lanham, MD: American Correctional Association, p. 47.

[40] Puzzanchera, C. (2003). *Delinquency Cases Waived to Criminal Court, 1989-1998*. Washington, DC: Office of Juvenile Justice and Delinquency Prevention. Available at: www.ncjrs.gov/pdffiles1/ojjdp/fs200135.pdf.

[41] Rainville, G. & S. Smith (2003). *Juvenile Felony Defendants in Criminal Courts: Survey of 40 Counties*. 1998. Washington, DC: U.S. Department of Justice.

[42] del Carmen, R. & C. Trulson (2006). *Juvenile Justice: The System, Process, and Law*. Belmont, CA: Thomson-Wadsworth; Bartollas, C. & S. J. Miller (2005). *Juvenile Justice in America*, Fourth Edition. Upper Saddle River, NJ: Pearson/Prentice Hall.

[43] See the Office of Juvenile Justice and Delinquency Prevention's *Probation as a Court Disposition*. Retrieved 12/1/06 from: http://ojjdp.ncjrs.org/ojstatbb/probation/qa07102.asp?qaDate=2003.

[44] Austin, J., K. Johnson & R. Weitzer (2005). *Alternatives to the Secure Detention and Confinement of Juvenile Offenders*. Washington, DC: Office of Juvenile Justice and Delinquency Prevention; Barton, W. (2006). "Incorporating the Strengths Perspective into Intensive Juvenile Aftercare." *Western Criminology Review* 7, 2: 48-53; Snyder, H. & M. Sickmund (1999). *Juvenile Offenders and Victims: 1999 National Report*. Washington, DC: Office of Juvenile Justice and Delinquency Prevention, p. 98.

[45] Lipsey, M. (1992). "Juvenile Delinquency Treatment: A Meta-analytic Inquiry into the Variability of Effects." In T. Cook, D. Cordray, H. Hartman, L. Hedges, R. Light, T. Louis & F. Mosteller (eds.), *Meta-Analysis for Explanation: A Casebook*. New York: Russell Sage Foundation, p. 83-127.

[46] Austin, J., K. Johnson & R. Weitzer (2005). *Alternatives to the Secure Detention and Confinement of Juvenile Offenders*. Washington, DC: Office of Juvenile Justice and Delinquency Prevention; Snyder, H. & M. Sickmund (1999). *Juvenile Offenders and Victims: 1999 National Report*. Washington, DC: Office of Juvenile Justice and Delinquency Prevention.

[47] Morris, A. & G. Maxwell 1997. "Reforming Juvenile Justice: the New Zealand Experiment." *The Prison Journal*, 77, 2: 125-134.

[48] Snyder, H. & M. Sickmund (2006). *Juvenile Offenders and Victims: 2006 National Report*. Washington, DC: Office of Juvenile Justice and Delinquency Prevention.

[49] Snyder, H. & M. Sickmund (2006). *Juvenile Offenders and Victims: 2006 National Report*. Washington, DC: Office of Juvenile Justice and Delinquency Prevention, p. 172.

[50] Sharp, R. (1988). "The Early Offender Project: A Community-based Program for High Risk Youth." *Juvenile and Family Court Journal* 39, 1: 13-20.

[51] Barton, W. & J. Butts (1990). "Viable Options: Intensive Supervision Programs for Juvenile Delinquents." *Crime and Delinquency* 36, 2: 238-256.

[52] Zhang, S. & L. Zhang (2005). "An Experimental Study of the Los Angeles County Repeat Offender Prevention Program: Its Implementation and Evaluation." *Criminology and Public Policy* 4, 2: 205-236.

[53] Mackenzie, D. (2005). "The Importance of Using Scientific Evidence to Make Decisions about Correctional Programming." *Criminology and Public Policy* 4, 2: 249-258.

[54] Bureau of Justice Statistics (2006). *Prison and Jail Inmates at Mid-Year, 2005*. Washington DC: U.S. Department of Justice.

[55] Arthur, L. (2001). "Ten Ways to Reduce Detention Populations." *Juvenile and Family Court Journal*, 52, 1:29–36.

[56] Austin, J., K. Johnson & R. Weitzer (2005). *Alternatives to the Secure Detention and Confinement of Juvenile Offenders*. Washington, DC: Office of Juvenile Justice and Delinquency Prevention.

[57] McGonigle, S. & D. Swanson (2007). "Feds Knew About TYC Abuse Cases." *Dallas News*. Retrieved 8/8/07 from: http://www.dallasnews.com/sharedcontent/dws/news/texassouthwest/stories/080507dnmettycabuse.389a816.html. See also Blakeslee, N. (2007). "Hidden in Plain Sight: How Did Alleged Abuse at a Youth Facility in West Texas Evade Detection For so Long?" *Texas Observer*. Retrieved 8/8/07 from: http://www.texasobserver.org/article.php?aid=2428.

[58] Lane, C. (2005). "5-4 Supreme Court Abolishes Juvenile Executions." *Washington Post*, March 2: A1.

[59] Barton, W. (2006). "Incorporating the Strengths Perspective into Intensive Juvenile Aftercare." *Western Criminology Review* 7, 2: 48–53.

[60] Barton, W. (2006). "Incorporating the Strengths Perspective into Intensive Juvenile Aftercare." *Western Criminology Review* 7, 2: 48-53, p. 48.

[61] Barton, W. (2006). "Incorporating the Strengths Perspective into Intensive Juvenile Aftercare." *Western Criminology Review* 7, 2: 48-53, p. 49.

[62] See Cocozza, J. & J. Shufelt (2006). *Juvenile Mental Health Courts: An Emerging Strategy*. Delmar, NY: National Center for Mental Health and Juvenile Justice, Policy Research Institute. Retrieved 11/25/06 from: http://www.ncmhjj.com/pdfs/publications/JuvenileMentalHealthCourts.pdf?tr=y&auid=1879566.

[63] Barton, W. (2006). "Incorporating the Strengths Perspective into Intensive Juvenile Aftercare." *Western Criminology Review* 7, 2: 48-53, p. 49.

[64] Josi, D. & D. Seachrest (1999). "A Pragmatic Approach to Parole Aftercare: Evaluation of a Community Reintegration Program for High-Risk Youthful Offenders." *Justice Quarterly* 16: 51-80. See also Goodstein, L. & H. Sontheimer (1997). "The Implementation of an Intensive Aftercare Program for Serious Juvenile Offenders." *Criminal Justice and Behavior* 24: 332-359.

[65] Leschied, A., A. Cummings & L. Baker (2005). "Models of Supervision Relevant to the Delivery of Effective Correctional Service." In American Correctional Association, *What Works and Why: Effective Approaches to Reentry*. Lanham, MD: American Correctional Association, pp. 35-60.

[66] Barton, W. (2006). "Incorporating the Strengths Perspective into Intensive Juvenile Aftercare." *Western Criminology Review* 7, 2: 48-53.

[67] Barton, W. (2006). "Incorporating the Strengths Perspective into Intensive Juvenile Aftercare." *Western Criminology Review* 7, 2: 48-53.

[68] Howell, J. (1995). *Guide for Implementing the Comprehensive Strategy for Serious, Violent and Chronic Juvenile Offenders*. Washington, DC: Office of Juvenile Justice and Delinquency Prevention; Lipsey, M. (1992). "Juvenile Delinquency Treatment: A Meta-analytic Inquiry into the Variability of Effects." In D. Rosenbaum (ed), *Community Crime Prevention: Does it Work?* New York, NY: Russell Sage Foundation.

Chapter 11

The Function of Corrections

What You Need to Know

★ Correctional goals seem to occur in cycles and include: retribution, deterrence, incapacitation, and reform/rehabilitation.

★ The origin of the penitentiary was the Walnut Street Jail.

★ The contributions of Maconochie, Crofton, Brockway, and Augustus led to the modern-day probation and parole systems.

★ The rehabilitative era of the 1960s-1970s had ended by 1980, although its influence can still be detected in correctional programs.

★ Incarceration in prison or jail is the most frequent felony sentence (78%), but the largest percentage (59% as of 2003) of correctional offenders are on probation.

★ There are roughly 600,000-650,000 individuals who return from prison each year to their communities.

★ About seven million persons are under some form of correctional supervision, at a rate of about 3,150 per 100,000.

★ Women represent about 23 percent of probationers, 12 percent of parolees, and six percent of prisoners.

★ The three approaches to offender classification are clinical, actuarial, and risk/needs.

Criminal punishments have been around as long as there have been organized communities. Humans have been incredibly creative in inventing ways to inflict pain. At various times in history we have employed punishments that included: crucifying, drawing and quartering, boiling in oil, whipping, penal colonies, enslavement, forfeiture of all property, stocks and pillories, banishment, and many others. Historically, the goal of punishment was simply **retribution**, which basically means inflicting punishment proportional to the harm caused. However, to some extent, **deterrence** has also been a goal. Deterrence can be **specific deterrence** (what is done to an individual to deter him or her from future offending), or **general deterrence** (what is done to an individual to discourage others from future offending). Incapacitation was added as a goal with the development of places of confinement. **Incapacitation** simply means to become incapable, and in corrections, it means to make the offender incapable of committing crime. Also, in more recent eras, we have added the goal of **rehabilitation**, which means to change the individual in terms of values, attitudes, beliefs, and behaviors. Thus, the four goals of corrections or punishment have always been:

★   Retribution

★   Deterrence

★   Incapacitation

★   Reform/Rehabilitation

The cycles of punishment and correction continue, and today we remain in a more punitive era where rehabilitation is a less emphasized goal.

1. THE HISTORY OF PUNISHMENT AND CORRECTIONS

In the history of punishment, we have seen two competing approaches to punishment. On the one hand, there is a tendency to employ the community by shaming the offender (i.e., in the use of stocks and pillories); on the other hand, there has also been a tendency to banish the offender and remove him or her from the community. Most often, the two types of punishment response exist together in any given community or time.

Very early forms of justice, such as the Code of Hammurabi, detailed specific punishments for specific crimes and employed a harsh system of corporal and capital punishments for crimes. Early punishment systems also employed a proportional "eye for an eye" (**lex talionis**) form of punishment, but there were some elements of compensation to the victim instead of simply dictating physical retribution. In some societies, offenders were ordered to pay compensation, and only when they could not or would not, would corporal punishment be employed.

In medieval Europe, the term "**outlaw**" came to mean an individual who refused to abide by punishments ordered by authorities that were largely compensatory, meaning that they ordered the offender to pay back the victim in some way. When the individual declared themselves, through their non-conformance, as "outside the law," then more serious forms of punishment were employed. Very serious crimes warranted banishment; however, other forms of punishment in Europe and the American colonies kept the offender in the community and, in fact, depended on the community to enforce the punishment. Most punishments were public and the community participated. Box 11.1 shows some of the types of public punishments that were used in early American colonies. If the shame of these punishments did not deter future offending, repeat offenders were banished from the colony and/or branded to discourage them from living in other communities. Banishment from the colonies often meant death because it was hard to survive in the wilderness alone without the protection of the community.

ELDER ANDERSON IN THE PILLORY.

This engraving shows a man being punished in the stocks, or pillory, for perjury.

© Bettmann/CORBIS

The origin of the penitentiary in this country can be traced to the Walnut Street Jail and the Eastern Penitentiary in Pennsylvania. We will discuss penitentiaries in greater detail in Chapter 13. The penitentiary was a type of banishment because penitentiaries were, by design, far away from communities. Interestingly, the offenders were banished not only to protect the community from the offender, but also to protect the offender from the community! Originators of the penitentiary believed that the community was the cause of crime. The penitentiary, with its emphasis on obedience and sobriety, was considered

BOX 11.1

Forms of Public Punishment

Ducking stool Typically for women charged with being a "common scold" or, sometimes, for those accused of witchcraft. It was a board with chair on one end, dunked in the river or other body of water.

Brank Metal headgear, sometimes with a sharp spike that went under the tongue. Used for those accused of blasphemy or "common scolds."

Stocks The offender's head (and sometimes hands and feet) were secured in this wooden device in the town square. The public would participate by throwing vegetables, jeering, and scolding the offender.

a utopia where the offender could contemplate his or her evil ways and perform penitence. In fact, the name *penitentiary* is derived from this function.

The rise of the use of penitentiaries and prison colonies in the late 1770s and early 1800s spurred the creation of experiments that eventually led to community correctional alternatives like probation and parole. The most important contributors to modern concepts in corrections are described in Box 11.2. Alexander Maconochie's **mark system** in the Norfolk prison colony off the coast of Australia awarded prisoners marks or credits based on the work product of groups. Marks were exchanged for greater liberties. Eventually the inmate could even earn relative freedom on the prison colony-island and possibly early release. Sir Walter Crofton's Irish **ticket of leave system** allowed prisoners who behaved well to earn early release with a "ticket to leave" as long as they reported to the local constable's office in their community, which would then

BOX 11.2

Early Visionaries and Reformers

Alexander Maconochie (1787-1860)

Accomplishment

A Scottish naval officer who became a penal reformer, Maconochie's major contribution was the "mark system": prisoners could gain early release through work and program participation.

Sir Walter Crofton (1694-1796)

Accomplishment

Crofton's reforms included a graduated release program that could ultimately result in a conditional release called a "ticket of leave" in the 1850s. This program is the precursor for modern parole.

John Augustus (1785-1859)

Accomplishment

A Boston bootmaker who is considered the "father of probation," Augustus was a philanthropist who, for 18 years, posted bail for offenders then found them work and homes. He is credited with founding the investigations component of probation as his systematic probationary service was formulated based on criteria including moral character, age, and other mitigating factors.

Sources: Barry, J.V. (1958). *Alexander Maconochie of Norfolk Island.* Melbourne, Australia: Oxford University Press. Clear, T.R. and G.F. Cole (2002). *American Corrections*, Sixth Edition. Belmont, CA: Wadsworth Publishing Company. New York City Department of Probation. *A Brief History of Probation.* Retrieved 10/1/06 from: http://www.ci.nyc.ny.us/html/prob/html/history.html.

informally monitor the ex-prisoner's behavior in the community. Both of these "great experiments" can be described as precursors to parole. In this country, Zebulon Brockway, the first Superintendent of Elmira Reformatory, employed an early form of parole in the late 1800s. In his plan, inmates could earn a release back into the community through good behavior; an obvious forerunner of today's parole system.

Probation began with the volunteer efforts of John Augustus, a Boston shoemaker who, in the 1800s, convinced judges to release petty criminals into his custody instead of sending them to jail. He would then help the individuals get jobs and stay out of trouble in order to achieve their successful diversion from criminal sentencing.

The **Progressive Movement**, from 1890 through the early 1900s, saw a great deal of activity in the growth of private charities designed to deal with the problems of the poor in northeastern cities. Private charities and settlement houses sought to feed, clothe, and instill religious virtues in the immigrant populations. In settlement houses, such as the one run by Jane Addams, middle-class and upper-middle-class women literally moved into the ghetto and tried to recreate their middle-class community through lessons on housekeeping and etiquette in the settlement house.

Other than these few examples, the first half of the twentieth century was largely without innovation in corrections. Prisons were successful if they stayed off the front page of the newspaper. Although the legislation that created probation slowly spread across the country from its origins in Massachusetts, it wasn't until 1956 that all states finally passed enabling statutes. Between the Depression and the Vietnam War, there were no dramatic developments in correctional philosophy. That all changed in the 1960s.

1.1 The Rehabilitative Era

The period of the 1960s through 1974 has been called the **rehabilitative era**. Prisons were renamed correctional institutions, and guards were renamed correctional officers. Funding became available for prison treatment programs. There also developed a groundswell of support for community alternatives to prison. This period could also be referred to as the *prisoner rights* era. Federal courts began handing down decisions in prisoners' rights cases that supported the prisoners' complaints that prisons did not provide them with basic rights, such as due process and the right to be free from cruel and unusual punishment.

The 1967 President's Commission on Law Enforcement and the Administration of Justice's report encouraged communities to develop diversion programs to keep offenders from becoming more deeply embroiled in the justice system. One of the side effects of such programs, unfortunately, was **net-widening**. This term is used to describe how diversion programs designed for those sentenced to prison would be used for minor offenders instead. What happened, then, was not a reduction of the number of people involved in the corrections system, but an increase, because the same offenders continued to go to prison, and new offenders, who might have received only a suspended sentence before, were given the new types of sentences. Only those programs that diverted the offender *after* sentencing could be totally assured of truly diverting instead of widening the correctional population.

Part of this period can also be called the **Reintegration Era**. The term was coined to discuss the issue of inmates returning to the community and the problems they encountered. Philosophically, the approach adhered to the belief that the community was the best place to deal with most offenders and, if the offender had to be sent away to prison, then it should be for as short of a time as possible. After release, the offender has trouble reintegrating into society, and, in the reintegrative era, a number of programs were created to help ex-convicts in their re-entry. Some of the popular programs of this era included:

- ★ pre-release programs
- ★ halfway houses to transition back into the community
- ★ work furloughs/release programs
- ★ school-release programs
- ★ service-enriched parole

It should be noted that this period was also marked by the de-institutionalization of other groups, such as the mentally ill and juvenile offenders. There was an emphasis on "grassroots development," community empowerment, and a belief that institutions were the least desirable societal response to social deviants.[1]

Communities were enticed and encouraged to keep offenders in the community through grants and subsidies that paid counties a per diem for each offender who otherwise would have been sent to prison. Criminal Justice Partnership Acts gave financial incentives for counties to develop programs and partnerships among probation, jail, and other local agencies.

1.2 The Decline of the Rehabilitative Ideal

By the beginning of the 1980s, the rehabilitative/reintegration era was over. States were passing determinate sentencing statutes, furloughs and work release programs were being drastically curtailed, and the incredible increase in incarceration had begun. Probation and parole continued, of course, but the philosophy shifted to surveillance rather than service. Intensive probation programs originated in the early 1980s as a way to "beef up" this sentencing option and make it more palatable for judges who would otherwise send the offender to prison. The 1980s also saw the emergence of boot camps, created to provide tough, "shape up" incarceration experiences for young adults. Waivers to adult courts for juvenile offenders increased. Mandatory sentence laws for drug offenders were passed in many states. In the 1990s, three-strikes sentencing laws became more popular. By the end of the 1990s, correctional policy bore only the faintest resemblance to the rehabilitative era of the early 1970s. From the mid-1990s until today, the national crime rate has fallen dramatically while the imprisonment rate has continued to increase.

1.3 New Reentry Efforts

After 20 years of dormancy, it appears that a reintegration era may have returned. Three elements can be identified as forming this new era.

First, there has been a growing uneasiness with the incredible rise of incarceration. We now incarcerate in prisons or jails 738 of every 100,000 individuals in this country.[2] We use incarceration more than any similar western country and only such countries as Russia and South Africa share our tendency to incarcerate so many citizens.[3] A steady and growing voice in the academic and popular press have called into question the approach of building more prisons and incarcerating more and more people. One aspect of this criticism is the "collateral" damage that imprisonment creates. Collateral damage refers to the problems of the families left behind by offenders, and to the communities who lose large numbers of their citizens to imprisonment. It also refers to the civil disabilities that prisoners experience upon release from prison.

Second, there has been the recognition that the tens of thousands of people who have been incarcerated throughout the 1980s and 1990s are now being released. In states that abolished parole, the release comes with no substantive supervision. The statistic that has hit the news with force is that 650,000 offenders are being released into the community every year.[4] This has led to federal efforts to address the issue, such as the Second Chance Act of 2005.

> To read about the Second Chance Act, go to: http://judiciary.house.gov/HearingTestimony.aspx?ID=338

The third element that might have led to this new era of community emphasis in corrections is the **restorative justice movement**. This approach to corrections recognizes that the community is essential in crime prevention and crime control. Restorative justice programs keep the offender in the community and provide a means to meet the needs of the victim, the offender, and the community. Offenders who are banished are less likely to have a stake in the community while offenders who are embraced by the community are more likely to be reformed by the process of punishment.

The interest in returning offenders has been fueled by the 650,000 prisoners being released into the community each year. In one respect, this issue of ex-inmates is no different than the situation that has always existed. Ex-prisoners have always had problems with jobs, housing, and readjustment. In another sense, however, we face a different situation today because the scope of the problem is immense. The dramatic increase in incarceration has not only created the need for more prisons, but it has also created more ex-prisoners. Further, the scourge of drug addiction qualitatively changes the re-entry process from those ex-prisoners from 30 and 40 years ago. Still, many of their problems remain the same. One could almost have dusted off the reports from the 1970s, because the findings of those old reports were the same as the new ones. Not surprisingly, jobs and housing were, and continue to be, identified as factors in recidivism.[5]

One target of re-entry efforts is to address the range of **civil disabilities** — legal barriers that remove civil rights such as voting—that accompany a felony record. In 2001, it was reported that in 46 states, felons lose their right to vote and, in 14 of these states, the loss was permanent. It was estimated that 13 percent of the adult male population is disenfranchised in this way.[6] In 2004, only five states still retained a lifetime bar for some or all crimes. Seven other states had a bar that could be lifted if the offender applied for the voting right to be reinstated. Only two states (Maine and Vermont) had no restrictions on voting by offenders.[7]

2. PRISON VERSUS COMMUNITY CORRECTIONS

After a conviction, criminal offenders can be given a range of different punishments, but the two used most frequently are prison and probation. One in every 32 adult residents in this country is under correctional supervision.[8] Box 11.3 shows a breakdown of what percent of offenders in the criminal justice system are in each kind of supervision category. In this display, we see that probation holds the most offenders of any of the forms of correctional supervision. You might recall from Chapter 9, however, that felony offenders were more likely to receive a jail or prison sentence than a probation sentence. More than 78 percent of all felony offenders receive a prison or jail sentence. The reasons this table shows more individuals on probation than prison are: probation includes misdemeanant offenders (who are likely to receive probation) and individuals may spend more time on probation than they would spend in prison; therefore, the total number of offenders on probation is always larger

BOX 11.3

Correctional Population

Source: Bureau of Justice Statistics. Retrieved 6/2/05 from: www.ojp.usdoj.gov/bjs/. Prison and jail populations from *Prisoner and Jail Inmates Mid-Year 2004* and probation and parole numbers from *Correctional Populations, 2003 Year End*. Prison-1,410404; Jail-713,990; Parole-774,600; Probation 4,074,000.

than those in prison. Thus, one can say that a criminal offender is most likely to receive a prison or jail sentence as their punishment after conviction, but most criminal offenders in the corrections system are being supervised on a probation caseload. These two statements are not contradictory.

3. COSTS OF CORRECTIONS

It is difficult to determine the true costs of corrections. Some estimates include capital construction costs for prisons, while other estimates do not. Prison costs vary tremendously from state to state, and even within a state, maximum-security institutions cost more than minimum-security, and special-needs offenders cost more to house and care for than regular inmates. Intensive probation costs much more than regular probation, and probation sentences that use electronic monitoring are also more expensive. However, a rough estimate is that probation costs roughly $1.60 per day compared to a daily prison cost of $38.00.[9] This is a 1985 estimate. More current estimates are not much more. The cost of probation ranges from $1.24 to a high of $20.00 for intensive probation in New Jersey. The average cost of regular probation has been reported as $2.11 and the average cost for intensive probation as $9.66 (using an average of 16 states).[10] For instance, it is reported that it costs between $1.24 (Georgia) to $3.50 (Illinois) a day to supervise probationers. Intensive supervision, which has reduced caseloads and requires more probation officers, costs between $2.50 (Rhode Island) and $20 (New Jersey). This compares to the daily cost of prison that averages around $56.00 per day.[11] Prison costs are reported as $22,650 a year or $62.05 a day per prisoner.[12]

All costs associated with the criminal justice system have risen dramatically in the last 20 years, but the costs associated with corrections have risen by the biggest margin. While the total costs for police between 1982 and 2004 increased by 367 percent, and costs associated with the courts by 450 percent; the costs of corrections rose 585 percent over the same period. These increases are after the costs were adjusted for inflation.[13]

3.1 The "Collateral Costs" of Imprisonment

While imprisonment is obviously a necessary tool in the arsenal of correctional alternatives, there is a growing belief that it is used too much, with too many offenders being sent away from their communities with consequential negative effects on the individual, the family, and the community itself. In some communities, up to a quarter of all adult men are in prison on any given day.[14] The rate of imprisonment for black men is about six times higher than that for white men and the rate for Hispanic men is three times higher than that of whites.[15]

An analysis of incarceration patterns shows that certain neighborhoods in our cities are affected most heavily by incarceration. That is, some neighborhoods have disproportionate numbers of residents either away in prison or coming back from prison. What is the effect of imprisonment on these neighborhoods? One obvious result is that there is a shortage of men, leading to single head-of-households struggling to juggle work and parenthood. Another result is that the lifetime earnings of individuals are diminished because a prison sentence will affect one's employability forever. Another effect is that children will have to deal with the experience of having a parent in prison.

It is estimated that about 1.5 million children have a parent (or parents) in prison. Children of incarcerated women are especially affected because their living situation is often disrupted and, in fact, some estimates are that these children are moved an average of six times during the course of their mother's imprisonment. Children of men in prison are less likely to change their custody arrangements, because about 90 percent of them remain with their mother; however, statistics indicate that children who have family members in prison are six times more likely to be delinquent.[16] Of course, it may be the case that the removal of a violent family member is a positive factor in a child's life, but when a prisoner comes home, re-entry poses its own problems.

Researchers have found that imprisonment seemed to have some positive effects on a community, but it appears that when it reaches a certain level, there are some negative effects as well and the destabilization in families and communities may lead to more crime, not less. Some policy recommendations that have come from this research include the following:

1. Provide services to families of incarcerated offenders that include short-term financial assistance, crisis counseling, parenting classes, medical care, child care, and adult mentors for children;

2. Facilitate continued communication between the offender and his or her family that includes assistance with costs of telephoning and transportation to the prison.

3. Provide services to the children of incarcerated individuals that include counseling and assistance in maintaining contact with the incarcerated parent;

4. Provide assistance with comprehensive transition plans for release that includes job assistance, counseling, housing, and other services.

5. Reduce financial burdens of offenders that include supervision fees and court costs, at least in the short term, as well as financial restrictions that place barriers to successful re-entry (such as prohibitions against felons in public housing projects).

6. Increase access to low-cost drug treatment programs.

7. Provide services at neighborhood centers that include mentoring, awareness programs, and ex-offender counseling.[17]

4. OFFENDERS UNDER CORRECTIONAL SUPERVISION

In 1980, there were 1,842,100 individuals under some form of correctional supervision (probation, jail, prison, or parole); by 2005 there were more than seven million (7,056,000).[18] Of course the population has increased as well, but even the rate per 100,000, which holds the population constant, shows that the likelihood of correctional supervision has increased in dramatic ways. As mentioned previously, about one in every 32 adults were either in prison or under some other form of correctional control in 2005; this is about 3.2 percent of the entire population.[19]

In 1980, the rate for *any form* of correctional supervision was 1,132 per 100,000. By 1990 that rate had doubled to 2,348 per 100,000, and by 2000, it had increased again to 3,072 per 100,000.[20] In 2005, 3,150 citizens of every 100,000 were under some form of correctional supervision.[21] In effect, the rate of any form of correctional supervision has tripled in the last 25 years. It should be noted that the 2005 rate was slightly below that of 2004 (3,156) and 2003 (3,160); however, no one seriously believes that the rate will return to the lower rates of previous decades.

Of the seven million people under correctional supervision, close to five million were on probation or parole (4,946,944). In fact, the biggest portion of the increase in supervision numbers between 1990 and 2005 was in the number on probation, accounting for about half (53 percent) of the total growth of the correctional population, with prison inmates accounting for about 25 percent and jail and parolee populations making up the remainder of the increase.[22]

There is also a federal correctional system that receives criminal offenders from the federal courts. In 2003, 152,459 offenders were under the jurisdiction of the Federal Bureau of Prisons. Federal prisoners, as state prisoners, are now serving a much larger percentage (88 percent) of their sentence. About 109,712 federal offenders were under some form of community supervision.[23]

States have extremely varied supervision rates. For instance, while the state of New Hampshire has a probation supervision rate of 431 (per 100,000), Massachusetts has a supervision rate of 3,301 (per 100,000). This means that residents are almost eight times more likely to be under probation supervision

★ Exercise: In the State of . . .

Utilizing the Web site for the Bureau of Justice Statistics (**http://ojp.usdoj. gov/bjs/**), find your state's incarceration rate and compare it to surrounding states. Look for the number of people on probation and parole as well. You can find this information by following the links to BJS publications. How does your state compare to national averages?

in Massachusetts. States also have extremely varied rates of imprisonment. The south generally has a higher incarceration rate than the north. The states with the highest rates include Louisiana (at 1,138 per 100,000), Georgia (at 1,021), and Texas (at 976). The states with the lowest incarceration rates were Maine (at 272), Minnesota (at 300), and Rhode Island (at 313).[24]

As you might expect, individuals on probation tend to be less serious criminals than those who are sentenced to prison. Joan Petersilia reports that in a study of criminal records and case files of 16,500 males in 17 counties in 1980, the following factors were more likely to result in a prison sentence:

★   two or more counts

★   two or more prior convictions

★   on probation or parole status at time of arrest

★   drug addiction

★   use of a weapon during the crime or seriously injured victim

If an offender had three or more of these characteristics, there was an 80 percent probability of going to prison. Other factors that were influential were whether the offender used a private or public attorney, and whether the offender obtained pretrial release. All variables explained 75 percent of sentencing decisions; the remaining variance was not explained or predicted through the use of these variables.[25]

BOX 11.4

Characteristics of Offenders on Correctional Supervision

	Probation	Prison	Parole
Race			
White	56	34	40
Black	30	41	41
Hispanic	12	19	18
Crime Type:			
Violent crime	19	51	24
Drug crime	26	21	38
Property/other crime	54	23	26

Note: totals do not equal 100% because of other categories.

Source: Glaze, L. and S. Palla (2005). *Probation and Parole in the United States, 2004*. Washington, DC: U.S. Department of Justice; Harrison, P. and A. Beck (2005). *Prisoners in 2004*. Washington, DC: U.S. Department of Justice.

Today those factors are probably still predictive of receiving a prison sentence, however, it seems to be the case, as reported in the first chapter, that we are more likely to incarcerate all offenders today and for longer sentences. Box 11.4 compares those on probation, parole, and in prison by race, and type of crime.

4.1 Female Offenders

Women represent about 23 percent of the adult probation population, up from 21 percent in 1995. They account for about 12 percent of the parole population, up from about 10 percent in 1995.[26] They also represent about seven percent of the prison population, up from the six percent of 1995.[27] The idea that women receive "chivalry" and are typically sentenced less severely than male counterparts has received mixed findings from research studies. In general, there does seem to be a small but definite effect of gender on judicial sentencing but it seems to be moderated by race and whether the woman has dependents or not.[28]

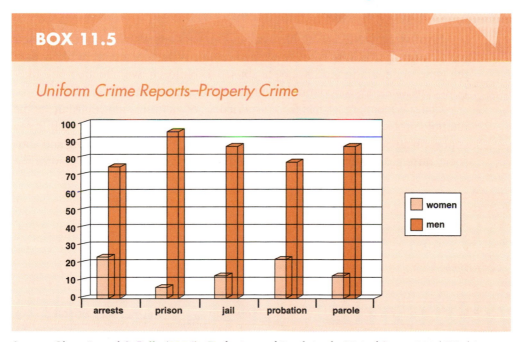

BOX 11.5

Uniform Crime Reports–Property Crime

Source: Glaze, L. and S. Palla (2005). *Probation and Parole in the United States, 2004.* Washington DC: Bureau of Justice Statistics. Harrison, P. and A. Beck (2005). *Prisoners in 2004.* Washington, DC: Bureau of Justice Statistics.

Women, many researchers argue, follow different pathways to crime and they require **gender-specific programming**, which matches prison and community correctional programs to women's specific needs and pathways to crime. These researchers and practitioners argue that women and men are different, and that, typically, corrections ignores their differences or does not respond to the differences in an appropriate way. The following are some of the differences noted between male and female offenders:

★   women are more likely to be primary caregivers of young children

★   they are more likely to have experienced childhood physical and/or sexual abuse

★   they are more likely to report physical and sexual abuse victimization as adults

★   they are more likely to have drug dependency issues

★   they are less likely to be convicted of a violent crime

★   they are less likely to have any stable work history

★   they are more likely to indicate psychosocial problems

★   they are more likely to have an incarcerated parent

★   they are more likely to come from a single-parent household

★   they are more likely to suffer from serious health problems, including HIV/AIDS[29]

Prior victimization (both physical and sexual) sets women apart from their male counterparts. While both male and female offenders are more likely than the general population to have been abused as children, women are more likely to experience abuse continuing into adulthood, as seen in Box 11.6.

Cathy Widom argues that these experiences of victimization contribute to the multiple problems females offenders have in adulthood, including an inability to cope with stress, suicide, abuse of alcohol and drugs, sensation-seeking and anti-social attitudes, lower levels of self-esteem, and the lack of a sense of control.[30]

BOX 11.6

Female Offenders' Victimization

Percent who have been . . .	Probation	Jail	Prison
Ever physically or sexually abused	41	48	57
Before age 18	16	21	12
Physically abused	15	10	18
Sexually abused	7	10	11
Both physically and sexually	18	27	28

Source: Greenfield, L. and T. Snell (1999). *Special Report: Women Offenders*. Washington, DC: Bureau of Justice Statistics.

Researchers have found that certain factors in the lives of black women set them on a path to crime. For instance, sexual abuse in the home leads to running away, which in turn leads to drug use and shoplifting. Relationships with drug-dealing male partners also lead to drug arrests for women.[31] Beth Ritchie, in particular, has detailed the way in which black women's gender and race influence the choices they make in life.[32]

Critics argue that we don't know the risk factors for women in community corrections as well as we do those of men, and we miss important factors in women's lives that might lead them to crime.[33] Other authors, such as Patricia Van Voorhis, point to specific factors that have been identified in prior research with female offenders that may be risk factors for women. These are:

★   marital status and suicide attempts

★   family structure of childhood home

★   childhood abuse, depression, and substance abuse

★   single parenting and reliance on public assistance

★   dysfunctional relationships

★   victimization

Special needs of women may include childcare, victimization trauma counseling, self-esteem counseling, financial assistance, healthcare, and mental health care.[34]

One major difference between female and male offenders is their relationship with children. As mentioned above, female offenders are more likely to be custodial parents and the financial and emotional strain of raising young children has an impact on their ability to stay crime or drug-free while on some form of community correction status. There have also been laws passed that have complicated the potential for success. The "Personal Responsibility and Work Opportunity Reconciliation Act (PRWORA)" of 1996 replaced Aid to Families with Dependent Children (AFDC) with a state block grant system that made it more difficult for single women as heads of households to receive state aid. Another section of the same Act created a lifetime ban on receiving any federal assistance to those who were convicted of a state or federal felony offense involving the use or sale of drugs. This draconian law affects only drug offenders, not those convicted of murder, robbery, or any violent crime. States may opt out of the program, but to do so means losing federal funding.

In 1996, the "One Strike Initiative" authorized local Public Housing Authorities to obtain criminal conviction records of applicants from law enforcement agencies and bar those with felony drug convictions from living in public housing. Another impediment to ex-offenders was created with the Higher Education Act of 1998, which barred anyone with a drug conviction from receiving federal loan money for education. Finally, the Adoption and Safe Families Act of 1997 mandates termination of parental rights after a child has been in foster care for 15 months. This means that women serving even relatively short prison sentences may lose their parental rights and/or women who must go to residential drug programs may lose their children if they need to depend on foster care to provide a home for their children while they are in treatment. This has influenced many women to make more informal arrangements for their children's care with, perhaps, less-than-desirable family members or friends. Women would rather not depend on state assistance because they fear losing their children permanently. These programs make the transition to the community extremely difficult for many female offenders who are very likely to have drug convictions.

Barbara Bloom and Barbara Owen and others have recommended that corrections approach the issue of correctional supervision for female offenders with the following objectives:

★   enhance supervision and treatment

★   validate assessment instruments on female samples

★   use single-gender caseloads

★   create policies and practices that acknowledge female offenders' special relationships with children, families, and significant others

★   create policies and practices that provide culturally relevant services and supervision to address substance abuse, trauma, and mental health

★   provide services appropriate to women's socioeconomic status

★   promote partnerships with other social service agencies[35]

5. CLASSIFICATION AND RISK ASSESSMENT

One of the most important activities of correctional professionals is classification and risk assessment. We want to know which offenders are more likely to reoffend, especially by committing violent crime. Once an offender has been sentenced, "client assessment" is concerned with two basic elements: risk and need. Prediction/assessment may be clinical, actuarial, or a combination of the two.

The **clinical approach** is when psychologists or psychiatrists employ interviews, social histories, and psychological tests to make predictions on future offending. In Box 11.7, some of the common personality characteristics associated with criminal offending are displayed.

The **actuarial approach** uses patterns of behavior and predicts risk based on prior behavior of those with similar characteristics. For instance, the U.S. Parole Commission developed the "Salient Factor Score." This instrument classified parolees into high, medium, and low levels of risk of re-offending based on the following factors:

★   Prior convictions/adjudications

★   Prior commitment(s) greater than 30 days

★   Age at current offense

★   Commitments during past three years

BOX 11.7

Psychological Profile of Criminals

★ antisocial/anti-authority attitudes

★ pro-criminal associates

★ egocentric thinking

★ weak problem-solving skills

★ family conflict

★ risk-seeking

★ early misbehavior

★ below average verbal intelligence

★ poor school performance

★ troubled relationships

★ preference for unregulated activities

★ low levels of skills

★ low levels of self-respect

★ low self-control

★ drug or alcohol issues

★ impulsivity

Source: C. Bartol and A. Bartol (2005). *Criminal Behavior: A Psychological Approach*, Seventh Edition. Upper Saddle River, NJ: Prentice Hall.

★ Status on probation/parole

★ Correctional escape

★ Heroin/opiate dependence[36]

In general, actuarial approaches are better predictors of recidivism than are clinical assessments. For instance, in one study of 2,850 probationers, the best predictors were found to be stability of employment, marital status, and number of past convictions.[37] Similarly, another study of 266 felony probationers found that the best predictors of recidivism were sex, employment, and prior record.[38] A study that compared the two approaches' ability to predict recidivism among sex offenders showed that the actuarial approach outperformed clinical assessments by a wide margin.[39]

The most sophisticated classification and assessment assigns treatment to the offender's risk and needs. As far back as the 1970s, correctional programs existed that attempted to match treatment to offenders, using a variety of personality inventories to assess the psychological profile of the individual offenders. More current classification systems also combine the offenders' risk and needs to improve the ability to predict recidivism.

5.1 Risk/Needs Approach

The *risk/need assessments* approach combines the clinical and actuarial approaches. This classification uses risk instruments that are stable and don't change (i.e., demographic, file, and historical information). The classification also includes dynamic, changeable items (i.e., personality tests and clinical interviews). The types of information collected include: physical health, vocational/financial situation, education, family and social relationships, residence and neighborhood, alcohol use, drug abuse, mental health, attitude, past and current criminal behavior. This approach tracks changes in the offender during the course of the supervision period because education, mental health, attitude, and drug use will change over time, affecting the offender's risk level (likelihood of reoffending).

This approach looks at the offender's needs in areas such as medical care, mental health, education, housing, and so on. Research continues to search for needs that are criminogenic (those that influence the offender to make criminal choices), versus those that are not. While it is a benefit to the offender if a correctional system addresses his or her needs, only criminogenic needs are high priority in a correctional program.

One of the pervasive findings of these evaluations is that intensive treatment is not recommended for all offenders. It seems to be the case that high-risk offenders are more likely to benefit than low-risk offenders when both participate in intensive treatment programs, such as halfway houses or intensive probation. In fact, correctional supervision interventions have been shown to result in *increased* recidivism among low-risk offenders as compared to control samples. In the largest study of this kind, Christopher Lowenkamp and his colleagues analyzed 97 correctional programs with 13,676 offenders involved and found that the programs that adhered to the principle of assigning services based on risk were the most successful in achieving a reduction in recidivism.[40]

Proponents argue that it is important to classify and match offenders to the type of treatment they need, not only because it is a waste of resources to do otherwise, but also because the treatment program may actually influence a low-risk offender to recidivate. Why would low-risk offenders be more inclined to recidivate when exposed to a correctional intervention? It might be that low-risk offenders would have naturally avoided making any more criminal choices, but that correctional supervision brings them into contact with other criminal offenders. It could also be that being monitored identifies behaviors that are violations, but these behaviors would not have entered the radar screen of the criminal justice system except for the correctional supervision.

Researchers are also looking at the correctional program itself. The Correctional Program Assessment Inventory measures how well a program adheres to the principles of risk, need, and responsivity as described above. Studies have shown that higher scores for the programs are associated with better success rates for offenders in the programs.[41]

5.2 Classifying Female Offenders

There have been few studies that attempt to validate or replicate the risk instruments described in the previous section with female offenders because there are so few women in the system. Earlier studies indicated that classification systems in use in prisons that were developed and validated with samples of male offenders "overclassified" female prisoners, meaning they indicated that women needed more secure settings than probably were necessary. Factors such as child abuse, mental health, substance abuse, and employment predicted women's institutional behavior, but age, time to serve, crime of conviction and prior offenses were not associated with institutional behavior of women even though they were factors that were predictors for men.[42]

In the few studies that have examined the predictive ability of classification instruments for female offenders, some researchers have found that these instruments effectively predict recidivism for women as well as for men.[43] However, at least one evaluation indicated that the classification instrument used was not as successful in predicting women's recidivism on parole as well as economic factors. Women who were given state support (welfare) were 83 percent less likely to recidivate than those who did not receive economic support.[44] These authors, as others, caution that factors such as poverty may be predictive of recidivism and, therefore, the "need" becomes a "risk" and increases an offender's risk score and that, in turn, increases the level of social control. The problem with this is that someone's status, not behavior, influences the level of punishment one endures, and second, the level of control often is related to the risk of recidivism (the more closely an offender is monitored, the more likely infractions will be found).

Current research, funded by the National Institute of Corrections, is concerned with testing whether the risk factors and needs identified above are predictive of women's future behavior, and further, whether the existing assessment tools accurately predict women's behavior. The researchers are testing certain potential risk factors for female offenders, such as self-efficacy, self-esteem, parenting, relationships, and abuse. The study is collecting information from female offenders, such as information about children, marital status, education, public assistance, and other factors.[45] With continuing study, researchers may find an appropriate adaptation of the assessment tools that were developed for male offenders.

5.3 False Positives and False Negatives

The difficulty inherent in any type of prediction device is the high number of **false positives** (errors involving predictions of recidivism that do not occur). There are likely many more false positives than **false negatives** (errors failing to predict recidivism that does occur), because program staff are more inclined to err on the side of caution. Some argue that our ability to predict violence will always be problematic because it is a relatively rare event.[46] Also, corrections professionals may be more concerned with *not* identifying a potentially dangerous offender than in accurately identifying someone who would not reoffend.

The level of risk willing to be taken determines the cutoff scores that are used for classification purposes. If you are worried about making false positives, then you will lower the cutoff score for high-risk offenders and assign more offenders to high-risk categories. This may make sense if one is dealing with violent offenders and makes no sense at all if one is dealing with low-level minor offenders because the cost would be greater to provide supervision than to accept a higher level of risk.

6. CONCLUSION

We have seen that the history of corrections and punishment consists of cycles of retribution and reform. Other correctional goals include deterrence and incapacitation. The modern-day penitentiary began with the Walnut Street Jail in the late 1700s. Modern parole began with the efforts in the 1800s of Alexander Maconochie and Walter Crofton and, in this country, Zebulon Brockway. John Augustus is considered the father of probation with his efforts in the late 1800s. The rehabilitation era existed for only a short time in the late 1960s and 1970s.

Today we are in an era when prison rates are very high. Incarceration is, in fact, the sentence most frequently received by felony offenders, although there are more correctional offenders on probation than in prison or on parole. Costs of corrections are extremely high and have increased by more than 500 percent in the last 25 years. There are seven million people under some form of correctional supervision today.

Researchers continue to try to find ways to identify and respond to the reasons these individuals choose to commit crime. The current best practices look both at the individual offender, using actuarial and clinical factors to determine their risk of recidivism, and the correctional program itself, measuring how well it does what it is supposed to do.

REVIEW QUESTIONS

1. What are the goals of punishment/corrections? What were the goals of the earliest forms of punishment?

2. Discuss the origins of the penitentiary, parole, and probation.

3. Describe the rehabilitative era. When did it end?

4. Why is re-entry considered an important issue today?

5. What is the most frequently given felony sentence? What type of correctional supervision has the largest number of offenders?

6. What is the typical cost of probation versus prison? What are the "collateral" costs of incarceration?

7. How many offenders are under some form of correctional supervision? What is the rate of probation supervision? What states have the highest imprisonment rates?

8. What are the differences between female and male offenders?

9. What are the three types of classification? Describe them.

10. Explain false positives and false negatives.

VOCABULARY

actuarial approach – a classification system that uses patterns of behavior and predicts risk based on prior behavior of those with similar characteristics

civil disabilities –legal barriers that remove civil rights such as voting, that accompany a felony record

clinical approach – a classification system that employs interviews, social histories, and psychological tests to make predictions about future offending

deterrence – when crime has been prevented by discouraging an offender from committing further crime

false positives – errors involving predictions of recidivism that do not occur

false negatives – errors failing to predict recidivism that does occur

gender-specific programming – matches prison and community correctional programs to women's specific needs and pathways to crime

general deterrence – what is done to an individual to discourage others from future offending

incapacitation – to hold incapable; in corrections, it means to make the offender incapable of committing crime

lex talionis – proportional "eye for an eye" form of punishment

mark system – program awarded prisoners marks or credits based on the work product of groups; marks were exchanged for greater liberties

net-widening – the situation in which minor offenders are placed in new diversion programs instead of prison-bound offenders the program was designed for

outlaw – an individual who refused to abide by punishments ordered by authorities that were largely compensatory, meaning that they ordered the offender to pay back the victim

Progressive Movement – from 1890 through early 1900s, private charities responded to the problems of the poor in northeastern cities

rehabilitation – to change the individual's values, attitudes, beliefs, and behavior

rehabilitative era – the 1960s-1970s; prison treatment programs were expanded along with innovative community alternatives

reintegration era – referred to a time when re-entry programs were developed that helped inmates adjust back into the community

restorative justice movement – approach that keeps the offender in the community and provides a means to meet the needs of the victim, the offender, and the community

retribution – a goal of punishment that inflicts harm proportional to the harm caused

specific deterrence – what is done to an individual to deter him or her from future offending

ticket of leave system – early Irish system that allowed prisoners who behaved well to earn early release with a "ticket to leave" as long as they were supervised by local police

FOR FURTHER READING

Bazemore, Gordon and Mara Schiff (eds.) (2001). *Restorative Community Justice: Repairing Harm and Transforming Communities*. Cincinnati, OH: Anderson Publishing.

Braswell, Michael C., John Fuller, and Bo Lozoff (2001). *Corrections, Peacemaking, and Restorative Justice*. Cincinnati, OH: Anderson Publishing.

Mauer, Marc (2003). *Comparative International Rates of Incarceration: An Examination of Causes and Trends*. Washington, DC: The Sentencing Project.

Pollock, Joycelyn (2005). *Women, Prison, and Crime*. Belmont, CA: Wadsworth Publishing.

Ritchie, Beth (1996). *Compelled to Crime: The Gender Entrapment of Battered Black Women*. New York: Routledge.

Travis, Jeremy, and Michelle Waul (2004). *Prisoners Once Removed: The Impact of Incarceration and Reentry on Children, Families and Communities*. Washington, DC: Urban Institute Press.

Van Ness, Daniel W. and Karen Heetderks Strong (2006). *Restoring Justice: An Introduction to Restorative Justice*, Third Edition. Newark, NJ: LexisNexis/Matthew Bender.

Van Voohis, Patricia, Michael Braswell, and David Lester (2007). *Correctional Counseling and Rehabilitation*, Sixth Edition. Newark, NJ: LexisNexis/Matthew Bender.

Whitehead, John T., Joycelyn M. Pollock, and Michael C. Braswell (2003). *Exploring Corrections in America*. Newark, NJ: LexisNexis/Matthew Bender.

---

[1] McCorkle, R. & J. Crank (1996). "Meet the New Boss: Institutional Change and Loose Coupling in Parole and Probation." *American Journal of Criminal Justice* 21, 1: 1-25.

[2] Harrison, P. & A. Beck (2006). *Prison and Jail Inmates and Midyear 2005*. Washington, DC: Bureau of Justice Statistics. Retrieved 9/2/06 from: http://www.ojp.usdoj.gov/bjs/pub/pdf/pjim05.pdf.

[3] Mauer, M. (2003). *Comparative International Rates of Incarceration: An Examination of Causes and Trends*. Washington, DC: The Sentencing Project. Retrieved 9/2/06 from: http://www.sentencing-project.org/pdfs/pub9036.pdf#search=%22international%20incarceration%20rates%22.

[4] Austin, J. (2001). "Prisoner Reentry: Current Trends, Practices and Issues." *Crime and Delinquency* 47, 3: 314-334, p. 314.

[5] See, for instance, Travis, J. & M. Waul (2004). *Prisoners Once Removed: The Impact of Incarceration and Reentry on Children, Families and Communities*. Washington, DC: Urban Institute Press.

[6] Travis, J. & J. Petersilia (2001). "Reentry Reconsidered: A New Look at an Old Question." *Crime and Delinquency* 47, 3: 291-313.

[7] Re-Entry Policy Council (2004). "Voting Restrictions for People with Felony Convictions." Retrieved 12/30/05 from: http://www.reentrypolicy.org/documents/votingrestrictions.pdf.

[8] Glaze, L. & T. Bonczar (2006). *Probation and Parole in the United States, 2005*. Washington, DC: Bureau of Justice Statistics.

[9] Camp, G. & C. Camp (1985). *Corrections Yearbook*. South Salem, NY: Criminal Justice Institute.

[10] Camp, G. & C. Camp (2000). *Corrections Yearbook*. South Salem, NY: Criminal Justice Institute.

[11] Camp, C. & G. Camp (1999). *The Corrections Yearbook* 1999. Middletown, CT: Criminal Justice Institute, p. 39.

[12] Stephan, J. (2004). *State Prison Expenditures*. Washington DC: Bureau of Justice Statistics.

[13] Bureau of Justice Statistics (2007).*Expenditures and Employment Extracts*. Retrieved 8/14/07 from: http://ojp.usdoj.gov/bjs/.

[14] Mauer, M. (2000). *Race to Incarcerate*. Washington, DC: The Prison Project.

[15] Bonczar, T. & A. Beck (1997). *Lifetime Likelihood of Going to State or Federal Prison*. Washington, DC: Bureau of Justice Statistics.

[16] Pollock, J. (2005). *Women, Prison, and Crime*. Belmont, CA: Wadsworth Publishing.

[17] Clear, T., D. Rose & J. Ryder (2001). "Incarceration and the Community: The Problem of Removing and Returning Offenders." *Crime and Delinquency* 47, 3: 335-351.

[18] Glaze, L. & T. Bonczar (2006). *Probation and Parole in the United States, 2005*. Washington, DC: Bureau of Justice Statistics.

[19] Glaze, L. & T. Bonczar (2006). *Probation and Parole in the United States, 2005*. Washington, DC: Bureau of Justice Statistics.

[20] Glaze, L. & S. Palla (2005). *Probation and Parole in the United States, 2004*. Washington, DC: Bureau of Justice Statistics.

[21] Glaze, L. & T. Bonczar (2006). *Probation and Parole in the United States, 2005*. Washington, DC: Bureau of Justice Statistics, p. 2.

[22] Glaze, L. & S. Palla (2005). *Probation and Parole in the United States, 2004*. Washington, DC: Bureau of Justice Statistics, p. 2.

[23] Bureau of Justice Statistics (2007). Retrieved 8/14/07 from: http://ojp.usdoj.gov/bjs/fed.htm#Corrections.

[24] Harrison, P. & A. Beck (2006). *Prison and Jail Inmates at Mid-year, 2005*. Washington, DC: Bureau of Justice Statistics.

[25] Petersilia, J. (2002). *Reforming Probation and Parole*. Lanham, MD: American Correctional Association, p.27.

[26] Glaze, L. & S. Palla (2005). *Probation and Parole in the United States. 2004*. Washington DC: Bureau of Justice Statistics.

[27] Harrison, P. & A. Beck (2006). *Prison and Jail Inmates at Mid-Year, 2005*. Washington, DC: Bureau of Justice Statistics.

[28] For a review, see Pollock, J. (1999). *Criminal Women*. Cincinnati, OH: Anderson Publishing.

[29] Pollock, J. (2002). *Women, Prison and Crime*. Belmont, CA: Wadsworth; Bloom, B. (2004). "Women Offenders in the Community: The Gendered Impact of Current Policies. *Community Corrections Report 12*, 1: 3-6. Chesney-Lind, M. (2000). "Women and the Criminal Justice System: Gender Matters." *Topics in Community Corrections: Responding to Women Offenders in the Community*, p. 7-11. Washington, DC: National Institute of Corrections.

[30] Widom, C. (2000). "Childhood Victimization and the Derailment of the Girls and Women to the Criminal Justice System." In National Institute of Justice, *Research on Women and Girls in the Criminal Justice System*, pp. 27-35. Washington, DC: National Institute of Justice.

[31] Henriques, Z. & N. Manatu-Rupert (2001). "Living on the Outside: African American Women Before, During, and After Imprisonment." *The Prison Journal* 81, 1: 6-19.

[32] Ritchie, B. (1996). *Compelled to Crime: The Gender Entrapment of Battered Black Women*. New York: Routledge.

[33] Chesney-Lind, M. (2001). *The Female Offender*. Thousand Oaks, CA: Sage.; Funk, S. (1999). "Risk Assessment for Juveniles on Probation." *Criminal Justice and Behavior* 26: 44-68.; Holtfreter, K. & M. Morash (2003). "The Needs of Women Offenders: Implications for Correctional Programming." *Women and Criminal Justice* 13: 137-160.

[34] Van Voorhis, P. (2005). "Classification of Women Offenders: Gender-Responsive Approaches to Risk/Needs Assessment." *Community Corrections Report* 12, 2: 19-20.

[35] Bloom, B. (2004). "Women Offenders in the Community: The Gendered Impact of Current Policies. *Community Corrections Report 12*, 1: 3-6. Bloom, B., B. Owen & S. Covington (2003). Gender-Responsive Strategies: Research, Practice and Guiding Principles for Women Offenders. Washington, DC: National Institute of Corrections.

[36] Van Voorhis, P. (2007). "An Overview of Offender Classification Systems." In P. Van Voorhis, M. Braswell & D. Lester, *Correctional Counseling and Rehabilitation*, Sixth Edition., pp. 133-160. Newark, NJ: LexisNexis/Matthew Bender, p. 139.

[37] Sims, R. & M. Jones (1997). "Predicting Success or Failure on Probation: Factors Associated with Felony Probation Outcomes." *Crime and Delinquency* 43, 3: 314-327.

[38] Morgan, K. (1994). "Factors Associated with Probation Outcome." *Journal of Criminal Justice* 22, 4: 341-353.

[39] Hanson, R. & M. Bussiere (1998). "Predicting Relapse: A Meta Analysis of Sexual Offender Recidivism Studies." *Journal of Consulting and Clinical Psychology* 66, 3: 348-362.

[40] Lowenkamp, C. & E. Latessa (2005). "Increasing the Effectiveness of Correctional Programming Through the Risk Principle: Identifying Offenders For Residential Placement." *Criminology and Public Policy* 4, 2: 263-290; Andrews, D., J. Bonta & J. Wormith (2006). "The Recent Past and Near Future of Risk and/or Need Assessment." *Crime and Delinquency* 52, 1: 7-27; Lowenkamp. C., E. Latessa & A. Holsinger (2006). "The Risk Principle in Action: What Have We Learned From 13,676 Offenders and 97 Correctional Programs." *Crime and Delinquency* 52, 1: 77-93.

[41] Andrews, D., J. Bonta & J. Wormith (2006). "The Recent Past and Near Future of Risk and/or Need Assessment." *Crime and Delinquency* 52, 1: 7-27.

[42] Van Voorhis, P. & L. Presser (2001). *Classification of Women Offenders: A National Assessment of Current Practices*. Washington, DC: National Institute of Corrections.

[43] Coulson, G., G. Ilacqua, V. Nutbrown, D. Giulekas & F. Cudjoe (1996). "Predictive Utility of the LSI for Incarcerated Female Offenders." *Criminal Justice and Behavior* 23: 427-439.; Lowenkamp, C., A. Holsinger & E. Latessa (2001). "Risk/Need Assessment, Offender Classification, and The Role of Childhood Abuse." *Criminal Justice and Behavior* 28, 5: 543-563.

[44] Holtfreter, K., M. Reisig & M. Morash (2004). "Poverty, State Capital, and Recidivism Among Women Offenders." *Crime and Public Policy* 3, 2: 185-208.

[45] Van Voorhis, P. (2005). "Classification of Women Offenders: Gender-Responsive Approaches to Risk/Needs Assessment." *Community Corrections Report* 12, 2: 19-20.

[46] Auerhan, K. (2006). "Conceptual and Methodological Issues in the Prediction of Dangerous Behavior." *Criminology and Public Policy*, 5, 4: 771-778.

Chapter 12

Pretrial Diversion and Probation

What You Need to Know

★ Pretrial release is different from pretrial diversion programs (which are also different from intermediate sanctions).

★ Benefit of clergy was an early form of diversion.

★ Day reporting centers, electronic monitoring, restitution, day fines, and community service can be used in both pretrial diversion programs and probation.

★ There are about 4,200,000 offenders on probation; in 2005 they comprised about 58 percent of all those under any form of correctional supervision.

★ Rates of probation vary tremendously across the states.

★ About 55 percent of probationers are white, 30 percent are black, and 13 percent are Hispanic.

★ Probation began with the efforts of John Augustus in 1841.

★ Probation involves the presentence, investigative function and the post-sentence, supervision function.

★ Conditions are rules of probation.

★ Caseloads average around 150, but vary tremendously from intensive supervision or specialized caseloads to minimum supervision caseloads.

★ About 60 percent of offenders successfully complete their probation sentence.

Once a criminal suspect is arrested, they are "in the system." After arrest, the suspect is brought to the jail and "booked." He or she must see a magistrate, usually within 48 hours.[1] It is almost from this moment that a variety of opportunities for diversion may occur. Diversion from the system can occur in numerous ways. In an earlier chapter, we discussed bail and ROR programs that simply divert the defendant from spending time in jail while awaiting trial. Other forms of diversion completely replace any adjudication. **Community corrections** refer to any form of correctional alternative that does not involve incarceration in prison. The term includes pretrial, post-trial or post-prison supervision. In Table 12.1 we attempt to show the possible types of community-based correctional sentences that exist. We will discuss the pretrial diversion programs in this chapter, along with probation, the most common form of diversion from prison.

BOX 12.1

Community Corrections in the Criminal Justice System

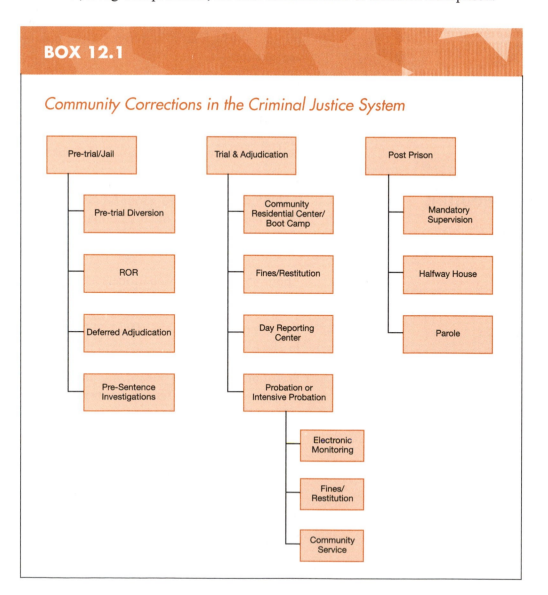

1. DIVERSION

The purpose of all the forms of **diversion** is to "divert" the offender from the system because of a belief that it is better for the offender and better for the system. It is better for the offender because he or she will suffer less stigma and disruption to work and family. It is better for the system because scarce resources (such as jail and prison beds) can be used for more serious offenders. Diversion is warranted when:

★ it can be done with little or no risk to the public; and

★ it does not offend the principles of justice.

There have always been some forms of diversion from formal punishment. For instance, descriptions of The Bay of Sanctuary in Hawaiian society indicate that those accused of crimes could escape punishment by swimming across and remaining on the other side of the bay. In early Europe the **benefit of clergy** was provided to those who could prove they were members of the clergy. Individuals who were facing trial and punishment in secular courts could have their cases dismissed with the expectation that ecclesiastical courts would take over and punish the clergy member. However, as time went on, the benefit became available to anyone who could read Psalm 54. It became, in effect, a type of diversion for those who, for whatever reason, the court chose to give the benefit of clergy.

2. TYPES OF DIVERSION PROGRAMS

We will distinguish **pretrial release programs** from deferred adjudication programs. While Release on Recognizance (ROR) or court surety programs are simply a means by which suspects may avoid having to pay bail before their adjudication, a pretrial diversionary program, successfully completed, takes the place of formal adjudication. The latter requires enabling legislation and is usually comprised of:

★ an evaluation by pretrial services staff of eligibility,

★ a contract that clarifies exactly what the defendant must do for successful completion, and

★ a mechanism by which the defendant's case is disposed of, usually through a court order that disposes of the case without a conviction.

Pretrial diversion comes before any finding of guilt. Offenders who are eligible and successfully complete a pretrial diversion program may honestly say they have never been convicted of a crime, because they haven't. Typically, once an offender is chosen for a pretrial diversion program, they may encounter one or more of the programs described, such as day reporting, community service, electronic monitoring, and so on. These programs may also be **intermediate sanctions**, because they are often added to a regular probation sentence. Thus, if any of these programs is part of a deferred adjudication program, it is considered a diversion program; however, if it is added to a regular probation sentence, it is considered an intermediate sanction.

Where they exist, most pretrial diversion programs evaluate all defendants for eligibility. A sentencing statute and/or office policy usually sets eligibility. Factors that go into deciding whether an offender is eligible would include:

* ★ Crime
* ★ Prior record
* ★ Drug history
* ★ Employment
* ★ Residential stability
* ★ Evidence of mental illness

Very often offenders in pretrial diversion programs are required to pay restitution (paying back the victim or the community), perform some form of community service, and/or pay a fine and court costs. The probation department often conducts the supervision for pretrial diversion programs, although the pretrial clients may be supervised via a specialized caseload or office. In many ways, this type of supervision is virtually indistinguishable from probation. Defendants may also be placed in drug treatment programs, helped to get back into school or vocational training, or assisted with job placement.

The main difference to remember between pretrial diversion and probation is that a diversion program (and deferred adjudication) will result in no conviction if successfully completed, but a probation sentence is handed down after a finding of guilt (or a guilty plea) and conviction. Both pretrial diversion programs and probation may utilize the same variety of programs, including: day reporting centers, electronic monitoring, restitution and/or fines, and community service.

2.1 Day Reporting Centers

Probationers or pretrial releasees may be required to "check in" to day reporting centers as a condition of their supervision. These centers offer both supervision and services; usually an array of job counseling and placement, educational, and social services are accessed at the sites. The concept was borrowed from Great Britain in the mid-1980s. The center may be public or privately operated, and provide services to probationers and/or pretrial diversion clients.[2]

Evaluations are mixed.[3] In a survey of 54 day reporting centers, Parent found that centers reported an average "negative termination" rate of about 50 percent; however, the range was from 14 to 86 percent. Negative termination included rule violations as well as new arrests. Centers that were run by private agencies, those that had curfew restrictions, and those with stricter policies had more negative terminations.[4] Because the studies show such a range of outcomes, it is difficult to make any generalizations about the effectiveness of such centers.

2.2 Electronic Monitoring

Electronic monitoring (EM) emerged in the mid-1980s as a supplement to traditional probation or parole supervision, or house arrest. It is now used in conjunction with bail and personal recognizance release, deferred adjudication programs, as part of a suspended jail sentence, as a condition of probation, as a condition of intensive probation, or as a condition of parole release. The most recent celebrity-criminal who had to wear an electronic monitoring device was Martha Stewart, who was released from her house arrest and monitoring in August of 2005.

Florida's Palm Beach program is cited as being the first of this type in the country.[5] Evidently the idea came to a New Mexico judge from a "Spider Man" comic strip. The judge enlisted the aid of an engineer to design the device.[6] Programs now exist in virtually all U.S. states as well as several other countries. Electronic monitoring basically uses an electronic device strapped to the ankle or wrist of the offender. The monitor operates in such a way that an alarm sounds when the offender is too far away from a transmitting detector, often located in the offender's telephone. The program can be set up so that the offender can travel from home to work and back again, but an alarm sounds if he or she is not home by a certain time.

Such programs always cost less than prison or jail; however, cost savings are moderated by the fact that judges may be more likely to give longer community supervision sentences than jail sentences. Further, such cost comparisons typically do not include treatment services that seem to be an essential part of any community sanction.[7] Even accounting for these factors, however, researchers have found that EM programs offer significant savings over incarceration. For example, Lilly et al. reported that Palm Beach County, Florida, conservatively estimated their savings at $130,000 for 26 months by using house arrest with EM and, for a seven-year period, the savings were about $600,000.[8]

Recidivism rates in EM programs have been reported as low as eight percent, and as high as 70 percent.[9] Some researchers found that there was little difference between the recidivism rates between EM programs and a matched sample, controlled for risk level, that complete either a prison sentence, or a traditional probation sentence.[10] Note that even if an EM program results in no significant reduction in recidivism compared to more traditional sentencing, it arguably should be labeled a success if it reduces costs. However, at least one meta-analysis found that electronic monitoring increased recidivism by about five percent over control groups.[11]

It is also important to note issues such as denial rates and completion rates. If a program has a low recidivism rate, it may be because very few are accepted into the program, or the final evaluation does not count the large number who dropped out of or were removed from the program before completion. Denial rates are often high; one study reported that only 24 percent of those who applied for the program were accepted.[12] Others note that the following factors are predictors of failure on electronic monitoring programs: gender (male), age (younger), unemployment, criminal history, marital status (single), type of crime (drug or property), and length of time on EM (longer).[13]

The new generation of electronic monitoring employs global positioning to not only monitor whether an offender returns home when he or she is supposed to, but also to track the offender's movements throughout the day. For instance, the Florida Department of Corrections in 1997 implemented EM-PACT (Electronic Monitoring Protection And Crime Tracking; formerly known as CrimeTrax), an electronic monitoring program that incorporates a global positioning system (GPS). The program automatically monitors the location of parolees and suspects out on bail.

Placing offenders on GPS monitoring rather than incarcerating them realizes significant savings. While one study indicated that it costs $49.75 daily to incarcerate an offender, house arrest cost only $20.33 with a satellite monitor, and $11.16 without.[14] The extra cost of GPS monitoring may be justified if the alternative is a prison sentence, but not if the alternative would be regular supervision in a diversion program or a regular probation sentence.

2.3 Restitution/Day Fines

The use of economic sanctions pre-dates most written forms of law. Offenders may be assessed a fine, restitution, court costs and/or probation supervision. Some jurisdictions charge offenders for services as well, including the cost of drug tests. The two types of economic sanctions we will discuss here are day fines and restitution.

Criminal fines may be set by statute, case law, or office policy but, in general, are proportional to the seriousness of the crime. Usually fines may be used to punish property crimes and public order crimes, but not violent crimes, which are considered too serious. In Europe, even violent crimes are likely to be resolved through the use of fines. In England 38 percent of all felonies and 39 percent of violent crimes are punished by fine. In Germany 81 percent of adult crimes and 73 percent of violent crimes are punishable by fine.[15]

The trouble with set fines is that any amount is experienced quite differently depending on one's economic situation. A fine of $1,000 may be a minor nuisance to a middle-class offender but an impossible burden to a poor, unemployed offender. Therefore, **day fines** are common in Europe and are also used in some jurisdictions in the United States. Day fines are set by the amount of income the offender has—i.e., if the offender is making minimum wage, his daily earnings would be about $42; therefore a fine of 10 days would be about $420. However, a professional may earn $416 a day and his fine would be $4,160. The theory is that each amount would be experienced in the same way by the two offenders. Day fine schedules sometimes also take into account number of dependents. Several jurisdictions use day fine systems. In a U.S. Department of Justice study of day fines, it was found that collection was sometimes a problem, but most professionals working in the criminal justice system liked the concept.[16]

Restitution is an order by the court that requires the offender to compensate the victim for the injury or loss suffered in the crime. It can be attached to a pretrial diversion program, included as a condition of probation, consist of a stand-alone sentence along with custody in a residential restitution center, or be added to a prison sentence. In 1984, the *Victims of Crime Assistance Act* and the *Federal Comprehensive Crime Control Act* ordered courts to consider restitution to victims as part of a criminal sentence. States followed with their own state legislation enabling judges to set restitution amounts as part of a criminal sentence. Today every state has enabling legislation and 29 states mandate restitution unless there are compelling reasons not to do so. However, even with these laws, it is said that restitution is imposed in only 14 percent of all felony cases.[17]

Victim-centered restitution includes the victim in the determination of the amount to be compensated. The offender either pays the victim directly or through the court, but there is a direct link between the offender and his or her victim. The idea behind restitution is that the offender will become more responsible and law-abiding when they see the harm they caused and are successful in compensating the victim. In other forms of restitution programs, the victims are not involved in the process and/or the money is paid to a state victim compensation or restitution fund. This form of restitution may be considered not much more meaningful than a fine. It certainly does not encourage the offender to think about the victim.

One study found that restitution orders were more commonly imposed on female offenders, property offenders, those with no prior record, and white offenders.[18] Studies indicate that restitution orders are difficult to enforce. One study indicated that only about a third of the total restitution ordered in a Chicago court was ever paid over a three-year period. Enforcement practices such as registered letters or telephone solicitations threatening adverse action raised the percentage of compliance substantially, as did declaring "amnesty days," where accrued interest would be deducted from the amount owed.[19]

2.4 Community Service

Community service might be considered symbolic restitution. It can also be used in place of a fine, especially for those who have no financial resources to pay any type of fine, even a day fine, because they have no income. There are two basic types of community service programs and philosophies that we will call "restorative service" and "punitive service."

Restorative service programs attempt to connect the offender to the victim through some process of recognizing the harm and injury done to the specific victim and arriving at an agreement between the offender and victim as to the appropriate action. For instance, the offender may repair the damage he caused or provide some other type of service to the victim. More often, the service is to a class of victims rather than the offender's specific victim, but it is still meaningful and related to the offense. For instance, an offender who committed fraud against an elderly victim may provide volunteer services to a nursing home. A doctor who committed Medicare fraud may be required to serve in a free or low-cost health clinic. A college student who pleads guilty to DWI may be required to assist in a high school alcohol awareness program.

Punitive service may not be linked to the victim at all, nor have any relationship to the crime. For instance, washing police cars, picking up trash on the side of the road, clearing vacant lots for the city, etc., are examples of community service orders, but they hold little meaning for the offender other than deterrence.

Some of the issues that have been discussed in relation to community service as a sanction include:

★   supervision costs

★   appropriate settings

★   liability

★   reasonableness (number of hours, types of work)

Obviously, someone has to monitor the community service order. Typically, it is the probation department that makes sure community service orders are completed. Supervision costs money—thus, some programs charge the offender for participation in the program. This presents a problem for offenders who do not have the financial resources to pay the service cost. The costs involved in supervising offenders certainly diminish the economic value of the service itself. Further, if the offender is placed in a community agency without supervision from a correctional supervisor, then the supervision costs are passed to the recipient agency.

While assisting with youth or the elderly is a more meaningful type of community service, there are serious questions as to whether these settings are appropriate for some offenders. Nursing home residents are targets for financial crime, children are targets for sexual predators. If the community service work is done in the community, i.e., winterizing or renovating homes for the poor, then these residents are vulnerable to crimes committed by the offenders. There are also issues in how many placements can be found in any community that are relevant, meaningful, and do not subject anyone to undue risk. It may be the case that there are far fewer placements than offenders who are given a community service order.

Liability issues are raised when offenders are placed in schools, youth centers, or nursing homes. The reason so many community service hours involve picking up garbage or washing police cars is because those settings do not create undue risk or liability. Probation departments that supervise offenders who victimize those during or because of a community service order may be exposed to legal liability for negligence. If offenders are injured during their community service work, the agency may be liable if there is negligence. In many cases, such workers may access worker's compensation funds. Public and private programs may have to carry liability insurance to cover injuries experienced by offender-workers.

Another complication for low-income, employed offenders is that often community service orders dictate when an offender must put in the hours. In some cases, it is impossible to complete community service hours and keep one's job. Disabled offenders are at a disadvantage in those programs that only offer community service in the form of physical labor; therefore, some offenders may receive a jail or prison sentence instead of community service, simply because of their inability rather than their unwillingness to participate.

The Web site for the Washington State Department of Corrections describes their community service program as one of the largest in the country. In existence since 1987, felony offenders are offered the opportunity to complete as many as 240 hours of community service in lieu of incarceration. Offender work crews perform various projects for community groups, cities, counties, or the state. Evaluations indicate that the program is extremely cost-effective and helps to reduce the number of offenders in jails and prisons.

> To read about Washington's program, see the official Web site http://www.doc.wa.gov/aboutdoc/offendercrews.asp

3. PROBATION

Probation is a Latin word meaning "period of proving" or "trial." Probation is both the sentence and a status. A criminal defendant may receive a sentence of probation, and once on probation, it becomes a legal status of reduced liberty. Probationers are subject to a higher level of supervision than ordinary citizens, and have less privacy from governmental scrutiny. The sentence of probation comes with a set of conditions that are rules for behavior. Either they specify required behaviors (like reporting once a month), or they prohibit certain behaviors (such as opening a bank account without the probation officer's approval). Typically, a probation sentence comes with the threat that, if revoked, the offender will receive a prison sentence.

Probation may be granted by a judge, jury, or as a result of plea bargaining. Most states have statutes that restrict who can be sentenced to probation. Typically, serious offenders who have committed murder or kidnapping are specifically excluded from receiving a probation sentence. Also, some states do not allow repeat offenders to receive probation.

> To find out about the American Probation and Parole Officers Association, go to: http://www.appa-net.org/

State statutes may set the maximum length of probation. In many states, it is never more than five years, but in other states, such as Texas, the maximum length is set at 10 years. In most states, there is a provision for early discharge. If the probationer has successfully completed a period of supervision and met all requirements, then the probation officer has the discretion to ask the judge to grant an early discharge.

In 2005 there were about 4,162,536 probationers in this country and the rate of probation supervision nationwide was 1,858 per 100,000 citizens. The number of people on probation varies tremendously from state to state, as does the rate per population. For instance, in 2005, Texas had 428,836 probationers, but North Dakota only had 3,739. Of course, the two states' populations are very different, but even rates, which standardize by population, show extreme variations. New Hampshire supervised 457 people per 100,000 on probation, while Massachusetts supervised 3,350 per 100,000.[20] Determinate sentence states are more likely to use probation than states with indeterminate sentencing.[21]

According to the Bureau of Justice Statistics, in 2005:

★   about 23 percent of probationers were women

★   about 55 percent of probationers were white, 30 percent were black, and 13 percent were Hispanic

★   about 57 percent were sentenced directly to probation (as opposed to a split sentence, suspended sentence, or other)

★   about half are on probation for felony sentences

★   the most common offense was drug law violations (28 percent), followed by DUI (15 percent)

★   about 59 percent successfully complete probation [22]

The number of adults on probation has risen more than 40 percent since 1990.[23] However, as a percentage of total sentences, probation sentences have been decreasing, as has the percentage of probationers as a percentage of the total population of those under correctional supervision. Petersilia reported in 2002 that about 80 percent of all misdemeanants and 60 percent of all felons receive probation.[24] The latest figures indicate that now only 31 percent of all felons are receiving probation; 41 percent receive a prison sentence and 28 percent receive a jail sentence. For those who do receive probation, the average sentence is about three years.[25] In 1990, about 61 percent of all those under some form of correctional supervision were on probation, but by 2004, only 59 percent.[26] In 2005, only 58 percent of all those under some form of correctional supervision were on probation.[27] Even though probation receives less than 10 percent of state and local government expenditures, it deals with almost 60 percent of all offenders.[28]

The Bureau of Justice Statistics reports that the per capita rate of women on probation rose 40 percent between 1990 and 1998. Only nine percent of women on probation were convicted of violent crimes; 44 percent were sentenced for property crimes and 46 percent were sentenced for drug or alcohol crimes. Nearly two-thirds of female probationers are white, a much higher percentage than that found in jails or prisons. Only about a quarter of women on probation were married (but that was a higher percentage than those in jail or prison). About 60 percent had at least a high school degree. About 40 percent reported being physically or sexually abused.[29]

Research indicates that women are less likely to re-offend than men.[30] One research study of 195 female probationers found that they were less likely to return to drug dealing if they were employed, involved in a relationship, or living with their children. They were less likely to engage in other crimes if they had stable living conditions or were living with a husband or significant other, but there was no effect on the return to drug crimes. This, the researchers note, illustrates the importance of relationships and supports prior research that found that living with a significant other in the drug trade increased a woman's likelihood of also becoming involved.[31]

Minority groups are disproportionately represented in prison populations, but not in community corrections populations. It seems to be the case that minorities are less likely than whites to be sentenced to diversion programs than prison. According to the Bureau of Justice Statistics, the percent of minorities as a percent of the total probation population has not increased significantly in the last 10 years. While about 55 percent of all probationers are white, blacks constitute about 30 percent and Hispanics only about 13 percent.[32] Unfortunately, not much is known about minorities on probation, unlike the substantial literature describing their experience in this nation's prisons. There are conflicting findings on whether blacks are less likely to get probation; some studies show a race effect, but other studies do not. The percent of people on probation who are Hispanic roughly reflects their percentage of the population.[33]

3.1 The History of Probation

The standard history of probation begins with the work of John Augustus. He was a Boston boot maker who was in court one day in 1841 and decided to intervene in the case of a drunk who was being sent to jail. A strong believer in the temperance movement, he decided to post bail for the man, who was charged with being a common drunk. Augustus asked the judge to defer sentencing for three weeks and release the man into his custody because he thought that he could help the man get his life in order. Evidently, his attempts were met with scorn from law enforcement, but for the next 18 years, from 1841 until his death in 1859, he bailed out more than 1,800 adults and children. He selected carefully and only chose first-time offenders. Once released, he helped them find employment or a place to live and reported their progress to the court. Most of the offenders released into his custody were charged with violations of vice or temperance laws.[34] His work continued and spread after he died and, in 1878, Massachusetts hired its first probation officer. In 1901, New York passed a statute authorizing probation for adults. Volunteers or police officers supervised probationers. Early probation officers were usually retired sheriffs and policemen who worked directly for the judge.

In the early 1900s, federal judges used a form of suspended sentence to give federal offenders a second chance. In 1925, the federal government created an enabling statute for federal probation. There was a very slow increase in the number of federal probation officers, with only 62 officers in 1931. Of course there were not that many federal criminals until the "federalization" of drug laws in the 1970s-1980s when the number of federal drug laws that paralleled similar state laws increased exponentially.

It was not until 1956 that all states had enabling legislation that allowed for probation sentences to be handed out by judges. In Box 12.2, we see that the enabling statutes for probation continued to be created well into the middle of the twentieth century.[35]

BOX 12.2

Enabling Statutes Passed Creating Probation

Before 1900	Massachusetts (1878), Missouri (1897), Rhode Island (1899)
1900–1905	California, Connecticut, Maine, Maryland, Michigan, New Jersey, New York, Vermont
1906–1910	Colorado, Georgia, Indiana, Kansas, Minnesota, Nebraska, Ohio, Pennsylvania, Wisconsin
1911–1915	Alabama, Arizona, Delaware, Idaho, Illinois, Montana, North Dakota, Oklahoma, Oregon, Tennessee, Washington
1916–1920	North Carolina
1921–1923	Arkansas, Utah
After 1923	Alaska, Florida, Hawaii, Iowa, Kentucky, Louisiana, Mississippi, Nevada, New Hampshire, New Mexico, South Carolina, South Dakota, Texas, West Virginia

Source: Johnson, F.R. (1928). *Probation for Juveniles and Adults.* New York: Century, pp. 12-13.

In the 1970s, probation came to the forefront of the public and policy-makers' attention and a series of reports indicated that it was not successful in its promise to reform offenders. Probation suffered the same fate as all "rehabilitative" programs in the 1980s, when politics and public sentiments moved toward a more punitive approach with offenders. Although probation never went away, the major innovation in these decades was intensive supervision, which involved more intensive supervision, not necessarily more intense programming. Unlike parole, however, probation was never abolished in any state and continues to absorb a large majority of offenders, either as the only correctional sentence they ever receive, or, for some, the first step on their way to prison.

3.2 Administration

There are a number of ways probation can be administered and every state is slightly different. The most common model is that of a state executive agency that provides hiring and procedural standards. Other states have purely local executive administration. In other states, probation is administered through the judicial branch of government, either from the state level or local level. Some states have a mixed model in which none of the above categories fits exactly as a description of how probation is administered. In more than half of all states, the state provides centralized hiring, training, and standards.[36] In Box 12.3, state models are identified as they existed in 1999.

The major reason for the trend to centralize probation is funding. When probation is administered as a county agency, there is variation in hiring standards and pay scales. Counties vary in their ability to fund probation and so

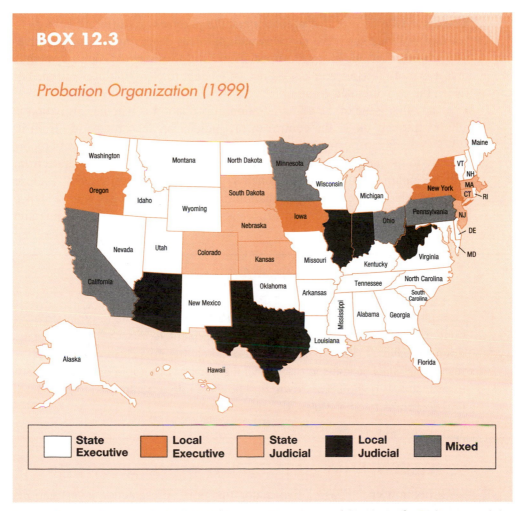

BOX 12.3

Probation Organization (1999)

Legend:
- State Executive
- Local Executive
- State Judicial
- Local Judicial
- Mixed

Source: From information in: N.I.C. 1999. State Organizational Structures for Delivering Adult Probation Services. Accessed via Web 2/14/07 from www.ncic.org/pubs/1999/015249.pdf.

there may be wide disparities in the quality of supervision. Furthermore, procedures may be different so that offenders who move from one county to the next find a completely different probation experience. Centralized systems can standardize budgets and provide consistency in employees and procedures.

Local administration may exist with state guidelines. States provide financial assistance to counties with the expectation and requirement that they meet certain hiring and other standards. Counties may be reimbursed on a per-offender basis for every offender that is kept in the county rather than sent to state prison. Community Corrections Acts provide incentives to counties to keep offenders in the community by funding local sentences (jail or probation instead of prison).[37]

Some states that administer probation from a centralized executive model combine probation and parole caseloads. The two supervision models are similar, of course, even though the reporting is different. While probation officers submit progress reports and violation reports to the sentencing court, parole officers submit such reports to the parole board or paroling authority. There are also those who believe that probationers and parolees are different enough to warrant different supervision styles with parolees deserving a more punitive, as opposed to service-oriented, supervision. One advantage of such a system is that it is more flexible and can more easily adapt to changing populations between the two offender groups.

The other issue in the administration of probation is whether probation is administratively under the control of the judicial branch or separate from it. While probation officers in some states are located in the courtroom and report directly to the judge; in most states the probation department is separate from judicial authority. In executive branch systems, there typically exists a close working relationship between probation officers and the judges who sentence to probation, but the probation officer is not the employee of the court and belongs to a separate agency.

★ Exercise: **In the State of . . .**

Using the Internet, find out whether Box 12.3 is still accurate for your state (hint: Google your state's probation department to discover what the administrative structure looks like). Also check the most current Bureau of Justice Statistics bulletins to discover if the number of people on probation in your state is going up or down, and how the rate of sentencing to probation compares to other states.

4. PRESENTENCE AND SUPERVISION FUNCTIONS

Probation encompasses two major functions: presentence investigations and recommendations and probation supervision. In larger jurisdictions, these functions are separated and assigned to different offices or divisions within the agency. In smaller jurisdictions the same officer may perform both functions.

The presentence function includes gathering information about offenders before sentencing. This begins with an interview with the offender, often in jail, if the offender is detained. The offender answers a series of questions relating to their past and current situation and then the officer checks the facts. The probation officer writes up the finding and makes a sentencing recommendation to the court. Information that may be included in a presentence report includes:

- ★ Defendant's risk (typically computed through a risk score system)
- ★ Circumstances (work, family, education)
- ★ All sentencing options
- ★ Recommendation

About half of all states require a presentence investigation in all felony cases. Another 16 states define the investigations as discretionary. In only two states are presentence investigations required prior to misdemeanor sentencing.[38]

There is a high correlation between the recommendation in the presentence investigation and the judge's sentence. It is unclear whether the high correlation between the probation officers' recommendations and the judges' sentences is because the judge follows the officer's recommendation, or whether it is because probation officers, who are often attached to the court and spend most of every day in the judge's courtroom, become familiar with how the judge would sentence and so they recommend accordingly.[39] It should also be noted that, in many jurisdictions, the sentence is the result of plea bargaining. In those cases, the prosecutor and defendant agree to a specific term and the judge either approves or disapproves. In these cases, if the presentence report is done at all, it is done before adjudication in order to help the prosecutor determine the appropriate sentence to offer or accept.

One of the legal issues that occurs with PSRs is confidentiality. In an early case, the Supreme Court held that information in the PSR could not be kept from the offender if he or she had been sentenced to death. Due process required the offender be able to know the information in the report in order to contest it as inaccurate or misleading. It could be, for instance, that the sentencing recommendation was based on hearsay and unproven allegations by co-workers, family members, or victims. If the offender did not know what was in the report, there would be no way to defend against unfair or untruthful allegations.[40] So far, however, the Court has refused to extend this reasoning to any sentence other than death; thus, whether the report is available to the defense is based on the law and procedural rules of the jurisdiction. The Federal Rules of Criminal Procedure, for instance, require that the PSR be made available to the defendant unless it might "disrupt rehabilitation," when the information was obtained with a promise of confidentiality, or when harm may result to any person because of the disclosure.[41]

The probation sentence also includes **conditions**. Conditions are the rules of probation. There are general conditions (such as to report to the probation officer), but also sometimes very specific conditions that are customized to the offender and his or her crime. Some of the possible conditions that might be attached to a probation order include standard conditions, i.e., reporting and notifying the probation officer of any change of address; punitive conditions, i.e., fines or community service; and treatment conditions, i.e., drug or alcohol treatment.[42]

While the probation officer may suggest conditions be added to the probation order in the PSR, only judges can impose conditions and only judges can drop or change conditions. Standard conditions may be pre-printed on the probation order. They are consistent for all probationers and cover fairly obvious rules, such as: "Don't commit another crime." Box 12.4 displays some common standard conditions.

BOX 12.4

Standard Conditions of Probation

★ Obey all laws

★ Do not possess firearm

★ Report as directed to probation officer

★ Permit home visits and searches

★ Avoid alcohol and illegal drug use

★ Maintain suitable employment

★ Notify of address changes

★ Do not associate with known criminals

★ Pay all fines and fees

It should be noted that many states have instituted fees for probation and payment of these fees is added as a condition to the probation sentence. Probationers are charged anywhere from $10 to $40 per month to be on probation. Sometimes there is a sliding scale based on income.[43] Paying the supervision fee is one of the conditions of probation and offenders may have their probation revoked if they refuse to pay. Although the offender can be required to pay court costs, fines, restitution, and even probation fees, the court cannot revoke probation solely for an inability to pay. Of course, if the offender is deemed able to pay and refuses, it is legally acceptable to revoke the probation order and send the offender to prison.[44]

Violating a condition of probation will not automatically result in a revocation and prison sentence; however, the judge has the legal authority to revoke probation if any conditions are not met. There is evidence that the number of special/punitive conditions have increased. This in itself may result in a greater likelihood of violations and increase the risk of failure because very restrictive conditions (such as never entering a bar) are difficult to live with for many years.[45]

So-called **Scarlet Letter conditions** are those where the judge creates a condition designed to humiliate or call attention to the wrongdoing of the offender. Some argue that these types of conditions subject the offender and his or her family to needless humiliation; others argue that the tailored conditions mean more than standard punishments. Some of the more unusual conditions include requiring sex offenders to post signs in their front yard warning people away, requiring DWI felons to put bumper stickers on their car identifying themselves as drunk drivers, requiring an individual to seek the forgiveness of his church, and so on.[46]

Any condition of probation must have a legitimate purpose, and sometimes the purpose may be rehabilitative. On the other hand, even treatment that is deemed too humiliating may be thrown out by the court. A court in Florida agreed with an offender that his probation condition, which involved

FOCUS ON ETHICS

You are a probation officer in the town you grew up in. You have been supervising a caseload for about a year and generally enjoy your job. You are assigned a new probationer that turns out to be the old boyfriend of your older sister in high school. You felt a little strange about being his probation officer, especially because you had a kind of little sister crush on him when he was dating your sister. You asked your supervisor about whether there were any policies or procedures about knowing your probationers, and he explained to you that in a small town it was bound to happen sooner or later. He asked you if you could make objective opinions about him. You said you could, but now, six months later, you find out that he has tested positive for drugs on a random test. He explains to you that it was just one time when he was at a party and, other than that, he has been doing well on probation, has a job, is paying child support for his two kids, and it wouldn't be fair to file a violation report. You have nothing to base it on, but suspect that he has started using again. He argues that you probably wouldn't file a report for anyone else, but are considering it for him because you are afraid of being perceived of treating him with favoritism. The fact is that there is a rule in the office that dirty tests automatically require a violation report, but the general practice is to give the offender a break if the officer feels that it was an aberration. What should you do?

wearing a diaper in a treatment program, was not acceptable.[47] On the other hand, a Nevada court upheld a condition that required those convicted of DWI to do community service with a label that identified them to passersby as "drunk drivers."[48]

Another issue that has arisen concerns the power of the probation officer to search. Typically, to search a home, a governmental agent must have a warrant that specifies with clarity what is being sought. Part of the probation order always requires the probationer to submit to periodic searches of one's home and/or person by the probation officer. This intrusion would never be justified toward a free person, but do probationers have all the rights of free people? The answer, obviously, is no, and courts have generally upheld the right of the probation officer to search without a warrant.[49]

The probation officer is not legally liable for any harm that comes from the sentencing recommendation because it is considered a quasi-judicial function. Thus, he or she is able to recommend probation without fear of being sued if the offender subsequently commits a crime, much in the same way as judicial immunity operates. Furthermore, the defendant cannot sue the probation officer (or court service officer) who prepares the presentence report for mistakes or false information. It should be noted that this type of immunity only applies to the quasi-judicial functions of the position; negligent supervision can be the basis for a lawsuit. For instance, a probationer may sue under Section 1983 for alleged violations of constitutional rights by the probation officer, or third parties may sue under some cause of action such as wrongful death if the officer's gross negligence in supervision resulted in the death of someone at the hands of the probationer. These cases are rare, however, because the standard of negligence is set fairly high.

4.1 Supervision

The other major function of probation, obviously, is supervision of probationers. Probation has followed a casework approach to service delivery. The **casework model** is typical of social work and involves the professional interacting with each "client" individually, serving as the primary and, sometimes, only service provider. This contrasts with other approaches that might have been taken, such as an investigative approach, in which officers simply perform a type of police function of tracking and patrolling probationers to attempt to catch them doing something wrong and/or investigating allegations and charges. Another model might be that of a service broker, where the probation officer refers offenders to different types of professionals (similar to the primary physician idea of HMOs). However, in the casework model, each probation officer is completely responsible for everyone on their caseload, and each offender on the caseload has a relationship with one probation officer. Interestingly, one of the complaints of probationers is that there is a great deal of turnover in probation offices and "their officer" may change frequently.

As long ago as 1960, the federal probation system assigned probationers to supervision levels based on their crime and risk level. Most were assigned a medium classification level and they were supervised in 50-person caseloads. Those who posed minimal risk to the public were placed in caseloads of 70 to 130 cases. However, those who had higher risk level scores were placed in intensive caseloads of only 20 offenders per officer.[50]

Typically, a probation officer has a general or specialized caseload and may supervise anywhere from 25 (in intensive or specialized caseloads) to more than 100 offenders, with the average at about 130.[51] There has been no definitive research indicating that there is an ideal caseload. Standards promulgated since the 1940s advocate a caseload no larger than 30, but the typical caseload has always been much higher.[52]

The number of contacts made each month with probationers depends on their classification level. While intensive supervision probationers might be seen as often as nine times a month with three field contacts, regular probationers may only be seen once, and those on a "mail in" status never see a probation officer—they just mail in or call in their report.[53] Petersilia, for instance, describes Los Angeles County, where 1,869 officers supervise 96,388 probationers. However, 65 percent of these probationers are in an automated, minimum-supervision caseload. There are no face-to-face meetings with probation officers; offenders simply participate in a video orientation program, mail in their reports and a computer alerts a probation officer if they are out of compliance. The ratio for this type of supervision is about 1,000 probationers to one officer.[54]

Most often, probation supervision involves a contact once a month when the probationer comes into the probation office to see the officer and fill out a report, and a "field contact" once a month, where the officer meets the offender in his or her own home or workplace. In these contacts, the officer checks to see if conditions are being met, whether the offender is still employed, and whether court costs are being paid. Offenders may also be required to submit to urinanalysis and the probation officer monitors those test results as well. Probation officers also make "collateral contacts," which are meetings with family members, neighbors, and employers to gather more information about the probationer.

Periodically, the officer writes a progress report to the sentencing judge. When an offender receives probation, the judge maintains control over the offender so the progress reports go to the judge and, if there is a violation report filed, the sentencing judge might hear a motion to revoke probation filed by the prosecutor.

4.2 Models of Supervision

Even though all probation officers have basically the same duties, there are differences in the way the duties are performed. The different approaches taken may be because of individual differences between officers or because of office policies. The different approaches may be characterized by the types found in Box 12.5.

BOX 12.5

Probation Officer Typology

Service Officer – this officer is more focused on the offender's needs and attempts to develop a relationship with each offender on the caseload; they may make allowances for violations of conditions based on individual circumstances

Surveillance Officer – this officer is more focused on surveillance and monitoring the offender's performance in completing the requirements and staying out of trouble; these officers emphasize the enforcement duties of the job; they strive to see that if the probationer breaks any laws or violates any condition, he or she is off the streets quickly and efficiently

Broker Officer – this officer balances service and surveillance, but does not attempt to provide direct counseling or service; rather, the officer uses other community resources and refers the client to the appropriate agency or service provider

Burned out Officer – this officer doesn't emphasize either service or surveillance and does the minimum amount of work necessary to stay out of trouble.

Source: Klockars, C. (1972). "A Theory of Probation Supervision." *Journal of Criminal Law, Criminology, and Police Science* 63, 4: 550-557.

4.3 Interstate Compact

After the creation of probation, it was soon apparent that probationers either would have to stay in the state they were sentenced in until they completed the probation order, or there was going to have to be some sort of shared supervision contract between the states. The **Interstate Compact** was created in September 1937 in Kansas City. All states participate and now these offenders represent about three percent of the total national probation and parole population. Each state has a state interstate compact office that accepts case transfers from other states. The offender must abide by the conditions in both states. Even if there was no supervision fee in the sentencing state, the offender may be required to pay one in the receiving state. Generally, the sending state sets the amount of time the offender is supervised, but the receiving state sets the level of supervision. In 2002, the Interstate Compact was replaced with a new Compact and new organization. Today the Interstate Compact for Adult Offender Supervision is the national body that coordinates the interstate agreements.

For further information on the Parole and Probation Compact Administrators' Association, see www.interstatecompact.org.

Some states may not allow certain types of offenders (i.e., sex offenders). On the other hand, some will not accept misdemeanants for supervision (evidently seeing those minor offenders as not worth the resources expended). There is no payment made to the receiving state; the idea is that as people move in and out of states, participating states will receive and send probationers in roughly equal proportions. The Parole and Probation Compact Administrators' Association meets twice a year to review standards and guidelines and policies.

5. RECIDIVISM

About 60 percent of all probationers successfully complete their probation and are discharged from probation. Only about 15 percent of probationers are revoked and sent to prison. The remainder **abscond**, which means they leave supervision and are unable to be located) (3 percent), are revoked without incarceration (13 percent), or have unspecified reasons, such as death, for leaving probation supervision.[55]

When a probationer violates probation, it may be revoked and he or she is sent to prison. What due process protects the individual from governmental error in the decision to revoke? The answer was addressed by the Supreme Court about 30 years ago. The first case that arose occurred in Washington, which used deferred sentencing. In **deferred sentencing**, the decision to sentence to prison, and the length of the possible prison sentence, is not established during the sentencing hearing immediately after conviction. In *Mempa v. Rhay*,[56] Jerry Mempa pled guilty to joyriding and received a two-year probation sentence with a deferred prison sentence. Because he was suspected of being involved in a burglary, the prosecutor moved for revocation and the sentencing court revoked his probation and sentenced him to 10 years in prison. Although there was a hearing, Mempa had no attorney present to help with his defense. Upon appeal, the Supreme Court held that because the state used deferred sentencing, and the decision and length of imprisonment was not set at the time of the original sentencing, the probation revocation hearing became, in essence, a sentencing hearing, and the offender deserved all the Sixth Amendment rights, including counsel.

Not surprisingly, Washington and other states stopped using deferred sentences with probation and instead began using suspended sentencing. In **suspended sentences**, the judge actually hands down a prison sentence, but then suspends it, pending successful completion of probation. If probation is revoked, the suspended sentence would be imposed. The revocation hearing in this instance is definitely not a sentencing hearing because all decisions regarding sentencing have been made.

In *Gagnon v. Scarpelli*,[57] Scarpelli received a suspended sentence and probation. He committed a burglary while on probation and, without a hearing, his probation was revoked and the suspended sentence imposed. He argued that this was a violation of due process. While the Supreme Court agreed that no Sixth Amendment rights applied because the revocation hearing was not a sentencing hearing, they decided that revocation still involved a protected liberty interest and, thus, due process (coming from the Fourteenth Amendment) applied. The "process due" or the steps needed to insure no error in the governmental deprivation of liberty were more problematic. The Supreme Court had just decided *Morrissey v. Brewer*,[58] a parole revocation case, and so they used that as a guide to determine how serious the deprivation was and what process was due. Arguably, a probation revocation was more serious than a parole revocation because the probationer, unlike the parolee, had never been in prison. Thus the due process protections required should be somewhat more than when someone faced parole revocation.

The court held that whether the proceeding was more like an administrative hearing, or more like a judicial hearing, hinged on whether the offender admitted guilt or not (or, put another way, when there was a factual issue of guilt). If there were questions regarding guilt or innocence, or if the offender could not understand the proceedings because of mental disability or language difficulties, then counsel might be required. However, if it was simply a matter of the offender absconding or some other clear violation of conditions, then no counsel was required. The elements of due process required for probation revocation, as specified by the court, are set out in Box 12.6.

BOX 12.6

Due Process Protections for Probation Revocation

★ Notice of alleged violations of probation and evidence

★ Opportunity to appear and to present evidence and witnesses

★ Right to confront adverse witnesses

★ Neutral decision maker

★ Written report

★ *Conditional* right to counsel

In practice, many states allow the probationer to have counsel if they request it. Remember that the right to counsel is not so much the issue of whether they have a right to be there; if an offender can afford to hire a lawyer, they are almost always allowed in a variety of proceedings. The issue concerning whether counsel is a right is important because if it is a right, then the state must provide indigent offenders with public defenders.

The Supreme Court has ruled that probationers do not have Fifth Amendment rights when being questioned by a probation officer; and probation officers do not have to give *Miranda* warnings before asking offenders about criminal activities unless the offender is already in custody.[59] Furthermore, at least one court has held that they can be punished for not responding to probation officers' questions about alleged violations, and also prosecuted or have their probation revoked if they do admit criminal activities to their probation officer.

If an offender violates one or more conditions of probation, the probation officer may file a violation report. The prosecutor's office may then file a motion to revoke probation or initiate the hearing before the judge that may end in a revocation of probation. This response is discretionary, however, and some probation officers may work with the offender to try to resolve the issue before filing the report. For instance, if the violation is not paying restitution and court costs, the probation officer may require the probationer to pay the arrears and monitor spending for a month. If the probationer has a "dirty" urine test, the probation officer may ask the offender to go into treatment.

However, if the probation officer finds out that the probationer has been arrested for a new crime, or believes that the **technical violations** (violations of rules rather than new crimes) warrant judicial intervention, then a violation report is filed. In the report, the officer presents the charges (the violations), and summarizes the proof. There is also a recommendation, much in the same way that the PSR recommends to the judge at the initial sentencing hearing.

After hearing the evidence, the judge decides whether to continue on probation, continue on probation but with modified conditions (i.e., imposing curfew, treatment, intermediate sanction, more conditions), or revoke probation and send the person to prison. In cases of new crimes, the decision is usually to send to prison. Depending on the state, the time spent on probation may not be counted at all toward the completion of the sentence. In this case, an offender may have already served four years on a probation sentence, but upon revocation, began serving the original five-year prison sentence with no credit for time served on probation. In some states, the judge has the discretion to consider time served or not.

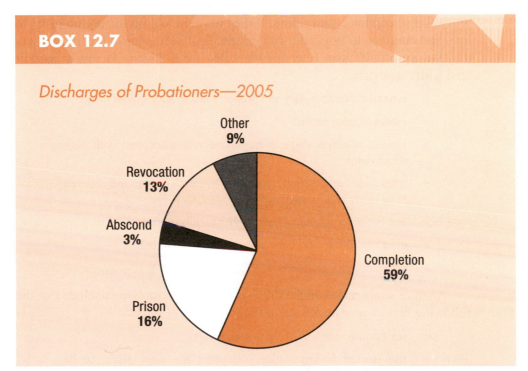

BOX 12.7

Discharges of Probationers—2005

Other 9%

Revocation 13%

Abscond 3%

Prison 16%

Completion 59%

Source: Glaze, L. and T. Bonczar (2006). *Probation and Parole in the United States, 2005.* Washington, DC: Bureau of Justice Statistics, p. 6.

In 1986, 74 percent of probationers successfully completed their term. In 1992, 67 percent were successful, but by 1998, only 50 percent successfully completed probation.[61] Today the number is back up to 60 percent.[62] In Box 12.7, the Bureau of Justice Statistics information is used to show the discharges of probationers.

One study found that most probationers failed within the first three months of probation and they failed because of technical violations, not new crimes. In this study, it was found that Michigan probationers were likely to fail because of such violations as:

★   failed drug tests

★   failure to attend or successfully complete programming

★   failure to perform community service

The single most common violation of all failed probationers (33 percent) was "failure to report." However, most probationers were charged with more than one violation. About 17 percent of those who were revoked had been arrested for assaultive crimes, including assaults with a dangerous weapon, criminal sexual conduct, and home invasion. The single most predictive factor relating to committing a new assaultive crime was the crime of conviction being assault.[63]

5.1 Factors Associated with Recidivism

There are obvious factors that influence whether offenders will succeed on probation or commit a new crime. If they have no job, no money, no place to live, and continue to associate with criminals, it seems fairly predictable that they will re-offend. Joan Petersilia identified the following factors as associated with recidivism:

★   type of crime (burglary and property crime have higher rates)

★   extent of prior record

★   income at arrest (high unemployment is associated with high recidivism)

★   household composition (those who live with spouse and children have lower recidivism)

★   age (younger offenders have higher recidivism rates)

★   drug use (drug users have higher recidivism rates)

★   program participation[64]

Another study reviewed the findings of prior research to conclude that the following factors may be related to failure:

★   sex (women are less likely to recidivate)

★   age (mixed findings; older offenders are more likely to be arrested for serious felonies, but in general younger offenders more likely to re-offend)

★ race (mixed findings)

★ education (higher levels are associated with success)

★ marital status (mixed, but most find marriage is related to success)

★ employment (associated with success on probation)

★ prior criminal history (associated with failure, especially property offenders).[65]

6. CONCLUSION

Diversion programs have the potential to keep appropriate offenders in the community and reduce total correctional costs. There are a number of programs that have diverted offenders from entering the system, such as deferred adjudication programs that use such features as restitution and electronic monitoring. For all diversion programs, the question that must be answered is whether the cost savings and benefit to the offender is worth the risk to public safety. To answer this question, prediction and classification instruments must be improved and the implementation of such programs must adhere to standards and guidelines set out by program developers.

The majority of criminal offenders have experienced probation. About 60 percent successfully complete their probation sentence. Although probation has the potential to be a sufficient and effective correctional sanction, there are a number of problems with the implementation of probation, which include:

1. An unclear mission;

2. Overstated and/or unspecified objectives that are difficult to measure;

3. Inadequate standards and training;

4. Lack of substantial results;

5. A history of inadequate funding;

6. Isolation from the public and a lack of public awareness;

7. Lack of strategic planning and effective management techniques; and

8. A weak constituency.[66]

If probation is to be used more often for first time and non-violent offenders and thereby reduce the total cost of corrections, it must overcome these issues and present a more palatable sentencing alternative to decisionmakers.

REVIEW QUESTIONS

1. Distinguish among pretrial release programs, pretrial diversion programs, and intermediate sanctions.

2. Discuss what benefit of clergy was and why it is called an early form of diversion.

3. Briefly describe day reporting centers, electronic monitoring, restitution, day fines, and community service.

4. How many people are on probation? What percent of all correctional offenders are on probation? What is the percentage of felony defendants who receive a sentence of probation?

5. Describe what percentage of probationers are women and what special issues face women on probation. Describe what percentage of probationers are minorities.

6. Describe the contributions of John Augustus.

7. Describe the state, local, and mixed models of probation administration.

8. Describe the elements that make up the presentence report, and discuss the issues of confidentiality and what conditions are placed on probation orders.

9. Describe the models of supervision.

10. Discuss the due process rights of probationers facing revocation.

VOCABULARY

abscond – to leave supervision without permission

benefit of clergy – early form of diversion where those who could prove they were members of the clergy by reading Psalm 54 were released from secular adjudication

casework model – involves the professional interacting with each "client" individually, serving as the primary, and sometimes only, service provider

community corrections – any form of correctional alternative that does not involve incarceration in prison

conditions – rules of probation

day fines – fines set by the amount of income the offender has, i.e., the fine is three days of income, rather than a dollar amount

deferred sentencing – a sentence where the decision to sentence to prison, and the length of the possible prison sentence, is not established during the sentencing hearing

intermediate sanctions – more than a suspended sentence, less than a prison sentence

interstate compact – agreement between states to supervise transferred probationers

pretrial release programs – a means by which suspects may avoid having to pay bail to gain release before their trial

punitive service – type of community service that may not be linked to the victim at all, nor have any relationship to the crime, i.e., washing police cars

restitution – an order by the court that requires the offender to compensate the victim for the injury or loss suffered in the crime

restorative service – type of community service that attempts to connect the offender to the victim through some process of recognizing the harm and injury done to the specific victim, i.e., providing a service to the victim or class of victims

Scarlet Letter conditions – a condition designed to humiliate or call attention to the wrongdoing of the offender.

suspended sentence – the judge actually hands down a prison sentence, but then suspends it, pending successful completion of probation

technical violations – violations of rules rather than new crimes

victim-centered restitution – includes the victim in the determination of the amount to be compensated, and then the offender either pays the victim directly or through the court

FOR FURTHER READING

Abadinsky, Howard (2005). *Probation and Parole: Theory and Practice*. Upper Saddle River, NJ: Prentice-Hall.

Johnson, Herbert and Nancy T. Wolfe (2003). *History of Criminal Justice*, Third Edition. Cincinnati, OH: Anderson Publishing Co.

Mair, George (2004). *What Matters in Probation*. London: Willan Publishers.

Petersilia, Joan (2002). *Reforming Probation and Parole*. Lanham, MD: American Correctional Association.

Timasheff, N. (1941). *One Hundred Years of Probation, 1841-1941*. New York: Fordham University Press.

---

[1] *County of Riverside v. McLaughlin*, 500 U.S. 44 (1991).

[2] Parent, D., J. Byrne, V. Tsarfaty, L. Valade, L. Esselman (1995). *Day Reporting Centers. Issues and Practices in Criminal Justice*, Vol. 1. Washington DC: National Institute of Justice.

[3] Jones, R. & J. Lacey (1999). *Evaluation of a Day Reporting Center for Repeat DWI Offenders*. Washington, DC: National Highway Traffic Safety Administration.

[4] Parent, D. (1996). "Day Reporting Centers: An Evolving Intermediate Sanction." *Federal Probation* 60, 4: 51-54.

[5] Lilly, J., R. Ball, G. Curry & J. McMullen (1993). "Electronic Monitoring of the Drunk Driver: A Seven-Year Study of the Home Confinement Alternative." *Crime and Delinquency* 39: 462-484.

[6] Bonta, J. S. Wallace-Capretta & J. Rooney (2000). "Can Electronic Monitoring Make a Difference? An Evaluation of Three Canadian Programs." *Crime and Delinquency* 46, 1: 61-75.

[7] Lilly, J., R. Ball, G. Curry & J. McMullen (1993). "Electronic Monitoring of the Drunk Driver: A Seven-Year Study of the Home Confinement Alternative." *Crime and Delinquency* 39: 462-484.

[8] Lilly, J., R. Ball, G. Curry & J. McMullen (1993). "Electronic Monitoring of the Drunk Driver: A Seven-Year Study of the Home Confinement Alternative." *Crime and Delinquency* 39: 462-484.

[9] Gibbs, A., & D. King (2003). "The Electronic Ball and Chain? The Operation and Impact of Home Detention with Electronic Monitoring in New Zealand." *The Australian and New Zealand Journal of Criminology*, 36, 1-17.

[10] Bonta, Wallace-Capretta, & Rooney (2000). "Can Electronic Monitoring Make a Difference? An Evaluation of Three Canadian Programs." *Crime and Delinquency* 46, 1: 61-75.

[11] Gendreau, P., C. Goggin, F. Cullen & D. Andrews (2000). "The Effects of Community Sanctions and Incarceration on Recidivism." *Forum* 12, 2: 10-13.

[12] Maxfield, M., & T. Baumer (1990). "Home Detention with Electronic Monitoring: Comparing Pretrial and Postconviction Programs." *Crime and Delinquency*, 36, 521-536.

[13] Lilly, J.R., R. Ball, G.D. Curry & J. McMullen (1993). "Electronic Monitoring of the Drunk Driver: A Seven-Year Study of the Home Confinement Alternative." *Crime and Delinquency*, 39, 462-484

[14] Stutzman, R. (2002a). "Ankle Monitors Show a Higher Rate of Success." *Orlando Sentinel*. December 29: B1; Stutzman, R. (2002b). "State Takes Eyes Off Inmates. *Orlando Sentinel*. December 29:B2.

[15] Hillsman, T. & J. Greene (1992). "The Use of Fines as an Intermediate Sanction" In J. Byrne, A. Lurigio & J. Petersilia (eds.), *Smart Sentencing: The Emergence of Intermediate Sanctions*, pp. 123-141. Newbury Park, CA: Sage Publications.

[16] Bureau of Justice Assistance (1996). *How to Use Structured Fines as an Intermediate Sanction*. Washington, DC: U.S. Department of Justice.

[17] Ruback, R., G. Ruth & J. Shaffer (2005). "Assessing the Impact of Statutory Change: A Statewide Multi-level Analysis of Restitution Orders in Pennsylvania." *Crime and Delinquency* 51, 3: 318-342, p. 319.

[18] Ruback, R., G. Ruth & J. Shaffer (2005). "Assessing the Impact of Statutory Change: A Statewide Multi-level Analysis of Restitution Orders in Pennsylvania." *Crime and Delinquency* 51, 3: 318-342, p. 334.

[19] Lurigio, A. & A. Davis (1984). "Does a Threatening Letter Increase Compliance with Restitution Orders?" *Crime and Delinquency* 36, 4: 537-548.

[20] Glaze, L. & T. Bonczar (2006). *Probation and Parole in the United States, 2005*. Washington, DC: Bureau of Justice Statistics, p. 3.

[21] Petersilia, J. (2002). *Reforming Probation and Parole*. Lanham, MD: American Correctional Association, p. 49.

[22] Glaze, L. & T. Bonczar (2006). *Probation and Parole in the United States, 2005*. Washington, DC: Bureau of Justice Statistics.

[23] Petersilia, J. (2002). *Reforming Probation and Parole*. Lanham, MD: American Correctional Association, p. 3.

[24] Petersilia, J. (2002). *Reforming Probation and Parole*. Lanham, MD: American Correctional Association, p. 3.

[25] Bureau of Justice Statistics. *Criminal Sentencing Statistics*. Retrieved 1/11/05 from: http://www.ojp.usdoj.gov/bjs/sent.htm.

[26] Glaze, L. & S. Palla (2005). *Probation and Parole in the United States, 2004*. Washington, DC: Bureau of Justice Statistics.

[27] Glaze, L. & T. Bonczar (2006). *Probation and Parole in the United States, 2005*. Washington, DC: Bureau of Justice Statistics.

[28] Glaze, L. & T. Bonczar, (2006). *Probation and Parole in the United States, 2005*. Washington, DC: Bureau of Justice Statistics.

[29] Greenfield, L. & T. Snell (1999/2000, revised). *Women Offenders*. Washington DC: Bureau of Justice Statistics. Retrieved 2/24/07 from: http://www.ojp.usdoj.gov/bjs/abstract/wo.htm.

[30] Gray, M., M. Fields & S. Maxwell (2001). "Examining Probation Violations: Who, What, and When." *Crime and Delinquency* 47, 4: 537-557.

[31] Griffin, M. & G. Armstrong (2003). "The Effect of Local Life Circumstances on Female Probationers' Offending." *Justice Quarterly*, 20, 2: 213-225.

[32] Glaze, L. & T. Bonczar (2006). *Probation and Parole in the United States, 2005*. Washington DC: Bureau of Justice Statistics.

[33] Steffensmeier D., J. Ulmer & J. Kramer (1998). "The Interaction of Race, Gender, and Age in Criminal Sentencing." *Criminology* 36: 763-797.

[34] Friedman, L. (1993). *Crime and Punishment in American History*. New York: Basic Books, p. 18.

[35] Friedman, L. (1993). *Crime and Punishment in American History*. New York: Basic Books.

[36] Petersilia, J. (2002). *Reforming Probation and Parole*. Lanham, MD: American Correctional Association, p. 37.

[37] Petersilia, J. (2002). *Reforming Probation and Parole*. Lanham, MD: American Correctional Association, p. 38.

[38] Petersilia, J. (2002). *Reforming Probation and Parole*. Lanham, MD: American Correctional Association, p. 25.; Walker, S. (1998). *Popular Justice: A History of American Criminal Justice*, Second Edition. New York: Oxford University Press.

[39] Rosecrance, J. (1988). "Maintaining the Myth of Individualized Justice: Probation Presentence Reports." *Justice Quarterly* 5, 2: 235-256.

[40] *Gardner v. Florida*, 430 U.S. 349 (1977).

[41] Federal Rules of Procedure 32(c)(2)(A-D). *See Julian v. U.S. Department of Justice*, 806 F2d. 1411 (9th Cir. 1986).

[42] Bonczar, T. & L. Glaze (1999). *Probation and Parole in the United States*, 1998. Washington DC: U.S. Department of Justice.

[43] Petersilia, J. (2002). *Reforming Probation and Parole*. Lanham, MD: American Correctional Association, p. 40.

[44] *Beardon v. Georgia*, 461 U.S. 660 (1983).

[45] Petersilia, J. (2002). *Reforming Probation and Parole*. Lanham, MD: American Correctional Association, p. 31.

[46] Ginzberg, J. (1992). "Compulsory Contraception as a Condition of Probation: The Use and Abuse of Norplant." *Brooklyn Law Review* 58: 979-1019.

[47] *Bienz v. State*, 434 So. 2d 913 (Fla. Dist. Ct. App. 1977).

[48] *Blanton et al. v. City of North Las Vegas*, 489 US 538 (1989).

[49] *Griffin v. Wisconsin*, 483 U.S. 868 (1987).

[50] Hoffman, P. (1997). "History of the Federal Parole System: Part 2 (1973-1997). *Federal Probation* 61, 4: 49-57.

[51] Camp. G. & C. Camp (2001). *The Corrections Yearbook*. Middletown, CT: Criminal Justice Institute, Inc., p.3.

[52] Camp. G. & C. Camp (2000). *The Corrections Yearbook*. Middletown, CT: Criminal Justice Institute, Inc.

[53] Camp. G. & C. Camp (2000). *The Corrections Yearbook*. Middletown, CT: Criminal Justice Institute, Inc. p. 35.

[54] Camp. G. & C. Camp (2000). *The Corrections Yearbook*. Middletown, CT: Criminal Justice Institute, Inc. p. 35.

[55] Glaze, L. & T. Bonczar (2006). *Probation and Parole in the United States*, 2005. Washington, DC: Bureau of Justice Statistics, p. 6.

[56] 389 U.S. 128 (1967).

[57] 411 U.S. 778 (1973).

[58] 408 U.S. 471 (1972).

[59] *Minnesota v. Murphy*, 465 U.S. 420 (1984).

[60] *United States v. Chapman*, U.S. App LEXIS 12301 (2000).

[61] Bonczar, T. & L. Glaze (1999). *Probation and Parole in the United States*, 1998. Washington, DC: Bureau of Justice Statistics, p. 6.

[62] Glaze, L. & S. Palla (2005). *Probation and Parole in the United States*, 2004. Washington, DC: Bureau of Justice Statistics, p. 6.

[63] Gray, M., M. Fields & S. Maxwell (2001). "Examining Probation Violations: Who, What, and When." *Crime and Delinquency* 47, 4: 537-557.

[64] Petersilia, J. (2002). *Reforming Probation and Parole*. Lanham, MD: American Correctional Association, p. 58.

[65] Gray, M., M. Fields & S. Maxwell (2001). "Examining Probation Violations: Who, What, and When." *Crime and Delinquency* 47, 4: 537-557.

[66] Fitzharris, T. (1984). "The Federal Role in Probation Reform." In P. McAnany, D. Thomson & D. Fogel (eds.), *Probation and Justice*. Cambridge, MA: Oelgeschaler, Gunn and Hain.

Chapter 13

Prisons and Jails

What You Need to Know

★ There are more than two million people incarcerated in prisons and jails as of 2005.

★ Incarceration rates vary across states and across countries.

★ The United States incarceration rate is 738 per 100,000, which is higher than any other Western country.

★ The Walnut Street Jail was the origin of the penitentiary concept.

★ Two systems of penitentiaries emerged — the separate system and the congregate system.

★ Prison subculture is explained through the deprivation or importation theory and includes the values of strength, loyalty, and violence. Men's and women's prison subcultures are different.

★ Prisoner rights litigation revolves around the Fourteenth, Eighth, and First Amendments.

★ The eras of prisoner rights include the *hands-off* era, the *prisoner rights* era, and the *due deference* era.

A prison sentence is the second most severe punishment that can be inflicted upon a criminal offender. For most of us, our perceptions of prison are shaped by movies (*The Shawshank Redemption*) and television shows (*Oz*). Some of these dramatizations have been realistic, some sensationalistic, and some ridiculous. Scriptwriters may never get it right because prison is an abnormal environment that becomes normal for the persons who live and work there. It is, at the same time, boring and terrifying; banal and soul destroying; it is a place of despair, but for some, a place of opportunity.

This country uses imprisonment as punishment more than any other Western nation. There are currently more than two million people incarcerated in prisons and jails. The United States' incarceration rate is the highest of the Western nations. It has not always been this way.

1. THE HISTORY OF PRISONS

Although the idea of solitary penitence was practiced in ecclesiastical institutions in Europe, its development as a secular punishment was purely American.[1] The **penitentiary** in America began with the **Walnut Street Jail** in Philadelphia in 1790. In 1790, the Society for Alleviating the Miseries of Public Prisons was able to get legislation passed that reformed the Walnut Street Jail. Women were segregated from men, and the worst offenders were segregated from others. Food, clothing, and medical care were provided by the Society.

Most importantly, the mission of the institution changed from mere incapacitation to reform. Inmates were expected to contemplate their evil ways in their solitary cells and reform themselves through penitence. By the 1800s, the Walnut Street Jail was extremely overcrowded and conditions had deteriorated to the point where Eastern State Penitentiary was built to replace the jail. Here, the solitary system was pursued to an even greater degree, and this institution became one of the models for the penitentiary system.[2] The penitentiary was designed to isolate criminals from the contagion of the corrupt influences of the city. Prison advocates argued that prisoners would experience solitude, work, and penitence, and that this experience would transform them into good, sober citizens.

Two distinct versions of the penitentiary emerged in the 1800s: the *separate* and *congregate* systems. The **separate system** originated in Philadelphia at the Walnut Street Jail (1790) and later at Eastern Penitentiary (1829). This system is sometimes called the Philadelphia or **Pennsylvania system**. The regimen was one of solitary confinement and manual labor. Prisoners were kept in their cells at all times. The **congregate system** was first introduced at Auburn Prison (1817), and is often called simply the **Auburn system**. Prisoners of this system slept in solitary cells, but worked and ate together. Silence was strictly enforced, however, to prevent them from being corrupted by each other. Regimentation and harsh punishment were used to control inmates, but also to reform them to become obedient and sober workers. Separation, obedience, and labor became the "trinity" around which officials managed the penitentiary.[3] Convicts were "men of idle habits, vicious propensities, and depraved passions," who had to be taught obedience as part of their reformation.[4] The **lockstep march** was an iconic image of these prisons where prisoners shuffled together, bound by one hand on the opposite shoulder of the man in front. This was the only exercise available to inmates until the 1900s—it was eventually abolished in the first several decades of the twentieth century.[5]

Advocates of the two systems argued for years about which was a better system. The similarities between the two were just as striking as the differences. Both employed a vision of the penitentiary as a place where inmates would be transformed to obedient citizens. Reformation was the dominant theme of the 1870 Prison Congress, which laid out the "Principles of Corrections," and these were endorsed again, almost without change, in the 1970 Prison Congress. The 1870 and 1970 Prison Congresses endorsed such philosophical principles as:

★   Corrections must demonstrate integrity, respect, dignity, fairness.

★   Sanctions imposed by the court shall be commensurate with the seriousness of the offense.

★   Offenders shall have the opportunity to engage in productive work, participate in programs and other activities that will enhance self-worth, community integration, and economic status.[6]

The Auburn model became the template for future building, largely because it allowed factory work to partially offset the costs of imprisonment. Interestingly, the separate system became a more common model for prison building in Europe.

There were few women sentenced to prison in the 1800s. Those who were confined to penitentiaries were often caged in attics, left unsupervised, and subjected to sexual abuse.[7] Early prisons also did not house many blacks, at least until after the Civil War, because they more often were punished by slave owners.

In the late 1800s, the **reformatory era** brought new ideas to the philosophies of imprisonment. Elmira Reformatory, dating from 1870, was created for young men and had a mission of reform through education and strict discipline. While reformatories for men utilized militaristic drills and staffing, reformatories for women sought to recreate home-like environments through the use of cottages. Matrons were expected to serve as role models of what women should be like.[8] Approximately 21 women's reformatories were built between 1860 and 1935. The women sent there typically were young, white women who had committed minor crimes. Even those who had committed only public order or juvenile crimes, such as running away or being promiscuous, might have been sent to a reformatory. Black women, older white women, and women who had committed serious crimes, were sent to custodial prisons for women. These women continued to be housed in a wing or building at the men's prison. Eventually reformatory institutions lost their mission and the boundaries blurred between custodial prisons for women and reformatories.

Robert Johnson calls the maximum-security prisons throughout the first half of the twentieth century **Big Houses**.[9] In prisons of the early to mid-1900s, prisoners worked, sometimes in meaningless labor, such as the infamous rock pile. There was no purpose, and no institutional mission, other than incapacitation and punishment. The only thing that the prison did well was keep inmates behind its massive walls and out of the public's view.

Early prisons in southern states were more likely to follow an agricultural model, rather than an industrial or factory model. In fact, some argue that they were extensions of the slave plantation.[10] Newly emancipated blacks and others were sentenced to hard labor in the fields of landowners. These landowners leased prisoners' labor from the state prison to replace the newly freed slaves. Prisoners also labored on the infamous chain gangs. Black female prisoners were subjected to the same harsh treatment as the men, while white women were more often assigned as house servants to the wardens and other administrators.[11]

Until about the 1960s, prisons were segregated by policy, and blacks had little power. Early sociological discussions of prisons did not mention black prisoners at all. Gresham Sykes' classic study, *The Society of Captives* (1958/1966), describes Trenton State Prison in 1950. The prison society, as Sykes described it, was a world of the strong preying on the weak. A few prisoners were able to obtain a range of goods, including alcohol and sex, by barter or money from the outside. Prisoners were expected to "do their own time," and ignore the victimization of their fellow inmates. In the Big House prisons of the north and the southern plantation prisons, prisoners received the minimal resources necessary to sustain life.

The **correctional institution** emerged gradually, and by the 1950s one began to see the rhetoric of reform. Gradually, prisons began to offer prisoners more privileges, such as yard and recreational privileges; more liberal mail and visitation policies; and occasional movies or concerts. The more important development, however, was the beginning of educational, vocational, and therapeutic programs. In fact, by the 1970s there was a burst of optimism and hope that the prison could become a place of change. In some places, radical ideas were considered, such as the plan for college classes to be held on prison grounds for inmates, officers, and townspeople alike. Inmates were released through a variety of work and educational release. Some colleges even had dorms for prisoners where they would check in and out for class.

Women's correctional institutions also followed the mission of reform. Niantic prison in Connecticut, for example, was described, during this period, as "nice and cozy" where officers and inmates would meet in groups to discuss things and inmates were allowed to make their rooms their own personal space through pictures and possessions.[12] Some women's prisons even experimented with having apartment-like minimum-security buildings, where female inmates could go out to work in the community, returning to the prison-based apartment at night.

However, despite these examples, promises of reform did not necessarily translate into realities for most prisoners, and prisons erupted into riots, first in the 1950s, and then, 20 years later, in the 1970s. The Attica prison riot, and lesser known riots in other prisons during the same period, have been attributed to frustrated expectations that prisons would offer meaningful programs. Another important element, however, was the greater politicization of inmates, especially minority inmates, who often had been involved in organizations such as the Black Panthers on the street. The Black Awareness movement of the 1960s and 1970s spurred the prisoners' rights movement, but it also may have spurred changes in the prison subculture. Prison, although becoming officially desegregated via judicial decisions, became increasingly self-segregated along racial and ethnic lines.[13]

The 1970s was a time of great change for prisons. The unrest on the street seeped into prisons and led to prisoners demanding more rights; race conflict emerged and often escalated into violence; and the beginning of the scourge of drugs (which exploded in the next decade) began to affect the prison subculture and raised the stakes of the prison black market economic system. In the 1980s, the tremendous increase in the numbers of individuals being sent to prison exacerbated all these problems.

The correctional institution's rhetoric of reform gave way fairly quickly to the warehouse prison of today. Even women's prisons have changed. For example, Niantic prison, described earlier, was supplanted by York prison for women, a huge concrete-and-steel "confinement model" prison. Here, as well as all across the country, women were told they were going to be treated like inmates rather than women, and the unique characteristics of women's prisons were systematically eliminated.[14]

The contemporary prison provides a much better life for prisoners than at earlier times in history. Prisoners get enough to eat and they have probably better medical care than they would have access to on the street. However, because of the crushing burden of numbers, reform or rehabilitation is not a central mission, which is why we call contemporary prisons **warehouse prisons**. Most prisoners are simply housed and fed until release.

2. INCREASED IMPRISONMENT

Today, the incarcerated population in America exceeds two million persons.[15] Two-thirds (1,438,701) of this number are in prison, and the rest are incarcerated in jails. The prison population alone grew about 93.5 percent from 1990 to year-end 2005—from 743,382 to 1,438,701 prisoners in just 15 years.[16]

To better understand the increased use of imprisonment, we will examine rates per 100,000. Rates allow us to compare incarceration across different populations; therefore, we know, when comparing two different years or two different states, the change is not due to population fluctuations. There are two different types of rates that you might see for incarceration. The first is the total incarceration rate, which includes both federal and state prisons and *jails*. The total United States rate in 2005 was 738 per 100,000. The other rate, more commonly used, is the imprisonment rate, which is just the number of people

BOX 13.1

Incarceration Rates

Source: M. Cahalan (1986). *Historical Corrections Statistics in the United States, 1850-1984.* Rockville, MD: Westat, Inc.; Bureau of Justice Statistics (1997). *Sourcebook of Criminal Justice Statistics.* Washington DC: Bureau of Justice Statistics (1998). *State and Federal Prisoners, June 30, 1998.* Washington DC: Bureau of Justice Statistics. P. Harrison and J. Karberg (2003). *Prison and Jail Inmates at Midyear 2002.* Washington DC: Bureau of Justice Statistics.

BOX 13.2

Prison and Jail Incarceration Rate, Selected States, 2005

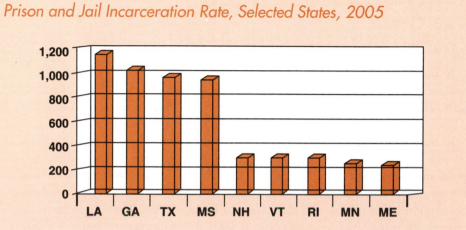

Source: Harrison, P. and A. Beck (2006). *Prison and Jail Inmates at Midyear 2005.* Washington, DC: Bureau of Justice Statistics.

incarcerated in state or federal prisons, excluding jails, per 100,000. In 2005, this rate was 488 per 100,000. In Box 13.1 the incarceration rates for the last 150 years are displayed and we see that the use of prisons has increased dramatically only within the last three decades.

It is also the case that the rate of incarceration varies tremendously between the states. In Box 13.2, the total incarceration rate (including jails) is used to show the variability between the states with the highest rates and the states with the lowest rates. While Louisiana incarcerates 1,138 per 100,000 of its citizens, Maine only incarcerates 273 per 100,000. What accounts for this difference? There is no good answer to that question, although people have explored the issue for decades.

Rates also allow us to compare the United States to other countries. In Box 13.3 we see that the United States uses incarceration as a punishment much more frequently than similar countries. Only a few countries have similar rates to the United States, and most of our "sister" countries, such as England, Canada, Australia, France, and Germany have much lower incarceration rates.

The prison population of the United States contains disproportionate numbers of racial minorities relative to their proportion in the general population.

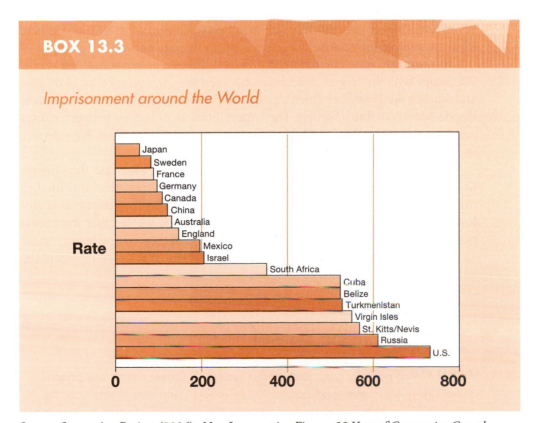

BOX 13.3

Imprisonment around the World

Source: Sentencing Project (2006). *New Incarceration Figures: 33 Years of Consecutive Growth.* Retrieved 8/18/07 from: http://www.sentencingproject.org/Admin/Documents/publications/inc_newfigures.pdf.

BOX 13.4

Rates by Race/Ethnicity and Gender

	Males	Females
Total	1,371	129
White	709	88
Black	4,682	347
Hispanic	1,856	144

Source: Harrison, P. and A. Beck (2006). *Prison and Jail Inmates at Midyear 2005*. Washington, DC: Bureau of Justice Statistics.

The incarceration rate for black men is an amazing 4,682, which is almost seven times higher than that of white men, whose rate was 709 in 2005. In Box 13.4, we can see the relative rates across race/ethnicity and gender groups.

Interestingly, race/ethnicity and gender differences vary across the states. The states with the largest differences between the incarceration rates of men and women are New York (men's rate is 16.5 times higher than women's) and Rhode Island (16 times higher). The largest differences in rates between whites and blacks is Iowa (14 times higher for blacks), and Connecticut, New Jersey, and Vermont (12 times higher for blacks).[17]

Women's incarceration rates continue to rise at a faster rate than men's. Since 1995, women's annual increase has averaged 4.7 percent, compared to men's average of three percent. The actual number of women in prison is still low (7 percent), but it has been rising. In Box 13.5, we see that the prison population is still largely male, and that, even though they comprise only about 13 percent of the total population in the United States, black men represent the largest group in this country's prisons.

★ Exercise: In the State of . . .

Find the Web page for your state prison system. Discover how many prisons there are in your state and how many prisoners. Find out, if you can, the breakdown by race/ethnicity and gender. You might also find this information from the Bureau of Justice Statistics Web site.

BOX 13.5

Prison Population, 2005, By Gender and Race/Ethnicity (Percent)

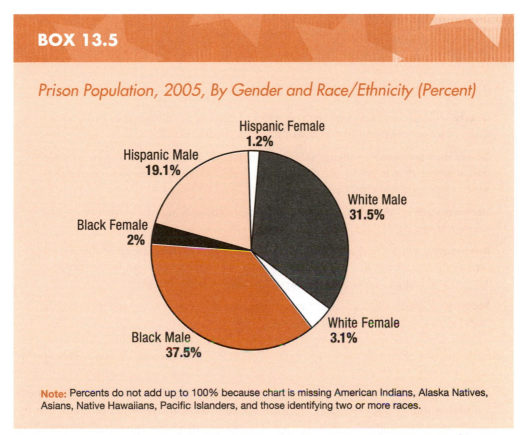

Note: Percents do not add up to 100% because chart is missing American Indians, Alaska Natives, Asians, Native Hawaiians, Pacific Islanders, and those identifying two or more races.

Source: Harrison, P. and A. Beck (2006). *Prison and Jail Inmates at Midyear 2005*. Washington, DC: Bureau of Justice Statistics, p. 8.

3. PRISON LIFE

Many prisoners are young, members of a minority group, and undereducated. About half of prisoners are violent offenders who are facing long sentences and are serving longer proportions of their sentence in prison. Prisons contain "disproportionate numbers of the least mature, least stable, and most violent individuals in American society."[18] In the prison world, the values that most of us live by are turned upside down. In prison, violence is respected and victims are despised.

3.1 Deprivation and Importation

All inmates are subject to what Sykes[19] called the deprivations of prison life. They are described in Box 13.6. These deprivations are said to result in the prisoner subculture. For instance, because of the deprivation of heterosexual relationships, predatory rapists exist in prison and are not considered homosexual. Instead, negative stigma attaches to the victims and they are referred to as "punks."

BOX 13.6

Sykes' Deprivations of Imprisonment

Liberty — includes restrictions on the freedom of movement and deprivation of contact with family members and friends and others from the free world.

Goods and services — inmates' inability to obtain these reduces them to an infantile state whereby they must depend on staff to provide everything from socks and underwear to shampoo and toothpaste.

Heterosexual relationships — refers to the deprivation of "normal" sexual contact in prison settings.

Autonomy — refers to the fact that inmates are not free to make decisions about their own lives; they are not free to do what they want, when they want, and how they want. They are told when to eat, sleep, and work by being treated like a child.

Security — inmates are in a constant state of anxiety about their safety and there is little that they can do to avoid danger.

Source: Sykes, G. (1958). *The Society of Captives*. Princeton, NJ: Princeton University Press, p. 78.

A competing perspective on the development of prisoner subcultures explains that it does not develop from the deprivations of imprisonment, but instead is brought into or is imported to prison from the outside.[20] Researchers subscribing to the **importation hypothesis** believe that the prisoner subculture is derived from the pre-prison characteristics of the people coming into prisons rather than prison deprivations themselves. Research provides support for both of these explanations of the prisoner subculture.

Prisonization is the process of being socialized to the prison subculture.[21] The "**inmate code**" is described as a *sub rosa* (subcultural) set of rules by which prisoners "should" run their lives in the prison setting. Early descriptions of the inmate code portrayed a world where convicts "did their own time," shunned guards, and never lost their "cool," even in the face of extreme provocation. The prisoner who followed the code valued loyalty, autonomy, and strength. The most violent inmate is the person most respected and admired. Violence is often rational, directive, and useful as it indicates toughness, strength, and the ability to "take care of business."

Group loyalty is also an important factor in the prisoner subculture. Snitching may be the most heinous prison "crime." There are a disproportionate number of names for a snitch in the prison setting, including "rat," "squealer," "snitch," "cheese-eater," and "stool pigeon." One of the most gruesome attacks on snitches occurred during the New Mexico prison riot in 1980. Inmates took over the New Mexico Prison and eventually reached Cellblock 4, the housing area for snitches. Using acetylene torches, rioters broke into the protective custody unit and tortured, maimed, and murdered the men found there.[22]

Officials and inmates alike often scorn the person identified as a snitch. Ironically, officials indicate they could not run the prison without informers. Snitching is present in both female and male subcultures, but subcultural sanctions against this behavior were (and are) more serious in prisons for men.[23]

Giallombardo[24] was one of the few researchers who made any attempt to describe the female prisoner subculture. In her study of Alderson, a federal prison for women, she found that different themes were emphasized in the female prisoners' world compared to men. She found that the principle of "do your own time," was rejected in the women's culture. Researchers continue to find that women are more likely to confide in each other and have more interactions with staff.[25]

The male and female inmate codes have changed from when early researchers began writing about prisoner subcultures. Inmate solidarity has eroded considerably, if it ever existed at all.[26] Younger and more violent offenders entering prisons have ignored the old-timers' admonitions to stay loyal and keep a low profile. Perhaps one of the greatest change agents for the inmate subculture has been the influx of younger and more violent inmates, who appeared to take control of some prisons in the 1980s. These "lowriders" or "state raised youth" who entered prisons in the 1980s had little respect for the inmate code, were ready to use violence in any situation, on any inmate, at any time, for even the slightest provocation.[27]

Today's prison subculture often forces inmates to choose between isolation or affiliation with gangs for protection. Today, race is an extremely central issue in prisons.[28] Blacks, who comprise less than 13 percent of the American population have become the majority in prisons for men. In fact, it has been said that it is the one place in society where their power is clear: "I was in jail, the one place in America that black men rule."[29]

Racial gangs exist in all major prison systems in the United States. Probably the best-known gangs formed in Illinois, California, and Texas. In Illinois and California, prison gangs were imported from the streets in the 1960s and 1970s. The formation of the Mafia and Nuestra Familia in California resulted in black inmates forming the Black Guerilla Family and white inmates forming the Aryan Brotherhood to protect themselves.[30] In Texas, there was negligible gang activity during the same period because prisons were dominated by **Building Tenders** (BTs), inmates who were authorized by staff to control inmates by any means necessary.[31] After a court case forced the state to abandon the BT system, the power vacuum was filled by emerging gangs.[32] The gang's struggle for dominance resulted in more homicides during a two-year period than the previous 20 years.[33] Gangs in Texas prisons now include the Texas Syndicate (Hispanic), the Aryan Brotherhood of Texas (white), and the Bloods and Crips (black).

Some research indicates that gangs among female prisoners are growing whereas others have found little evidence of this phenomenon.[34] Perhaps the comparative lack of gang membership among female prisoners may be related to the pseudo-family groupings that exist (and will be discussed in the next section). Female pseudo-families cross racial lines and provide protection, services, and group belonging in similar ways to gang membership. It is likely that women do not form gangs because there is less of a need for protection.

3.2 Prisoner Argot, Argot Roles, and Prison Sex

Prison slang, or argot, is the language of prisoners and thought to be an important part of the prison subculture. Ironically, correctional officers learn the prison argot and use it as adeptly as inmates.[35] Lerner[36] described argot he learned as a new prison "fish." Being a college-educated inmate, Lerner was called a "lawdog" or someone who could assist other inmates to file and read court papers. Other argot he encountered included "dawg," which was slang for a friend or associate; "toads," which was a derogatory name for white inmates; and "fishcops," who were new correctional officers. "Shit," "smack," "crap," "H," and "brown" are some of the many names for heroin. Argot for marijuana may be the most numerous with traditional names from "Mary Jane," "grass," or "Aunt Mary," to less recognized names such as "lubage," and "mutha." Slang for drugs in general includes the term "junk."[37] Argot terms for drugs are so numerous that every conceivable combination and potency of a drug may have several different names.

Prisoner roles (or **argot roles**) serve to classify and describe inmates based upon their behavior before prison, as well as what they do in prison. Gresham Sykes identified several prisoner roles in an early study, including that of rats (informers), centermen (those aligned with correctional officers), gorillas (aggressive predators), merchants (involved in the underground or black market in prison), wolves (sexual aggressors), punks (those forced into homosexual activity against their will), fags (those who engage in homosexuality voluntarily), real men (old-style convicts who do their own time), ball busters (those frequently involved in violent confrontations), toughs (affiliated with violent crime), and hipsters (drug-involved criminals).[38] At the time, drugs were just beginning to be a factor in the subculture.

Clarence Schrag's (1944) roles have perhaps become the most well-known. He described prisoner roles such as the square john, right guy, con politician, and outlaw. The "square john" was the type of inmate who did not have an extensive criminal record and identified more with prison officers than other inmates. Other inmates did not trust him. The "right guy" is characterized as the old-style convict. He was respected for his criminal profession, usually being a professional thief, bank robber, or a member of organized crime. He was respected as a leader in the yard and was not afraid of violence, but used it sparingly and selectively. The "con politician" was a title ascribed to inmates who held the most formal leadership roles in prison, for example, as a representative of the inmate council, and were very visible in interaction with the prison administration. The "outlaw" inmate was characterized as one who did not follow any code of behavior, even the inmate code.[39]

There has not been as much research on female role types. Giallombardo described numerous social roles among female prisoners including snitchers (informers), inmate cops (affiliated with correctional officers), squares (square john equivalents), jive bitches (those who stirred up trouble), rap buddies or homies (friends), boosters (shoplifters), pinners (a trusted inmate who serves as a lookout when illicit activities are undertaking), and a number of roles associated with homosexuality—penitentiary turnouts, butches, lesbians, femmes, stud broads, tricks, commissary hustlers, chippies, kick partners, cherries, punks, and turnabouts.[40]

Homosexuality in men's prisons was (and is) characterized by violent assaults and coercion where older and more experienced convicts (wolves) offered protection to younger more inexperienced inmates (punks) for sexual favors and commissary articles. Violence, intimidation, and exploitation is associated with homosexuality in prisons for men.[41] Aggressive and dominant inmates get powerful names such as "wolf" and "daddy," where submissive and weak inmates are "punks" and "fags." Only "punks" and "fags" are identified as homosexuals and there is little distinction between those who are forced into such a role and those who were homosexual before prison.

Alternatively, homosexuality in women's prisons was (and is) more often consensual and (femmes) voluntarily engage in relationships with other women who assume the male role (butches). Either woman may or may not have lived a homosexual lifestyle outside of prison. Most violence in women's prisons occurs when partners become jealous and attack their partner, or the per-

BOX 13.7

Argot Roles in Men's and Women's Prisons

Men's Prisons	Women's Prisons
Sykes	*Giallombardo*
real men	boosters
gorillas	pinners
centermen	squares, inmate cops
merchants	homies
rats	snitchers
wolves	jive bitches
punks	rap buddies
fags	
ball busters	
toughs	
hipsters	
right guy	
square johns	
con politician	
outlaw	

ceived "other woman." Less frequently, women manipulate others into a relationship, typically because the target has family who put money in her inmate account for commissary.

Another unique feature of homosexual relationships among women prisoners is the concept of **pseudofamilies**. Pseudofamilies are make-believe family systems that include all the familial roles including fathers, mothers, daughters, sisters, cousins, and so on. Women relate to each other more or less consistently with their roles. Parents advise and counsel, siblings share, and husbands and wives may (but not necessarily) engage in sex.[43] These types of relationships are less frequent today than in the past, perhaps because of more liberal visitation policies that allow closer contact with real families.

In both men's and women's prisons, it is difficult to gauge the extent of homosexual behavior. In women's prisons, relationships include note-writing and hugging, propositioning and harassment, and genital sexual relations.[44] Many studies have used unreliable estimates of homosexual activity, such as estimates from officers or other inmates. There is also sexual victimization in prisons for both men and women. In one study, about 15 to 20 percent of a prisoner sample reported "minor" forms of sexual victimization (rubbing, fondling, or harassment) happened to them at least once, or was the "worst incident" of sexual victimization experienced by them. Actual completed rapes seem to be less frequent in both men's and, especially, women's prisons. About one to seven percent of inmates reported at least one episode of forced rape.[45] The Prison Rape Elimination Act (PREA) passed by Congress and signed into law by President Bush in 2003 has placed a renewed emphasis on such victimizations in prisons.

An increasingly common alternative to gang membership, or participation in pseudofamilies or prison homosexuality, is isolation. Some inmates have always chosen this option by avoiding the yard, staying in their cells, and developing few relationships with a few other prisoners. Barbara Owen described how many female inmates avoid going to the yard because that is where those in the mix hang out (referring to drugs, homosexual activity, and fighting).[46] Both male and female inmates seek out niches and sanctuaries in prison.

4. PRISONERS' RIGHTS

What legal rights should prisoners have? Prior to the 1960s, they had very few. In fact, the **hands-off era** (1900-1960) was called that because federal and state courts rarely accepted grievances that prisoners brought to their attention. In fact, in *Ruffin v. Commonwealth*,[47] a Virginia court basically said that a prisoner was a "slave of the state." State and federal courts rejected prisoner appeals for the following reasons:

1. Deferral to the expertise of administrators. They believed that management of a prison should be left to the experts.

2. "Slave of the state" argument: They believed that prisoners only had privileges (that could be taken away) rather than rights.

3. Federalism. Federal courts hesitated to interfere with the business of the state prison.

4. "Opening the door." Judges didn't want to open the door to an increase in such prisoner rights litigation.[48]

Actually, that is what happened in the **prisoner rights era** (1960-1980). Prisoner petitions increased tremendously. However, after 1980, in the **due deference era** (1980-today), judges became more likely to give "due deference" to the expertise of prison administrators when faced with prisoner litigation. In 1996, Congress passed the *Prison Litigation Reform Act* (**PLRA**),[49] which significantly reduced prisoner petitions through a number of measures, including limiting attorney fees, and punishing those who file "frivolous" lawsuits.

Generally, prisoners' rights lawsuits allege violations of the Fifth or Fourteenth Amendment (due process), the Eighth Amendment (cruel and unusual punishment), and the First Amendment (freedom of religion and expression).

4.1 Due Process

Recall that due process may apply whenever the government seeks to deprive one of life, liberty, or property. Being able to have access to the courts of this nation is a fundamental element of due process. In the past, prison authorities would confiscate letters and legal documents and prevent inmates from having their grievances relayed to the courts. In a series of cases, the U.S. Supreme Court and other courts prohibited prison officials from blocking the inmates' access to the court system.[50] The Supreme Court also made it clear that inmates should have meaningful assistance to access the courts, even if it had to take the form of **jailhouse lawyers**, inmates who help other inmates file petitions for a fee, or law students.[51] The Court also held that legal mail could not be censored,[52] and that prisoners should have access to either law libraries or legal services.[53] However, in more recent decisions, the United States Supreme Court has restricted the right of access to the courts and/or the ability to seek damages if the prison does not provide meaningful access.[54]

The **due process clauses** of the federal constitution prohibit both state and federal authorities from taking life, liberty, or property without due process of law. Prisoners challenged the adequacy of due process protections in disciplinary hearings and received the right to have at least a notice of charges and a hearing before being punished by segregation or loss of good time.[55] Later cases reduced due process rights solely to the loss of good time, and curtailed the level of proof required before punishment could be administered.[56] Prisoners never received the right to any due process protections before being transferred, even if it was to a prison far away or to a higher security classification.[57]

4.2 The Eighth Amendment: Corporal Punishment and the Use of Force

The Eighth Amendment prohibits cruel and unusual punishment and has been the basis for outlawing **corporal punishment** in prisons.[58] Later, **totality**

of circumstances cases involved multiple conditions of confinement that, as a whole, constituted cruel and unusual punishment. Conditions that were cited in these cases included high levels of violence (either or both inmate-on-inmate or officer-on-inmate), lack of medical care, lack of sanitation, little or no programming, no assistance for the mentally ill or mentally retarded, and overcrowding. In some of the most egregious cases, prisoners won. As conditions improved across the country, prisoners were less likely to win such cases.

Lack of medical care for prisoners has also been defined as cruel and unusual punishment.[59] In these cases, a deliberate withholding of medical care that constitutes an unnecessary and wanton infliction of pain can be a violation of the Eighth Amendment. The key, however, is that it has to be a *deliberate* lack of care, and medical negligence does not constitute a constitutional violation. The Eighth Amendment has also been used to challenge prison treatment programs that involved the infliction of pain. Behavior modification programs must obtain free, voluntary, and knowing consent from inmates, otherwise such pain constitutes cruel and unusual punishment.[60]

4.3 First Amendment Rights

The following issues derive from the First Amendment: (1) access to prisons and prisoners by the press, (2) freedom of speech and communication, (3) freedom of association and visitation, and (4) freedom of religion.

In a series of court cases in the 1970s, the Supreme Court identified prisoners' rights to have access to the press, although the press had no greater right of access to prisons than did the general public.[61] The Supreme Court also held that the prison could not stop prisoners from writing to outside citizens about prison conditions. The justices declared that restrictions on prisoners' right of correspondence must be related to a governmental interest: specifically security, order, or rehabilitation .[62]

In the 1980s, courts upheld prison authorities' bans on inmate-to-inmate correspondence.[63] Other restrictions that were upheld included the publishers-only rule, where prisoners can only receive publications from official distributors. Furthermore, any publications that are deemed to be a threat to the security or order of the institution can be confiscated.[64] As would be expected, courts have never been very sympathetic to freedom of speech claims by prisoners. Prison authorities have the right to punish prisoners for angry racial comments, work stoppages, and protests.

Prisoners have virtually no rights of association. Numerous cases have categorized visitation as a *privilege* that may be curtailed or denied for just cause, not a *right*. In a recent case, the Supreme Court approved rigorous restrictions on visitation in a Michigan prisoner's challenge.[65]

Freedom of religion is a primary constitutional right guaranteed by the First Amendment. Prisoners have the right to practice their religious beliefs as long as they do not impinge upon the state's interest in safety, security, and order. Courts use the **rational relationship test** to balance the individual's interest against the state's. As long as the state's rule or procedure is rationally related to a legitimate state interest, the state will win any challenge to regulations that prohibit an inmate from practicing his or her religion.[66] Obviously, prisoners' rights are not the same as those of free people. Any right must be balanced against the state's right to run a safe and secure prison.

5. JAILS

Jails and prisons are often confused, but they are very different institutions. Jails are local detention facilities that house pretrial detainees and misdemeanants, as well as a variety of other detainees. Most jails are run by the county sheriff and are located in the county seat. There are also state jails that house both felons and misdemeanants and regional jails that serve several counties and are run by administrators, not sheriffs. More Americans see the inside of a jail than a prison, and the time spent in jail is, for the most part, shorter; however, the jail experience is still disruptive and traumatic to many prisoners. Suicide is a real problem in jails, as are other medical emergencies such as drug withdrawals or overdoses. The rate of suicide in jail is five to six times higher than for comparable individuals outside of jail.[67] Jail personnel must deal with all these issues, perhaps without knowing the history of the individual; thus, insulin shock may look like an alcoholic stupor, or a defendant complaining of pain may be suffering mild drug withdrawal or life-threatening appendicitis. Inmates are often housed for short periods in "bullpens" or large cells. This raises the risk of victimization and creates a sanitation problem when too many people are housed in a small space, especially when some are intoxicated. Unpleasant smells, unremitting noise, and fear of the unknown characterize many individuals' first experience in jail.

Before the 1700s, jails (or gaols) were usually horrific places of confinement that housed the sick along with the healthy, women with men, and children with adults. The so-called **fee system** meant that prisoners had to pay for their room and board. Typically, stays in jails were short. The individual was held only until corporal punishment could be carried out, whether that was by whipping, the stocks or pillory, or hanging. In many cases, individuals were held for debt. In those cases, the person could be held indefinitely until he or his family could pay his debts. If they were unable, then the individual might be subject to transportation or indenture to the colonies.

Houses of corrections and bridewells may have taken the place of the jail as the place of confinement for the itinerant and poor. These institutions, such as St. Brigit's Well, first established in 1553, required inmates to earn their keep with labor.[68] The idea was that the poor, petty criminals and orphaned children should learn a trade and become productive. Arguably, this was an improvement over the gaols. In 1777, Sheriff John Howard wrote about his findings after traveling around England visiting gaols. He recommended major reforms in the way jails were run, including classification, segregating women and children, individual cells, eliminating the fee system, and providing religious instruction.[69]

In the colonies, the keeper and his wife ran the jail as a large house under the direction of the local sheriff. The fee system was also in use in this country. Like England, the imprisoned inmates were held only until they were acquitted at trial or punished. Minor offenders and debtors may have stayed longer, but the early history of the jail was simply as a temporary holding facility until punishment could be carried out.

Historical records show that there were very few women held in jails and the majority of inmates were white men. Common crimes included everything from theft to murder. While hanging was the punishment for more than 200 crimes in England, the colonies were less likely to impose capital punishment, probably because laborers were in short supply.[70]

5.1 Jail Populations

In 2005, there were 3,365 jails in the country with an average daily population under supervision of 819,434. Nine percent of this population was under some form of community release from the jail (community service, work release, weekend reporting, electronic monitoring, or other programs).[71] This does not take into account the numbers of people who have been in and out of jail during the year. There are more than 11 million separate entries and exits from jail each year.[72] About a third of all felony sentences are to local jails.[73] Since 1995, the nation's jail population has increased 31 percent.[74]

The average population in jails is about 180; however, many jails hold less than 50 inmates. On the other hand, there are extremely large jails that hold thousands of inmates. The 50 largest jails housed nearly a third of all jail inmates in 2002.[75] Today, four states (California, Texas, Florida, and Georgia) hold a third of the nation's total population.[76] The largest jail system in the country is Los Angeles County, with a daily population average of 18,512 inmates (in 2004). This is actually down from their highest population in 2002 of close to 20,000. New York City follows with an average population of 13,751 and Cook County, Illinois (Chicago) with 10,155.[77]

The majority of those in jail have not been convicted. About 38 percent are convicted and the rest are awaiting trial or final adjudication on either a new charge or a probation or parole violation.[78] Box 13.8 shows that about nine out of 10 jail inmates are men, although the percentage of women is increasing. As in prisons, the percentage of blacks is disproportionate to their percentage of the total population; however, the percentage of Hispanics more closely resembles their percentage of the population.

For information on jails collected by the federal government, go to the Bureau of Justice Statistics Web site: www.ojp.usdoj.gov/bjs/

One of the major differences between prisons and jails is that jails hold a greater variety of types of prisoners, and many have not been convicted or sentenced. In Box 13.9, some of the types of individuals who are incarcerated in jails are listed.

BOX 13.8

Gender, Race and Ethnicity, and Conviction Status of Jail Inmates

Characteristics	Percent of Jail Inmates			
	1995	**2000**	**2004**	**2005**
Total	100.0	100.0	100.0	100.0
Gender				
Male	89.8	88.6	87.7	87.3
Female	10.2	11.4	12.3	12.7
Race/Hispanic Origin				
White	40.1	41.9	44.4	44.3
Black	43.5	41.3	38.6	38.9
Hispanic	14.7	15.1	15.2	15.0
Other	1.7	1.6	1.8	1.7
Conviction Status				
Convicted	44.0	44.0	39.7	38.0
Male	39.7	39.0	34.8	33.2
Female	4.3	5.0	4.9	4.8
Unconvicted	56.0	56.0	60.3	62.0
Male	50.0	50.0	53.0	54.2
Female	6.0	6.0	7.3	7.7

Source: Harrison, P. and A. Beck (2006). *Prison and Jail Inmates at Midyear 2005.* Washington DC: Bureau of Justice Statistics. Notes omitted, p. 8.

In general, most people in jail are either misdemeanants serving sentences or pretrial detainees awaiting adjudication because they cannot make bail. It may come as a surprise to many that as many as two-thirds of jail inmates were employed prior to their arrest. Unfortunately, many will lose their job before they are released. About 1.6 percent of jail inmates are under 18. Almost 70 percent used drugs regularly before incarceration and about half had used in the month prior to their arrest.[79]

Between 1983 (227,541) and 2004 (784,538), the jail population increased 244 percent.[80] As with prison populations, the jail population has risen dramatically in the last 20 years and the rate of confinement has increased as well. In 1983, the rate of confinement to jail was 96 per 100,000 residents; by 1995 it was 193 per 100,000; and in 2005, it was 252 per 100,000.[81] This means that,

BOX 13.9

Jail Inmates

★ defendants pending arraignment, trial, or sentencing

★ probation, parole, bail-bond violators

★ absconders

★ juvenile detainees

★ mentally ill (pending transfer to mental institution)

★ military violators (pending transfer to military facilities)

★ contempt violators

★ material witnesses

★ state prisoners waiting transfer

★ misdemeanants

BOX 13.10

Jail Population by Age and Gender, 1990 – 2005

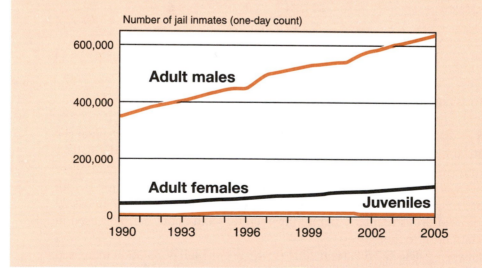

Source: Bureau of Justice Statistics Correctional Surveys (The National Probation Data Survey, National Prisoner Statistics, Survey of Jails, Census of Jail Inmates, and The National Parole Data Survey) as presented in *Correctional Populations in the United States, 1997*, and *Prison and Jail Inmates at Midyear, 2005*. Washington, DC: Bureau of Justice Statistics.

in addition to there simply being more people in jail, we also are more likely to jail those accused of crimes, or hold them longer, or be less likely to release them on pretrial alternatives.

Women have increased their percentage of the total population from less than 10 percent in the 1980s to about 12 percent today. Box 13.10 shows this increase relative to that of men.

As Box 13.11 shows, the rate of jail incarceration for minorities is disproportionate to their percentage in the population. Blacks are five times as likely to be incarcerated in jail as whites and three times as likely as Hispanics.

BOX 13.11

Jail Incarceration Rate—2005

	Number	Rate (per 100,000)
Total	747,529	252
Gender		
Male	652,958	447
Female	94,571	63
Race/Hispanic Origin		
White	331,000	166
Black	290,500	800
Hispanic	111,900	268
Other	13,000	88

Source: Harrison, P. and A. Beck (2006). *Prison and Jail Inmates at Midyear 2005*. Washington DC: Bureau of Justice Statistics, Notes omitted, p. 8.

About 13 percent of all black men are in prison or jail (compared to only 3.6 percent of Hispanic and 1.7 percent of white men).[82] What this means is that in some communities, jail is not strange or unusual, it is a part of life. This does not mean that it is not damaging, however, and the thrust of diversion programs is to stop the cycle of jail to prison and back again.

As with the explosive growth of this nation's prison population, larger jail populations come at a cost. Counties that experience double-digit increases in their jail populations are unable to accommodate these numbers without cutting the budget of other governmental services. Part of why it is difficult for jails to meet national standards is that county commissioners or other budget decision-makers do not have any incentive to increase jail budgets unless there are security concerns. Jail inmates are not likely to be important constituents for politicians; they are unlikely to vote and they have no advocates in the community.

Jails can be considered, to some extent, the depositories for the marginally functioning in society. It has been estimated that the percentage of jail inmates with serious mental health issues such as schizophrenia, severe depression, and mania is four times higher than the general population and the rate of substance abuse is four to seven times higher. Estimates of how many inmates have mental health issues range from 10 to 30 percent; one jail survey found that 20 percent of inmates had a mental health issue.[83] Others report that 600,000 to 700,000 individuals with mental health issues cycle through our jails every year.[84]

According to the Bureau of Justice Statistics, about 64 percent of all jail inmates have some type of mental health problem. About 21 percent have been clinically diagnosed or treated within the 12 months before incarceration. Percentages of jail inmates who exhibit symptoms of mental illness diagnoses illustrate the prevalence of the problem and include mania (54 percent), clinical depression (30 percent), and psychotic disorders (24 percent). In this study, it was found that women, whites, and young inmates were more likely to exhibit mental health problems. About 75 percent of women in jails exhibited mental health problems compared to 63 percent of male inmates. About 71 percent of whites, 63 percent of blacks, and 51 percent of Hispanics were found to have a mental health problem. Jail inmates with mental health problems are more likely to have had past incarcerations, used drugs, have experienced homelessness, have experienced past physical or sexual abuse, have parents who abused drugs or alcohol, and are more likely to violate facility rules.[85]

The deinstitutionalization of the mentally ill that occurred in this country in the late 1970s occurred because of court cases such as *Wyatt v. Stickney*.[86] In this case, the court held that the mentally ill could not be held indefinitely unless they could be shown to pose a danger to self or others. The original intent was that community mental health centers would be better places to serve the mentally ill than housing them in large mental hospitals. Unfortunately, that promise has not been fulfilled to the degree that many advocates had hoped, thus many mentally ill individuals "slip through the cracks;" not sick enough to be institutionalized, but not well enough to fully function in today's society.

Arguably, female jail inmates have more severe problems with drugs and with mental health problems than do their male counterparts, no doubt in part due to childhood abuse.[87] Box 13.12 shows that female jail inmates are more likely than male inmates to have experienced childhood sexual and physical victimization. Even though male inmates may be underreporting such experiences to some extent, it is clear that women in jail often come from dysfunctional families and suffer from the effects of sexual victimization.

5.2 The Jail Experience

Coming into the jail, an inmate may spend the night in a holding cell, sometimes called a "bullpen" or "drunk tank." This one large cell may hold many offenders, and a toilet (or toilets) in the same room with no screen or privacy may be the only provision for sanitation needs. After a first appearance, the suspect may be transferred to a different section of the jail. He or she is

BOX 13.12

Physical or Sexual Abuse Before Current Admission
Abuse Percentage of Jail Inmates

	Total	Male	Female
Ever	16.4	12.9	47.5
Before 18	14.3	11.9	36.6
After 18	4.7	2.3	26.7
Physically abused	13.3	10.7	37.2
Sexually abused	8.7	5.6	37.1
Raped	6.6	3.7	32.2

Source: Harlow, C. (1998). *Profile of Jail Inmates 1996.* Washington DC: Bureau of Justice Statistics, p. 11.

fingerprinted, showered, and given jail issue clothing, which is often an overall that may be several sizes too big. If the inmate is showing signs of medical distress, a quick exam by a medical professional may occur.

Most jail inmates do not stay long. The average length of stay in jail is three to 20 days; pretrial detainees have an average stay of three days. Those who make bail may be out in 24 hours, but those who cannot make bail, or are serving a misdemeanor sentence, may be there for months. Large jails such as those in Los Angeles, Chicago, and New York City bear no resemblance to the very small rural jails that still exist all across the country. The smallest jails may have less than 20 inmates in the basement of a county courthouse. A few sheriff's deputies are responsible for them and food may be catered in rather than cooked on-site. These types of jails are all but extinct in today's trend of regional jails, but they do exist. On the other side of the spectrum, counties like Los Angeles run jail systems that are larger than most state prison systems. Some large systems have state-of-the-art surveillance technology and programming that rivals what can be found in prisons. Large urban jails probably have a subculture that more closely resembles what one would find in a prison and inmates get their first sense of the inmate code in these local jails.

Jails now often conform to standards promulgated by the state or the American Jail Association, and may be accredited by the American Correctional Association. Standards cover everything from sanitation to staffing to programming. The adoption of standards, however, has been slow and very few jails are accredited. The major problem, of course, is funding. Jails are a low priority for counties when budgets are written and because many jails are small, it is more difficult for them to meet the standards because it is more costly on a per-prisoner basis.

Because the jail is considered a temporary correctional facility, there is less emphasis on programs. Some of the larger jails may have programs such as work-release and GED tutoring. They may also have parenting classes and other life skills training. However, other jails have virtually nothing to occupy the time of the inhabitants, so inmates spend all day watching television and playing cards.

For information on the American Jail Association, see: http://www.corrections.com/aja/

Very few jailed inmates are placed in alternative supervision. The Bureau of Justice Statistics reported that in 2005 only nine percent of jail inmates were on some form of alternative supervision. Within this nine percent, 21 percent were in some type of pretrial diversion (jail administered); and the rest were in these programs: community service (22 percent); electronic monitoring (16 percent); weekend reporting (20 percent); work release (10 percent); or treatment program (3 percent).[88]

Jails are often understaffed and there are few career incentives to motivate workers. Often the officers in a jail are sheriff's deputies who are waiting to get a street patrol assignment. Sometimes sheriffs use the jail assignment as punishment or as a probation assignment for new deputies. In some jurisdictions, the position is a separate hiring line from that of deputy, but many hired as jail officers aspire to be deputies. The lesser status assigned to the jail officer is often reflected in lower pay scales. According to the Department of Labor, the average hourly wage for jail officers in 2001 was only about $16.00.[89]

The new generation jail and its direct supervision model, which places officers inside the living units instead of outside long tiers or pods, requires officers to interact more with inmates, which would demand a higher level of communication skill and ability on the part of officers. It is possible that eventually these demands will translate into higher wages and a better status for jail officers. Early evidence indicates that these jails present better working conditions for officers and they respond with fewer absentee days and reduced misconduct.[90]

6. CONCLUSION

Prisons are a necessary element in society, built to house seriously violent offenders. In the United States, we may have exceeded the cost benefits of this sanction by overuse. We now incarcerate more people than any other nation. It was not always this way and the rise in incarceration rates has only occurred within the last 30 years.

The history of prisons is marked by periodic cycles of reform. The penitentiary arose with the Walnut Street Jail. The two models of the penitentiary were the separate system and the Auburn system, but it was the Auburn system that became the model for subsequent building. The reformatory era in the late 1800s and early 1900s followed the first penitentiaries. The "Big House" was the type of prison that existed through the 1900s until about the 1960s. The "Correctional Institution" followed the "Big House"; however, we now talk about the "Warehouse Prison" where there are few, if any, programs.

Prisoners have more freedoms, rights, and access to a few, but better programs today. Prisoners are more likely to be young, violent, drug- and gang-related; thus, the increased freedom creates more opportunity for violence. It is a world of power and violence. The prisoner subculture may be somewhat different for women. There seems to be less violence, fewer gangs, and more consensual relationships.

Prisoners in the United States are supposed to retain all the rights of free people except those that are inconsistent with institutional needs of order, security, and rehabilitation. Most prisoner lawsuits allege violations of the Fourteenth, Eighth, or First Amendments. Although prisoners won several cases in the 1970s, more often today, courts (following the due deference approach) uphold the policies and procedures of the prison. Still, prisons have progressed a long way from the harshness of the Big House in the early 1900s.

Jails are not prisons. There are differences in the type of people housed, their sentences, programming, and administration. Generally, jails are local, supervised by the county sheriff, and receive funding from the local jurisdiction rather than the state. Like prisons, they are much better places to be today than in the past, although there are still management problems. Dostoevsky's observation that a society can be judged by the state of its prisons is as true today as it has been throughout history.

REVIEW QUESTIONS

1. Describe incarceration rates and compare the United States to other countries.

2. What was the origin of the penitentiary? Distinguish between the *separate* and the *congregate* systems.

3. Describe the reformatory, the "Big House," the "Correctional Institution," and the "Warehouse Prison" and identify when they developed.

4. List and discuss Sykes' deprivations of imprisonment and describe the deprivation and importation theory of prisoner subcultures.

5. Compare and contrast the male and female prisoner subcultures. Describe prison argot, argot roles, homosexuality, and the inmate code.

6. Discuss how the prison subculture today is different from the 1940s through the 1960s.

7. Discuss the three eras of prisoner rights: *hands-off, prisoner rights,* and *due deference.*

8. What are some of the rights at issue under the Fourteenth Amendment? The Eighth? The First?

9. Describe some differences between jails and prisons.

10. Who is housed in jails and how are they different from those in prison?

VOCABULARY

argot – the language of a subculture (in this case, prisoners)

argot roles – prisoner roles; they serve to classify and describe inmates based upon their behavior before prison, as well as what they do in prison

Auburn system – congregate prison system where prisoners work, eat, and exercise together but have separate cells, created in Auburn, New York, prison (1817)

"Big Houses" – Robert Johnson's name for prisons of the early to mid-1900s

Building Tenders (BTs) –Texas inmates who were authorized by staff to control inmates by any means necessary

congregate system – first introduced at Auburn Prison (1817); prisoners slept in solitary cells, but worked and ate together

corporal punishment – physical punishment

correctional institution – prisons in the 1950s; prisoners had more privileges, such as yard and recreational privileges

due deference era – (1980 to today); judges are more likely to give "due deference" to the expertise of prison administrators when faced with prisoner litigation

due process clauses – in the Fifth and Fourteenth Amendments to the federal Constitution; they prohibit both state and federal authorities from taking life, liberty, or property without due process of law

fee system – in early jails prisoners had to pay for their room and board

hands-off era – (1900-1960); referred to federal and state courts rarely accepting grievances prisoners brought to their attention

importation hypothesis – theory that the prisoner subculture is derived from the pre-prison characteristics of the people coming into prisons rather than prison deprivations themselves

inmate code – is described as a set of subcultural rules for prisoners

jailhouse lawyers – inmates who help other inmates file petitions for a fee

lockstep march – in congregate prison systems prisoners shuffled together, bound by one hand on the opposite shoulder of the man in front

"The Mix" – the subculture of women's prisons; referring to the activities associated with drugs, homosexual activity, and fighting

penitentiary – began with Walnut Street Jail in 1790, prisoners were kept in single cells and expected to reform through penitence

Pennsylvania system – another name for Philadelphia system or separate system; prisoners were in solitary confinement and performed manual labor in their cells

PLRA – *Prison Litigation Reform Act*; passed in 1995, this legislation severely restricted prisoners from filing lawsuits against prison officials

prisoner rights era – (1960-1980); period when prisoner petitions increased tremendously and major prisoner rights cases were decided

prisonization – process of being socialized to the prison subculture

pseudofamilies – make-believe family systems that include all the familial roles including fathers, mothers, daughters, sisters, cousins, etc.

rational relationship test – one of the tests used by the courts to balance the individual's interest against the state's; if the contested rule or procedure is rationally related to a legitimate state interest, the state will win the challenge

reformatory era – late 1870s through early 1900s, period when reformatories, such as Elmira Reformatory, were built

separate system – type of prison system that originated in Philadelphia at the Walnut Street Jail (1790) and later at Eastern State Penitentiary (1829); inmates were housed in single cells

totality of circumstances – type of Eighth Amendment case that argues that multiple conditions of confinement, as a whole, constituted cruel and unusual punishment

Walnut Street Jail – origin of the concept of the penitentiary in the United States; built in Philadelphia in 1790, founders instituted single cells, classification, and expectation of reform through penitence

warehouse prisons – a name for contemporary prisons because prisoners do not receive many programs and are simply housed and fed until release

FOR FURTHER READING

Johnson, Robert (2002). *Hard Time: Understanding and Reforming the Prison.* Belmont, CA: Wadsworth.

Lerner, James (2002). *You Got Nothing Coming: Notes From a Prison Fish.* New York: Broadway Books.

Pollock, Joycelyn (2002). *Women, Prison, and Crime*, Second Edition. Belmont, CA: Wadsworth.

Pollock, Joycelyn (2004b). *Prisons and Prison Life: Costs and Consequences.* Los Angeles, CA: Roxbury.

Rafter, Nicole (1990). *Partial Justice: Women, Prisons, and Social Control,* Second Edition. Boston, MA: Northeastern University Press.

Rolland, Mike (1997). *Descent Into Madness: An Inmate's Experience of the New Mexico State Prison Riot.* Cincinnati, OH: Anderson Publishing.

Rothman, David (1971). *The Discovery of the Asylum: Social Order and Disorder in the New Republic.* Boston, MA: Little, Brown.

---

[1] Hirsch, A. (1987). "From Pillory to Penitentiary: The Rise of Criminal Incarceration in Early Massachusetts." In K. Hall (ed.), *Police, Prison and Punishment: Major Historical Interpretations.* New York: Garland, pp. 344-434.; McKelvey, B. (1987). "Penology in the Westward Movement." In K. Hall (ed.), *Police, Prison and Punishment: Major Historical Interpretations.* New York: Garland, pp. 457-479.

[2] Zupan, L. (1991). *Jails: Reform and the New Generation Philosophy.* Cincinnati: Anderson Publishing.

[3] Crosley, C. (1986). *Unfolding Misconceptions: The Arkansas State Penitentiary, 1836-1986.* Arlington: Liberal Arts Press.

[4] Rothman, D. (1971). *The Discovery of the Asylum: Social Order and Disorder in the New Republic.* Boston: Little, Brown.

[5] Johnson, R. (2002). *Hard Time.* Belmont, CA: Wadsworth/ITP.

[6] American Correctional Association (1970/revised 2002). Retrieved 1/2/04 from: www.aca.org/past-presentfuture/principles.asp.

[7] Rafter, N.H. (1990). *Partial Justice: Women, Prisons, and Social Control,* Second Edition. Boston: Northeastern University Press, p. xxvi.

[8] Rafter, N.H. (1990). *Partial Justice: Women, Prisons, and Social Control,* Second Edition. Boston: Northeastern University Press; Freedman, E. (1981). *Their Sister's Keepers: Women's Prison Reform in America,* 1830-1930. Ann Arbor: University of Michigan Press.

[9] Johnson, R. (2002). *Hard Time.* Belmont, CA: Wadsworth/ITP.

[10] Crouch, B. & J. Marquart (1989). *An Appeal to Justice: Litigated Reform of Texas Prisons.* Austin: University of Texas Press.

[11] Rafter, N.H. (1990). *Partial Justice: Women, Prisons, and Social Control,* Second Edition. Boston: Northeastern University Press.

[12] Rierden, A. (1997). *The Farm: Life Inside a Women's Prison.* Amherst: University of Massachusetts Press, p. 2.

[13] Carroll, L. (1974). *Hacks, Blacks and Cons: Race Relations in a Maximum Security Prison.* Lexington, Mass: Lexington Books.

[14] Rierden, A. (1997). *The Farm: Life Inside a Women's Prison.* Amherst: University of Massachusetts Press.

[15] Harrison, P. & A. Beck (2006). *Prison and Jail Inmates at Midyear 2005.* Washington, DC: Bureau of Justice Statistics.

[16] Harrison, P. & A. Beck (2006). *Prison and Jail Inmates at Midyear 2005.* Washington, DC: Bureau of Justice Statistics; Harrison, P. & A. Beck (2003). *Prison and Jail Inmates at Midyear 2002.* Washington, DC: Bureau of Justice Statistics.

[17] Harrison, P. & A. Beck (2006). *Prison and Jail Inmates at Midyear 2005.* Washington, DC: Bureau of Justice Statistics, p. 10.

[18] Jacobs, J. (1982). "The Limits of Racial Integration in Prison." *Criminal Law Bulletin* 18: 117-153.

[19] Sykes, G. (1958). *The Society of Captives.* Princeton: Princeton University Press.

[20] Irwin, J. & D. Cressey (1962). "Thieves, Convicts, and the Inmate Culture." *Social Problems* 10 (Fall): 142-155.

[21] Clemmer, D. (1958). *The Prison Community*. New York: Holt, Rinehart and Winston.

[22] Morris, R. (1980). *The Devil's Butcher Shop: The New Mexico Prison Uprising*. Albuquerque, NM: University of New Mexico Press.

[23] Owen, B. & D.L. MacKenzie (2004). "The Mix: The Culture of Imprisoned Women." In M. Stohr & C. Hemmens (eds.), *The Inmate Prison Experience*. Upper Saddle River, NJ: Pearson, pp.152-172.

[24] Giallombardo, R. (1966). *Society of Women: A Study of a Women's Prison*. New York: Wiley.

[25] Pollock, J. (2002). *Women, Prison, and Crime*, Second Edition. Belmont, CA: Wadsworth; Girshick, L. (1999). *No Safe Haven: Stories of Women in Prison*. Boston, MA: Northeastern University Press; Owen, B. (1998). *"In the Mix": Struggle and Survival in a Women's Prison*. Albany, NY: State University of Albany Press.

[26] Irwin, J. (1980). *Prisons in Turmoil*. Boston: Little, Brown and Company; Hassine, V. (1999). *Life Without Parole: Living in Prison Today*. Los Angeles: Roxbury.

[27] Irwin, J. (1980). *Prisons in Turmoil*. Boston: Little, Brown and Company.

[28] Jacobs, J. (1977). *Stateville: The Penitentiary in Mass Society*. Chicago: University of Chicago Press. Carroll, L. (1974). *Hacks, Blacks and Cons: Race Relations in a Maximum Security Prison*. Lexington, MA: Lexington.

[29] McCall, N. (1995). *Makes Me Wanna Holler: A Young Black Man in America*. New York: Vintage, p. 149.

[30] Irwin, J. (1980). *Prisons in Turmoil*. Boston: Little, Brown and Company.

[31] Crouch, B. & J. Marquart (1989). *An Appeal to Justice: Litigated Reform of Texas Prisons*. Austin: University of Texas Press.

[32] *Ruiz v. Estelle*, 503 F. Supp. 1265 (1980).

[33] Crouch, B. & J. Marquart (1989). *An Appeal to Justice: Litigated Reform of Texas Prisons*. Austin: University of Texas Press.

[34] Mahan, S. (1984). "Imposition of Despair: An Ethnography of Women in Prison." *Justice Quarterly* 1: 357-385; Greer, K. (2000). "The Changing Nature of Interpersonal Relationships in a Women's Prison." *The Prison Journal* 80: 442-468.

[35] Hargan, J. (1934). "The Psychology of Prison Language." *Journal of Abnormal and Social Psychology* 30: 359-361; Lerner, J. (2002). *You Got Nothing Coming: Notes From a Prison Fish*. New York: Broadway Books; Sykes, G. & S. Messinger (1960). "The Inmate Social System." In R. Cloward (ed.), *Theoretical Studies in the Social Organization of the Prison*. New York: Social Science Research Council, pp. 6-10.

[36] Lerner, J. (2002). *You Got Nothing Coming: Notes From a Prison Fish*. New York: Broadway Books.

[37] Trulson, C. (2005). "The Social World of the Prisoner." In J. Pollock (ed.), *Prisons Today and Tomorrow*. Sudbury, MA: Jones and Bartlett Publishers, pp. 79-124.

[38] Sykes, G. (1958). *The Society of Captives*. Princeton: Princeton University Press, p. 84-108.

[39] Schrag, C. (1961). "Leadership Among Prison Inmates." *American Sociological Review* 19: 37-42.

[40] Giallombardo, R. (1966). *Society of Women: A Study of a Women's Prison*. New York: Wiley, p. 105-123.

[41] Hanser, R. & C. Trulson (2004). "Sexual Abuse of Men in Prison." In F. Reddington & B. Kreise (eds.), *Sexual Assault: The Victims, the Perpetrators, and the Criminal Justice System*. Durham, NC: Carolina Academic Press.

[42] Pollock, J. (2002). *Women, Prison, and Crime*, Second Edition. Belmont, CA: Wadsworth.

[43] Gagnon, J. & W. Simon (1968). "The Social Meaning of Prison Homosexuality." *Federal Probation* 32: 23-29.

[44] Struckman-Johnson, C. & D. Struckman-Johnson (2000). "Sexual Coercion Rates in Seven Midwestern Prison Facilities for Men." *The Prison Journal* 80: 379-390.

[45] Hanser, R. & C. Trulson (2004). "Sexual Abuse of Men in Prison." In F. Reddington & B. Kreise (eds.), *Sexual Assault: The Victims, the Perpetrators, and the Criminal Justice System*. Durham, NC: Carolina Academic Press; Struckman-Johnson, C. & D. Struckman-Johnson (2000). "Sexual Coercion Rates in Seven Midwestern Prison Facilities for Men." *The Prison Journal* 80: 379-390.

[46] Owen, B. (1998). *"In the Mix": Struggle and Survival in a Women's Prison*. Albany, NY: State University of Albany Press.

[47] 62 Va. 790 (1871).

[48] National Advisory Commission on Criminal Justice Standards and Goals (1973). *Report on Corrections*. Washington, DC: U.S Government Printing Office, p. 18.

[49] 42 U.S.C. § 3626.

[50] *Ex parte Hull*, 61 S. Ct. 640 (1941).

[51] *Johnson v. Avery*, 89 S. Ct. 747 (1969); *Procunier v. Martinez*, 94 S. Ct. 1800 (1974).

[52] *Wolff v. McDonnell*, 94 S. Ct. 2963 (1974).

[53] 97 S. Ct. 1491 (1977).

[54] *Lewis v. Casey*, 116 S. Ct. 2174 (1996), *Shaw v. Murphy*, 121 S. Ct. 1475 (2001).

[55] *Wolff v. McDonnell*, 94 S. Ct. 2963 (1974).

[56] *Superintendent, Massachusetts Correctional Institution, Walpole v. Hill*, 105 S. Ct. 2768 (1985); *Sandin v. Conner*, 115 S. Ct. 2293, 2303 (1995).

[57] *Meachum v. Fano*, 96 S. Ct. 2532 (1976); *Olim v. Wakinekona*, 103 S. Ct. 1741 (1983).

[58] *Jackson v. Bishop*, 404 F.2d 571 (8th Cir. 1968).

[59] *Estelle v. Gamble*, 97 S. Ct. 285 (1976).

[60] *Knecht v. Gillman*, 48 F.2d 1136 (8th Cir. 1973).

[61] *Pell v. Procunier*, 94 S. Ct. 2800 (1974}), *Saxbe v. Washington Post*, 94 S. Ct. 2811 (1974).

[62] *Procunier v. Martinez*, 94 S. Ct. 1800 (1974); *Pell v. Procunier*, 94 S. Ct. 2800 (1974).

[63] *Turner v. Safley*, 107 S. Ct. 2254 (1987).

[64] *Thornburgh v. Abbot*, 109 S. Ct. 1874 (1989).

[65] *Overton v. Bazzetta*, 123 S. Ct. 2162 (2003).

[66] *0 'Lone v. Estate of Shabazz*, 107 S. Ct. 2400 (1987).

[67] Hayes, L. (2005). "Suicidal Signs and Symptoms." *Corrections Forum* 14, 6: 36.

[68] American Correctional Association (1983). *The American Prison: From the Beginning*. Lanham, MD: ACA.

[69] Morris, N. & D. Rothman (1995). *The Oxford History of the Prison*. New York: Oxford University Press.

[70] Moynahan, J. & E. Stewart (1980). *The American Jail: Its Development and Growth*. Chicago: Nelson-Hall.

[71] Harrison, P. & A. Beck (2006). *Prison and Jail Inmates at Midyear 2005*. Washington DC: Bureau of Justice Statistics.

[72] Kerle, K. (2002). "Women in the American World of Jails: Inmates and Staff." *Margins* 2, 1: 41-61.

[73] Bureau of Justice Statistics (2004). *State Court Sentencing of Convicted Felons*, Statistical Tables. Washington DC: U.S. Department of Justice. Retrieved 1/11/05 from: http://www.ojp.usdoj.gov/bjs/pub/pdf/scscf02.pdf.

[74] Harrison, P. & A. Beck (2006). *Prison and Jail Inmates at Midyear 2005*. Washington DC: Bureau of Justice Statistics, p. 8.

[75] Harrison, P. & J. Karberg (2003). *Prison and Jail Inmates at Midyear 2002*. Washington DC: Bureau of Justice Statistics.

[76] Harrison, P. & A. Beck (2006). *Prison and Jail Inmates at Midyear 2005*. Washington DC: Bureau of Justice Statistics.

[77] Harrison, P. & A. Beck (2005). *Prison and Jail Inmates at Midyear 2004*. Washington DC: Bureau of Justice Statistics.

[78] Harrison, P. & A. Beck (2005). *Prison and Jail Inmates at Midyear 2005*. Washington DC: Bureau of Justice Statistics, p. 8.

[79] *Sourcebook of Criminal Justice Statistics 2003*, Table 6.21. "Percent of Jail Inmates Reporting Drug Use. Retrieved from: http://www.albany.edu/sourcebook/pdf/t621.pdf.; Harrison, P. & A. Beck (2005). *Prison and Jail Inmates at Midyear 2004*. Washington DC: Bureau of Justice Statistics.

[80] *Sourcebook of Criminal Justice Statistics, 2003*. "Number of Jail Inmates, Average Daily Population, and Rated Capacity, Table 6.14." Retrieved 1/22/2006 from: http://www.albany.edu/sourcebook/pdf/t614.pdf.; Harrison, P. & A. Beck (2005). *Prison and Jail Inmates at Midyear 2004*. Washington DC: Bureau of Justice Statistics.

[81] Harrison, P. & A. Beck (2005). *Prison and Jail Inmates at Midyear 2004*. Washington DC: Bureau of Justice Statistics. Harrison & Beck (2005). *Prison and Jail Inmates at Midyear 2004*. Washington DC: Bureau of Justice Statistics, p. 10.

[82] Harrison, P. & A. Beck (2005). *Prison and Jail Inmates at Midyear 2004*. Washington DC: Bureau of Justice Statistics.

[83] Bell, A., N. Jaquette, D. Sanner, C. Steele-Smith & H. Wald (2005). "Treatment of Individuals with Co-Occurring Disorders in County Jails." *Corrections Today* 67, 3: 86-91; Teplin, L., K. Abram & G. McClelland (1996). "Prevalence of Psychiatric Disorders Among Incarcerated Women: Pretrial Jail Detainees." *Archives of General Psychiatry* 53: 505-512.

[84] White, T. & E. Gillespie (2005). "Mental Health Programs: Addressing the Unfunded Mandate." *Corrections Today* 67, 6: 108-113.

[85] James, D. & L. Glaze (2006). *Mental Health Problems of Prison and Jail Inmates*. Washington DC: Bureau of Justice Statistics.

[86] 325 F. Supp. 781 (M.D. Ala. 1971).

[87] Veysey, B., K. DeCou & L. Prescott (1998). "Effective Management of female Jail Detainees with Histories of Physical and Sexual Abuse." *American Jails* (May/June): 50-63.

[88] Harrison, P. & A. Beck (2006). *Prison and Jail Inmates at Midyear 2005*. Washington DC: Bureau of Justice Statistics, p. 7.

[89] U.S. Department of Labor (2006). *Occupational Wages in the United States*. Washington DC: Bureau of Labor Statistics. Retrieved 2/20/07 from: http://www.bls.gov/oes/current/oes_nat.htm#b33-0000.

[90] Zupan, L. (1991). *Jails: Reform and the New Generation Philosophy*. Cincinnati, OH: Anderson Publishing.

Chapter 14

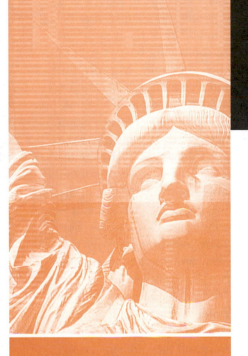

Parole and Re-Entry

CHAPTER OUTLINE

What You Need to Know

★ Parole is release *from* prison while probation is typically release *instead* of prison (usually).

★ There are almost 784,408 adults on parole; about 12 percent are women.

★ The contributions of Maconochie, Crofton, and Brockway led to modern parole.

★ Only 15 states still have full discretionary release parole systems.

★ The rate at which eligible inmates actually receive parole varies widely from state to state, and even within a state over different periods.

★ Inmates have no due process rights regarding the parole release decision, but they do have due process rights before their parole is revoked.

★ About two-thirds of parolees are rearrested.

★ About 40 percent of all admissions to prison are of parolees who have had their parole revoked.

Many people do not understand the difference between parole and probation. It used to be quite simple, in that probation was a sentence to supervision in the community *instead of* a prison sentence and parole was a supervised release *from a* prison sentence. With **split sentencing** and **shock incarceration**, the terms became less clear because those forms of sentencing involve a short period of incarceration before being supervised in the community by probation officers. The better differentiation to make today would be in the administration of the two types of correctional supervision. Recall that probation is administered by probation officers who report to the sentencing judge. While probation itself may be under the executive branch or the judicial branch, it is always the sentencing judge who determines revocation or makes changes to the conditions attached to the probation order. Parole officers, on the other hand, submit their violation reports to the paroling authority. Parole may be a division of the institutional corrections division or an independent agency. The parole board is the releasing body and also conducts violation hearings or, in larger states, delegates that function to hearing officers. The sentencing judge is not involved at all in parole decisions. One other difference between probation and parole is that while probation exists in all 50 states, some states have abolished parole.

Parole is intimately tied to the **indeterminate sentence**, where the release date is not set by the sentencing judge. The idea of indeterminate sentencing is that offenders should be rewarded for their good behavior. Once reformed, they should be released. That release is typically to parole and they are supervised in the community for the remainder of the time of their sentence. Some states, however, have abolished indeterminate sentencing, and parole along with it. Cases in which released prisoners killed their victims while on parole, such as Richard Allen Davis (who killed Polly Klaas); Jesse Timmendequas, the paroled sex offender who killed Megan Kanka; and Henry Lee Lucas, who killed several people after being paroled in Texas, have spurred some states to abolish parole entirely. The fact is that although all prisoners eventually will be released, early release to parole does carry with it some risks. However, it is estimated that parole costs about one-tenth of holding someone in prison; therefore, in some states, parole continues to be essential in the effort to keep down the cost of corrections.

1. CHARACTERISTICS OF THE PAROLE POPULATION

In 2006, there were 784,408 adults on parole. About half of all parolees were in California, Texas, Michigan, Pennsylvania, or Illinois.[1] Parole populations can fluctuate greatly; for instance, between 1990 and 2000, California's population increased by 72 percent, while Texas experienced only a 6.7 percent increase. This was because California reinstituted parole after having abolished it for many years.[2] In 2005, the rate per 100,000 people in parole custody status for the nation was 350; however, it was only three in Maine because this state is largely determinative in sentencing structure, compared to 1,214 per 100,000 in the District of Columbia and 787 per 100,000 in Pennsylvania.[3]

According to the Bureau of Justice Statistics, at year-end 2005, one in every 286 people in the United States was under parole supervision. As a percentage of all releases from prison, discretionary releases to parole have declined dramatically. Before 1980, almost two-thirds of releases from prison were offenders being released on discretionary parole.[4] About 55 percent of all releases in 1980 were to discretionary parole, but by 2004, only 22 percent were released to discretionary parole. Mandatory parole releases increased from 19 percent to 39 percent over the same period. Mandatory supervision means when the offender serves a full term and then is required to be under a period of mandatory supervision in the community after release. Other forms of releases from prison, including expiration of sentence ("maxing out"), probation, and other conditional releases remained stable.[5]

Most parolees have served prison sentences for drug offenses (37 percent of all parolees). The rest of the parolee population is made up of property offenders (25 percent), violent offenders (25 percent), and all others (13 percent).[6]

The Bureau of Justice Statistics reports that as a percentage of the total, blacks decreased from 45 percent of all parolees in 1995 to 40 percent in 2005. Whites increased from 34 percent to 41 percent and Hispanics declined slightly from 21 percent to 18 percent.[7]

Blacks are more likely to serve longer sentences before being paroled. In 1999, blacks served, on average, about 37 months before discretionary parole, while whites served 34 months and Hispanics served 33 months. Hispanics served the longest when looking specifically at drug offenses (31 months compared to 28 months for blacks and 27 months for whites).[8]

The success rate for parolees is lower than that of probationers. Only about 46 percent were successfully discharged in 2004. About 40 percent are returned to prison under either a new charge (12 percent of all parolees) or through revocation (27 percent). About 10 percent abscond, and the rest are considered either "unsuccessful," transferred, or die.[9] States seem to vary tremendously in their patterns of success. While about 83 percent of Massachusetts parolees successfully complete parole, only 18 percent of parolees in Utah do.[10]

These percentages are of a "snapshot" of parolees taken at the end of 2004. The better way to evaluate recidivism, however, is to track ex-prisoners after release. Researchers at the Bureau of Justice Statistics tracked ex-prisoners in three states in 1984 for three years after their release and then did the same thing again for a new sample of ex-prisoners in 1994. They found that for all crime categories, more of them were rearrested within three years of release in 1994 than in 1984. About 68 percent of the ex-prisoners were rearrested in 1994, an increase from the 63 percent in 1984. Property offenders were more likely to be rearrested than any other category of criminal, although drug and public order offenders showed the largest increases in recidivism, when comparing the 1984 and 1994 samples. Interestingly, while arrest figures had increased, reconviction numbers did not, except for drug offenders, which increased significantly. This study showed that more than half of the releasees

(51.8 percent) were returned to prison within three years, either because of a new crime or a technical violation of parole.[11]

More recently, the Bureau of Justice Statistics analyzed nonviolent offenders who were released from prison on parole.[12] Non-violent offenders included property, drug, and public order offenses. From their study, we learn the following:

★ About three out of four inmates leaving state prisons had been convicted of a nonviolent crime. Property offenders and drug offenders each accounted for about a third of those exiting prisons.

★ The single largest offense category was drug trafficking (1 in 5 nonviolent releasees).

★ Nine out of 10 parolees were men.

★ Two-thirds of parolees were racial minorities.

★ Four in 10 had less than high school education.

★ Two-thirds said they had been using illegal drugs in months leading up to prison.

★ About one-quarter were alcohol dependent prior to imprisonment.

★ One-third were using alcohol at the time of the offense.

★ About 95 percent had an arrest history and 80 percent had at least one prior conviction.

★ About one-third had been arrested for a violent offense.

★ They had served an average of a third of their sentence.

★ Sixty-four percent had committed their current offense while on parole, probation, or escape.

★ Seven in 10 were rearrested within three years, half were reconvicted, and a quarter returned to prison.

★ One in five were rearrested for a violent crime.[13]

The results from this study suggest that the bulk of offenders released from prison will recidivate, but not all return to prison.

About eight percent of parolees were women in 1990, about 10 percent were women in 1995. By 2000 the figure was 12 percent of the total number of parolees.[14] In 2005, their percentage remained stable at about 12 percent.[15] Women on parole experience a multitude of problems. Many of them are the same problems that male parolees face, but some are different, or experienced in different ways. Women are more likely than men to have histories of drug and alcohol use, long-term unemployment, few or no skills, and a history of sexual abuse.[16]

In one study of Texas releasees, it was found that women were more likely than male offenders to have serious histories of drug use, but less likely to have received any treatment. About 42 percent reported daily cocaine use before prison, compared to only 17 percent of the men. More men expected to live with families than women.[17] In this same study, female parolees reported less family support and more negative family influences than did men.

In a study of Boston female parolees, community service referrals were correlated with lower recidivism. In a two-year follow-up, those who completed community programs in employment, drug treatment, and other social service programs were significantly less likely to recidivate. The study found that one-third of the women did not recidivate, another third had a low violation level, and the last third had a high violation level. Those who were least likely to recidivate included older women, minorities, those with few or no children, and those who had committed a personal offense with a low number of prior arrests.[18]

Some programs report recidivism of women at 3.2 to 13 percent after two years.[19] However, national statistics are much higher. According to the Bureau of Justice Statistics, about 45 percent of female parolees were returned to prison or had absconded. National statistics indicate that probably the most significant factor in recidivism is having a prior arrest history. While only 21 percent of the women with only one prior arrest recidivated, nearly 8 in 10 of those with 11 or more priors were rearrested. Those who had employment and stable living arrangements were more likely to succeed on parole.[20]

One study reported on the types of needs identified at intake from a sample of 546 female parolees. Researchers found that if a female parolee was employed, had stable living arrangements, and was assessed as needing and receiving some type of drug and/or alcohol program intervention, she was less likely to fail on parole. The study found that many female parolees had drug and alcohol treatment needs, as well as employment, housing, and other needs that were not assessed or addressed. The authors speculate that parole is more custodial than treatment oriented, and point out that these needs are associated with failure on parole, therefore they should be addressed.[21]

One of the differences between male and female offenders is that it seems as though women's relationships with men are more central to their offending; thus, upon parole they are less likely to stay out of trouble if they are in a relationship with a criminal partner. It is also true that women are less likely to have relationships to return to and they are wary of old partners who may be instrumental in their falling back into drug use.[22]

Several research efforts have documented the difficulties of women after release. Patricia O'Brien followed 18 women after release and documented their difficulties in adjusting to life on the outside. The financial and emotional difficulties of reuniting with children are the most important distinguishing factor between male and female offenders. Interestingly, women seem to be more likely than men to view their parole officers as a positive force, and look to them for assistance and resource referrals.[23]

Mary Dodge and Mark Pogrebin also interviewed female parolees and found that one of their greatest concerns was the difficulty of gaining custody of their children. To regain custody if the child is under state control, the female offender must show she has participated in drug treatment (if she was identified as a drug addict), maintain steady employment, and have a decent and stable home for the child. Because just meeting the requirements of daily living and the further demands of parole officers is difficult, the extra burden of children is sometimes too much for female parolees and they either cannot or do not even try to regain custody.[24]

2. ADMINISTRATION OF PAROLE

Parole is either a division under the state's department of corrections, a separate agency, or a variation of these two models. The advantage of the parole system being part of the department of corrections is that communication is generally smoother and the paroling authority may be more responsive to prison overpopulation. On the other hand, some argue that is exactly why the paroling authority should be separate from the prison system. In some states, only the parole board is separate from the department of corrections, but parole officers and all employees related to supervision are part of the corrections department. This removes the discretionary release decision makers from the auspices of the agency, but not supervising officers.

3. THE HISTORY OF PAROLE

Parole comes from French word *parol* (*parole d'honneur*) referring to "word" as in giving one's word or honor.[25] The idea of releasing prisoners from incarceration can be traced all the way back to the punishment of **transportation**, which involved sending prisoners from England to the colonies and, after the American Revolution, to Australia. These prisoners were not paroled in the sense that we think of today, but they were released from confinement into the community, and leased to a landowner who used their labor. The last shipment of convicts to Australia was as late as 1868.[26]

Alexander Maconochie (1787-1860) developed an early form of parole on Norfolk Island. Norfolk Island was a prison colony 1,000 miles off the coast of Australia where felons who committed additional crimes after being transported to Australia were sent. Maconochie's **mark system** consisted of stages of increasing responsibility. At the highest stage of responsibility, the offender could live almost independently, albeit on the island, and the final stage was a form of early release. Maconochie eliminated harsh punishments and improved the living conditions of the offenders incarcerated on Norfolk Island, but his tenure was short-lived. He held the job of prison superintendent only from 1840 until 1843, at which point he was removed because of his perceived leniency. He also tried to implement similar ideas in Birmingham Borough prison in 1849 but was dismissed two years later—again, on charges that he was too lenient.[27]

Sir Walter Crofton (1815-1897) developed a concept much more similar to today's parole. His **ticket of leave**, implemented around 1853, was a form of the mark system. Offenders were released early from prison upon going through graduated stages of responsibility and earning marks along the way for good behavior. When the offender had earned enough marks, he received his "ticket to leave" prison and returned to his community. The offender was required to report to police and, supposedly, a police inspector helped find the offender a job and supervised his release.

In 1870, a Prison Congress was held in Cincinnati, Ohio, which gathered together many of the major prison policymakers and reformers of the era. At the Congress, Crofton's idea was disseminated and led directly to the concept of graduated liberties found in the "Declaration of Principles" from the Congress.[28] Zebulon Brockway (1827-1920), a major participant of the Prison Congress, was appointed superintendent of Elmira Reformatory in New York in 1877.

This new institution was supposed to be different from the earlier penitentiary in that it reformed young, malleable inmates through education and discipline. Although Brockway was associated with corporal punishments, he also implemented indeterminate sentences and parole release. Inmates of Elmira were young men (16 to 30) who were placed in "Second Grade," which was the highest form of custody. After six months of good conduct, they were promoted to "First Grade." Continued good behavior would earn an early release. Offenders were released to six months of supervision, supervised by volunteer guardians. It wasn't until many years later that parole was implemented with paid employees.[29]

Gradually throughout the late 1800s and early 1900s, states adopted some form of early release or parole, but it may not have included any concept of supervision, or supervision was provided haphazardly, or by volunteers. In 1907 New York became the first state to implement what we consider parole:

- ★ an indeterminate sentence
- ★ a system for granting early release
- ★ post-release supervision by paid employees
- ★ the possibility of revocation and return to prison

By 1927, only three states (Florida, Mississippi, and Virginia) did not have parole systems. By 1942, all states had a parole system, although some continued to use volunteer parole officers.[30] The federal system of parole came later than state parole, but was fully implemented by 1932. In 1973, federal parole guidelines were established that set out guidelines for sentence length based on offense severity and likelihood of recidivism.[31]

It took longer for all states to establish public parole systems than it did for states to create state probation agencies. Also, unlike probation, some states have since abolished parole. In the "rehabilitative era" of the 1970s, the majority of inmates were released on parole. For instance, in 1977, 72 percent of all prisoners were released via parole. However, the use of parole declined dramatically in the 1980s and 1990s and, by 1997, only 28 percent of all prisoners were released via parole.[32] At the federal level, the Comprehensive Crime Control Act of 1984 created the U.S. Sentencing Commission, which established sentencing guidelines that specified fixed terms. Federal parole was abolished and replaced with mandatory post-release supervision.

In the late 1970s and 1980s, parole came under criticism from both liberals and conservatives. Liberals were upset that there were no guidelines or rules in how parole boards granted parole or such guidelines were not transparent so there was no way for an offender to ensure their success or appeal the decision to refuse parole. Conservatives criticized parole for being too lenient and letting violent offenders out too early.

Joan Petersilia, an authority on probation and parole, describes the criticisms that led to the demise of parole as involving these major arguments:

★   There was no perceived scientific support for rehabilitation or evidence that correct programming could ever reform criminals;

★   There was a moral problem with tying release to prison behavior because one didn't necessarily predict the other;

★   Not knowing one's release date was a form of cruel punishment; and

★   Paroling authorities had uncontrolled discretion with no guidelines.[33]

Because of extreme dissatisfaction with parole and criticism of how it was implemented, Maine abolished parole in 1976 and, in 1977, California and Indiana abolished their parole release decision power and established determinate sentencing. Other states followed and, by the end of 2000, 15 states had abolished parole; 21 states allowed parole for only some types of prisoners, and just 15 states still had full parole discretion.[34] In Box 14.1, states are grouped according to the type of parole release decisionmaking that exists.

BOX 14.1

Status of Parole Release, 2002

Full Release Power   Alabama, Colorado, Idaho, Kentucky, Montana, Nevada, New Jersey, North Dakota, Oklahoma, Pennsylvania, Rhode Island, South Carolina, Utah, Vermont, Wyoming

Limited Release Power   Alaska, Arkansas, California, Connecticut, Florida, Georgia, Hawaii, Iowa, Louisiana, Maryland, Massachusetts, Michigan, Missouri, Nebraska, New Hampshire, New York, South Dakota, Tennessee, Texas, West Virginia, Wisconsin

No parole   Arizona, Delaware, Illinois, Indiana, Kansas, Maine, Minnesota, Mississippi, New Mexico, North Carolina, Ohio, Oregon, Virginia, Washington, federal system

Source: Petersilia, J. (2002). *Reforming Probation and Parole.* Lanham, MD: American Correctional Association, p. 111.

★ Exercise: In the State of . . .

Find out whether your state has discretionary parole, limited discretionary parole, mandatory release, or none of the above. (Basically confirm whether the information in Box 14.1 is correct. How many adults are being supervised by a parole supervision authority in your state (if any)?

During the same period when discretionary parole declined, the rate of revocations in the states that retained parole rose. Parole boards evidently became more cautious in granting parole and in leaving parolees on the street after violation reports had been filed. In 2001, 40 percent of prison admissions were parole revocations, compared to about half that number in 1980.[35]

Interestingly, several states (North Carolina, Florida, California, and Colorado) that had abolished the parole granting authority have now reinstated it, no doubt because of prison overcrowding. Today, only Maine and Virginia have no parole or post prison supervision.[36] Other states have a form of mandatory supervision after release that is set based on a percentage of time served and good time awarded. The offender is subject to revocation and return to prison until the full expiration of the original sentence.

4. SUPERVISION ISSUES

As explained above, the parole board is the paroling authority in most states (although it may be called something else). In states that retain their system of parole, the inmate is eligible for parole according to statute; typically when one-half or two-thirds of the sentence has been served. Just because an inmate is eligible for parole does not mean that he or she receives it. The decision to grant parole is made by the paroling authority and is based on the severity of the crime and the inmate's behavior in prison. Some states use more formal guidelines for granting parole; in others, the decision is more discretionary. Even in states that have abolished parole, there is still discretionary parole for those inmates who were sentenced before the state legislature abolished discretionary parole. However, there is no doubt that fewer individuals are receiving parole today than in the past. In 1977 just four percent of prisoners **maxed out**, meaning they served their full term with no early release. By 2002, close to 20 percent of prisoners were "maxing out" of prison. This means that they have no conditions on their release and no supervision.[37] In some states, this percentage is even higher.

The rate of parole (the ratio of offenders who receive parole to those who are eligible) fluctuates widely between states and, sometimes, within a state over different time periods or different regions. Texas, for instance, is divided into different regions, and there is quite a wide disparity in the parole approval rates. For instance, while one region approves only 38 percent of low-risk eligible offenders, another region in the state approves 58 percent of low-risk offenders. The approval rates for high risk range from 0.5 to 15 percent.[38] In 2005, only about half of offenders who were at the lowest risk level were approved for parole and only about 40 percent of those at the second-lowest level were approved.[39]

The paroling authority may be called different things in different states, but the board is typically made up of a number of individuals who have the discretion to grant parole. In many states, the board also offers recommendations to the governor on pardons. The positions are typically political appointments and consist of no more than 10 members who may come from a variety of backgrounds, including law enforcement, education, and business. The appointment is typically a term lasting from three to six years; however, in some states the appointment is indefinite. Depending on the state, these members may have the power to grant parole, set parole decision dates, rescind parole, issue warrants and subpoenas, set conditions, restore offenders' civil rights, and grant final discharges. Some or all of these duties may be delegated.

There are about 200 individuals on state parole boards or paroling authorities across the nation. These 200 individuals are responsible for releasing roughly 128,708 offenders each year, setting the conditions for an additional 288,679 offenders who are released under some form of mandatory supervision, overseeing the supervision of the 643,452 parolees on parole, and being responsible for the 227,690 offenders whose parole is revoked each year.[40] There is a great deal of turnover on these boards and not much training. In some states, parole board members are only part-time and/or receive no compensation.

Generally, only a subset of the full board holds release hearings. Parole hearings last an average of 12 to 15 minutes. In some states, the board may not meet personally with the offender at all. The board may or may not allow the offender to appear personally and/or present witnesses and evidence in support of his or her release. The board considers a variety of factors in their release decision, including the seriousness of the offense, the amount of time served, the offender's age, juvenile history, criminal history, number of prison infractions, other arrests, participation in programs, and letters of support or protest.

Regardless of whether they have expertise in the area of corrections, the ability of parole board members to accurately judge when an offender is no longer a risk to the community has always been questionable. Studies show that board members pay most attention to the severity of the crime in making the release decision, not what the offender has done in prison. Other factors that weigh in the decision include prior criminal record, attitude toward family responsibilities, attitude toward authority, and attitude toward the victim.[41] About 96 percent of the states now also offer the opportunity for victims and district attorneys to provide input on the decision.[42] Recent research has found that victims can affect the decision of the parole board. In cases where victims attend the hearing or send letters, offenders are less likely to receive parole.[43]

Many states and the federal government have moved away from the idea of a **clinical assessment decision**, meaning that board members should be able to read the file and interview the inmate and predict his or her ability to be successful on release, to an **actuarial decision**, meaning that statistics are used to predict success based on demographics of those who have been successful. In effect, it is similar to how the insurance industry predicts that 16- to 21-year-old men are more likely than other groups to have accidents and, therefore, charge much higher premiums for them.

Parole guidelines are similar to sentencing guidelines because they give a presumptive term or guideline for how long the offender should serve in prison based on offense characteristics and characteristics of the offender. Risk factors typically include age at first admission to an incarceration facility, history of revocations, prior incarcerations, employment history, commitment offense, age, gang membership, education and/or training completions while incarcerated, disciplinary conduct, and custody level. These factors go into a risk score that is used, along with an offense severity score, to establish the guidelines.

Generally, prisoners receive parole hearings with board members. In these hearings, a future parole date is set according to a guideline system utilizing crime and offender characteristics. In subsequent hearings, the parole date may be re-evaluated. In most cases, prison violations would result in setting the date further in the future. When the presumptive date gets close, there will be a hearing at which time the parole is either granted or put off to a future tentative release date.

The Supreme Court held that parole release was not a right; therefore states did not have to follow strict due process guidelines in parole release hearings.[44] This means that states can set up any type of procedure deemed expedient in the decision to grant parole, or eliminate the privilege entirely.[45]

Parole board members are immune from liability if parolees murder or victimize others. The Supreme Court has held that officials must be immune from tort liability for their decisions.[46] This quasi-immunity is similar to that held by judges and probation officers when they are using their discretion to make sentencing recommendations on pre-sentence reports. On the other hand, parole officers who supervise a caseload may be liable in Section 1983 actions if, acting in the course and duty of employment, they violate an offender's constitutional rights.[47]

The power to parole is different than the power to **pardon** convicted offenders, which is basically a release and forgiveness of criminal culpability. This power rests in the executive power of the president and governors. Section 2 of the U.S. Constitution gives the president pardon power over federal crimes. Similar provisions exist in most state constitutions for governors to pardon state crimes. In many states, the parole board is called the board of pardons and paroles because the board makes recommendations to the governor on pardons. While a pardon is basically forgiveness and removes the conviction, a commutation is simply a reduction of sentence.

The decision to pardon can be controversial. In 1974, President Gerald Ford pardoned former president Richard Nixon. While some argued this act closed the door on a difficult time in the nation's history and began the healing process after the Watergate scandal, others argued that the nation never reached closure over the incident. In 1993, President George Bush pardoned former Defense Secretary Caspar Weinberger over the Iran-Contra affair—an act that, again, stirred controversy. The most controversial pardons, however, were made by President Clinton in 2001. He offered clemency to FALN members, a terrorist group dedicated to the freedom of Puerto Rico. He also pardoned Dan Rostenkowski for the misuse of public funds, as well as several federal prisoners who had long mandatory sentences for drug crimes. He pardoned Patricia Hearst, Roger Clinton, Susan McDougal, Henry Cisneros, and Marc Rich for wire fraud, racketeering, and tax evasion. The last pardon was heavily criticized because Rich had been a major contributor to Clinton's campaign.

State governors have received less press for their pardoning or commutation powers. President George W. Bush received recognition, both positive and negative, for refusing to commute Karla Faye Tucker's capital sentence to a life sentence in 1998. She was executed amidst worldwide criticism.

There have been scandals regarding the parole process as well. In 1978, Ray Blanton, then-Governor of Tennessee, and three aides were charged with accepting money in return for approving parole and pardon requests. Two were convicted and sentenced to prison. In 1991, a scandal emerged when it became known that James Granberry, an ex-parole commission member in Texas, received money from prisoners' families as a "parole advisor." Evidently he charged between $500 and $2,000 to help prisoners' quests for parole. He was indicted by a federal grand jury for lying to a federal magistrate in 1992 about what he was doing. It was later discovered that, while on the board, he voted to parole a car dealer's son in exchange for reduced lease payments on a car.[48]

4.1 Caseload Supervision

Generally, parole caseloads are smaller than probation caseloads. The average caseload today is about 70 and twice what some consider to be an ideal size.[49] Only about 14 percent of parolees are under some form of intensive parole. A very small number (about three percent) are under some form of specialized supervision (such as sex offenders). Intensive parole and specialized caseloads cost more than twice what regular parole costs per year.[50]

Intensive parole is similar to intensive probation programs in that smaller caseloads allow officers to more intensely supervise offenders. For instance, in one state's intensive parole program, offenders who are high risk because they have committed an act of violence are supervised in caseloads of 14. Officers see the offender at least 15 times per month with at least six "face to face" contacts, six drivebys, and one home visitation. Offenders are on 24-hour electronic monitoring and must submit and have approved a 24-hour schedule of where they will be every hour of the day.[51]

Caseloads may be assigned to officers based on geography, classification level, offender type, or random assignment. Some argue that it would be better for caseloads to be assigned geographically so that officers would be able to coordinate with community police officers and share information about parolees and their family members in a given neighborhood. In one study it was found that in a high-crime neighborhood, 43 different probation officers supervised 218 probationers instead of concentrating all probationers under a few officers who would be better informed about the neighborhood. This same principle applies to parole as well.[52] Parolees generally are localized in a few zip codes that are also typically marked by high crime, dysfunctional families, and poverty. Furthermore, most of the neighborhoods do not have any services available in the immediate vicinity.[53]

4.2 Parole Conditions

Similar to probationers, all parolees are required to abide by conditions established at the time of the parole release. Generally, standard conditions are like those of probation; the offender must report monthly, notify the officer of any moves, hold a job, not commit a crime, and so on. Parolees are increasingly expected to pay supervision fees and/or victim compensation fees. Other conditions may be treatment oriented, such as participating in a treatment program or obtaining a GED; or custody oriented, such as following a curfew, or not going anywhere near children. A list of typical conditions is offered in Box 14.2.

As with probation, violating any of these conditions might result in a parole officer writing a violation report. There may also be a revocation hearing in front of the parole board or a hearing examiner. Technical violations are those that involve only breaking one or more of the conditions. Parolees are also sometimes revoked for committing new crimes, with or without formally prosecuting the new crime.

BOX 14.2

Parole Conditions

- ★ Pay supervision fees and restitution
- ★ Not use controlled substances except by prescription
- ★ Submit to drug testing
- ★ Remain in the state
- ★ Find gainful employment or participate in education
- ★ Obtain permission to change residence
- ★ Submit to searches of home and visits to workplace
- ★ Consent to search of person
- ★ Obey all laws
- ★ Cooperate in all ways with parole officer
- ★ Not possess any weapons

4.3 Re-Entry Concerns

Re-entry assistance has increased in recent years with support from the federal government. In his 2004 State of the Union address, President Bush made special mention of the need for reentry services and advocated a $300 million federal initiative to provide financial support for state programs to give parolees and releasees a "second chance" through job training, transitional housing, and other forms of support. States were given grants to create such programs. Many researchers and writers are urging states to reexamine the dramatic decline of discretionary parole and the high return-to-prison rates as wasteful spending of correctional dollars.[54]

There has been a great deal of press lately about the fact that more than 600,000 inmates return to the community every year. Many of these are released to parole. It bears noting that a large number of these offenders received very little assistance in prison to learn how to avoid criminal decisions, drugs, or negative lifestyles.[55] It is reported that prison treatment programs only comprise one to five percent of prison budgets each year.[56] The number of prisoners who participated in vocational programs dropped from 31 percent in 1991 to 27 percent in 1997; the number who had participated in education programs dropped from 43 percent to 35 percent, and the number who received any formal substance abuse treatment dropped from 25 percent to 10 percent.[57]

One study points out that the pre-release programs that were more popular in past decades may have been instrumental in reducing recidivism. Researchers found that, of 3,244 Massachusetts inmates released between 1973 and 1976, those who participated in both a pre-release and furlough program had a nine percent recidivism rate; those who only participated in furloughs had a 17 percent recidivism rate; those who participated only in the pre-release program had a 26 percent rate; and those who participated in neither had a 29 percent recidivism rate (holding prisoner age and prior record constant).[58] Even assuming that those who were allowed to participate in furloughs might have been better risks overall, this does indicate that pre-release programs should be considered essential tools in reducing recidivism.

Some argue that the problems of parolees are more serious today than they have been in the past, partly because of a lack of in-prison programming, and partly because prisoners have more barriers to overcome.[59] Of those released from prison on parole or mandatory release, three-fourths have a history of substance abuse and one in six suffer from mental illness. However, only one-third have received substance abuse or mental health treatment while in prison. The percentage of all prisoners who are participating in such programs has declined from 25 percent a decade ago to only 10 percent today. Further, two to three percent of releasees are HIV-positive; one-third were unemployed at the time of current arrest; about 40 percent have no GED or high school; and 11 percent have a learning disability.[60]

In a study of releasees in one state, utilizing a sample of 414 men and 262 women, it was found that 37 percent had no high school degree or GED; and only half of the sample had held a job for two years or more prior to their prison term. Eighty-seven percent of this sample indicated they would need some or a lot of help in finding a job. Only 15 percent had a job waiting for them upon release. About 60 percent of this sample had not received any drug treatment, even though close to 60 percent reported cocaine use and a quarter reported heavy daily use. A significant percentage of this sample (almost 20 percent) reported mental health problems and about 30 percent reported a diagnosis of depression.[61]

In California, it has been reported that there are only 200 shelter beds available for parolees, but 10,000 who have no home to be released to. Also, there are only four mental health clinics, but 18,000 who require psychiatric services, and only 750 drug treatment beds for 85,000 substance abusers.[62] Furthermore, only about six percent of releasees in California participated in any kind of pre-release program.[63] On the other hand, the state of Washington has a very comprehensive pre-release system that assesses risk and need. The state also offers pre-release services in prison. Between 30 and 40 percent of released prisoners spend time in community residential release centers.[64]

In past decades, many inmates took advantage of furloughs to help them look for a job or get reacquainted with family before release. That is no longer the case. For instance, in the 1970s, California granted 15,000 furloughs a year; however, in 2001 no furloughs were granted.[65] The "Willie Horton" incident refers to Michael Dukakis's ill-fated campaign for president that was damaged by the widespread dissemination of the case of Willie Horton, a furloughed Massachusetts inmate who committed murder while on furlough. Dukakis, as governor, was not directly responsible for the decision to release Horton, but the voters held him accountable.[66]

For more information about reentry issues for offenders, see the Legal Action Center's report on roadblocks to reentry at http://www.lac.org

About 37 percent of parolees have been committed for a drug offense,[67] yet many received no drug treatment. In fact, it is reported that in Texas, 900 offenders were approved for parole in 2006 but remained in prison simply because the release decision included a condition of entering a drug treatment facility, and none were available.[68]

Jobs are a key to success on parole but parolees have major barriers to overcome. Many have very poor job histories and few or no skills. The stigma of being an ex-felon is a tremendous barrier to finding quality employment even if the offender has a marketable skill. Only about 15 to 50 percent of offenders have a job waiting for them upon release.[69] Issues that must be overcome in order to obtain decent employment in addition to a lack of a job history and few skills include drug abuse, lack of transportation, restrictions imposed by parole (i.e., curfews and reporting requirements), statutory exclusions for licenses and certifications, and a lack of socialization to workplace culture. Even after a job is secured, retention is a problem.

Transitional jobs are those that the offender may obtain immediately upon release. These are important even if they provide no long range future.

Such jobs, to be adequate, must be relatively low skilled, with frequent pay periods, providing close supervision and mentoring, perhaps some subsidies to help the parolee begin life on the outside, and some training for more lucrative employment.[70] Some programs operated by community corrections departments meet most of these elements either through a partnership with a private employee or a community work project employing ex-offenders.

In many cases, families are unlikely to be of much assistance to the parolee. In a Texas study, two-thirds of the sample reported that at least one family member had been convicted of a crime. More than a third reported that a family member was currently in prison. Two-thirds reported having a family member with a serious drug or alcohol problem. Most (54 percent) had children under 18 years old, and 59 percent of these people had lived with one or more children prior to imprisonment.[71]

The Urban Institute has several reports on re-entry issues available on its Web site, http://www.urban.org

It may be that prisoners who leave prison underestimate the difficulties they will encounter upon release. In the Texas study, almost 80 percent believed it would be easy to renew relationships with family and 82 percent thought their family would be supportive. About 63 percent expected to live with family after prison, and about half (54 percent) expected financial support from their families. Further, 65 percent who did not have housing lined up thought that it would be easy or very easy to find housing, and 72 percent thought it would be easy to stay out of trouble. Fully 84 percent thought it would be easy to stay out of prison after release, and 81 percent thought it would be easy to avoid any parole violations. Most also thought it was unlikely that they would commit a crime (87 percent) or use drugs (81 percent).[72] Despite their optimism, parolees indicated they needed education (73 percent), job training (72 percent), and financial assistance (73 percent).[73]

Another study also documented unrealistic positivism from young offenders before release. In this study, interviews with young offenders before release were compared to interviews with young offenders who were revoked on parole. Those who were revoked exhibited a fatalism regarding their return to prison. They admitted that their expectations of release were unrealistic and led to a letdown after release when practical matters such as jobs and housing overwhelmed them.[74]

It may come as a surprise to some people that, upon conviction of a felony, some individuals permanently lose their right to vote. In fact, only Maine and Vermont have no restrictions on voting by ex-felons. **Civil disabilities** refers to those rights that are lost or compromised after a criminal conviction. Many disabilities exist, including rights regarding voting, employment, jury service, eligibility to hold public office, and the right to own a firearm. Many states require some criminals to register; for example, every state requires sex offenders to register.[75] Parolees may also be barred from public housing and public assistance.

According to Joan Petersilia, the states that have the most exclusionary policies generally are in the south but also include Texas, Arizona, Kansas, and Nebraska. The most inclusive states (with the fewest civil disabilities for returning felons) are generally in the northeast, but also include Indiana, Ohio, Oregon, and Utah.[76]

5. RECIDIVISM AND REVOCATION

Similar to probation officers, a parole officer may file a violation report when a parolee violates any of the conditions of his or her parole and/or commits a new crime. These reports go to the paroling authority, rather than the sentencing judge, and the revocation hearing will be conducted by parole board members or, in some states, hearing officers that have been given the power invested in the paroling authority. Parole board members or these hearing officers have the power to change conditions or revoke parole and send the offender back to prison. In the federal system, recall that parole has been abolished. However, there is a mandatory period of post-release supervision, and federal offenders who violate the supervision conditions will go before their sentencing judge. In this case, it is a judicial proceeding to determine whether revocation and a return to prison are warranted.

As discussed earlier, a prison inmate has no right to parole and no rights to any particular due process elements in a parole release hearing, unless such rights are created by the state. However, once parole has been granted, the Supreme Court has recognized it as a protected liberty interest and due process applies before parole can be revoked. In *Morrissey v. Brewer*,[77] the Court held that the following elements must be granted before parole revocation:

★ Bifurcated hearing (preliminary and full hearing)[78]

★ Written notice of parole violation

★ Disclosure to parolee of evidence against him

★ Opportunity to be heard in person and to present witnesses and documentary evidence

★ Conditional right to confront and cross-examine (denied if there is reason to keep identity of witnesses secret, for example, police informers).

★ Neutral and detached hearing body

★ Written statement of fact finders as to evidence against and reasons for decision.

This court decision led to a dramatic change in the way some states operated their parole system. It required parole officers to participate in revocation hearings held by parole board members or specially hired hearing officers. Generally, the preliminary hearing should take place where the parolee is located at the time of the violation. Many offenders waive the preliminary hearing, and the full revocation hearing is often located in the prison after the offender is sent back. In another case, the Supreme Court held that Oklahoma's "pre-parole" status was equivalent to parole and, therefore, *Morrissey v. Brewer's* due process analysis applied when the state sought to deprive the pre-parole participants of their liberty.[79]

When an offender is revoked and sent back to prison, it used to be the case that the years spent on parole did not count as part of the sentence; therefore an offender could have served five years of a 10-year term, been paroled, spent four years on parole and then be revoked and sent back to prison with five years remaining on his sentence. Now, many states have statutory restrictions on how long an offender can be returned to prison—for instance, in Georgia, the maximum amount of time is two years.[80]

The parole revocation hearing is described as an administrative or quasi-judicial hearing and, therefore, the due process protections than an individual would have in a criminal trial do not exist. As stated above, there is no right to counsel and the right to cross-examine is conditional. Further, some courts have held that the exclusionary rule does not apply. This means that even if evidence obtained through an illegal search could not be used to prosecute new charges, it can be used in a parole revocation hearing.[81]

It is a sad fact that there is a high failure rate on parole. According to a 1994 Bureau of Justice Statistics study, two-thirds of parolees are rearrested within three years of release. In this study, one in three were arrested in the first six months, 44 percent in the first year. This study showed that property offenders were most likely to recidivate (about three-quarters) compared to two-thirds of drug offenders and 62 percent of public order and violent criminals.[82]

In 2001, about 37 percent of all admissions to prison nationwide were for parole revocations.[83] Revocation can occur either through a new arrest (and prosecution), or for **technical violations** (which are not crimes but simply rule violations). In 1997, about three out of five parolees who were revoked were sent back for technical violations, not new crimes.[84] Interestingly, successful discharges from parole are more likely for those released on discretionary parole rather than mandatory supervision. In Box 14.3, Bureau of Justice Statistics information shows that in 2000, about half of all state discretionary parolees were successfully discharged but only about a third of those released on some form of mandatory supervision were. Supporters of parole argue that this means that parole boards are able to identify those who pose less risk to the public.

In a study of parole releases and revocations in Tennessee, it was found that cohorts who were released between 1993 and 1999 experienced increasing likelihoods of being returned to prison on technical violations rather than new charges. About 40 percent of the 1993 cohort were returned to prison after two years of release and about 63 percent of those returns were for technical violations. The 1997 cohort had a higher percentage of revocations (about 48 percent) and of those, a higher percentage were revoked for technical violations (about 77 percent). The 1999 cohort had a lower rate of revocations (40 percent again), but the percentage of technical violations remained at 79 percent of the total who were revoked.[85]

BOX 14.3

Percent of Parole Discharges Successfully Completed, by Type, 1983-2000

Year	All Parole Exits	Discretionary	Mandatory
1983	54%	55%	48%
1984	56	68	47
1985	51	57	37
1986	44	56	35
1987	42	56	33
1988	35	52	23
1989	35	51	24
1990	36	52	24
1991	41	53	25
1992	42	51	30
1993	43	55	34
1994	40	52	30
1995	41	54	28
1996	42	56	30
1997	41	56	31
1998	41	55	32
1999	40	54	33
2000	41	54	35

Source: Bureau of Justice Statistics (2003). *Probation and Parole in the United States, 2002.* Bureau of Justice Statistics (2001). *Trends in State Parole*, 1990-2000.

The analysis of the results of this study is problematic. It seems clear that the parole release rate in a state can swing up and down depending, no doubt, on political pressures to parole or not because of crowded prisons (which would increase the number of releases) or a public "get-tough" attitude (which would decrease releases). The large number of returns based on technical violations seems to indicate that the revocation process may be too harsh and intermediate community sanctions should be used because the violations are not necessarily new crimes; however, it may be the case that prosecutors are urging parole authorities to use revocations in lieu of new charges and prosecutions. If an offender is going back to prison anyway, new charges and a new sentence may be redundant. There is no way to know whether technical violations are overused, or used in lieu of new charges, without further research.

5.1 Factors Associated with Failure

A number of studies have looked at what factors seem to be associated with recidivism while on parole or supervised release. In one study of 167 participants in a "day reporting" program, it was found that the factors associated with success were age (older offenders were more likely to be successful), family responsibilities, and no drug use history. In fact, those with a drug history were three times more likely to fail. Further, offenders with three or more criminal counts and those who received institutional detention were more likely to fail, as were repeat offenders and those with longer sentences.[86] Many studies find that failure is most likely to occur in the first three months of release; therefore it is recommended that all services be concentrated at the front end of release, in the first three months.

Contrary to what some believe, there is good evidence that some programs can reduce recidivism by as much as 30 percent. Programs that use cognitive-behavioral content, address drug addiction, and provide extended support in the community have particularly positive results.[87]

Intermediate sanctions are options to use for parolees who violate their parole but not seriously enough to warrant a return to prison. Such sanctions may include loss of privileges, increased reporting, drug tests, curfews, electronic monitoring, and even short stays in a community incarceration facility in some jurisdictions. Graduated sanctions have reduced the returns to prison; for instance, in Georgia, the use of such sanctions helped to increase the successful completion of parole from 61 percent in 1998 to 72 percent in 2002.[88] Other states, such as Washington, have also attempted to reduce their rate of returns to prison by using a type of sentencing grid for parolees that provides for graduated sanctions for technical violations and petty crimes.[89]

6. CONCLUSION

Parole has a long history and is derived from the idea that offenders should be rewarded when they reform their behavior. Unfortunately, it has always been difficult to determine whether their behavior has changed. Parole is one-tenth the cost of prison, so it is a cost savings as well as a reward to the offender. Despite the cost savings, however, the use of parole has declined considerably from the 1970s when the majority of inmates were released on parole. Today, there are about 800,000 parolees.

The decision to release on parole is made by a paroling authority (typically a parole board); however, only about 15 states still retain full discretionary release. About 14 states have no discretionary release (although there may be a mandatory supervision period after release), and the rest of the states have limited discretionary release (for certain crimes or offenders). Parolees have no due process rights in relation to the release decision; however, after they receive parole, there are due process rights that apply before their parole can be revoked and they can be sent back to prison.

Only about a third of all parolees are successfully discharged. High failure rates are associated with parolees who have prior drug histories and criminal records. It should also be noted that it appears that parolees are more likely today to be revoked for technical violations instead of new crimes. Regardless, as long as failure rates remain high, the future of parole is uncertain.

In a national report of parole for state and federal policymakers, the authors advocated the following changes or new directions for parole:

★ Reassess risk and need measures

★ Enhance the offender's motivation to change through the use of positive rewards and positive interactions with parole officers

★ Target the needs of the offender through the concepts of risk, need, and responsivity

★ Use cognitive-behavioral programs when appropriate

★ Increase the use of positive reinforcements rather than negative

★ Provide prosocial supports for offenders

★ Measure success and provide feedback to decision maker[90]

REVIEW QUESTIONS

1. What is the difference between probation and parole? What is the difference between discretionary parole and mandatory supervision?

2. How many people are on parole? What percent are women? What is the racial/ethnic breakdown? What percent have committed violent crimes? What percent successfully complete parole?

3. What are the differences between female and male parolees' problems when returning to the free world?

4. What are the early forerunners of modern parole? Describe them.

5. Why was parole criticized and abandoned in some states?

6. Describe the legal rights of inmates/parolees to due process. Discuss specifically the due process elements identified in *Morrissey v. Brewer*.

7. How many people are returning to the community from prison each year? What are the problems that face them?

8. How many parolees are rearrested within three years? What are the factors associated with failure on parole?

9. What percent of prison admittees are parolees who have had their parole revoked? What are intensive parole and intermediate sanctions and how might these be utilized to reduce the numbers returned to prison?

10. What are the suggestions offered to improve parole?

VOCABULARY

actuarial decision – decision based on statistics

civil disabilities – civil rights that are lost or compromised after a criminal conviction

clinical assessment decision – prediction based on personal interview and clinical judgment

indeterminate sentence – when the release date is not set by the sentencing judge

intermediate sanctions – options short of a return to prison, including loss of privileges, increased reporting, drug tests, curfews, and electronic monitoring

mark system – Maconochie's program of stages of increasing responsibility based on good behavior

maxed out – serving the full term with no early release

parol (*parole d'honneur*) – "word" as in giving one's word or honor

pardon – basically a release and forgiveness of criminal culpability

parole guidelines – give a presumptive term or guideline for how long the offender should serve in prison before receiving parole, based on offense characteristics and characteristics of the offender

split sentencing and **shock incarceration** – type of sentence involving a short period of incarceration before being supervised in the community by probation officers

technical violations – not crimes but simply rule violations

ticket of leave – Crofton's plan of early release based on good behavior

transitional jobs – those that the offender may obtain immediately upon release and involve certain characteristics, such as frequent pay

transportation – punishment of being sent from England to the colonies and, after the American Revolution, to Australia

FOR FURTHER READING

Burke, Peggy and Tonry, Michael (2006). *Successful Transition and Reentry for Safer Communities: A Call to Action for Parole*. Silver Spring, MD: Center for Effective Public Policy.

Jones, Mark (2004). *Community Corrections*. Prospect Heights, IL: Waveland Press.

O'Brien, Patricia (2001). Making It in the "Free World": *Women in Transition from Prison*. Albany, NY: SUNY Albany Press.

Petersilia, Joan (2002). *Reforming Probation and Parole*. Lanham, MD: American Correctional Association.

Travis, Jeremy and Sarah Lawrence (2002). *Beyond the Prison Gates: The Status of Parole in America*. Washington DC: The Urban Institute. May be accessed via http://www.urban.org/UploadedPDF/310583_Beyond_prison_gates.pdf.

---

[1] Glaze, L. & T. Bonczar (2006). *Probation and Parole in the United States, 2005*. Washington, DC: Bureau of Justice Statistics.

[2] Petersilia, J. (2002). *Reforming Probation and Parole*. Lanham, MD: American Correctional Association, p. 145.

[3] Glaze, L. & T. Bonczar (2006). *Probation and Parole in the United States, 2005*. Washington, DC: Bureau of Justice Statistics, p. 3.

[4] Burke, P. & M. Tonry (2006). *Successful Transition and Reentry for Safer Communities: A Call to Action For Parole*. Silver Spring, MD: Center for Effective Public Policy, p. 19.

[5] Glaze, L. & T. Bonczar (2006). *Probation and Parole in the United States, 2005*. Washington, DC: Bureau of Justice Statistics, p. 8.

[6] Glaze, L. & T. Bonczar (2006). *Probation and Parole in the United States, 2005*. Washington, DC: Bureau of Justice Statistics, p. 9.

[7] Glaze, L. & T. Bonczar (2006). *Probation and Parole in the United States, 2005*. Washington, DC: Bureau of Justice Statistics, p. 9.

[8] Hughes, T., D. Wilson & A. Beck (2001). *Trends in State Parole, 1990-2000*. Washington, DC: Bureau of Justice Statistics.

[9] Glaze, L. & S. Palla (2005). *Probation and Parole in the United States, 2004*. Washington, DC: Bureau of Justice Statistics, p. 9.

[10] Hughes, T., D. Wilson & A. Beck (2001). *Trends in State Parole, 1990-2000*. Washington, DC: Bureau of Justice Statistics, p. 11.

[11] Bureau of Justice Statistics. Retrieved 1/10/06 from: http://www.ojp.usdoj.gov/bjs/reentry/recidivism.htm.

[12] Ducrose, M. & C. Mumola (2004). *BJS Fact Sheet: Profile of Nonviolent Offenders Exiting State Prisons*. Washington, DC: U.S. Department of Justice.

[13] Ducrose, M. & C. Mumola (2004). *BJS Fact Sheet: Profile of Nonviolent Offenders Exiting State Prisons*. Washington, DC: U.S. Department of Justice.

[14] Glaze, L. & T. Bonczar (2006). *Probation and Parole in the United States, 2005*. Washington, DC: Bureau of Justice Statistics.

[15] Petersilia, J. (2002). *Reforming Probation and Parole*. Lanham, MD: American Correctional Association, p. 145; Glaze, L. & T. Bonczar (2006). *Probation and Parole in the United States, 2005*. Washington, DC: Bureau of Justice Statistics, p. 8.

[16] Greenfield, L. & T. Snell (2000). *Women Offenders*. Washington, DC: Bureau of Justice Statistics.

[17] LaVigne, N. & V. Kachnowski (2005). *Texas Prisoners' Reflections on Returning Home*. Washington, DC: Urban Institute.

[18] Pearl, N. (1998). "Use of Community-Based Social Services to Reduce Recidivism in Female Parolees." *Women and Criminal Justice* 10, 1: 27-52.

[19] Prichard, D. (2000). "Project ReConnect Responds to Women Offenders on a Personal Level." In National Institute of Corrections, *Topics in Community Corrections: Responding to Women Offenders in the Community*, pp. 26-31. Longmont, CO: NIC Information Services.

[20] Greenfield, L. & T. Snell (2000). *Women Offenders*. Washington, DC: Bureau of Justice Statistics.

[21] Schram, P., B. Koons-Witt & F. Williams (2006). "Supervision Strategies and Approaches for Female Parolees: Examining the Link Between Unmet Needs and Parolee Outcome." *Crime & Delinquency*, 52, 3: 450-471.

[22] Ritchie, E. (2001). "Challenges Incarcerated Women Face as They Return to Their Communities: Findings from Life History Interviews." *Crime and Delinquency* 47, 3: 368-389.

[23] O'Brien, P. (2001). *Making it in the "Free World": Women in Transition from Prison*. Albany, NY: SUNY Albany Press.

[24] Dodge, M. & M. Pogrebin (2001). "Collateral Costs of Imprisonment for Women: Complications of Reintegration." *The Prison Journal* 81, 1: 42-54.

[25] Petersilia, J. (2002). *Reforming Probation and Parole*. Lanham, MD: American Correctional Association, p. 129.

[26] Hughes, R. (1986). *The Fatal Shore*. New York: Vintage Books.

[27] Barnes, H. & N. Teeters (1959). *New Horizons on Criminology*, Third Edition. Englewood Cliffs, NJ: Prentice-Hall.

[28] Petersilia, J. (2002). *Reforming Probation and Parole*. Lanham, MD: American Correctional Association, p. 130.

[29] Rothman, D. (1980). *Conscience and Convenience*. Boston: Little, Brown & Co.

[30] Petersilia, J. (2002). *Reforming Probation and Parole*. Lanham, MD: American Correctional Association.

[31] Hoffman, P. (1997). "History of the Federal Parole System: Part 2 (1973-1997)." *Federal Probation* 61, 4: 49-57.

[32] Petersilia, J. (2002). *Reforming Probation and Parole*. Lanham, MD: American Correctional Association, p. 131.

[33] Petersilia, J. (2002). *Reforming Probation and Parole*. Lanham, MD: American Correctional Association, p. 135.

[34] Petersilia, J. (2002). *Reforming Probation and Parole*. Lanham, MD: American Correctional Association, p. 111.

[35] Burke, P. & M. Tonry (2006). *Successful Transition and Reentry for Safer Communities: A Call to Action for Parole*. Silver Spring, MD: Center for Effective Public Policy, p. 22.

[36] Petersilia, J. (2002). *Reforming Probation and Parole*. Lanham, MD: American Correctional Association, p. 112.

[37] Petersilia, J. (2005). "Meeting the Challenges of Prisoner Reentry." In American Correctional Association, *What Works and Why: Effective Approaches to Reentry*, pp. 175-192. Lanham, MD: American Correctional Association, p. 179.

[38] Ward, M. (2006). "Parole Rules Aren't Being Followed, Panel Says." *Austin American-Statesman*, November 15: B7.

[39] Levin, M. (2006). *The Role of Parole in Solving the Texas Prison Crowding Crisis*. Austin, TX: Texas Public Policy Foundation. Available at: www.TexasPolicy.com, p.3.

[40] Burke, P. & M. Tonry (2006). *Successful Transition and Reentry for Safer Communities: A Call to Action for Parole*. Silver Spring, MD: Center for Effective Public Policy, p. 25.

[41] Burns, R., P. Kinkade, M. Leone & S. Phillips (1999). "Perspectives on Parole: The Board Members' Viewpoint," *Federal Probation* 63, 1: 16-22.

[42] Burke, P. & M. Tonry (2006). *Successful Transition and Reentry for Safer Communities: A Call to Action for Parole*. Silver Spring, MD: Center for Effective Public Policy, p. 25.

[43] Morgan, K. & B. Smith (2005). "Victims, Punishment and Parole: The Effect of Victim Participation on Parole Hearings." *Criminology and Public Policy* 4, 2: 333-360.

[44] *Greenholtz, Chairman, Board of parole of Nebraska, et al. v. Inmates of the Nebraska Penal and Correctional Complex*, 442 U.S. 1 (1979).

[45] Note that states may "create" a right by statutory language, i.e., in *Board of Pardons et al. v. Allen et al.*, 482 U.S. 369 (1987), the use of the word "shall" in the enabling statute created a parole right which was then deemed to be a protected liberty interest.

[46] *Martinez v. California*, 444 U.S. 277 (1980).

[47] See, for example, *Mee v. Ortega*, 967 F.2d 423 (10th Cir. 1992).

[48] Jones, M. (2004). *Community Corrections*. Prospect Heights, Ill: Waveland Press.

[49] Travis, J. & J. Petersilia (2003). "Reentry Reconsidered: A New Look at an Old Question." *Crime and Delinquency* 47, 3: 3-15.

[50] Petersilia, J. (2002). *Reforming Probation and Parole*. Lanham, MD: American Correctional Association, p. 158.

[51] Reentry Council (2003). *Report of the Re-entry Policy Council*. New York: Council of State Governments. Available at: www.reentrypolicy.org., p. 362.

[52] Reentry Council (2003). *Report of the Re-Entry Policy Council*. New York: Council of State Governments. Available at: www.reentrypolicy.org., p. 360.

[53] Watson, J., A. Solomon, N. LaVigne & J. Travis (2004). *A Portrait of Prisoner Reentry in Texas*. Washington, DC: Urban Institute, p. 76.

[54] Austin, J. & T. Fabelo (2004). *The Diminishing Returns of Increased Incarceration: A Blueprint to improve Public Safety and Reduce Costs*. Washington, DC: The JFA Institute.

[55] Petersilia, J. (2002). *Reforming Probation and Parole*. Lanham, MD: American Correctional Association, p. 154.

[56] Petersilia, J. (2005). "Meeting the Challenges of Prisoner Reentry." In American Correctional Association, *What Works and Why: Effective Approaches to Reentry*, pp. 175-192. Lanham, MD: American Correctional Association, p. 178.

[57] Watson, J., A. Solomon, N. LaVigne & J. Travis (2004). *A Portrait of Prisoner Reentry in Texas*. Washington, DC: Urban Institute, p. 21.

[58] LeClair, D. & S. Guarino-Ghezzi (1991). "Does Incapacitation Guarantee Public Safety? Lessons from the Massachusetts Furlough and Prerelease Programs," *Justice Quarterly* 8, 1: 9-36.

[59] Petersilia, J. (2005). "Meeting the Challenges of Prisoner Reentry." In American Correctional Association, *What Works and Why: Effective Approaches to Reentry*, pp. 175-192. Lanham, MD: American Correctional Association, p. 176.

[60] Petersilia, J. (2005). "Meeting the Challenges of Prisoner Reentry." In American Correctional Association, *What Works and Why: Effective Approaches to Reentry*, pp. 175-192. Lanham, MD: American Correctional Association, p. 176.

[61] LaVigne, N. & V. Kachnowski (2005). *Texas Prisoners' Reflections on Returning Home*. Washington, DC: Urban Institute.

[62] Reentry Council (2003). *Report of the Re-Entry Policy Council*. New York: Council of State Governments. Available at: www.reentrypolicy.org., p. 1.

[63] Petersilia, J. (2002). *Reforming Probation and Parole*. Lanham, MD: American Correctional Association.

[64] Austin, J. (2001). "Prisoner Reentry: Current Trends, Practices and Issues." *Crime and Delinquency* 47, 3: 314-334.

[65] Petersilia, J. (2005). "Meeting the Challenges of Prisoner Reentry." In American Correctional Association, *What Works and Why: Effective Approaches to Reentry*, pp. 175-192. Lanham, MD: American Correctional Association, p. 176.

[66] Feld, B. (2003). "The Politics of Race and Juvenile Justice: The "Due Process Revolution" and the conservative reaction." *Justice Quarterly* 20, 4: 765-800, p. 791.

[67] Glaze, L. & T. Bonczar (2006). *Probation and Parole in the United States, 2005*. Washington, DC: Bureau of Justice Statistics, p. 9.

[68] Ward, M. (2006). "Parole Rules Aren't Being Followed, Panel Says." *Austin American-Statesman*, November 15: B7.

[69] Reentry Council (2003). *Report of the Re-entry Policy Council*. New York: Council of State Governments. Available at: www.reentrypolicy.org., p. 384.

[70] Reentry Council (2003). *Report of the Re-entry Policy Council*. New York: Council of State Governments. Available at: reentrypolicy.org., p. 362.

[71] LaVigne, N. & V. Kachnowski (2005). *Texas Prisoners' Reflections on Returning Home*. Washington, DC: Urban Institute.

[72] LaVigne, N. & V. Kachnowski (2005). *Texas Prisoners' Reflections on Returning Home*. Washington, DC: Urban Institute, p. 6.

[73] LaVigne, N. & V. Kachnowski (2005). *Texas Prisoners' Reflections on Returning Home*. Washington, DC: Urban Institute, p. 7.

[74] Hanrahan, K., J. Gibbs & S. Zimmerman (2005). "Parole and Revocation: Perspectives of Young Adult Offenders." *The Prison Journal* 85, 3: 251-269.

[75] Petersilia, J. (2002). *Reforming Probation and Parole*. Lanham, MD: American Correctional Association, p. 163.

[76] Petersilia, J. (2005). "Meeting the Challenges of Prisoner Reentry." In American Correctional Association, *What Works and Why: Effective Approaches to Reentry*, pp. 175-192. Lanham, MD: American Correctional Association, p. 182.

[77] 408 U.S. 471 (1972).

[78] While earlier analyses of this case concluded the court meant that two hearings were required, later writers and some lower court holdings have determined that there can be one hearing as long as all elements are present. See del Carmen, R. S. Ritter & B. Witt (2005). *Briefs of Leading Cases in Corrections*. Newark, NJ: LexisNexis/Matthew Bender, p. 176.

[79] *Young v. Harper*, 520 U.S. 143 (1997).

[80] Jones, M. (2004). *Community Corrections*. Prospect Heights, Ill: Waveland Press.

[81] *Pennsylvania Board of Probation and Parole v. Scott*, 524 U.S. 357(1998).

[82] Langan, P. & D. Levine 2002. *Recidivism of Prisoners Released in 1994*. Washington, DC: Bureau of Justice Statistics. See also Solomon, A., V. Kachnowski & A. Bhati (2005). *Does Parole Work: Analyzing the Impact of Post Prison Supervision and Rearrest Outcomes. Research Report*. Washington, DC: The Urban Institute.

[83] Burke, P. & M. Tonry (2006). *Successful Transition and Reentry for Safer Communities: A Call to Action for Parole*. Silver Spring, MD: Center for Effective Public Policy, p. 14.

[84] Reported in Reentry Council (2003). *Report of the Re-entry Policy Council*. New York: Council of State Governments. Available at: www.reentrypolicy.org., p. 391.

[85] Wilson, J. (2005). "Bad Behavior or Bad Policy? An Examination of Tennessee Release Cohorts, 1993-2001." *Criminology and Public Policy*, 4, 3: 485-519.

[86] Roy, S. (2004). "Factors Related to Success and Recidivism in a Day Reporting Center." *Criminal Justice Studies*, 17, 1: 3-17.

[87] Burke, P. & M. Tonry (2006). *Successful Transition and Reentry for Safer Communities: A Call to Action for Parole*. Silver Spring, MD: Center for Effective Public Policy, p. 15.

[88] Reentry Council (2003). *Report of the Re-entry Policy Council*. New York: Council of State Governments. Available at: www.reentrypolicy.org., p. 392.

[89] Reentry Council (2003). *Report of the Re-entry Policy Council*. New York: Council of State Governments. Available at: www.reentrypolicy.org., p. 395.

[90] Burke, P. & M. Tonry (2006). *Successful Transition and Reentry for Safer Communities: A Call to Action for Parole*. Silver Spring, MD: Center for Effective Public Policy, p. 17-18.

Chapter 15

CHAPTER OUTLINE

Looking Toward the Future: Criminal Justice in the 21st Century

What You Need to Know

★ Crime has declined but is starting to inch upward again.

★ The community has always been identified as a factor in criminal choice.

★ Social disorganization theory is not unlike the Chicago or ecological school idea that crime was localized in distressed neighborhoods.

★ Restorative justice changes the major focus of the justice system from punishment to restoring the victim to a state of wholeness.

★ Restorative justice programs include victim-offender mediation, community reparation boards, family conferences, and circle sentencing.

★ September 11, 2001, dramatically changed the governmental focus, agency structure, and laws regarding counterintelligence and protection of the public against the threat of terrorist acts.

★ A controversial element of the USA PATRIOT Act is extending the right to use roving wiretap warrants, which apply to any telephone the suspect calls.

★ The Department of Homeland Security has a budget of more than $30 billion. It includes all or part of the FBI, Customs, Border Patrol, and 19 other agencies.

What is the future of criminal justice in our country? Of course it is impossible to accurately predict what may occur in the future, but it is important to ponder the possibilities and prepare for them. In this last chapter, we will take the time to look forward. It should be clear that the criminal justice system is a massive, multifaceted, non-organization of police, courts, and corrections across 50 states and the federal government. It affects literally millions of individuals in this country. Change is unlikely to be systemic or coordinated. On the other hand, we can identify trends and the possible directions that might be taken by the many different agencies that make up the system of criminal justice.

Crime has dramatically decreased since the early 1990s—so much so that homicide rates are at 30-year lows, and all forms of personal and property crimes have decreased to levels not seen since the 1970s. Even so, it seems to be the case that citizens are not aware of this good news because media outlets tend to emphasize violent crimes disproportionately to their prevalence. Television reality "cop shows," court shows, and prime-time dramas focus on violent crimes and obscure the reality that crime may not be the major problem that people think it is.

In the last few reporting periods, we have seen a slight rise in crime, certainly in some reporting jurisdictions. This may be a troubling harbinger of things to come. One of the clear issues of the day is what to do about the 600,000 individuals released from prison each year, many of whom have been in prison since the early and mid-1980s. These individuals have served long periods of time, decades even, without any meaningful programs to help them conquer addictions and adapt to their freedom on the street. Are these individuals beginning to affect the crime rate? Perhaps a slowing economy might be why crime is now beginning a slight upward trend. Or the numbers may be simply artifacts of reporting changes. We will need to watch carefully to track whether crime rates will continue to rise.

We have, throughout this book, concentrated primarily on domestic crime and state and local responses to it. One thing that cannot be ignored since 9/11 is that the United States must prepare for future terrorist attacks. We briefly mentioned the Department of Homeland Security in an earlier chapter, but the response to terrorism must be a shared effort among all levels of law enforcement and public safety. Therefore, we come to an interesting observation.

1. TWO DIRECTIONS

In thinking about the future of the criminal justice system, or, more accurately, the various components of the *non-system* of criminal justice, it seems that an interesting juxtaposition of future trends must be considered. The first is that the system has been, for the last couple decades, moving toward, in fits and starts, a more community-oriented view of the causes of crime, prevention, and enforcement. Such things as community policing, community courts, re-entry programs, and restorative justice all have the basic theme that crime is a community problem and any solution to it must be found in the community.

Another factor, however, that has dramatically changed the criminal justice system is the threat of terrorism, and the legislative changes and executive response to it. This threat has led to a greater centralization of law enforcement, and greater federal powers to investigate and prosecute. Thus, we have two almost countervailing tendencies that will influence the future; the first would lead to decentralized, community responses to crime, and the second to increasing federalization and expanded powers of investigation.

The most monumental event of the decade was, of course, September 11, 2001, which will take its place in United States history beside such tragedies as the bombing of Pearl Harbor. The effects of this tragedy cannot be underestimated. In addition to the loss of lives, we must also consider the psychological effects of fear, the crippling costs of military efforts in Afghanistan and Iraq, and the continuing costs of protection here at home, including costs associated with TSA and the Department of Homeland Security.

The governmental response to the threat of terrorism within the boundaries of the country has dramatically reshaped the organization and mission of federal law enforcement. It has also created new questions for the courts to resolve and pitted federal courts against the executive branch in arguments regarding torture, renditions, executive privilege, civil liberties, and the security classification of government documents. Fear of crime has now been eclipsed by fear of terrorism, and new legal and ethical questions regarding the appropriate response to this threat have taken center stage in national debates.

So that brings us to an interesting paradox. We have, on the one hand, seen a renewed interest in community responses to crime, as evidenced by the popularity of restorative justice programs and a federally supported initiative to respond to the problems of re-entry of prisoners. These are examples of trends that tend to energize individual communities to deal with the issues of crime and juvenile delinquency by placing resources and the responsibility of crime prevention at the community level. Community responses are often less punitive, and require more comprehensive social responses to the problems of crime in the community.

On the other hand, we have also witnessed a series of federal responses to terrorism that centralizes resources, and promotes greater powers for the federal branch of government. Even conservative pundits are beginning to express concern at the cost of the "war on terror," as well as the expansion of federal crimes and the role of federal investigation and law enforcement in domestic crime fighting. Some argue, in fact, that the responses that have occurred after 9/11 are threatening the bedrock of state "police power" (the power of states to define and enforce most criminal laws), and even the very civil liberties that define our country.

So, in this last chapter, we will explore these disparate directions, looking at the policies and underlying philosophies and rationales of each. They seem to represent two different directions that the country can take. Some might argue they must be different because they respond to different threats.

2. THE ROLE OF THE COMMUNITY IN CRIME

There is a long history in criminology of looking at the community as criminogenic. Recall from an earlier chapter that the ecological or Chicago school of crime theory discovered that high crime rates existed in mixed zones, which are areas of the city where the functions of retail, residential, and commerce were mixed. These researchers further discovered that the **mixed zones** also were likely to display high levels of other social ills, such as alcoholism and mental illness in addition to crime. Further, indicators such as graffiti, abandoned houses, vandalism, and low home ownership characterized the zone.[1] The Chicago school approach led to 60 years of attempting to more closely describe in what way the community and/or the residents within the community influenced the individual to commit crime.

Social disorganization theory today continues this theoretical thread, and theorists such as Robert Sampson postulate that indicators of social disorganization, i.e., lack of social "capital," are also indicators of high crime.[2] A strong community can prevent criminal behavior. The following quote describes this idea:

> When multiple members of a community act for each other's benefit, an overarching sense of good will and community spirit develops. When there are patterns of such reciprocity, a sense of community capital emerges, and this capital can reap strong returns in reducing crime and establishing standards of conduct among its members. . . . even in impoverished, inner city neighborhoods, social capital can suppress criminal activity. [3]

Others, such as Robert Bursik and Harold Grasmick, also examine the informal controls on an individual that come from family, school, church, and neighborhood. They argue that formal controls, such as police, tend to undercut these more personal controls.[4]

The importance of the community on crime is recognized by such efforts as community policing. The idea behind this innovation was that the community itself needed to be involved and police officers could strengthen community resolve to conquer crime by acting as facilitators and resource mediators. Even community policing efforts become complicated, however, when attempts are made to draw the boundaries of good and bad, offender and victim, too simplistically. Some researchers note that community residents express mixed feelings toward the gang members whom the criminal justice system targets as offenders. In one sense, these youths are the problem because they create crime and scare away business development. In another sense, however, they are the community, because they are the sons and brothers of residents.[5]

Criminogenic communities have more comprehensive and pervasive social problems. Typically, the communities that offenders come from and go home to are characterized by long-standing poverty from lack of jobs and business development. Schools are sub-performing and drop-out rates are high. The residents are heavy users of government services. In fact, in a justice mapping research project in New Orleans (before Hurricane Katrina) it was found that there existed "million dollar blocks." These were areas of the city where more than a million dollars was spent incarcerating, returning, and revoking offenders from that street. Further, there is a substantial overlap between neighborhoods that are recipients of TANF (Temporary Assistance to Needy Families) and those who receive a disproportionate share of offenders (released on parole or probation).[6] Obviously, the best approach to the "crime problem" is to deal with the community's needs as a whole. For instance, all residents could benefit from revitalization efforts, and these efforts would also provide alternatives to criminal opportunities.

More generally, research is beginning to show that the huge increase in incarceration that occurred since the 1980s has not necessarily been helpful to the communities hardest hit by crime. Todd Clear and his associates found that a "**tipping effect**" occurred at high rates of imprisonment where imprisonment seemed to result in more crime in certain communities. Positive effects of incarceration included removal of problem family members and reducing the number of dangerous individuals in the community, but negative effects also occurred. In fact, there was an apparent increase of crime in the neighborhoods that experienced high incarceration rates.[7]

Further study with focus groups indicated that community members saw incarceration as both a positive and negative force in the community. Negative elements included the stigma attached to returning offenders for the offender and his or her family, the financial impact of imprisonment for both the offender and his or her family, and the difficulty of maintaining interpersonal relationships through a prison sentence. High levels of incarceration reduce the number of potentially positive role models for children, result in transient populations, and affect the ability of the community to control its members through informal and affective ties.[8]

It should be noted that one can argue that there may be a *correlation* between crime and high levels of imprisonment but it is difficult to show causation. Also, the correlation between high levels of imprisonment and low respect for formal social control agencies is also silent on directionality and so it could just as easily be that these factors lead to high imprisonment, not the other way around. In reviewing all the evidence, however, it seems that incarceration has mixed effects. It reduces crime by the removal of criminal offenders; on the other hand, if a community experiences high levels of incarceration, it increases social mobility and social disorganization, and weakens the ability of the community to utilize parochial methods of control.[9] The best policy recommendations based on the above research include limited incarceration and enriched services to the communities that experience moderate to high rates of incarceration. The community should be helped to reach a point where it can control its members through informal private means of control.

It cannot be ignored that prisoners almost always eventually get out and return to the community. Recently, there has been attention to the issue of the 600,000 prisoners who are released to the community each year. Community efforts are seen as essential in responding to the problem of huge numbers of prisoners being released. Because they will be returning to communities, these communities must be involved in efforts to help ex-offenders adapt and become productive citizens. Re-entry efforts have included job training/placement, drug treatment, and housing assistance, as these are identified as the major problems of those released from prison.

Another aspect that has been noted is that ex-offenders lose civil liberties that most of us take for granted. In most states, ex-offenders no longer have the right to vote (14 states permanently take away this right), serve on juries (31 states permanently take away this right), or possess firearms (28 states permanently take away this right). In about half of all states, ex-offenders cannot hold public office, and close to half of all states allow imprisonment to be used as a reason for permanent deprivation of parental rights.[10] You might think that these deprivations are either rightfully withheld from those who broke the law, or that the offender should have thought of this result before they committed the crime, but the opposing argument is that we want the offender to become a productive, law-abiding citizen. If he or she does so, is it fair to withhold all the rights of citizenship indefinitely?

The following quote is from the report of the Reentry Policy Council, a bi-partisan agency that brings together federal, state, and local representatives, as well as representatives from institutional corrections, community corrections and law enforcement, to address the problems of reentry for criminal offenders.

> Although the re-entry phenomenon is currently understood as a criminal justice issue, solutions to the challenges that are posed by so many people returning to their neighborhoods from prison cannot be found within the justice system alone. Instead, these solutions will require a coordinated effort among a range of actors stretching from state officials to neighborhood associations.[11]

3. RESTORATIVE JUSTICE PROGRAMS

Restorative justice programs basically change the paradigm of the justice system. Instead of finding guilt or innocence and inflicting punishment, restorative justice seeks to "restore" all individuals to a state of wholeness. While this may involve restitution to the victim or some form of compensation in response to injury or loss, the approach also takes into consideration the relative needs of the victim and offender. Community members are also involved to help resolve the issues that led to the criminal event. Restorative justice efforts, in effect, reduce the need for reentry programs because, in many cases, the offender never leaves the community. Without banishment to state prison or county jail, there is no re-entry difficulty.

Many different types of programs fall under the restorative justice umbrella, but they all have in common the idea of doing more than simply punishing the offender. The roots of restorative justice go back as far as Roman or Grecian law, based on repayment to the victim rather than punishment of the offender.[12] In the 1960s and 1970s, during the rehabilitative and reintegration era, restorative justice programs were popular and fit in with the community empowerment and grass-roots model of President Johnson's "War on Poverty." Box 15.1 presents some of the ideas of restorative justice.

BOX 15.1

Restorative Justice

★ The process of justice employs local leadership, is informal, and invites participation from community members.

★ The goal is to repair the harm done to a community member by another community member in a way that will restore the health of the community relationship.

★ The authority of the justice is through the customs and traditions accepted by all members.

Source: Schweigert, F. (2002). "Moral and Philosophical Foundations of Restorative Justice." In J. Perry (ed.), *Repairing Communities through Restorative Justice*, pp. 19-37. Lanham, MD: American Correctional Association, p. 25.

Examples of tribal justice are often used to illustrate the origins and philosophy of restorative justice. For instance, the family group sentencing conference that is used by the Maori people of New Zealand, or the Peacemaking Panel of the Skokomish tribe in North America, are examples where tribal justice is more interested in resolving and repairing the harm done by the crime than inflicting punishment on the offender. All community members are involved in the resolution and participate in the decisionmaking in these types of models.[13]

Four types of restorative justice models related to criminal justice sentencing and corrections are:

Victim-offender mediation. This is the most common and is more than 20 years old. Some programs are called Victim-Offender Reconciliation Programs or Dialog Programs. There are more than 320 programs in the United States and many more in Europe. They involve the victim and offender meeting and discussing the event and coming to an agreement about restitution and reparation. The idea is to promote healing on the part of the victim, and responsibility on the part of the offender. The program may be implemented as a diversion from prosecution or as a condition of probation. Research has found that victims are more satisfied when they have an opportunity to go through these programs (79 percent compared to 57 percent). Victims were also significantly less fearful of being victimized. Offenders were more likely to complete their restitution and recidivism was lower for those who went through mediation as compared to traditional sentencing.

Community Reparative Boards. This model has been more common in the juvenile system and has been in use since the 1920s. It re-emerged with greater popularity in the 1990s and may be called youth panels, neighborhood boards, or community diversion boards. The goals of the program are to promote citizen ownership of the sentencing process, and provide an opportunity for victims and community members to confront the offender in a constructive manner. The idea is also to reduce dependence on formal justice processing. Basically, citizens are involved in a sentencing decision and the experience is more of a dialogue between the offender and the board, who look at long-term solutions rather than retribution.

Family Group Conferencing. This type of program comes directly from the dispute resolution tradition of the Maori as described above. In fact, it was adopted into national legislation in New Zealand in 1989. A similar model is taken from the Wagga Wagga people of South Australia and uses police officials to administer the conferencing. In these models, police (or another agency) set up a family conference of the offender, victim, and the families of both, as well as others involved. The goal is to have everyone participate, to have the offender come to a greater understanding of how the crime affected others, and to allow others to help make sure that the collective decision is carried out. Participants generally report higher levels of satisfaction than those who go through traditional justice models.

Circle Sentencing. This model is an updated version of tribal justice processes of North American indigenous peoples and is very similar to the models above. The key elements are that everyone involved with the victim and offender participates. In this model, they sit in a circle and everyone gets a turn to speak. After everyone has a chance to speak, the circle decides what should be done. The goal is to promote healing, to provide the offender an opportunity to make amends, to address the underlying causes of criminal behavior, to build a sense of community, and to promote and share community values.[14]

There are some criticisms and potential problems with the restorative justice concept. Some argue that it is not an appropriate response for serious violent crimes. Some argue that victims may not want to participate, or that they may feel pressured to forgive the offender or feel "ganged up" on by the offender's family and friends.[15] Generally, however, research indicates that victims are more satisfied when the focus is on their needs and when the offender takes responsibility for and makes right the offense.

★ Exercise: In the State of . . .

Do a computer search to discover if there are any restorative justice programs in your state. If they exist, where are they? Which type of program exists?

Although restorative justice programs received a great deal of attention and even federal funding in the mid through late 1990s, after 9/11, federal dollars were shifted to other priorities. Restorative justice programs haven't gone away, but they tend to be localized and are more common with juvenile offenders than adult offenders.

4. TERRORISM AND OUR RESPONSE

Some people argue that this country was created by terrorism because the Revolutionary War began with attacks by dissidents against the established government of the king. "One man's terrorist is another's freedom fighter" is an overused phrase, but has some truth to it. Terrorist tactics have been used at various times in this nation's history by groups such as the Ku Klux Klan, which used lynching and burning to instill terror in newly freed slaves. Such tactics were revitalized during the Civil Rights movement of the 1960s. Race riots and arson have been episodic reactions by minorities in this country to the perceived oppression of the dominant majority. Even direct attempts to destabilize the government have occurred. Bolshevik terrorists attempted 38 bombings against capitalist figures such as J.P. Morgan and John D. Rockefeller in 1919, and the Weather Underground, the Symbionese Liberation Army, and the Black Panthers used armed robberies to finance their terrorism in the 1960s and 1970s, which included bombing public buildings.[16]

As terrorism has been present from the beginning of this country's history, so, too, have been government efforts to combat it. The first Alien and Sedition Acts were passed a mere 22 years after the birth of the United States in 1798. The Alien Act gave the government the right to deport those thought to be a danger to the country, and the Sedition Act gave the government the right to punish those who spoke against the government's actions. These Acts were criticized by many prominent individuals as being contrary to the First Amendment and eventually disappeared; however, the Bolshevik bombings and advocacy of communism led to the Espionage Act of 1917 and the 1918 **Sedition Act**. During the early 1900s, the United States government, fearful that Russian immigrants would import their revolution as well, had thousands arrested. Under the Sedition Act, anyone who expressed support for Communism could be arrested. Attorney General Palmer arrested 16,000 Soviet resident aliens in 1918 and 1919, and detained them without charges and without trial.

The government targeted emerging labor unions, especially the Industrial Workers of the World movement, as threats to the nation, and widespread violence occurred on both sides. The fear and official reaction to the Bolsheviks reached a pitch at the anniversary of the Russian revolution on November 7, 1919. The fear that they would begin a major assault on that day never materialized.[17]

The next chapter in the government's campaign against communism was carried out by Palmer's assistant, J. Edgar Hoover, who was appointed in 1924 and rose to prominence as director of the FBI. His continued investigation of Communists eventually led to the McCarthy hearings (House Un-American

Activities Committee) in the 1950s. Throughout the 1960s and 1970s, the FBI continued to infiltrate and investigate groups and individuals that were considered threats to the nation. At one point, Hoover had a card index of 450,000 people who were identified or suspected of having left-wing political views.[18]

It should be noted that there were seriously violent groups that did advocate and use violence, such as the Symbionese Liberation Army, who utilized kidnapping and robberies and the Black Panthers, who used armed robbery and hijacking to advance their cause. However, the focus of investigations carried out by the government also included those who, in hindsight, did not pose a danger to the government, such as Martin Luther King Jr., Hollywood actors who espoused liberal views, and student and community groups that advocated nonviolent means of protest.

It was the abuses of the powers granted by anti-terrorist legislation, as well as the misuse of government intelligence, by those in the Nixon administration, that led to Congress dramatically curtailing the powers of federal law enforcement in the 1970s. The Senate created the Select Committee on Intelligence in 1976, and strengthened the Freedom of Information Act. In 1978 the Foreign Intelligence Surveillance Act (FISA) was created and mandated procedures for requesting authorization for surveillance. A secret court was created (the Foreign Intelligence Surveillance Court), which consisted of seven federal district court judges appointed by the Supreme Court's Chief Justice. Federal law enforcement officers were required to obtain permission from the court to conduct surveillance. They had to show that their target was an agent of a foreign power and information was in furtherance of counterintelligence. FISA originally approved only electronic eavesdropping and wiretapping, but was amended in 1994 to include covert physical entries, and later in 1998 to permit pen/trap orders and business records.[19]

Typical search warrants are obtained only on a showing of probable cause that the target of the search will be found in the location specified, and that it is evidence or an instrumentality of a crime. On the other hand, FISA approval may be obtained merely upon a showing that the target is a foreign power or agent and the search is relevant to a counterintelligence investigation. If the target is a U.S. citizen, there must be probable cause that their activities may involve espionage.[20]

After the Cold War ended, the United States shifted its attention to right-wing radical groups in this country who advocated violent means to oppose the government and, to a lesser extent, international groups, such as the PLO. Hamas and Hezbollah later became targets after they claimed responsibility for violent attacks and spoke out against the United States. Through the 1980s and 1990s, the activities and rhetoric of such groups became more and more anti-American and many analysts argued that the United States, in addition to Israel, was or would become a central target of terrorist actions.

The government did not sit idle, of course. President Reagan utilized National Security Decision Directives rather than seeking public laws from Congress to craft and employ a government response to the growing international threats. These directives established a hierarchy of authority regarding response to threats via aviation and kidnapping. Public Laws were also passed, including:

★ Act to Combat International Terrorism (1984), which sought international cooperation

★ Public Law 99-83 (1985), which allowed funding to be cut off to countries that supported terrorism

★ Omnibus Diplomatic Security and Antiterrorism Act (1986), which expanded the jurisdiction of the FBI to overseas when investigating acts of terrorism against U.S. citizens abroad or at home [21]

Two of the most important pre-9/11 anti-terrorist laws were passed during the Clinton administration. The Omnibus Counterterrorism Act of 1995 greatly expanded the role of the federal government over local and state law enforcement in investigating and prosecuting acts of terrorism, such as bombings, within the boundaries of the United States, and also expanded the U.S. jurisdiction overseas when committed against U.S. embassies. It also criminalized fundraising for groups defined as terrorist. It expanded federal law enforcement authority to use "pen registers" and "trap and trace" devices, which track telephone calls. It also created the power of federal law enforcement to seek a wide range of personal and business documents with "national security letters," rather than warrants, when investigating terrorism.

This Act was replaced by the Anti-Terrorism and Effective Death Penalty Act of 1996, which incorporated most of the provisions discussed above, and added others, such as expanding the authority of INS to deport accused terrorists and other resident aliens, and increasing the penalties for such crimes. The other part of the Act applied to all offenders, and changed habeas corpus protections, eliminating multiple appeals and removing legal barriers to executions.[22]

Prior to 9/11, few of us were aware of this nation's counter-terrorism laws and few citizens gave serious thought to the threat of terrorism. There were prior events that should have alerted us to the possibility of a major attack: the 1993 bombing of the World Trade Center, the attacks on the USS Cole and the attacks on U.S. embassies in Africa, and the stated aim of Osama Bin Laden to "cut off the head of the snake," meaning the United States and, more specifically, United States' economic dominance in the world. Generally, however, the FBI was largely concerned with domestic terrorism. This focus was not misplaced given the tragedy of the Oklahoma City bombing by Timothy McVeigh and Terry Nichols and the presence of other radical groups that still exist and have expressed and indicated a willingness to use violence to advance their goals.

In the aftermath of the terrorist attacks on September 11, 2001, Congress enacted the USA PATRIOT Act to combat terrorism and created the Homeland Security Council, and then later the Department of Homeland Security. These two actions have had tremendous consequences for the organization and powers of investigative and justice agencies in the United States. We will discuss the USA PATRIOT Act first and then the Department of Homeland Security.

4.1 USA PATRIOT Act

On October 11, 2001, the 107th Congress enacted Public Law 107-56, which is titled "Uniting and Strengthening America by Providing Appropriate Tools Required to Intercept and Obstruct Terrorism Act." This Act is known as the **USA PATRIOT Act** of 2001. The purpose of the Act is "to deter and punish terrorist acts in the United States and around the world, to enhance law enforcement investigatory tools, and for other purposes." What many people don't realize is that there were already counter-terrorism laws in existence. As mentioned above, the 1996 Anti-Terrorism Act was signed by President Clinton and included most of the provisions of the USA PATRIOT Act. What was added to the USA PATRIOT Act were provisions that were expressly rejected by Congress in the earlier law. The numerous sections of the Act are included under 10 titles as set out in Box 15.2.

Title VIII of the Patriot Act, "Strengthening the Criminal Laws against Terrorism" revised Chapter 113B, titled "Terrorism" in the United States Code. The earlier Chapter included criminal penalties for a series of acts relating to terrorism, including: Use of Weapons of Mass Destruction, Acts of Terrorism Transcending National Boundaries, Financial Transactions, Providing Material to Terrorists, and Providing Material Support or Resources to Designated Foreign Terrorist Organizations.

BOX 15.2

USA PATRIOT Act

Title I — ENHANCING DOMESTIC SECURITY AGAINST TERRORISM
- ★ Amends Posse Comitatus Act
- ★ Enhances President's power to confiscate property and assets

Title II — ENHANCED SURVEILLANCE PROCEDURES
- ★ Eliminated restrictions on and expanded federal surveillance practices
- ★ Eliminated barrier between domestic and international investigations
- ★ Expanded use of pen register and trap-and-trace devices
- ★ Relaxed rules on obtaining warrants

Title III — INTERNATIONAL MONEY LAUNDERING ABATEMENT AND ANTITERRORIST FINANCING ACT OF 2001
- ★ Required banks to create anti-laundering procedures and audit functions
- ★ Expanded reporting mechanisms for suspicious transactions

Title IV — PROTECTING THE BORDER
- ★ Increased the number of border security agents
- ★ Improved monitoring capabilities

BOX 15.2 - *continued*

Title V — REMOVING OBSTACLES TO INVESTIGATING TERRORISM

★ Created domestic rewards for information leading to terrorist capture

★ Relaxed rules of no communication between domestic crime and international investigations of terrorism

★ Relaxed requirements for obtaining National Security Letters from "specific and articulable evidence" to "relevant"

★ Removed any rights of terrorists to have privacy over DNA or records

Title VI — PROVIDING FOR VICTIMS OF TERRORISM, PUBLIC SAFETY OFFICERS, AND THEIR FAMILIES

★ Expedited processes for obtaining aid for victims and their families

Title VII — INCREASED INFORMATION SHARING FOR CRITICAL INFRASTRUCTURE PROTECTION

★ Expanded the eligible participants in federal grants for information sharing

Title VIII — STRENGTHENING THE CRIMINAL LAWS AGAINST TERRORISM

★ Included acts of terrorism and assisting terrorists in the federal criminal code

★ Criminalized the act of providing funds to terrorist organizations

★ Removed statute of limitations for some crimes

★ Further delineated cybercrimes

Title IX — IMPROVED INTELLIGENCE

★ Restated removal of the "wall" between investigations of international terrorists and domestic criminals

★ Set priorities for national intelligence mission and policies

Title X — MISCELLANEOUS

★ Defined critical infrastructure components

★ Addressed fraudulent charitable solicitations

★ Prohibited anyone involved in money laundering from entering the country

Title 18 U.S.C. § 2331, as it existed prior to the PATRIOT Act, defined international terrorism as activities that "involve violent acts or acts dangerous to human life that are a violation of the criminal laws of the United States or of any State, or that would be a criminal violation if committed within the jurisdiction of the United States or of any State" and that appear to be intended to do one or more of the following:

(i) to intimidate or coerce a civilian population;

(ii) to influence the policy of a government by intimidation or coercion; or

(iii) to affect the conduct of a government by assassination or kidnapping; and

(C) occur primarily outside the territorial jurisdiction of the United States, or transcend national boundaries in terms of the means by which they are accomplished, the persons they appear intended to intimidate or coerce, or the locale in which their perpetrators operate or seek asylum;

The PATRIOT Act amended § 2331 of Title 18 to include "by mass destruction, assassination or kidnapping" as one of the acts that constitutes terrorism. In addition, "domestic terrorism" was included and defined as those acts "dangerous to human life that are a violation of the criminal laws of United States or of any State and that appear to be intended to do one of the following:

(i) to intimidate or coerce a civilian population;

(ii) to influence the policy of a government by intimidation or coercion; or

(iii) to affect the policy of a government by mass destruction, assassination, or kidnapping; and

(C) occur primarily within the territorial jurisdiction of the United States.

Section 2332b is titled "Acts of Terrorism Transcending National Boundaries." This section expanded the concept of terrorism to include the actions of individuals who attack Americans outside of the boundaries of the United States. This expansion allowed for the prosecution of John Phillip Walker Lindh, who was charged under this Act with conspiracy to murder nationals of the United States, including American military personnel and other government employees serving in Afghanistan. He was not convicted of violating the statute, but was found guilty of other offenses.[23]

Title 18 U.S.C. § 2339A, "Providing Material Support to Terrorists" provides that whoever, within the United States, provides material support or resources or conceals or disguises the nature, location, source, or ownership of material support or resources, knowing or intending that they are to be used in preparation for carrying out a violation of the sections indicated, or in preparation for, or in carrying out, the concealment or escape from the commission of such violations, shall be fined under this title, imprisoned not more than 10 years, or both. This section was amended by the USA PATRIOT Act by striking out "within the United States" and by adding sections of the law covered by the Act. The effect of deleting "within the United States" makes the provisions enforceable when the acts described occur outside the United States.

Title 18 U.S.C. § 2339B, "Providing Material Support or Resources to Designated Foreign Terrorist Organizations" was amended in part by the PATRIOT Act to include the idea that foreign terrorist organizations were defined by the federal government, specifically the President, and an individual who contributed money to such an organization for its charitable activities would still be guilty of violating the law and subject to a long term of imprisonment.

The other elements of the PATRIOT Act that have been controversial are those that expand federal powers of investigation. Title II, "Enhanced Surveillance Procedures," substantially changed the provisions of the FISA described earlier. Specifically, the Act lowered the standard required to obtain permission to use surveillance against suspects; roving wiretaps were authorized that allowed agents to tap any phone the suspect might use; further, pen registers were allowed that followed any phone number called by the suspect. The PATRIOT Act also authorizes law enforcement agencies charged with investigating terrorism to share investigative information with domestic law enforcement investigators and vice versa.

In summary, some of the provisions that are most controversial include:

★ Expanding the range of crimes trackable by electronic surveillance

★ Allowing the use of roving wiretaps to track any phone a suspect might use

★ Allowing the "sneak and peek" search (not notifying suspects of searches)

★ Allowing federal warrants to search records with less than probable cause

★ Lowering barriers of information sharing between domestic and international investigations

★ Creating new tools for investigating money laundering (by requiring banks to file reports on suspicious behaviors).

On March 7, 2006, Congress approved the renewal of the USA PATRIOT Act. Three provisions of the Act will be reviewed in four years, the other provisions of the Act have been made permanent. The bill created a "National Security Division" in the Department of Justice. It continued the "roving wiretap" provision of the USA PATRIOT Act, as well as the power of federal officials to access library, business, and medical records without probable cause.[24]

Generally, the public has been supportive of the USA PATRIOT Act. In 2003, only 28 percent of those polled believed that it gave the government too much power over individual liberties, and 51 percent believed that people had to give up some individual freedom to fight terrorism.[25]

4.2 The Department of Homeland Security

Nine days after 9/11, President Bush created the Homeland Security Council and a cabinet-level position was created called the Homeland Security Advisor, with Tom Ridge appointed to fill the position. Then, in March 2003, the Department of Homeland Security was created with the mission to prevent terrorist attacks within the United States and to minimize damages from any attacks. The Department of Homeland Security consolidated 22 federal agencies and more than 180,000 federal employees under one umbrella agency. It had a budget of $30 billion in 2005 and $31.4 billion in 2006.[26]

The major impetus for the agency was 9/11 and the finding that one of the reasons the terrorists were able to accomplish their goal was poor communication among the FBI, the CIA, and the FAA. For instance, while the CIA knew that two of the hijackers had attended Al Qaeda meetings in the Middle East, the FBI knew (or at least a field office knew) that several of the hijackers were acting suspiciously by taking flying lessons. Together, those bits of information might have been enough to prevent the disaster.[27]

While the CIA is not one of the agencies that has been merged into the Department of Homeland Security, the idea of a national intelligence center is at the heart of the effort, and the CIA director is no longer the titular head of the U.S. intelligence function, as that role has shifted to the Department of Homeland Security. The Immigration and Naturalization Service was dismantled and the functions distributed to two agencies, U.S. Immigration and Customs Enforcement (ICE), and the U.S. Customs and Border Protection Agency, which also subsumed and redistributed the functions of the Border Patrol and U.S. Customs. The Customs and Border Protection Agency has about 40,000 employees; together, the two agencies employ 55,000 people.

We have all felt the effects of the nation's efforts to prevent terrorism. Travelers endure searches and a constant revision of rules concerning what can be carried onto airplanes. The national threat alert system is a routine part of news broadcasts, although whether people pay any attention to them is another matter. The vigilant efforts have met with success because there has not been a single successful terrorist incident within the borders of the country. Since 2001, nearly 200 suspected terrorists or associates have been charged with crimes and, according to authorities, 100 terrorist plots disrupted.[28]

4.3 Other Responses to Terrorism

In addition to the PATRIOT Act and the creation of the Department of Homeland Security, the United States has been involved in other actions in response to the threat of terrorism. The war in Iraq is beyond the scope of this book, but some of the controversial decisions of the Bush administration are extremely relevant to the system of criminal justice because they illustrate the centrality of law in our lives. Issues such as detaining "enemy combatants," limiting habeas corpus, the use of torture during interrogation, and conducting wiretaps without court orders are legal issues, and our earlier discussion of due process is directly relevant.

When the United States is engaged in war, and soldiers are captured on the battlefield, the Geneva Convention (1864/1949) specifies how they should be treated. The Convention, which the United States joined, dictates that no ordinary soldier should be tried and punished for fighting, as long as he had not committed war crimes, as defined by treaty and convention. Further, certain minimum standards exist for the care of prisoners of war, and they are supposed to be protected from interrogation, other than the information of name, rank, and serial number.

President Bush signed an Executive Order shortly after the invasion of Afghanistan that defined those captured as "enemy combatants" rather than soldiers. As such, they were said to be outside the protections of the Geneva Convention. Eventually, 680 "enemy combatants" were transported to Guantanamo Bay, Cuba, and held in a military installation there, without charges, without access to attorneys, and without any constitutional or legally recognized protections. The use of the "enemy combatant" status had not been used since World War II, when it was applied to six German spies who entered the United States illegally to conduct sabotage. The Bush Administration's position has been that the individuals held in Guantánamo were not captured in a normal war and they are not soldiers in the traditional sense, therefore the protections of the Geneva Convention do not apply, including the protection against interrogation (and the use of coercive and torture-like tactics) to obtain information.

Opponents argue that the Executive Order places limitless power in the President to define anyone as an unlawful combatant outside the oversight of any other body, including the Supreme Court. In an earlier case, the Supreme Court held that holding detainees without access to federal courts was illegal according to current law; however, the justices indicated that Congress could enact a new law that would allow such action. In response, Congress passed the Military Commissions Act, which stripped habeas corpus protections from detainees and subjected them to a military tribunal rather than due process via the courts. The writ of **habeas corpus** is an ancient due process right that protects individuals from the power of the government to hold them unlawfully or unfairly. Amidst a firestorm of controversy, the Supreme Court declined to hear the case that challenged this provision of the Act. However, in late June, 2007, the Supreme Court reversed itself and decided to hear the case, which is scheduled to be heard as early as December of 2007.[29]

In the meantime, less than half of the detainees are still being held. Many of them have been released to their home countries. Some are now suing the United States for illegal detention and torture in international courts.[30] The administration's position was that enemy combatants were not subject to the protections of the Geneva Convention and there have been news reports of the use of extreme interrogation tactics at Guantanamo, as well as at the infamous Abu Ghraib prison in Iraq. Opponents argue that by ignoring the mandates of the Geneva Convention, American prisoners have less protection from enemy forces. For instance, presidential contender John McCain, himself a prisoner of war and victim of torture during the Vietnam War, was a staunch opponent of the Bush Administration's attempt to short-circuit Congress's condemnation of torture tactics. These issues illustrate differences between what some consider legally and ethically appropriate in war against our enemies, and what is legally and ethically appropriate against American citizens. Yet it was inevitable that some American citizens would also become identified as participating in terrorist actions.

The definition of enemy combatants was later extended to American citizens fighting against coalition forces in Afghanistan and Iraq. José Padilla is an American citizen who was arrested on American soil as an enemy combatant.

In 2002, shortly after he was arrested at O'Hare Airport under a material witness warrant, he was transferred to a military base under a presidential order that he be declared an enemy combatant. Governmental authorities alleged that he was instrumental in a plot to explode a "dirty bomb" in this country. What they did know was that he had probably been in a terrorist training camp in Pakistan or Afghanistan. Advocates argued that he could not be considered an enemy combatant because he was an American citizen, and these advocates fought to restrict the ability of the government to use the enemy combatant status against citizens who were not members of foreign armies. The Supreme Court sent the case back for technical reasons and, after it had been through the federal appellate process again, declined to issue a writ of certiorari. However, before it was scheduled for a final appeal, the government asked for and received permission to remove the case from the military tribunal system to a federal district court in Miami. After being tried in a civilian federal court, on August 16, 2007, after being held for about five years, Padilla was convicted of all charges, including conspiracy to murder, kidnap, and maim U.S. citizens, and conspiracy to provide material support for terrorists. The government had dropped all the other charges.

Proponents of governmental actions argue that the U.S. government has every right to provide a different type of due process to those accused of being terrorists and that military tribunals are an acceptable alternative to the court system. They argue that civilian courts are unable to hear cases involving terrorists because juries might feel intimidated, that governmental security prohibits the exposure of much of the evidence relied upon, and that it is too difficult to try such cases with the evidence and procedural rules of such courts. On the other hand, opponents argue that American citizens should never be held without access to the courts and that many citizens could be labeled as enemy combatants, given the vagueness of the term.

In 2006, a controversy arose after it was revealed that federal officers had been using wiretaps without warrants. A Presidential Order signed in 2002 allowed the National Security Agency to monitor international telephone calls and international e-mail messages of thousands of people inside the United States without first obtaining a warrant. The concern expressed by opponents of the practice is that the National Security Agency has traditionally been involved in investigations external to the borders of the United States and that the secret court (Foreign Intelligence Surveillance Court) has hardly ever turned down a government request for a warrant when asked for one. The 1978 law that created the court has been interpreted to bar all domestic wiretapping, even for national security, unless it is sanctioned by a warrant, and the secret court was created to grant such warrants. On the other hand, the administration's position is that Congress authorized the President to take any and all steps required to combat terrorism in the wake of 9/11.[31] This issue remains unresolved.

The process of **rendition** is when federal agents find, detain, and carry away suspected terrorists in other countries without the country's approval or permission and against their sovereign laws. The United States argues that it has the jurisdiction to do so as a protection for its own security. Other countries argue that such actions are simply criminal. There are outstanding warrants in Italy against a CIA Bureau Chief and several agents for the rendition of an Italian citizen; Italy defined such action as kidnapping. Renditions are also associated with **torture-by-proxy**, the practice of the United States to hand over suspects to governments that use torture methods condemned by international treaties that the United States has signed. While some argue that extraordinary threats call for extraordinary methods; others argue that the United States is very quickly losing international support and by flouting the criminal laws of other countries, it encourages lawlessness and may be sowing the seeds of new terrorists by these actions.

4.4 State and Local Law Enforcement

Local law enforcement has obviously been greatly affected by the challenge of terrorism. As we all know, the first responders to a terrorist attack such as 9/11 are local and state public servants. Firefighters and police officers were the first to respond to the attacks on the World Trade Towers and the Oklahoma City federal building, and among those who died.

Since 9/11, more resources have been directed to **first responder training.** This type of training gives law enforcement officers the skills to approach, engage, and coordinate responses to major threats, such as terrorist actions. Local police, especially those in major metropolitan areas, must assume that they will be first responders when targets of terrorist attacks are located in their city. Bridges, buildings, schools, transportation, sports complexes, other venues where there are large crowds, and nuclear reactors and power plants are the likely targets of terrorists. Actually, there are a wide range of targets that might be vulnerable to terrorist attacks. In addition to those already mentioned, the water supplies of major cities can be contaminated with toxic agents, the banking industry can be immobilized by computers, the nation's ports can be blocked with explosions, or the nation's oil and gas supplies can be sabotaged—bringing to a standstill industry, commerce, and basic services. Federal agents are unable to protect all these targets. Police are the first line of defense, both in terms of preventive observation and surveillance, as well as response and intervention.

Narco-terrorism refers to the pattern of terrorist groups to use narcotics to fund their activities. Since 9/11, several major drug raids have uncovered ties between drug dealers and terrorist groups, such as Hezbollah. Opium from Afghanistan, although condemned by the Taliban, is now believed to be one of the largest sources of funding for Al Qaeda. It is clear that local drug investigations may end up becoming investigations of international terrorists. One of the biggest challenges, in fact, is to improve the communication between local law enforcement intelligence and federal Homeland Security personnel. Local law enforcement officials complain that the communication pattern tends to go one way only when they are expected to collect intelligence for federal agencies, but are not informed of threats in their jurisdiction. The lack of communication between the CIA and the FBI has been widely cited as one of the reasons that the 9/11 plot was not discovered and prevented, but the wider problem is the complete lack of any coordinated information sharing among the 20,000 law enforcement agencies and the Department of Homeland Security.

State and local law enforcement are now receiving more resources to address these new responsibilities. For instance, civilian analysts may be employed by state and metropolitan police agencies. These analysts track and analyze information that might lead to uncovering terrorist plots. Joint task forces between local and federal agents have also been funded. State anti-terrorism agencies have also been created to coordinate local law enforcement agencies in the state.

It is clear that, despite the importance of state and local law enforcement in preventing future terrorism, at present they may not have the training or resources to be as effective as they might be. Their arsenal of weapons may not even match that of a well-armed militia group, the surveillance equipment may be inadequate to monitor suspected terrorists, and their communication networks may be deficient. Further, local officers may not be trained to investigate even domestic cybercrime, much less terrorists who use cybertactics. Further, local agencies may not have the expertise to investigate, or training, to recognize biological threats.

Hurricane Katrina was a natural disaster, but many point to this as an example of how poorly prepared the United States is when responding to massive events such as 9/11 or a hurricane that devastates a major city. FEMA is the federal agency that is charged with responding to disasters of this magnitude and, many argue, the weaknesses of the agency were apparent. Local law enforcement did not escape criticism either and the event pointed out that more training and operational procedures are necessary to prevent the panic and disorganization that characterized the aftermath of Katrina.

Local law enforcement has also been faced with difficult decisions in balancing their investigative activities against individual liberties. Federal law enforcement has sometimes taken aggressive actions in response to the threat of terrorism, especially in regard to Muslim residents and individuals of Middle Eastern descent. Immediately after 9/11, more than 5,000 resident aliens were detained without charges. Many were subsequently deported for minor immigration violations. Those who were released alleged that they were subject to illegal detention and abuse during their imprisonment. The FBI also asked local law enforcement agencies to conduct surveillance and/or question Muslims and foreign residents without any reason other than their nationality or religion. The Portland, Oregon, Police Department gained notoriety when they refused the FBI's request that they conduct interviews with all foreign students in the area. Portland police supervisors thought that they had no authority to do so because the FBI did not articulate any reasonable suspicion, the questions were in areas that were constitutionally protected, such as their religion, and did not relate to criminal matters.[32]

Racial profiling was held to be unconstitutional when it is used as the only element in a decision to stop a minority as a suspect in drug crimes. After 9/11, however, racial profiling of Middle Eastern-looking men was used by airline employees, federal agents, and local law enforcement officers, and continues to lead to greater scrutiny of this group of travelers. Federal guidelines clearly condemn the use of racial profiling *except* for investigations involving terrorism or national security.[33]

Another area of controversy between federal and local law enforcement is the enforcement of immigration laws. Some cities and their police departments have refused to notify federal authorities when they may have reason to believe victims or witnesses of crimes are violators of immigration laws. Police departments that refuse to be the enforcers of federal laws argue that their role is domestic and involves only local security and crime fighting. These so-called sanctuary cities basically respond to crime victims or criminals, for that matter, without regard to any suspicion that the individual is an illegal alien. One assumes that even those departments, however, will cooperate with DHS authorities when the individual who comes to their attention may be even peripherally involved with others who may be terrorists. The fact is that immigration control is one of the most critical areas of protecting this nation from terrorists.

In these examples, as well as many others, it is clear that local law enforcement is a vital element in protecting the United States against terrorism. The legal issues involved when balancing due process and civil liberties against security are difficult and, ultimately, affect us all.

5. CONCLUSION

In this chapter we have examined the concept of community. Criminology has long identified the community as a crucial element in crime causation. In our response to crime, we have swung back and forth between banishment and involving the community in correctional responses. Early forms of parole and probation were based on a belief that the offender should be in the community if at all possible. Older forms of justice involved the community in developing the response to offenders that would take into account the needs of the offender, the victim, and the community. Today these programs are known as restorative justice.

There are such things as criminogenic communities—those where social capital is weak and the community is unable to utilize private and parochial controls on its members. These communities have high rates of incarceration, but also have high rates of poverty and a disproportional use of governmental services, such as TANF. Because offenders will return to these same communities while on parole, probation, or diversion programs, it is essential to consider the community and not just the offender in any response to crime.

Ironically, just as restorative justice efforts picked up momentum, we had a far greater threat to our national peace of mind than crime. The threat of terrorism has led to a massive restructuring of the federal investigative and justice agencies. State and local law enforcement have also responded, and funding priorities, training, and the mission of local law enforcement have changed.

Terrorists are thought of as outside the community and, certainly, the Middle Eastern men who hijacked and crashed the airplanes on 9/11 can be considered outsiders in very fundamental ways.

On the other hand, it is important to remember that there is also the threat of domestic terrorists, and these individuals were born and raised in the communities of the South, the Northwest, and other regions of the country. They grew up and lived in our communities and, for very specific reasons, decided that violence was an appropriate and acceptable response to their needs, in much the same way that an armed robber or a hired killer decides that violence is an acceptable solution. Even the Middle Eastern men who were "sleepers" and came from other countries spent years in this country, even raising families here. To what extent did the community affect them?

José Padilla, the citizen who was accused of being an enemy combatant, came from a poor Puerto Rican immigrant family. He was involved with gangs and had been in trouble with the criminal justice system since his youth. In fact, it is believed that he converted to Islam in prison. So we come full circle. We see that the challenge of responding to the threat of terrorism is not unrelated to the challenge of responding to crime. It is not difficult to imagine that the threat of future terrorism may lie within our own cities and communities. Poor and disenfranchised citizens who do not believe that the great wealth and opportunities that exist in this country are available to them are prime subjects for indoctrination by those spouting anti-American rhetoric. An individual like José Padilla might, in a previous decade, have spent his life in and out of prison for "ordinary" crimes. Instead, he felt the need to travel to the Middle East to join a group committed to this country's destruction. How many more Padillas exist in the tenements, streets, lockups, and prisons of this country? What methods will we approve to prevent them from hurting us? Is it possible that strengthening communities, meeting the needs of victims and offenders, scrupulously adhering to the law and ideals of due process, and making it clear that everyone is a valued part of the community, regardless of what they have done, might help to prevent terrorists as well as criminals? In the twenty-first century, the criminal justice system will most probably be dealing with the prevention of terrorism as well as crime.

REVIEW QUESTIONS

1. Discuss some of the programs or approaches that indicate the importance of community in the prevention of crime.

2. What is restorative justice and what are the principles behind it?

3. What are the four types of restorative justice sentencing programs?

4. What earlier examples of terrorism took place in this country and provide examples of the government's response?

5. What are the major controversial elements of the USA PATRIOT Act?

6. What is the FISA?

7. What major counter-intelligence agency is not part of the Department of Homeland Security? What agencies do fall under DHS?

8. What is the argument concerning the "enemy combatants" housed in Guantánamo Bay?

9. What methods/actions of government in response to terrorism possibly challenge the concept of due process?

10. Why might "ordinary" crime prevention efforts also respond to the threat of terrorism?

VOCABULARY

habeas corpus – an ancient due process right that protects individuals from the power of the government to hold them unlawfully or unfairly

mixed zones – areas of a city where the functions of retail, residential, and commerce were mixed; these zones have high crime

Sedition Act – made it illegal for anyone to express support for Communism or other enemies of the country

social disorganization theory – idea that indicators of social disorganization, i.e., lack of social "capital," are also indicators of high crime

rendition – the practice of finding, detaining, and carrying away suspected terrorists in other countries without the country's approval or permission and against their sovereign laws

tipping effect (of imprisonment) – while some imprisonment reduces crime in a community, at a certain level, imprisonment seems to result in more crime in certain communities

torture-by-proxy – the practice of the United States to hand over suspects to governments that use torture methods condemned by international treaties that the United States has signed

USA PATRIOT Act of 2001 – The purpose of the Act is "to deter and punish terrorist acts in the United States and around the world, to enhance law enforcement investigatory tools, and for other purposes."

FOR FURTHER READING

Bursik, Robert and Harold Grasmick (1993). *Neighborhoods and Crime: The Dimensions of Effective Community Control*. New York: Lexington.

Cole, David and James Dempsey (2002). *Terrorism and the Constitution*. New York: The Free Press.

Fagin, James (2006). *When Terrorism Strikes Home: Defending the United States*. Boston, MA: Allyn and Bacon.

Perry, John (ed.) (2002). *Repairing Communities Through Restorative Justice*. Lanham, MD: American Correctional Association.

Ward, Richard H., Kathleen L. Kiernan, and Daniel Mabrey (2006). *Homeland Security: An Introduction*. Newark, NJ: LexisNexis/Matthew Bender.

---

[1] See, for instance, Shaw, C. & H. McKay (1942). *Juvenile Delinquency and Urban Areas*. Chicago: University of Chicago Press.

[2] See, for instance, Sampson. R. (1988). "Local Friendship Ties and Community Attachment in Mass Society: A Multilevel Systemic Model." *American Sociological Review* 53: 766-779. Sampson, R. & W. Groves (1989). "Community Structure and Crime: Testing Social-Disorganization Theory." *American Journal of Sociology* 94: 774-802.

[3] Carey, M. (2005). "Social Learning, Social Capital, and Correctional Theories: Seeking an Integrated Model." In American Correctional Association, *What Works and Why: Effective Approaches to Reentry*, pp. 1-33. Lanham, MD: American Correctional Association, p. 9.

[4] Bursik, R. & H. Grasmick (1993). *Neighborhoods and Crime: The Dimensions of Effective Community Control*. New York: Lexington Books.

[5] Zatz, M. & E. Portillos (2000). "Voices from the Barrio: Chicano Gangs, Families, and Communities." *Criminology* 38, 2: 369-401.

[6] Reentry Policy Council (2005). "An Explanation of Justice Mapping: Three Examples." Retrieved 12/30/05 from: www.reentrypolicy.org/report/justice-mapping.php.

[7] Clear, T., D. Rose & J. Ryder (2001). "Incarceration and the Community: The Problem of Removing and Returning Offenders." *Crime and Delinquency* 47, 3: 335-351; Clear, T., D. Rose, E. Waring & K. Scully (2003). "Coercive Mobility and Crime: A Preliminary Examination of Concentrated Incarceration and Social Disorganization." *Justice Quarterly* 20, 1: 33-64.

[8] Clear, T., D. Rose & J. Ryder (2001). "Incarceration and the Community: The Problem of Removing and Returning Offenders." *Crime and Delinquency* 47, 3: 335-351.

[9] Lynch, J. & W. Sabol (2004). "Assessing the Effects of Mass Incarceration on Informal Social Control in Communities." *Criminology and Public Policy* 3, 2: 267-294.

[10] Hemmens, C. (2001). "The Collateral Consequences of Conviction," *Perspectives* 25, 1: 12-13.

[11] Reentry Policy Council (2005). "An Explanation of Justice Mapping: Three Examples." Retrieved 12/30/05 from: www.reentrypolicy.org/report/justice-mapping.php.

[12] Schweigert, F. (2002). "Moral and Philosophical Foundations of Restorative Justice," In J. Perry (ed.), *Repairing Communities through Restorative Justice*, pp. 19-37. Lanham, MD: American Correctional Association, p. 21.

[13] Schweigert, F. (2002) "Moral and Philosophical Foundations of Restorative Justice," In J. Perry (ed.), *Repairing Communities through Restorative Justice*, pp. 19-37. Lanham, MD: American Correctional Association, p. 28.

[14] Braithwaite, J. (2002). "Linking Crime Prevention to Restorative Justice." In J. Perry (ed.), *Repairing Communities through Restorative Justice*, pp. 55-66. Lanham, MD: American Correctional Association.

[15] Braithwaite, J. (2002). "Linking Crime Prevention to Restorative Justice." In J. Perry (ed.), *Repairing Communities through Restorative Justice*, pp. 55-66. Lanham, MD: American Correctional Association, p. 85.

[16] Fagin, J.(2006). *When Terrorism Strikes Home: Defending the United States*. Boston: Allyn and Bacon.

[17] Fagin, J. (2006). *When Terrorism Strikes Home: Defending the United States*. Boston: Allyn and Bacon, p. 39.

[18] Fagin, J. (2006). *When Terrorism Strikes Home: Defending the United States.* Boston: Allyn and Bacon, p. 51.

[19] Cole, D. & J. Dempsey (2002). *Terrorism and the Constitution.* New York: Free Press.

[20] Ward, R., K. Kiernan, & D. Mabrey (2006). *Homeland Security: An Introduction.* Newark, NJ: LexisNexis/Matthew Bender, p. 254.

[21] Fagin, J. (2006). *When Terrorism Strikes Home: Defending the United States.* Boston: Allyn and Bacon, p. 57.

[22] Fagin, J. (2006). *When Terrorism Strikes Home: Defending the United States.* Boston: Allyn and Bacon, p. 62.

[23] *United States v. Lindh*, 227 F. Supp. 2d 565 (E.D. Va. 2002).

[24] Cable News Network. Retrieved 7/4/06 from: www.cnn.com/2006/POLITICS/03/07/patriot.act/.

[25] Cited in Fagin, J. (2006). *When Terrorism Strikes Home: Defending the United States.* Boston, MA: Allyn and Bacon, p. 77.

[26] Ward, R., K. Kiernan, & D. Mabrey (2006). *Homeland Security: An Introduction.* Newark, NJ: LexisNexis/Matthew Bender, p. 68.

[27] Ward, R., K. Kiernan, & D. Mabrey (2006). *Homeland Security: An Introduction.* Newark, NJ: LexisNexis/Matthew Bender.

[28] Cited in Fagin, J. (2006). *When Terrorism Strikes Home: Defending the United States.* Boston, MA: Allyn and Bacon, p. 127.

[29] Hawke, A. (2007). *Primer: Guantanamo Detainees' Rights.* National Public Radio. Retrieved 8/25/07 from: http://www.npr.org/templates/story/story.php?storyID=11600605.

[30] Barnes, R. (2007). "Justices to Weigh Detainee Rights." *Washington Post*, Sat. June 30, 2007, A01.

[31] Ward, R., K. Kiernan, & D. Mabrey (2006). *Homeland Security: An Introduction.* Newark, NJ: LexisNexis/Matthew Bender, p. 254.

[32] Cited in Fagin, J. (2006). *When Terrorism Strikes Home: Defending the United States.* Boston, MA: Allyn and Bacon, p. 71.

[33] Cited in Fagin, J. (2006). *When Terrorism Strikes Home: Defending the United States.* Boston, MA: Allyn and Bacon, p. 305.

Index